T0325103

Urban Analytics with Social Media Data

The use of data science and urban analytics has become a defining feature of smart cities. This timely book is a clear guide to the use of social media data for urban analytics.

The book presents the foundations of urban analytics with social media data, along with real-world applications and insights on the platforms we use today. It looks at social media analytics platforms, cyberphysical data analytics platforms, crowd detection platforms, City-as-a-Platform, and city-as-a-sensor for platform urbanism. The book provides examples to illustrate how we apply and analyse social media data to determine disaster severity, assist authorities with pandemic policy, and capture public perception of smart cities.

This will be a useful reference for those involved with and researching social, data, and urban analytics and informatics.

Urban Analytics with Social Media Data

Foundations, Applications and Platforms

Tan Yigitcanlar and Nayomi Kankanamge

CRC Press
Taylor & Francis Group
Boca Raton London New York

CRC Press is an imprint of the
Taylor & Francis Group, an **informa** business

A CHAPMAN & HALL BOOK

First edition published 2023
by CRC Press
6000 Broken Sound Parkway NW, Suite 300, Boca Raton, FL 33487-2742

and by CRC Press

4 Park Square, Milton Park, Abingdon, Oxon, OX14 4RN

CRC Press is an imprint of Taylor & Francis Group, LLC

© 2023 Tan Yigitcanlar and Nayomi Kankanamge

Reasonable efforts have been made to publish reliable data and information, but the author and publisher cannot assume responsibility for the validity of all materials or the consequences of their use.
The authors and publishers have attempted to trace the copyright holders of all material reproduced
in this publication and apologize to copyright holders if permission to publish in this form has not
been obtained. If any copyright material has not been acknowledged please write and let us know so
we may rectify in any future reprint.

Except as permitted under U.S. Copyright Law, no part of this book may be reprinted, reproduced,
transmitted, or utilized in any form by any electronic, mechanical, or other means, now known or
hereafter invented, including photocopying, microfilming, and recording, or in any information
storage or retrieval system, without written permission from the publishers.

For permission to photocopy or use material electronically from this work, access www.copyright.
com or contact the Copyright Clearance Center, Inc. (CCC), 222 Rosewood Drive, Danvers, MA 01923,
978-750-8400. For works that are not available on CCC please contact mpkbookspermissions@tandf.
co.uk

Trademark Notice: Product or corporate names may be trademarks or registered trademarks and are
used only for identification and explanation without intent to infringe.

Library of Congress Cataloging-in-Publication Data

Names: Yigitcanlar, Tan, author. | Kankanamge, Nayomi, author. Title: Urban
analytics with social media data : foundations, applications and platforms /
Tan Yigitcanlar and Nayomi Kankanamge. Description: First edition. | Boca Raton :
CRC Press, 2022. | Includes bibliographical references and index. | Summary: "The
use of data science and urban analytics has become a defining feature of smart cities.
This timely book is a clear guide to the use of social media data for urban analytics.
The book presents the foundations of urban analytics with social media data, along
with real world applications and insights on the platforms we use today. It looks
at social media analytics platforms, cyberphysical data analytics platforms, crowd
detection platforms, city as a platform and city as a sensor for platform urbanism.
The title provides examples to illustrate how we apply and analyse social media data
to determine disaster severity, assist authorities with pandemic policy and capture
public perceptions on smart cities. This will be a useful reference for those involved
with and researching social, data and urban analytics and informatics"-- Provided by
publisher. Identifiers: LCCN 2021060849 | ISBN 9781032244976 (hardback) |
ISBN 9781032244952 (paperback) | ISBN 9781003278986 (ebook)
Subjects: LCSH: Smart cities. | City planning--Data processing. |
Web usage mining. | Big data. Classification: LCC HT165.5 .Y54 2022 |
DDC 307.1/216--dc23/eng/20220103 LC record available at https://lccn.loc.gov/2021060849

ISBN: 9781032244976 (hbk)
ISBN: 9781032244952 (pbk)
ISBN: 9781003278986 (ebk)

DOI: 10.1201/9781003278986

Typeset in Palatino
by KnowledgeWorks Global Ltd.

This book is dedicated to our beloved,

beautiful, and brilliant family members:

Susan, Ela, Selin

&

Indu, Lakshan

Contents

Part I   Foundations

Part II   Applications

Part III   Platforms

List of Figures

List of Tables

Foreword

We are caught in a series of moments, a time of intense political upheaval, a global pandemic, and a world impacted by the increasingly destructive impacts of climate change. It is of paramount importance that we consider the ways in which we navigate through these moments and empower our global citizenry in forging a new path forward. It is an honour then to introduce this new book which offers us promising new methodological directions in the face of significant global challenges. Yigitcanlar and Kankanamge waste no time in offering a rigorous appraisal of the issues facing society, but also the avenues presented to us in making the most of the technical tools at our disposal in navigating these rough seas.

The central thesis that is expertly prosecuted by Yigitcanlar and Kankanamge is that in a time of significant global challenge we must also appreciate that we also have an immense array of resources at our disposal. Big social data provides us with new ways to understand our shared concerns, and this is precisely where the authors begin, by appraising the various challenges and opportunities presented to us at the intersection of social media, big data, and urban analytics. Aptly described as 'foundations', these first chapters lay the groundwork of the key sites of interest, primarily social media data. These social media belong to ordinary users of large platforms like Twitter and Facebook, through to official government, commercial and NGOs use of these platforms.

The early chapters examine contemporary strategies employed by government departments, and the role that citizens can play in crowdsourcing information to inform disaster management. The focus on user engagement with and desire to assist in the sharing of localised and contextually relevant data that can be of use in addressing critical disaster incidents is a particularly noteworthy contribution. All too often users of social media are characterised as passive audiences, and these chapters provide counter-evidence to such claims and the wisdom of the crowd. While this does not attempt to dismiss the many significant and as yet unresolved issues facing social media platforms, much of which is outside the scope of the text, it does show how these platforms can be used as a force for good.

Moving through to applications, the book offers several concrete examples that showcase urban analytics utilising social media data. These chapters focus on topics such as disaster severity mapping, and public perceptions of both concrete issues such as the COVID-19 pandemic, and more abstract issues such as smart cities, artificial intelligence, and society. On the first, disaster severity mapping, the chapter expands on the foundational chapters in outlining approaches that seek to leverage localised expertise in mapping and responding to disasters in real-time. The use of the Brisbane floods resonated with me strongly, having been personally impacted by this significant weather event as a young postdoctoral research fellow in Brisbane. The Brisbane floods have been studied at length by leading digital media scholars such as Bruns, Burgess, Crawford, and Shaw, and this re-examination of the case lends further credibility to the findings and importance of the use of social media in crisis management.

The use of social media for appraising opinion dynamics is well-trodden ground. Almost since they have existed, there have been groups that are interested in using social media to understand public sentiment and attitudes. However, the twist offered here is how the use of geo-locative data can combine with other topics, sentiment, or attitudinal data in forming a view of how the public understands specific acute issues (e.g., the global pandemic), or more abstract concepts such as smart cities or artificial intelligence. The chapters offer a clear guide to how one can go about gathering, analysing, and interpreting such data, and how findings can be related to specific policy objectives.

The final section then offers the most exciting chapters of the book, which examine more speculative and novel approaches to utilising social and urban data in pursuit of more harmonious, inclusive, safer, and resilient cities. These final chapters examine issues at the intersection of social data as previously described, but with far more urban sensor data integration, and with a focus on platform level thinking. The key themes revolve around interoperability, and in helping cities function and react to the voice of the citizenry and their movements and interactions.

The use of Melbourne as a key site of interest is timely, given the recent focus of Melbourne City Council in increasing pedestrian mobility in the 'Hoddle Grid' of the CBD. Chapter 10, which takes a platform-level view of how a city can achieve greater crowd mobility is required reading for any city that wants to genuinely tackle significant health and environmental concerns of its citizens.

Beyond specific case studies though, the authors do well to re-engage near the conclusion of the book with a return to the concept of platform urbanism. Through a systematic literature review, the authors move beyond the concept alone to a pragmatic approach for how platform urbanism can be deployed at a local level by city councils and policymakers.

Yigitcanlar and Kankanamge have provided us with a timely intervention, offering a practical suite of tools, concepts, and workflows for engaging with social data through an urban informatics lens.

Professor Daniel Angus
School of Communication and Digital Media Research Centre
Queensland University of Technology, Brisbane, Australia

Preface

Due to the rapid urbanisation rates across the globe, the 21st Century is nick-named as the 'Century of Cities'. While at the first instance this nickname is associated with technological and governance excellence to provide ideal living, working, and leisure opportunities to citizens in more densely constructed high-quality urban localities, the reality is far from this desired future outcome. Most of the city-regions in the world today are troubled with environmental and socioeconomic inequalities and facing colossal challenges in sustainably managing the city and its sprawling development. Beyond this, climate refugees are a reality of our time and making even the most liberal and democratic countries turn their back to these highly vulnerable, and quickly increasing, groups.

In other words, in the age of climate change, pandemics and natural disasters, and ever-increasing socioeconomic inequalities cities are struggling big time to function, and operate their amenities and services, in an effective, efficient, and sustainable way. Policymakers, managers, planners, and practitioners are under extreme pressure to first understand the rapid changes happening along with the resulting and constantly evolving challenges, and then develop sound strategies and actions to implement and monitor.

This pressing issue has increased the importance of technocentric approaches to support policy efforts. Consequently, in recent years, urban analytics (and big data, which also brought the issue of how to make the best use of big data either voluntarily provided by the public or regulatorily collected by authorities) has become a critical support tool for urban policymakers, managers, planners, and practitioners. Nonetheless, as one of the largest and open access big data source, the exponential growth in social media, at the global level, has created an opportunity, in recent years, to use social media generated big data in urban analytics systems.

Against this background, the book thoroughly explores and sheds light on the utilisation of urban analytics with social media data in understanding and addressing the challenges and changes of our cities and societies, which are experiencing and confronting in the age of climate change, pandemics, and natural disasters.

First, the book provides a sound understanding of the key foundations of urban analytics with social media data, including urban big data and social media analytics, volunteer crowdsourcing and social media, and government utilisation of social media channels. Next, the book presents application examples of urban analytics with social media data, including social media analytics for determining disaster severity, assisting authorities in pandemic policy, and capturing public perceptions on smart cities and artificial intelligence. Last, the book offers examples and insights into platforms for urban analytics with big data, including social media analytics platforms, cyberphysical data analytics platforms, crowd detection platforms, City-as-a-Platform, and city as a sensor for platform urbanism.

The book is structured under three main parts and elaborated briefly as below:

Part 1: Foundations
This part of the book concentrates on providing a clear understanding on the key foundations of urban analytics with social media data. These foundations include urban big data and social media analytics, volunteer crowdsourcing and social media, and government social media channels.

Part 2: Applications
This part of the book concentrates on providing application examples of urban analytics with social media data. These examples include social media analytics for determining disaster severity, social media analytics for assisting authorities in pandemic policy, social media analytics for capturing public perceptions on smart cities, and social media analytics for capturing public perceptions on artificial intelligence.

Part 3: Platforms
This part of the book concentrates on providing examples and insights into platforms for urban analytics. These platform examples include social media analytics platform, cyberphysical data analytics platform, crowd detection platform, City-as-a-Platform, and city as a sensor for platform urbanism.

The authors of the book believe that social media is now a formal tool of communication across the globe, where it constantly generates crowdsourced big data that is invaluable for urban policymakers, managers, planners, and practitioners—and also for researchers and scholars—to use for understanding and tackling key urban and societal issues. The book, thus, offers an invaluable opportunity to urban policymakers, managers, planners, practitioners, and researchers by introducing the foundations of urban analytics with social media data, providing examples on the application areas of urban analytics with social media data, and presenting examples of the platforms for urban analytics with big data.

Authors

Tan Yigitcanlar is an eminent Australian researcher with international recognition and impact in the field of urban studies and planning. He is a Professor of Urban Studies and Planning at the School of Architecture and Built Environment, Queensland University of Technology (QUT), Brisbane, Australia. Along with this post, he carries out an Honorary Professor role at the School of Technology, Federal University of Santa Catarina, Florianopolis, Brazil, and the Founding Director positions of the *Australia-Brazil Smart City Research and Practice Network* and QUT's *Urban Studies Lab* and *City 4.0 Lab*. The main foci of his research interests, within the broad field of urban studies and planning, are clustered around the following three interdisciplinary themes: Smart technologies, communities, cities, and urbanism; Knowledge-based development of cities and innovation districts; and Sustainable and resilient cities, communities, and urban ecosystems. He is the lead Editor-in-Chief of *Elsevier's Smart Cities Book Series*, and carries out senior editorial positions in the following high-impact journals: *Land Use Policy, Sustainable Cities and Society, Cities, Journal of Knowledge Management, Journal of Urban Technology, Knowledge Management Research and Practice, Sustainability, Global Journal of Environmental Science and Management, Journal of Open Innovation: Technology, Market, and Complexity, Asia Pacific Journal of Innovation and Entrepreneurship, Measuring Business Excellence, Urban Science, International Journal of Information Management*, and *International Journal of Knowledge-Based Development*. He has disseminated his research findings extensively including over 250 articles published in high-impact journals, and 20 key reference books published by esteemed international publishing houses. His research outputs have been widely cited and influenced urban policy, practice, and research internationally. As of March 2022, his research was cited over 14,000 times, resulting in an h-index of 70 (Google Scholar). According to the 2020 Science-wide Author Databases of Standardised Citation Indicators, among the urban and regional planning scholars, he is ranked as #1 highly cited researcher in Australia, and #7 highly cited researcher worldwide. For this achievement, he was recognised as an 'Australian Research Superstar' in the Social Sciences Category at The Australian's 2020 Research Special Report.

Nayomi Kankanamge is a Sri Lankan early career researcher specialised in the field of urban and regional planning. She is a Lecturer at the Department of Town and Country Planning, University of Moratuwa, Katubedda, Sri Lanka. She obtained her PhD degree from the Queensland University of Technology, Brisbane, Australia. Her PhD study was supervised by Professor Tan Yigitcanlar. During her PhD study, she has received a High Achiever

Higher Degree Researcher Award from the Queensland University of Technology. The main foci of her research cluster around urban planning, social media analytics, and disaster management areas. Her specific expertise lies in analysing and interpreting crowdsourcing data and its impact in modifying the conventional urban planning approaches. She has authored over a dozen highly cited journal articles published in high-impact journals on the overall topic of urban analytics with social media data.

Part I

Foundations

This part of the book concentrates on providing a clear understanding of the key foundations of urban analytics with social media data. These foundations include urban big data and social media analytics, volunteer crowdsourcing and social media, and government social media channels.

DOI: 10.1201/9781003278986-1

Part I

Foundations

1

Urban Big Data and Social Media Analytics

1.1 Introduction

Today, in the age of climate change, pandemics, and natural disasters, cities are struggling to function, and operate their amenities and services, in an effective, efficient, and sustainable way. Policymakers, managers, planners, and practitioners are under extreme pressure to first understand the rapid changes happening along with the resulting and constantly evolving challenges, and then develop sound strategies and actions to implement and monitor. This issue has increased the importance of urban analytics, and also brought the data issues. Nonetheless, the exponential growth in social media, at the global level, has created an opportunity, in recent years, to use social media generated big data in urban analytics systems.

Data analytics is an integral part of the decision-making process in urban planning and development. In recent years, with the advancement of digital technologies and analytical capabilities of large datasets, urban analytics systems have started to highly benefit from big data—that is being generated from cities and societies. Besides, the opportunities offered with the wider use of social media channels and resulting user-generated data helps in urban analytics, social media analytics, and big data analytics to work together to produce input into urban planning and development decisions (Kankanamge et al., 2020a).

In conducting urban analytics, social media, as a big data type, can be used to present, such as, the structural changes to a city; and also, for instance, big data patterns in a city can show how governance influences cities' sustainability performance (Boeing et al., 2021; Kandt & Batty, 2021; Wey & Peng, 2021). The increasing opportunities of analytics for cities bring the need for understanding how urban analytics, social media analytics, and big data analytics work and also interact. A quick look at the literature reveals a trend on the common use of these analytical approaches for smart city, community/society, and governance domains (Kankanamge et al., 2020b; Yigitcanlar et al., 2021). Hence, this chapter focuses on urban analytics with social media big data from the angle of planning for smart cities, communities, and governance.

DOI: 10.1201/9781003278986-2

Smart cities, communities/societies, and governance utilise data as a mean to assist shaping, managing, and smoothly running urban services and amenities effectively and efficiently (Lim et al., 2018; Kandt & Batty, 2021). In order to capture the required data, smart cities employ Internet-of-Things (IoT) and other sensor technologies and methods. The data and analysis, in turn, assist in, for example, detecting and understanding air pollution levels, infrastructure failures, transport system delays, and environmental or public safety risks. Big data-driven urban analytics is a commonly used method in smart cities. Social media analytics is also beneficial for smart cities and communities/societies (Zeng et al., 2010; Kourtit et al., 2019). However, with social media analytics might come some the privacy concerns (Stieglitz et al., 2013; Ye et al., 2020). Smart governance also relies on sensor data captured and analysis, such as IoT, artificial intelligence (AI), and other related technologies (Stieglitz et al., 2013; Kourtit, 2019) to enhance the accuracy of policy and decision-making processes.

Along with the smart city movement, virality of social media use across the globe has led to urban analytics with social media big data to gain recognition as a mainstream method to investigate contemporary and future cities and understand the changes and challenges in urban systems and societies. This chapter aims to expand our understanding on what the opportunities and constraints of urban analytics with social media big data are. To achieve this aim, this chapter employed a systematic literature review approach to reveal the landscape and challenges and opportunities of social media, big data, and urban analytics. The findings generated insights into how urban analytics with social media big data is being used to investigate, understand and act upon the changes and challenges of our cities and communities/societies.

1.2 Literature Background

1.2.1 Big Data Analytics

Big data can be an untraditional type of data due to its size and complexity (Rathore et al., 2016; Sedkaoui & Khelfaoui, 2019). Big data is used to obtain real-time information that can identify urban form and machinery patterns. It also can be used to inform urban policy decisions (Pfeffer et al., 2015; Sedkaoui & Khelfaoui, 2019). Governance is very prevalent in big data and was found to be the mostly used application area, tied with 'smart cities' in the research pool relating to big data. As per the prevailing literature, it was evident that the IoT, general AI, blockchain data, and 5G/6G technologies were the mostly used methods of data collection within big data. Using these technologies, it was found that big data can be used to record productivity of an area or body of work, such as transport decisions, trends, growth prediction, overall supervision of urban form, and land use planning networks (Bibri, 2018; Babar & Arif, 2019; Huang & Wey, 2019; Lock et al., 2021).

In addition, big data is used frequently in studying city sustainability in terms of the natural and built environment (greenspace interaction) and sustainable transport options (Khalifa et al., 2016; Morgan, 2020). Big data is a type of research that is mostly suitable for large data retrieval and management. Nonetheless, it has been found that there are concerns of user confidence and reliability in big data being able to handle sensitive information, and other various types of data (Brower et al., 2019). There are research gaps in using this type of data but the discussion on how to resolve that and work on solutions has only just started to begin (Nigel et al., 2018).

1.2.2 Social Media Data Analytics

Social media data can come from platforms such as Twitter, Facebook, Airbnb, and general GPS tracking to name a few (Zeng et al., 2010; Moe & Schweidel, 2017). Social media data collection allows for the opportunity for geo-location tracking, which in turn allows for a more focused subject/study area, increasing the level of engagement. Society was the most commonly found application area in social media data analytics. This type of data analytics, in an urban planning sense, can be used to 'investigate applications of social media analytics towards identified problems' within an area, discover ethical implications, and assist in the management of flooding, fires, and other natural disasters (Nanda & Kumar, 2019; Pääkkönen et al., 2020; Zhang et al., 2020). To collect this data, the most used forms of technologies found in the research were IoT, machine learning, AI, smart surveillance based on AI, data mining, and GPS tracking forms of data collection. While social media data analytics is an advanced form of data collection for more personal and accurate data, privacy and data control have been found to be a major constraint and area of concern for communities (Stieglitz et al., 2013; Chen et al., 2016; Tang et al., 2017; Yang & Zeng, 2018; Yang et al., 2020; Ye et al., 2020; Zhang et al., 2020; Petrescu & Krishen, 2020)

1.2.3 Urban Analytics

Originating from 'urban analysis', urban analytics can be defined as a 'set of tools employed to deal with problems of big data, urban simulation and geodemographics' (Kandt & Batty, 2021). It is a combination of different analytical techniques such as social media analytics and network analysis that is being used to explore urban themes, cities, connectivity, and the inner workings of a city (Kourtit, 2019). A key theme seen within urban analytics was the theme of smart cities. Most urban analytics-related studies refer to land use planning and urban morphology, where approaches such as smart governance based on AI, cloud computing, smart grids, data sensing, and IoT are used as data collection and analyses tools. While urban analytics is a very useful research tool for land use planning and urban morphology purposes, it can also be used to help inform social studies such as cultural, amenity, and other community needs (Kourtit, 2019; Fleischmann et al., 2020;

Löfgren & Webster, 2020). Urban analytics provides opportunities for a number of studies from geo-processing studies, cultural studies, and the more common spatial studies (Behnisch et al., 2019). Despite urban analytics being used more in data collection and analyses, there seems to be limitations and gaps in this research arena. Further research on quantitative analysis of urban form, cultural analysis, and management, and using larger subject groups and broader research scopes are lacking in relation to urban analytics (Kaur & Garg, 2019; Kourtit et al., 2019; Fleischmann et al., 2020).

1.3 Methods

To undertake this study of urban analytics in social media analytics, a systematic literature review was completed. The research was separated into three different sections. They are: (a) Urban analytics; (b) Social media analytics; and (c) Big data analytics. This 'three-phase methodologic approach' has been adopted from (Yigitcanlar et al. 2018). The literature selection process is shown in Figure 1.1.

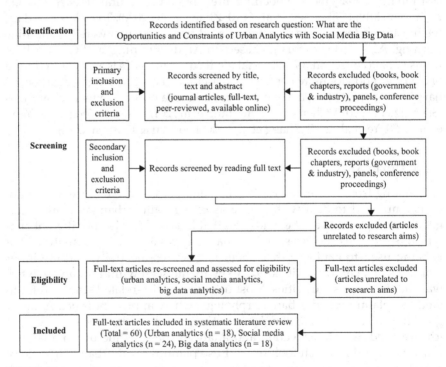

FIGURE 1.1
Literature selection procedure.

To approach the first phase, specific keywords were used to narrow down the search. These keywords, starting with the broader terms of 'urban analytics', 'social media analytics', and 'big data analytics', were further broken down to create a large word search. The keywords used in each category of 'urban analytics', 'social media analytics', and 'big data analytics' are provided in Table 1.1.

TABLE 1.1

Boolean Search

Phases	Boolean Search
Urban Analytics	("Conducting" OR "understand" OR "find" OR "coordinate" OR "organise" OR "guide" OR "orchestrate" OR "drive" OR "carry out" OR "perform" OR "communicate" OR "govern" OR "lead") AND ("urban" OR "city" OR "state" OR "town" OR "metropolitan" OR "region" OR "regional" OR "suburban" OR "metropolis" OR "megalopolis" OR "urban complex") AND ("analytics" OR "analysis" OR "analytical" OR "data" OR "science" OR "statistics" OR "investigate" OR "inquiring" OR "problem-solving" OR "rational" OR "search" OR "systematic" OR "information" OR "evidence") AND ("opportunities" OR "chance" OR "probability" OR "scope" OR "possibility" OR "prospect" OR "fortuity" OR "likelihood") AND ("constraints" OR "restriction" OR "pressure" OR "restraint" OR "limits" OR "limitation" OR "constriction" OR "obstacles") AND ("application areas" OR "study area" OR "field" OR "operation area" OR "locality" OR "case study" OR "priority area" OR "area of work" OR "focus area") AND ("method" OR "system" OR "process" OR "practice" OR "system" OR "program" OR "technique" OR "scheme" OR "way")
Social Media Analytics	("Conducting" OR "manage" OR "supervise" OR "regulate" OR "coordinate" OR "handle" OR "guide" OR "orchestrate" OR "drive" OR "carry out" OR "perform" OR "communicate" OR "govern" OR "administer" OR "lead") AND ("Social Media Analytics" OR "Social Media" OR "Social Data" OR "Twitter Data" OR "Social Media Findings" OR "Geo-Locational Social Media" OR " Geo-Locational Twitter" OR "Geo-Locational Data" OR "GPS" OR "Facebook Data" OR "Social Media Dataset") AND ("Analytics" OR "Analytical" OR "Investigative" OR "Inquiring" OR "Problem Solving" OR "Rational" OR "Systematic" OR "Scientific" OR "Thorough" OR "Conclusive" OR "Inquisitive" OR "Dissecting" OR "Questioning" OR " Searching" Or "Testing" OR "Exploratory") AND ("Opportunities" OR "Convenience" OR "Contingency" OR "Occasion" OR "Probability" OR "Fortuity") AND ("Constraints" OR "Restraint" OR "Pressure" OR "Duress" OR "Repression" OR "Suppression" OR "Impelling" OR "Impulsion") AND ("Application Areas" OR "Operation Area" OR "Employment Areas" OR "Exercise Areas" OR " Practice Areas" OR "Function Areas" OR "Application Field" OR "Operation Field" OR "Employment Field" OR "Exercise Field" OR "Practice Field" OR "Function Field") AND ("Methods" OR "Scheme" OR "Rule" OR "System" OR "Technique" OR "WAY" OR "Manner" OR "Mechanism" OR "Approach" OR "Mode" OR "Process" OR "Program" OR "Recipe" OR "Channel" OR "Course" OR "Proceeding" OR "Schema" OR "Tactic" OR "Usage" OR "Modus" or "Technic" OR "Ways and Means")

(Continued)

TABLE 1.1 *(Continued)*

Boolean Search

Phases	Boolean Search
Big Data Analytics	("Conducting" OR "manage" OR "supervise" OR "regulate" OR "coordinate" OR "handle" OR "guide" OR "orchestrate" OR "drive" OR "carry out" OR "perform" OR "communicate" OR "govern" OR "administer" OR "lead") AND ("Big Data" OR "Massive Data" OR "Macro Data" OR "Lots of Data" OR "Significant Data" OR "Large Amount of Data" OR " Lot of Information" OR "Mass Data" OR "Computer Data" OR "Large Data Volume" OR "Bulky Data" OR "Metadata" OR "Large Databases" OR "Large Data Sets" OR "Electronic Data") AND ("Analytics" OR "Analytical" OR "Investigative" OR "Inquiring" OR "Problem Solving" OR "Rational" OR "Systematic" OR "Scientific" OR "Thorough" OR "Conclusive" OR "Inquisitive" OR "Dissecting" OR "Questioning" OR " Searching" Or "Testing" OR "Exploratory") AND ("Opportunities" OR "Convenience" OR "Contingency" OR "Occasion" OR "Probability" OR "Fortuity") AND ("Constraints" OR "Restraint" OR "Pressure" OR "Duress" OR "Repression" OR "Suppression" OR "Impelling" OR "Impulsion") AND ("Application Areas" OR "Operation Area" OR "Employment Areas" OR "Exercise Areas" OR " Practice Areas" OR "Function Areas" OR "Application Field" OR "Operation Field" OR "Employment Field" OR "Exercise Field" OR "Practice Field" OR "Function Field") AND ("Methods" OR "Scheme" OR "Rule" OR "System" OR "Technique" OR "WAY" OR "Manner" OR "Mechanism" OR "Approach" OR "Mode" OR "Process" OR "Program" OR "Recipe" OR "Channel" OR "Course" OR "Proceeding" OR "Scheme" OR "Tactic" OR "Usage" OR "Modus" or "Technic" OR "Ways and Means")

Each search had a primary and secondary inclusionary and exclusionary criterion. The primary criteria were assessed against what type of source the search result was (e.g., article, book), with the secondary criteria being assessed against the results' relevance to the topic. The inclusionary and exclusionary criteria are shown in Table 1.2.

TABLE 1.2

Inclusion and Exclusion Criteria

Primary Criteria		Secondary Criteria	
Inclusionary	**Exclusionary**	**Inclusionary**	**Exclusionary**
Journal articles	Books	Urban analytics relevant to research aims	Articles unrelated to research aims
Full text	Book chapters	Social media analytics relevant to research aims	
Peer-reviewed	Reports (Government & Industry)	Big data analytics relevant to research aims	
Available online	Panels		
	Conference proceedings		

TABLE 1.3

Criteria for Formulation of Themes

Selection Criteria
1. Determine relative themes within urban analytics, social media analytics, and big data analytics
2. Investigate methods used to acquire urban analytic, social media analytics, and big data analytics data
3. Identify opportunities and constraints related to the analytic data found
4. Review the reliability and eligibility of the selected data
5. Final review of literature
6. Finalise the themes of the analytic data
7. Review literature under the selected themes

In the second phase, in total 60 journal articles were chosen and refined to reflect the broad scope of the topic. The criteria for the formulation of the urban analytic, social media analytics, and big data analytics themes are shown in Table 1.3.

The split of data focusing on each category was relatively even, with most being able to address more than one category at a time. To analyse these journal articles, a table was produced that showcases the key findings, as shown in this chapter's Appendix. This table includes the author, title of the article, specific journal the article is from, the aim and relevance to the topic, indication of the application area, as well as the technologies and methods used to collect the data.

The final phase is the reporting phase. The documenting and further analysis of the research was completed within this phase. This is to produce a thorough background and a discussion of the results, which includes general observations, an analysis of the technologies, and methods used in relevance to the application areas, as well as a more detailed and comprehensive overview of the opportunities and constraints of using and conducting research through urban analytics, social media analytics, and big data analytics.

1.4 Results

1.4.1 General Observations

From the selected 60 articles, nearly half were recently published, i.e., 2019 (n = 15; 25%), 2020 (n = 12; 20%), and 2021 (n = 1; 2%). A total of 25 articles (n = 25; 42%) were published between 2015 and 2018; the latter numbers corroborate an increased academic interest in this topic during the last six years, which is a stark contrast to the number of articles published between 2008 and 2013 (n = 4; 7%). In terms of application areas, all the articles were categorised under six smart city components: (a) Economy; (b) Society; (c) Environment;

TABLE 1.4

State-of-the-Art Technologies in Big Data Analytics

Category	Recurrent Technologies	Recurrent Application Areas
Big Data Analytics	IoT (n = 17), general AI (n = 10), Blockchain (n = 2), 5G (n = 2) (inform AI and cloud computing in following areas: Smart Grid (n = 2), Smart Transport (n = 6), Smart Governance (n = 12), Smart Energy (n = 2), Smart Economy (n = 2), Smart Surveillance (n = 1))	Governance (n = 10) Smart City (n =10) Economy (n = 6) Environment (n = 5) Community Planning (n = 3) Transport Planning (n = 3) Society (n = 3)

(d) Government; (e) Transport; and (f) Technology. As depicted in Table 1.4, all big data, social media, and urban analytics include in the subject areas of: (a) Economy, commerce, and marketing: (b) Community planning, society, and education; (c) Environment and sustainability; (d) Governance, smart city, politics, disaster, and stakeholder management, which are majorly monitored by government institutions; (e) Transport planning; and (f) Big data.

1.4.2 State-of-the-Art Technologies in Relevance to Application Areas

All of the technologies in the reviewed literature were classified under three sub-areas of social media analytics, big data analytics, and urban analytics.

1.4.2.1 Big Data Analytics

In the sphere of big data analytics (n = 18; 30%), the two most recurrent technological themes are IoT (n = 12; 20%) and general AI concepts (n = 7; 12%), which are supported by technologies such as Blockchain (n = 3) and 5G (n = 3). However, the most outstanding application areas are those related with smart city initiatives; specifically, governance (n = 10), smart city (n =10), economy (n = 6), environment (n = 5), community planning (n = 3), transport planning (n = 3), and society (n = 3).

From the ten sources that contain governance as an area of application, six (60%) adopted AI and IoT as the main technologies. The remaining four contained one of the smart city strategies seen in Table 1.4. AI and IoT are utilised to assist local governments in the process of delivering policies that reflect population needs that have been identified via these technologies (Hilbert, 2016; Rathore et al., 2016; Bibri, 2018; Sedkaoui & Khelfaoui, 2019; Morgan, 2020; Boeing et al., 2021; Lock et al., 2021). Big data analytics supported by IoT permits the retrieval and amalgamation of real-time data from different sources such as education providers, traffic data, healthcare, and surveillance. Big data analytics is a commonly used method in smart cities to capture and analyse urban data (Pfeffer et al., 2015; Bibri, 2018; Babar & Arif, 2019; Huang & Wey, 2019; Wey & Peng, 2021).

The latter overlaps with the smart city (n = 10) as an application area, where AI is utilised in the process of reading retrieved data as noted in sources (Hilbert, 2016; Nigel et al., 2018; Singh et al., 2019; Lock et al., 2021). This is essential in maintaining the layers of 'smartness' that characterises a smart city. For instance, smartness of a smart city enhances the interconnection and working synergy of goods and services (maintained via a technology capable of analysing clusters of seemingly disorganised big data) and use self-learning algorithms (which are capable of identifying recurrent patterns and structuring the big data) in order to enable readability of big data. Still, it is emphasised that qualitative big data reading requires a contextualisation for the type of data analysed, e.g., stakeholder sentiment in relation to quality of a specific good or service (Fan et al., 2014), while a quantifiable automation of the reading of qualitative data will result in skewed data reading results.

1.4.2.2 Social Media Analytics

As shown in Table 1.5, the results in social media analytics (n = 24; 40%) demonstrate a dominance of IoT technologies in social media analytics (n = 19; 32%). Secondly, machine learning or general AI concepts (artificial intelligence: n = 11; 18%) are the prominent. Further, AI has been applied in the form of smart surveillance algorithms (n = 5; 8%), with a single recurrence for GPS, virtual reality, wearable technology, smart environment, and smart education. The three overarching application areas were related to society (n = 18; 30%), followed by commerce/marketing (n = 8; 13%), politics (n = 6; 10%), and disaster management (n = 6; 10%) occupying the third place.

Society as an application area is dominated by IoT technologies as 13 out of 18 (70%) sources were supported by the aforementioned technology. The remaining five sources were informed by AI and self-learning smart initiatives, which are based on AI and cloud computing. These technologies are applied in the areas of smart education, smart surveillance, and smart environment. The possibilities that IoT provides in the deployment of social

TABLE 1.5

State-of-the-Art Technologies in Social Media Analytics

Category	Recurrent Technologies	Recurrent Application Areas
Social Media Analytics	IoT (n = 19), machine learning (n = 6), IT (AI) (n = 5), smart surveillance based on AI (n = 5), data mining (n = 3), GPS (n = 1), robotics (n = 1), virtual reality (n = 1), wearable technology (n =1), (inform AI and cloud computing in the areas of smart environment (n = 1) and smart education (n = 1))	Society (humanistic approaches) (n = 18) Commerce – Marketing (n = 8) Politics (n = 6) Disaster Management (n = 6) Smart Cities (n = 5) Stakeholder management (n = 3) Education (n = 1)

media analysis range from supporting retrieval of stakeholder data (by interconnecting social media activity in platforms such as Twitter and Facebook to movement activity via GPS tracking) to resulting in condensed data about a location's demographic activity as well as insights into the activity preferences of the public (Zeng et al., 2010; Zha et al., 2016; Moe & Schweidel, 2017; Stieglitz et al., 2018; Nanda & Kumar, 2019; Kordzadeh & Young, 2020; Yao & Wang, 2020; Pääkkönen et al., 2020).

As confirmed by the sources, social media analytics based on AI's self-learning algorithms also has the potential to inform policy-related decision-making that depends on an understanding of population behaviour (Stieglitz et al., 2013; Fan & Yan, 2015; Chen et al., 2016; Zhang et al., 2020). The policy drafting of transportation, education, healthcare, and disaster management strategies is directly informed by geo-tagged social media applications and type of stakeholder activity in those platforms (Zhu et al., 2018).

Management strategies also intersect with smart technologies based on AI and cloud computing. For instance, they are applied in the area of smart city creation with the help of mass retrieval of personal data via social media analysis. These result in the automated profiling of subjects that portray suspiciously lawless behaviour. IoT technologies further reinforce the capacity to utilise surveillance technologies and equipment by maintaining real-time communication between law enforcement and businesses (Chen et al., 2016; Zhu et al., 2018; Andriole, 2019; Zhang et al., 2020; de Andrade et al., 2021). The results also show the emergence of wearable technologies as tools that further add to social media data, specifically in the sphere of fashion technology which enables a profiling of stakeholders' personal activities and preferences.

1.4.2.3 Urban Analytics

Table 1.6 shows an emphasis on AI in the area of smart governance/government (n = 6) as a technology in the urban context followed by AI-based smart grid

TABLE 1.6

State-of-the-Art Technologies in Urban Analytics

Category	Recurrent Technologies	Recurrent Application Areas
Urban Analytics	Smart governance/government based on AI and cloud computing (n = 6), Smart grid/ smart city based on AI and cloud computing (n = 4), Data sensors (n = 4), IoT (n = 3), Spatial analysis (n = 2), Smart surveillance based on AI and cloud computing (n = 1), Digital information (n = 1)	Smart cities (n = 9) Urban form (n = 6) Government (n = 4) Big data (n = 2) Transport/ urban planning (n = 2) Society (n = 2) Sustainability (n = 1)

(n = 4), data sensors (n = 4), and IoT (n = 3) with AI-based smart surveillance and digital information with a single record. The most recurrent application areas were smart cities (n = 9), urban form (n = 6), government (n = 4), and transport/urban planning (n=2).

AI technologies in the areas of smart government and smart grid are inherently supported by IoT, 5G, and cloud computing (Clifton et al., 2008; Rabari & Storper, 2015; Puiu et al., 2016; Rathore et al., 2018; Fleischmann et al., 2020). This seeks to assist the organised development of an urban form by automating the process of city governance. Via big data analytics in the spheres of transportation, sustainability, and society, the government is equipped with tools to obtain filtered data. This has been retrieved via decentralised cloud networks. The self-learning algorithms of AI merge statistical data on spatial analysis and social matters with an estimate of trends being presented, and decision-making is directly informed by said data, resulting in the term "smart governance/government" (Kitchin et al., 2015; Lim et al., 2018; Kourtit, 2019; Osman, 2019; Löfgren & Webster, 2020;). Data sensors and IoT technologies cooperate to expand on urban planning data (Rabari & Storper, 2015; Rathore et al., 2018; Serasinghe Pathiranage et al., 2018).

The study findings pointed out the capacities of data sensors to retrieve spatial topographical data, identifying historical land use, and categorising the most proficient use for both occupied and vacant land. IoT unifies the separate procedures undertaken by sensors retrieving urban data (Stiglbauer et al., 2014; Zhu et al., 2018; Sebei et al., 2018). Instead of having a myriad of sensors retrieving sets of data within their own fields, e.g., traffic congestion, parking, surveillance, IoT technology enables the unification of sensor data retrieval. This results in a monolithic urban data sensor held together by a cloud network. Said agglomeration of data feeds the AI algorithm of city governance further supported by 5G (Hilbert, 2016; Lock et al., 2021) and cloud computing (Fan et al., 2014; Pfeffer et al., 2015; Hilbert, 2016; Boeing, 2018; Stieglitz et al., 2018; Brower et al., 2019; Kourtit, 2019; Zhang et al., 2020; Boeing et al., 2021; de Andrade et al., 2021; Locket al., 2021).

In the areas of society, transport, and sustainability, emphasis is given to AI, cloud computing, and IoT technologies in the form of smart surveillance, with the objective of enhancing law enforcement presence (Boeing, 2018; Lim et al., 2018; Löfgren & Webster, 2020). By leveraging the scope of coverage possible via AI/self-learning technologies, surveillance data retrieval is expected to identify activities in real time that may result in property or personal damage.

1.4.3 Opportunities and Constraints

As shown in Table 1.7 in this chapter's Appendix, a majority of reviewed articles contain both opportunities and constraints. These are applicable to big data, social media, and urban analytics. This represents that all these listed categories require further improvements, where they still contain limitations in their contemporary technologies and functions. On the other hand, these categories also contain beneficial potentialities towards their projected application areas, overall, in urban analytics. Opportunities and constraints of contemporary big data, social media, and urban analytics vary by their application areas, domains, and technologies, given that these categories are currently being utilised in different factors and manners. Accordingly, both big data and social media analytics have demonstrated their wide range of applicable domains, where urban analytics is limited to social and urban-related domains. In addition, overall opportunities justified those guidelines, problems, and solutions have been identified throughout obtained datasets and information. On the other hand, datasets and information obtained in all three categories sometimes tend to be limited and fragmented, which were insufficient for clearer identifications.

1.4.3.1 Big Data Analytics

Big data analytics play significant roles in utilities of urban analytics, given that it clearly identifies stakeholder preferences, statistical information (demographics, incomes, accessibilities, and educations), and smart city requirements (smart transport, education, governance, energy, etc.) in real time, throughout the utilisation of IoT. Identification of the listed factors is underpinned by technologies of big data analytics (As shown in Table 1.7 in this chapter's Appendix), where most of the technologies are IoT and smart city technologies.

Big data analytics help to make smarter decisions in urban developments, throughout providing real-time accessibility in more accurate and more structured information by dramatically reducing the uncertainty (Hilbert, 2016). For instance, literature reporting the case study findings from Paramaribo (Suriname) and Port of Spain (Trinidad and Tobago) disclose the use of big data analytics in mitigating water scarcity and crime prevention interventions (Pfeffer et al., 2015).

On the other hand, big data analytics provide opportunities but also hold restrictions for policy development and implementation, since it holds serious constraints such as privacy and human resource scarcity issues. According to Hilbert (2016), big data analytics jeopardise privacy, since any data on human subjects inevitably raise privacy issues, likely to social media analytics. Throughout big data analytics, it also promotes developments of AIs and other technologies and eventually dramatically reduces human resources by substituting human workers. Moreover, Hilbert (2016) has referred to Tversky and Kahneman's (1981) view: "From a theoretical standpoint, every decision is an uncertain, probabilistic gamble based on some kind of prior information (Tversky & Kahneman, 1981)", underpinning lack of reliability of big data analytics (Hilbert, 2016).

It was also justified that big data analytics tend to provide limited and fragmented datasets for the listed factors of urban analytics. This is majorly due to fragmentation in datasets occurring consequential to a failure to recognise contextual backing of the data involved. For instance, applying a quantitative approach to a set of data that is majorly qualitative, said dynamic results in a disfigurement of data and skews findings. This identifies the misapplication of big data analytics which could result in unsustainable urban growth and hinder the development of urban infrastructures.

1.4.3.2 Social Media Analytics

Social media analytics majorly contribute to identifying general perspectives from a wide range of participants and domains, such as residents, developers, companies and organisations, politicians, and governmental institutions. In addition, social media analytics towards urban analytics is majorly targeted to improving urban environments and smart city initiatives, especially throughout applications of IoT, GPS, data mining, and machine learning. These listed technologies contribute to developing movement activities as in social media platforms, such as Twitter and Facebook, which provides precise demographic activity, as well as insights into their preferences among a certain group of population.

Besides, the purpose of social media analytics is to enable identifying these listed stakeholder insight spaces, problems, and solutions, referring to their social media platforms and usages. These applications of social media analytics are further utilised in supporting decision-making frameworks in urban planning projects. Moreover, throughout evaluating the usages of social media platforms, developable factors and guidelines of social media analytics are also found, which refers to constraints of contemporary social media analytics.

Contemporary social media analytics contain a number of constraints, where it firstly refers to privacy and ethical issues that have been depicted as the major drawback. Also, there is an invasion of individual privacy due to the misuse of mobile government microblogs in China (Yang & Zeng, 2018; Kankanamge et al., 2019; Nanda & Kumar, 2019). Moreover, as findings are sometimes fragmented and inconsistent across contexts, industries, situations, and categories of products and services (Kordzadeh & Young, 2020), certain boundaries gathered interest and others did not, since interests vary across users. This further leads to shortage of contingency, as well as consequential unsustainable urban growth, and may fail to achieve the smart city initiatives.

1.4.3.3 Urban Analytics

Referring to Kandt and Batty (2021), the role and purpose of urban analytics is to be central in governance and planning, as well as to contribute to encountering long-term challenges in the smart city initiatives, majorly based on big data and social media analytics. Urban analytics, big data, and social media analytics demonstrate a close relationship, since social media and big data analytics act as base models for urban analytics and its technologies.

As the starting point in utilising big data and social media analytics towards the smart city initiatives, urban analytics is necessary for contemporary urban environments. Urban analytics is majorly focused on studying transportation, public safety, and sustainability within a smart city; it demonstrates that urban analytics and urban data tools are increasingly relevant and important to government bodies. Urban analytics firstly plays a significant role in urban transport, energy or policing, and intelligent traffic management. For instance, maximising efficiency in road spaces and minimising traffic congestion by predicting, based on real-time monitoring and datasets (Kandt & Batty, 2021). Moreover, urban analytics provide new hypotheses, requirements in real time, by utilising both small and big data in relevant manners, for small data to be just as important as big data for governance strategies and policy makings. Also based on big data and social media datasets, urban analytics also utilises a wide range of technologies and software such as ArcGIS and QGIS mapping system (Clifton et al., 2008; Yao & Wang, 2020).

Nevertheless, as corroborated with constraints of big data and social media analytics, their constraints directly affect contemporary urban analytics, especially limitations and fragmentations of big data analytics and privacy issues of social media analytics. Improvements in urban analytics majorly include requirements of further data metrics policies (Kourtit, 2019), as well as reliabilities and qualities of urban datasets (Löfgren & Webster, 2020) and visual, temporal, and spatial connectivity, and scaling measures of urban form (Boeing, 2018), due to inconsistencies, privacy, and ethical issues of social media datasets and analytics. Thus, for the purpose of more intelligent and reliable uses towards the smart city initiatives, more in-depth accurate identifications and developments are required within listed constraints of big data, social media analytics, in relation to urban analytics.

1.5 Discussion

The systematic literature review undertaken in this study allowed us to explore the current landscape in the relationship between social media, big data, and urban analytics. The result section demonstrated that recurrent technologies informing social media and big data analysis form the backbone for overarching urban analytics technologies (Fan et al., 2014; Hilbert, 2016; Stieglitz et al., 2018; Singh et al., 2019; Babar & Arif, 2019; Zhang et al., 2020;

Lock et al., 2021). The latter is demonstrable due to AI and IoT technologies combined appearing 56 times throughout the retrieved 60 literature pieces. AI and IoT were mostly found (52 out of 56 times) in the three most recurrent application areas; smart city (n = 24), community/society (n = 18), and governance (n = 14).

These results confirm that urban analytics, compounded with social media and big data, serves as a fundamental three-way collaboration to support the compilation of data in contemporary urban areas by leveraging the vast scope of coverage of social media and utilising big data analysis methods. Urban analytics is enabled to access key population data via social media and subsequently carry out big data analysis via self-learning algorithms (used in AI) that identify current and future population needs (Clifton et al., 2008; Puiu et al., 2016; Sebei et al., 2018; Babar & Arif, 2019; Morgan, 2020; Kordzadeh & Young, 2020; Ye et al., 2020; de Andrade et al., 2021)

Consequently, the intrinsic union of AI, IoT, and the smart initiative areas based on AI/self-learning machines as their main technologies with urban analytics via social media and big data throughout the retrieved sources corroborates that current academic research acknowledges the need to gain an in-depth understanding of the various ways in which urban analysis processes can be enhanced. This finding points towards an existing need within urban planning practice to automate incoming data reading due to increased amounts of data generated as a consequence of exponential urban growth (Zhu et al., 2018; Morgan, 2020; Yang et al., 2020; Lock et al., 2021; Dur & Yigitcanlar, 2015).

The dominant state-of-the-art technologies identified in the results section present characteristics that are equipped with a capacity to accomplish the synthesis of big data regardless of geographical origin (Kitchin, 2016; Zhu et al., 2018; Behnisch et al., 2019; Yao & Wang, 2020; de Andrade et al., 2021). IoT promises to unify the sources from which the majority of data comes (Babar & Arif, 2017; Morgan, 2020; Kordzadeh & Young, 2020; Pääkkönen et al., 2020; Lock et al., 2021; de Andrade et al., 2021); whilst AI promises to pinpoint previously unidentified gaps in knowledge in the retrieved data (Khalifa et al., 2016; Stieglitz et al., 2018; Huang & Wey, 2019; Yao & Wang, 2020; Löfgren & Webster, 2020). Consequently, this chapter identifies that the smart city based on big urban data analysis gravitates around three core concepts:

- Interconnected urban spaces via IoT as a means of data retrieval, leveraging social media platforms and interactive urban IoT devices.
- Automated big data analysis via self-learning algorithms built on artificial intelligence, covering areas from governance to environment via AI/smart initiatives.
- Analysis of big urban data resulting in customised strategic problem-solving.

Based on the latter elements, it is inferred that the future success of urban spaces in the age of information is directly associated with their growing capacity to incorporate technologies that facilitate the integration of seemingly unrelated data sources into a monolithic web of information. This could help to identify recurrent urban patterns and proposes solutions via self-learning algorithms driven by AI (Zeng et al., 2010; Pfeffer et al., 2015; Babar & Arif, 2019; Kourtit, 2019; Singh et al., 2019; Ye et al., 2020; Boeing et al., 2021). The manners in which said big data is organised and dissected transcend the technological platforms that enable the retrieval of said data, as are AI, IoT, and 5G. Methods consist mainly of ways that enable data categorisation, predominately via the use of social media platforms. For instance, in the case of geo-data twitter analysis tools that act as methods for the retrieval of large amounts of sentiment and opinion-based information to identify patterns in population preferences and attitudes (Pfeffer et al., 2015; Tang et al., 2017; Sarin et al., 2020; Yao & Wang, 2020; Petrescu & Krishen, 2020; de Andrade et al., 2021).

Performance-based approaches were also utilised as a method to determine the viability of using technologies such as AI, IoT, and cloud computing with a particular set of data. For instance, by determining the proficiency of those tools at enabling consistent and reliable data reading results. It was possible to discern which approaches were unsuitable for a particular set of data. It became clear that the suitability of the approach was not determined by the type of data, rather by the context from which said data originated (Clifton et al., 2008; Yang & Zeng, 2018; Singh et al., 2019; Brower et al., 2019). Subsequently, opinion-based data required an approach that accounted for contextual qualitative analysis, whilst numerical statistical datasets required an automated approach that enabled quantitative readings. Successful interpretation of data was inherently determined by using the appropriate method which was subsequently established via a cross-comparison of data-reading performance methodology (Fan et al., 2014; Moe & Schweidel, 2017; Babar & Arif, 2019; Ye et al., 2020).

Synthesis of large-scale urban data is only possible via advance urban analytic systems. The future of urban big data analysis through leveraging social media inherently relies on public officials' political willingness to propel the implementation of infrastructures that permit urban analytical systems based on cloud computing, AI, 5G/6G, and other relevant smart systems (Zhang et al., 2018).

From opportunities and constraints of each analytics, overall, it was justified that big data and social media analytics basically contribute towards development of intelligence-related technologies such as IoT and AI. Meanwhile, it was justified that smartness of these analytics could also jeopardise individuals and their privacy. Opportunities and constraints of big data and social media analytics have been summarised into urban analytics. They are directly being utilised towards central governance, planning, and indeed the smart city initiatives. In order to accomplish the smart city initiatives in more ethical (Kitchin, 2016; Nanda & Kumar, 2019; Löfgren & Webster, 2020; Petrescu & Krishen, 2020) and reliable (Hilbert, 2016; Löfgren & Webster, 2020) manner, throughout utilisations of listed analytics, constraints will have to be vanished by minimising listed factors and their consequences.

1.6 Conclusion[1]

This chapter has delivered a systematic literature review on the research question of: What are the opportunities and constraints of urban analytics with social media big data? This chapter assists in the understanding of how these types of research collaborate to produce data that can be used to present the structural changes to a city, big data patterns in a city, and show how governance influences cities (Boeing et al., 2021; Kandt & Batty, 2021; Wey & Peng, 2021).

The findings from the systematic literature review assisted in the findings of the opportunities and constraints associated with the research analytics and disclose that:

- Although big data analytics assists in providing real-time accessibility in more accurate and more structured information while significantly reducing uncertainty, it allows for privacy and human resource scarcity issues as well as limited and fragmented datasets of urban analytics.

- Social media analytics assists in identifying stakeholder insights, problems, and solutions as well as providing precise demographic activity, but does, however, include inconsistencies and major privacy and ethical issues.

- Urban analytics provides new hypotheses and real-time data, through utilising both small and big data in relevant manners, allowing small data to be just as significant as big data for governance strategies and policymaking. However, there is a need for further data metrics policies, reliability, and quality of urban datasets as well as visual, temporal, and spatial connectivity.

This chapter has identified that to advance urban analytics with social media big data, further studies and experiments are needed to encourage and discover more intelligent and reliable uses towards the smart city initiatives. More in-depth identification and developments are required to the outlined constraints of big data, social media analytics, in relation to urban analytics.

---

[1] Authors cordially thank Bridget Rowan, Andres Ruiz Maldonado, and Alex Ryu, and acknowledge their invaluable input in an earlier version of this chapter.

Appendix

TABLE 1.7
Review Summary Table

No	Author	Year	Title	Journal	Aim	Relevance	Application Area	Technologies	Methods	Opportunities	Constraints
1	Kandt, J., Batty, M.	2021	Smart cities, big data and urban policy: Towards urban analytics for the long run	*Cities*	To explore a system that categories urban analytics	Four characteristics of urban analytics were found 1. Focus on how real-time data can influence the slow structural changes of a city 2. Urban analytics enables a more focused analysis of big data patterns 3. the role politics plays within urban analytics Data provides an example of sensing technology	Government Smart Cities	AI and cloud computing in the area of Smart Governance	Contextual Analysis Long-term evidence of big data and urban policy.	Urban data provides new hypotheses and allows small data to be just as important as big data. Urban analytics is the starting point in accepting alternative rationalities	Tension between high-frequency data and the structural challenges cities face Epistemological and practical challenges coming from high-frequency data

(Continued)

TABLE 1.7 (Continued)
Review Summary Table

No	Author	Year	Title	Journal	Aim	Relevance	Application Area	Technologies	Methods	Opportunities	Constraints
2	Rathore et al.	2018	Urban Planning and building smart cities based on the Internet of Things using Big Data analytics	*Computer Networks*	To propose a system of interconnected sensors that retrieve urban related data via IoT; from pollution, congestion, and transport frequency	Studies the manner in which the deployment of sensor devices based on IoT technologies has the potential to further inform researchers about shifting and evolving trends within an urban ecosystem; further informing policy making decisions. Presents the linkage between big data retrieval via IoT and analysis.	Government Smart City	IoT AI	Systematic deployment of IoT devices throughout various urban goods and services, particularly, transport hubs, surveillance (CCTV), and traffic	To accumulate urban data via an interconnected network sustained by IoT sensor devices enables real time access to data; this permit to identify shifting dynamics within an urban setting, in demand and supply of various services.	IoT sensor devices require further implementation of self-learning software that prioritises certain data over other; increased amounts of data results in more complex readability
3	Sedkaoui, S., & Khelfaoui, M.	2019	Understand, develop and enhance the learning process with urban big data	*Information Discovery and Delivery*	To develop a system that categorises consumer sentiment via software	Precedent for predictive analysis in the form of behaviour patterns. Provides foundation for in-depth understanding of learning processes in population; informs urban decisions regarding stakeholders. Informs further research about the ways in which Big Data Analytics can be employed in improving stakeholder interactions.	Community Planning Society Governance	AI IoT	Machine-learning software retrieved behaviour patterns and categorised level of engagement	To test the effectiveness of a good or service at satisfying stakeholder expectation	Focuses on individual stakeholder feedback does not discuss agglomeration of multiple stakeholder feedback

(Continued)

TABLE 1.7 *(Continued)*

Review Summary Table

No	Author	Year	Title	Journal	Aim	Relevance	Application Area	Technologies	Methods	Opportunities	Constraints
4	Singh et al.	2019	Fog computing: From architecture to edge computing and big data processing	*Journal of Supercomputing*	To determine alternate infrastructure for storage of Big Data that maximises capacity	Determines communication structure of data retrieval devices throughout the city. In Big data relevance, cloud networks and the emerging fog computing designs are assessed in order to determine the most proficient and less disruptive computational architectures that permit the utilisation of the Internet of Things	Smart City Governance	IoT AI Blockchain Smart Grid	Comparison between cloud computing and fog computing, cross-referencing software. Pilot Crowd Number Test	Enhanced connectivity of IoT appliances, self-learning smart city via interactive cloud	IoT unites all appliances into one network, alteration in the transport system e.g., lead to disruptions in other areas
5	Fiore et al.	2019	An integrated big and fast data analytics platform for smart urban transportation management	*IEEE Access*	To explore the way in which the City Administration Dashboard proposed in this study enables urban big data reading and consequent decision making	The application of a local administration dashboard based on big data analysis monitors the transportation system of Curitiba; the technology utilises GPS to inform vehicles of routes as well as AVL to locate buses and predict increased passenger transit in the network.	Smart City Transport Governance	IoT AI	Automatic vehicle location and automatic fare collecting based on IoT sensor devices	Increased ability to foresee the withstanding capacity of a transport network via the use of sensor technologies, GPS and AVL; informing real time decision making	The administration of the service depends solely on big data analysis which relies on external devices for data retrieval, faults in devices jeopardises integrity of system

(Continued)

TABLE 1.7 *(Continued)*
Review Summary Table

No	Author	Year	Title	Journal	Aim	Relevance	Application Area	Technologies	Methods	Opportunities	Constraints
6	Nigel et al.	2018	Precomputing architecture for flexible and efficient big data analytics	*Vietnam Journal of Computer Science*	To assess existing systems utilised in optimising Big Data performance	Studies the architecture of data retrieval systems in urban ecosystems; Clarifies current gaps in knowledge about the ways in which computational systems/databases function and further inform future possibilities about the potential improvements in big data retrieval	Economy Smart City	AI and cloud computing in the area of Smart Economy IoT	Tested velocity of IoT closed system with time interval measuring software; compared performance between fog and cloud systems.	Informs the way in which IoT and big data systems are to be implemented in a closed habitat (cities)	Discussion is limited on solutions for gaps in knowledge
7	Pfeifer et al.	2015	Big data for better urban life? – an exploratory study of critical urban issues in two Caribbean cities: Paramaribo (Suriname) and Port of Spain (Trinidad and Tobago)	*The European Journal of Development Research*	To review population behaviour and concerns via geo-twitter Big Data analysis	Focuses on flooding, security, and poverty; informs city decisions. The prevalence, recurrence, and intensity of themes within a population are more easily identifiable via Big Data systems; consequently, providing a more holistic view of challenges which inform city policy making	Environment Community Planning Governance	AI and cloud computing in the area of Smart Governance AI and cloud computing in the area of Smart Grid	Geo-twitter analysis of population opinion about various issues afflicting their communities, results were utilised to create a map containing city areas where concern level were highest.	Direct feedback retrieval from population via geo-twitter sentiment analysis informing future city policy making	Big data strategy may potentially result in reduced direct interaction with community

(Continued)

TABLE 1.7 (Continued)
Review Summary Table

No	Author	Year	Title	Journal	Aim	Relevance	Application Area	Technologies	Methods	Opportunities	Constraints
8	Hillbert, M.	2015	Big data for development: A review of promises and challenges	*Development Policy Review*	To explore the way in which certain system infrastructure hinders performance of Big Data analytics.	Pinpoints the specific contexts in which Big Data can be hindered and ultimately perish, this article presents a view of the issues that need addressing in order to ensure the full deployment of Big Data systems in cities; specifically, self-learning algorithms that solve data inconsistencies.	Smart City	IoT 5G AI and cloud computing in the area of Smart Grid	Big data follows a pattern of behaviour which is studied in order to determine reliability of data.	Guides the implementation of IoT appliances and big data in cities	Most existing digital infrastructure is not designed to withstand IoT data loads
9	Fan et al.	2014	Challenges of Big Data analysis	*National Science Review*	To identify alterations needed in the employment of Big Data analytics to enhance processing performance.	Analyses challenges of existing computational infrastructure in city networks, this informs of specific frailties in the system which require further research and analysis for enhanced urban Big Data communication	Smart City	AI and cloud computing in the area of Smart Grid IoT	Cloud computing performance is recorded to determine the amount of big data handle by a cloud system potentially.	Informs of the use of qualitative input in big data analysis to predict urban trends	The process of quantifying qual data may result in skewed readings

(Continued)

TABLE 1.7 *(Continued)*

Review Summary Table

No	Author	Year	Title	Journal	Aim	Relevance	Application Area	Technologies	Methods	Opportunities	Constraints
10	Brower et al.	2019	Big qual: Defining and debating qualitative inquiry for large data sets	*International Journal of Qualitative Methods*	To develop a framework for the study of qualitative data using Big Data analytics.	Clarifies the importance of ensuring user confidence in the capabilities of big data in handling various types of data, focuses on the challenges that big data experiences in relation to qualitative data input. By presenting and highlighting the elements that need consideration in order to ensure the functionality of qualitative big data analysis, the ground for further improvement is provided	Transport Planning – Travel Behaviour Environment	AI and cloud computing in the area of Smart Governance AI and cloud computing in the area of Smart Energy	Comparison between cloud computing and fog computing, cross referencing software	The capacity to carry out Big Data Analytics on data containing public sentiment, imagery, and abstract variables	Framework is inherently limited as it must use quantitative means to interpret qualitative data which may result in corrupting qualitative data
11	Wey, W., & Peng, T.	2021	Study on Building a Smart Sustainable City Assessment Framework Using Big Data and Analytic Network Process	*Journal of Urban Planning and Development*	To explore the way in which smart city technologies can be utilised to increase ecological sustainability	Presents the way in which Singapore and Taipei achieved high sustainable city scores by dissecting urban data trends via big data analysis; prime governance indicators were identified	Smart City Governance	AI and cloud computing in the area of Smart Governance	Utilised ten quality governance indicators and assessed results of ten area via big data analysis	To view the way in which governance strategies affect urban trends, primarily by studying trends a score is given to governance strategy	More applications of this approach are required worldwide in order to establish its objectivity, in various contexts.

(Continued)

TABLE 1.7 (Continued)

Review Summary Table

No	Author	Year	Title	Journal	Aim	Relevance	Application Area	Technologies	Methods	Opportunities	Constraints
12	Boeing, G.	2019	Housing search in the age of big data: Smarter cities or the same old blind spots?	*Smart Cities, Housing and Community Development Policy*	To propose a quantitative use for existing Real Estate data and carry out Big Data Analytics in order to identify urban trends.	Dissects the potential sources from which a smart city can derive the information/data that inform its technological self-actualisation; in this case, it is presented that real estate listings are reliable datasets that have the potential of further informing about other urban variables such as inequality and lack of accessibility to resources	Smart City	AI and cloud computing in the area of Smart Transport AI and cloud computing in the area of Smart Infrastructure AI and cloud computing in the area of Smart Governance IoT	Systematic scanning of millions of Craigslist rental listings in the United States; followed by urban trends analysis via Big Data Analytics	Property data provides demographic, income, accessibility, education information which informs governance strategies	Amount and accessibility to rental listing data is determined by shifting supply and demand; reduced supply results in less data to be studied
13	Babar, M. & Arif, F.	2017	Smart urban planning using Big Data analytics to contend with the interoperability in Internet of Things	*Future Generation Computer Systems*	To develop a smart city scheme that uses big data analysis to determine needs in the urban grid	Presents the potential for the implementation on an interconnected network of IoT devices that inform city officials about transport, parking, environmental needs; retrieval of big data and consequent analysis automate decision making in northern Spain	Smart City Smart grid	IoT AI and cloud computing in the area of Smart Governance	Assessment of IoT device sensing capabilities and objectivity of data retrieved	To inform other jurisdictions about ways in which cloud networks informed by IoT censors can automate the process of city governance and policy making.	Further research is needed in the area of data acquisition via IoT devices, as fault in a device results in no data collection and interrupted governance.

(Continued)

TABLE 1.7 (Continued)
Review Summary Table

(Continued)

No	Author	Year	Title	Journal	Aim	Relevance	Application Area	Technologies	Methods	Opportunities	Constraints
14	Babar, M., Arif, F.	2019	Real-time data processing scheme using big data analytics in internet of things based smart transportation environment	*Journal of Ambient Intelligence and Humanised Computing*	To identify applications for IoT technologies in the context of smart transportation	Focuses on optimising the way in which travelling occurs within cities; Big Data can assist in the enhancement of productivity by achieving more sustainable transportation	Governance Smart City Economy	AI and cloud computing in the area of Smart Transport AI and cloud computing in the area of Smart Economy	NoSQL software for big data analysis performance recording	IoT in transport context merges data from various services, optimises transportation within cities	Further consideration must be given to qualitative data role in establishing transport corridors
15	Lock et al.	2020	The visual analytics of big, open public transport data – a framework and pipeline for monitoring system performance in Greater Sydney	*Big Earth Data*	To analyse the way in which visual data can be analysed via Big Data analytics to inform transport decisions	Systematic applicability of methods that have been designed and developed to facilitate the study of processes that require big data analysis in order to predict trends and growth; methodology predicted passenger growth over time, equipping city authorities of procedures that will be required to sustain said growth	Society Smart City – Urban Growth	AI and cloud computing in the area of Smart Transport 5G IoT Blockchain	General transit data was fed to the self-learning algorithm to determine transport infrastructure capacity	Permits to visualise future growth trends and determine needed transport infrastructure	Does not utilise data from other urban services in order to further inform decisions

TABLE 1.7 (Continued)
Review Summary Table

No	Author	Year	Title	Journal	Aim	Relevance	Application Area	Technologies	Methods	Opportunities	Constraints
16	Bibri, S.	2018	The IoT for smart sustainable cities of the future: An analytical framework for sensor-based big data applications for environmental sustainability	*Sustainable Cities and Society*	To assess existing literature discourse on the capabilities of IoT sensors and potentials data retrieval via this method.	The augmentation of the available data in urban contexts is presented in this study, as well as analytical frameworks that automate the reading of urban data via IoT networks built on cloud computing permit suitable decision making	Smart City Governance Transport	IoT	Optimised performance of smart devices (traffic lights) was measured via remote censors to determine Big data retrieval capacity of device	Provides a framework for maximising the retrieval capacity of data of various IoT devices by leveraging state-of-the art censor systems that enhance censing capabilities of IoT devices.	Censor technology is still in early stages that does not yet accommodate the full potential of big data analysis.
17	Huang, JY., Wey, WM	2019	Application of Big Data and Analytic Network Process for the Adaptive Reuse Strategies of School Land	*Social Indicators Research*	To develop a framework that assists in categorising potential uses for land based on retrieved urban data	Establish the feasibility and usability of land within Taipei; the precedent for future application of indicators as methods of Big Data categorisation will support future attempts to use Big Data Analytics as a way to systematically classify the use of city parts and their land use potential	Smart City – Land Use Governance Economy	AI IoT	Geo-data is analysed by deep-learning software to determine the feasibility and potential of land parcels according to distance from city centre.	Promises to gain the most utility out of existing land based on data analysis	May result in unfair distribution of land use from a socio-economic perspective

(Continued)

TABLE 1.7 (Continued)

Review Summary Table

No	Author	Year	Title	Journal	Aim	Relevance	Application Area	Technologies	Methods	Opportunities	Constraints
18	Morgan, C.	2020	Can Smart Cities Be Environmentally Sustainable? Urban Big Data Analytics and the Citizen-driven Internet of Things	*Geopolitics, History, and International Relations*	To explore via a literature review whether academic research sustains the environmental suitability of smart cities.	Explores the interaction between sustainability and enhanced city performance via an IoT device that feed big data retrieval; presents how urban sustainability can be attained via big data analysis; IoT sensor device technology potential in informing big data analysis is presented	Smart City Society Environment	IoT	Wireless IoT sensing device was assessed in accuracy of urban data retrieval; increased performance equalled increased sustainability score.	Provides insights into how IoT sensing devices can be utilised in big data retrieval with the objective of determining performance score and attain sustainable outcomes based on insights	The topic requires further research in regard to the inherent limitations of big data systems and how they impact the accuracy of performance score.
19	Khalifa et al.	2016	The six pillars for building big data analytics ecosystems	*Analytics Journal*	To test the design of big data analysis systems utilised in various urban contexts	Cohesive digital ecosystem interaction; organising data as a consequence and enabling readability through an interface that enables real-time analytics. This is essential in the implementation of IoT in smart cities	Governance Economy	AI and cloud computing in the area of Smart Grid AI	Hadoop data mining software categorises big data based on level of utility in informing the IoT system.	Ensures big data analysis processes remain consistent and do not corrupt future analysis	Due to broad analysis does not delve into different IoT uses and how each use requires different analysis design

(Continued)

TABLE 1.7 (*Continued*)

Review Summary Table

No	Author	Year	Title	Journal	Aim	Relevance	Application Area	Technologies	Methods	Opportunities	Constraints
20	Zeng et al.	2010	Social Media Analytics and Intelligence	*IEEE Intelligent Systems*	To evaluate applications of social media analytics and intelligence as in decision-making frameworks	Presents potentials within IoT, AI, and major components of social media analytics, towards richer and newer cities and their societies	Society Politics	IoT AI	User-generated content Consumer-generated media	Clear growth of applications, text mining, collaborative tagging, etc.	Could result in Possibilities of unsustainable growth Lack of structure and contingency
21	Moe et al.	2017	Opportunities for Innovation in Social Media Analytics	*The Journal of Product Innovation Management*	To evaluate social media analytics in terms of stakeholder engagement insights	Defines the relationship between social media platforms and stakeholder engagement, including citizens, businesses, organisations, and cities	Smart Education Marketing Consumer Science Disaster Management	IoT	Tags Privacy	Clear identification of stakeholder insight space, problems, and solutions	N/A
22	Zha et al.	2016	Social media analytics and learning	*Neurocomputing (Amsterdam)*	To summarise social media analytics in various emerging domains	Discusses applications of various social media analytics technologies and methods into urban and city contexts	Society Disaster Management	IoT Data Mining Machine Learning	Personalised search Community-based topic structuralisation Local features with adaptive region	Possibilities of improvements of applications in various domains	N/A
23	Kordzadeh et al.	2020	How Social Media Analytics Can Inform Content Strategies	*Journal of Computer Information Systems*	To identify social media analytics in user engagement and social content strategy developments	Identifies the use of social media analytics by companies and organisations for different purposes, throughout evaluating social media usage by users and competitors	Society Smart Health	IoT	Evaluations of likes, shares, and comments Evaluations of multimedia elements	Clear identification of improvable guidelines of social media analytics framework	Likelihood of conflicting results: Negative relation between post length, numbers of likes, comments, and shares

(Continued)

TABLE 1.7 *(Continued)*

Review Summary Table

No	Author	Year	Title	Journal	Aim	Relevance	Application Area	Technologies	Methods	Opportunities	Constraints
24	Yang et al.	2020	Location-Centric Social Media Analytics: Challenges and Opportunities for Smart Cities	*IEEE Intelligent Systems*	To discuss characteristics of location-based social media analytics and their opportunities and challenges in smart cities	Identifies the contexts, roles, opportunities, and applications of Location Based Social Networks (LBSN) in urban environments and smart city agendas	Society Smart Surveillance	IoT GPS	Location Based Social Networks (LBSN)	Clear identification of improvable guidelines of social media analytics framework	Invasion of privacy
25	Moss et al.	2015	Knowing your publics: The use of social media analytics in local government	*Information Polity*	To identify major stakeholders (such as residents, governments, etc.) throughout social media analytics and how to benefit them	Discusses the usage of social media by local governments, throughout social media data from public and others	Society Politics Governance	IoT	Semantic Polling Networked Public Sphere	Clear identifications of stakeholder needs and more effective communications among themselves	Invasion of privacy Likelihood of provoking conflicts among stakeholders
26	Yao, F., & Wang, Y.	2020	Towards resilient and smart cities: A real-time urban analytical and geo-visual system for social media streaming data	*Sustainable Cities and Society*	Explores how an urban analytical system based on geo-tagging tweets is capable of elaborating a landscape of urban events	Urban analytical system leveraging geo-mapping software ArcGIS interlinks mapping data with data retrieved via geo-tagged tweets; classifying a range of urban events and respective location; applications inform city authorities of issues.	Society – Stakeholder Engagement Politics	Artificial Intelligence (AI)	Geo-twitter sentiment analysis via the retrieval of key words determined recurrent themes in the urban ecosystem.	Provides insights into how to engage existing social media platforms in informing a geo-analysis of urban needs.	The system is prone to gaps in knowledge as sentiment word value may change according to tweet context.

(Continued)

TABLE 1.7 *(Continued)*

Review Summary Table

No	Author	Year	Title	Journal	Aim	Relevance	Application Area	Technologies	Methods	Opportunities	Constraints
27	Ye et al.	2020	Urban function recognition by integrating social media and street-level imagery	*Environment and Planning*	To attempt to predict human activity in the urban context by tagging verbs used in tweets	Presents how identifying recurrent verbs in a social media platform, in this case twitter, informs city officials of the most likely activities to be undertaken by a population; the latter further informs deep-learning algorithms.	Smart City Governance	Artificial Intelligence (AI)	Tagging recurrent verbs in tweets to determine and predict the activities to be carried out by a population.	Real time insights of potential activities to be carried out by a demographic informs city officials about strategies that are needed in order to sustain increased use of a good or service.	Public opinion on this form of activity is perceived as an infringement of privacy, consequently, reduced number of tweets may emerge.
28	Pääkkönen et al.	2020	Credibility by automation: Expectations of future knowledge production in social media analytics	*Convergence*	To investigate applications of social media analytics towards identified problems	Discusses the significance of credibility in social media analytics for smoother automation without any human interpretation along with businesses, organisations, and cities	Society Marketing	IoT Automation	Data-led thinking	Efficiency and business profit	Interference of human interpretation Significance of minimisation
29	Yang, S., & Zeng, X.	2018	Sustainability of government social media: A multi-analytic approach to predict citizens' mobile government microblog continuance	*Sustainability*	To investigate how mobile government microblogs affect the usage of social media by citizens	Demonstrates the significance of credibility and public-private partnership in mobile government microblogs, as well as hazards of excessive monitoring	Society Governance	IoT Smart Surveillance	Mobile government microblog	Enhanced interactivity, mobility, and value of usage intention	Excessive monitoring by government agencies Invasion of privacy

(Continued)

TABLE 1.7 (Continued)
Review Summary Table

No	Author	Year	Title	Journal	Aim	Relevance	Application Area	Technologies	Methods	Opportunities	Constraints
30	Stieglitz et al.	2018	Social media analytics – Challenges in topic discovery, data collection, and data preparation	*International Journal of Information Management*	To provide challenges and recommendations for social media analysts in various domains in relation to big data analytics	Discusses a wide range of social media analysis methods and their complexities, in terms of their domains (business, entertainments, science, crisis managements, and politics) and steps	Society Politics Stakeholder Management Marketing Science Event / Disaster Management	Information Technology (IT) AI and cloud computing in the area of Smart Surveillance	Data discovery, tracking, preparation, and analysis	More effective communication and participation in politics and journalism	Complexities within contemporary social media systems
31	Nanda, P. & Kumar, V.	2019	Social Media to Social Media Analytics: Ethical Challenges	*International Journal of Technoethics*	To underpin the significance of ethical implications of social media analytics, in individual and organisational perspectives	Demonstrates the significance of ethical implications of social media analytics by discussing its harness among companies, organisations, and cities to maintain reputation at last	Society Ethics	IoT	Ethical engagement	N/A	Unethical behaviours and consequential negative impacts
32	Chen et al.	2016	De-Biasing the Reporting Bias in Social Media Analytics	*Production and Operations Management*	To demonstrate challenges and necessity their of user-generated contents (UGC)	Presents user-generated contents (UGC) among different sentiments and various experiences of users, companies, organisations, and cities and its bias due to freedom of silence	Society Governance Smart City	IoT Smart Surveillance	User-generated content (UGC)	N/A	Bias within users and businesses Invasion of privacy

(Continued)

TABLE 1.7 (Continued)

Review Summary Table

No	Author	Year	Title	Journal	Aim	Relevance	Application Area	Technologies	Methods	Opportunities	Constraints
33	Zhang et al.	2020	Semi-automated social media analytics for sensing societal impacts due to community disruptions during disasters	*Computer-Aided Civil and Infrastructure Engineering*	To identify how social media analytics contribute to managing disasters and other catastrophes	Demonstrates the significance of effective decision-making in coordinations of societal impacts and disasters throughout social media analytics	Society Construction Smart City Disaster Management	AI and cloud computing in the areas of Smart Surveillance Smart Environment Smart Infrastructure	Social sensing of Disaster Impacts and Societal Considerations (SocialDISC)	Effectiveness in construction industries and their necessities	Invasion of privacy for construction workers
34	Petrescu Maria et al.	2020	The dilemma of social media algorithms and analytics	*Journal of Marketing Analytics*	To depict negative insights of contemporary social media usages and necessary ethics	Discusses the negative sides of modern social media platforms such as addictions and privacy breaches, as well as how it jeopardises smart city initiatives	Society Community Planning	IoT	Twitter extraction	N/A	Unethical behaviours and consequential negative impacts
35	De Andrade, S. C. et al.	2020	A multicriteria optimisation framework for the definition of the spatial granularity of urban social media analytics	*International Journal of Geographical Information Science*	To demonstrate how spatial analysis is conducted in identifying urban phenomena and demographic patterns	Discusses applications of social media analytics towards into spatial analysis in cities, throughout Twitter: Geo-tagged social media datasets	Society Smart City	IoT AI and cloud computing in the area of Smart Surveillance	Spatial analysis Twitter extraction Multi-criteria decision analysis (MCDA) Geo-tagged social media data	Developments in statistical analysis in cities	Dependent on hypothesis

(Continued)

TABLE 1.7 *(Continued)*
Review Summary Table

No	Author	Year	Title	Journal	Aim	Relevance	Application Area	Technologies	Methods	Opportunities	Constraints
36	Laurell et al.	2019	Exploring barriers to adoption of Virtual Reality through Social Media Analytics and Machine Learning – An assessment of technology, network, price, and trialability	*Journal of Business Research*	To identify applications, utilisations, and barriers Virtual Reality (VR) based on social media analytics	Demonstrates the trends and characteristics of Virtual Reality (VR) and relationship with social media analytics, as well as towards smart city initiatives	Social Robots Consumer Science Community Planning	Virtual Reality (VR) Machine Learning	Data discovery, tracking, preparation, and analysis	Benefits to customers for complementary products	Possibility of slow adoptions
37	Stieglitz et al.	2013	Social media and political communication: A social media analytics framework	*Social Network Analysis and Marketing*	To demonstrate applications of social media analytics towards political communications and discussions	Demonstrates how large and complex datasets are being utilised in business, organisations, and cities, including microblogging services and social network sites	Politics Governance Society	IoT	Microblogging Data tracking – Application programming interfaces (API)	Easier and clearer identifications of requirements of citizens and political organisations	Excessive transparency Invasion of privacy
38	Andriole, S.	2019	Social Media Analytics, Wearable Technology, and the Internet-of-Things	*IT Professional*	Discusses required understandings of Internet-of-Things (IoT), including social media platforms)	Discusses related potential impacts to Internet-of-Things (IoT), pilot sponsors, and project planning for managers, executives, and building-related workers, throughout widening and deepening insights by its analytics	Production Consumer Science Smart cities	IoT Wearable Technology	Pilot Project Planning	More convenient and effective production	Excessive reliance

(Continued)

TABLE 1.7 (*Continued*)

Review Summary Table

No	Author	Year	Title	Journal	Aim	Relevance	Application Area	Technologies	Methods	Opportunities	Constraints
39	Tang et al.	2017	Social Media Data Analytics for the U.S. Construction Industry: Preliminary Study on Twitter	*Journal of Management in Engineering*	Discusses applications of social media analytics in constructions	Discusses the significance of social media towards construction clusters (workers, companies, and unions)	Smart Cities Smart Buildings Politics	IoT Data Mining Machine Learning	Data discovery, tracking, preparation, and analysis Twitter extraction	Benefits in working conditions	Excessive transparency Invasion of privacy for workers
40	Fan, W., & Yan, X.	2015	Novel applications of social media analytics	*Information & Management*	To identify the relationship between user generated contents (UGC) and social media analytics	Presents brand new trends in social media platforms and applications towards smart city initiatives: user generated contents (UGC), providing a wide range of opportunities and challenges	Society Community Planning	IoT	User-generated content (UGC)	Smarter workflow for users, firms, corporations, state, and government agencies	Differentiated privacy results in terms of age, gender, etc.
41	Zhu et al.	2019	Geo-tagged social media data-based analytical approach for perceiving impacts of social events	*ISPRS International Journal of Geo-Information*	To discover the relationship between social media analytics and understandings of negative social events	Demonstrates how geo-tagged social media applications support significant social events, such as disasters and other catastrophes, in terms of extracting important and complex information	Society Disaster Management Community Planning	IoT AI and Cloud computing Machine Learning Natural Language Processing (NLP) Latent District Allocation (LDA)	Data discovery, tracking, preparation, and analysis – Geo-tagged social media data	Accurate identification of location-based data Easy applications	Inconsistent and limited accessibility to datasets

(Continued)

TABLE 1.7 (Continued)
Review Summary Table

No	Author	Year	Title	Journal	Aim	Relevance	Application Area	Technologies	Methods	Opportunities	Constraints
42	Shigibauer et al.	2014	Semantic social media analytics of CSR image: The benefit to know stakeholders' perspective	*Problems and Perspectives in Management*	To demonstrate the relationship between corporate social responsibility (CSR) and social media platforms	Demonstrates responsibilities of companies' or organisations' perceptions and expectations towards smart city initiatives, in relation to other stakeholders	Marketing Stakeholder Management	IoT Information Technology (IT)	Social sentiment analysis	Clear and concise identification of stakeholder insight space, problems solutions, and responsibilities	Complexity, informality, fragmentation Possibility of slow adoptions
43	Sebei et al.	2018	Review of social media analytics process and Big Data pipeline	*Social Network Analysis and Mining*	To review the entire social media analytics procedures in regard to critical support of big data analytics	Reviews the entire social media analytics procedures in regard to critical support and relationship with big data technologies	Smart Cities Smart Buildings Smart Health Politics Disaster Management	IoT Data Mining Machine Learning	Sentiment analysis, classification Social network analysis Data discovery, tracking, preparation, and analysis	Accurate, concise, and broad applications in various domains	Remaining challenges in big data analytics
44	Kourtit, K.	2019	Cultural heritage, smart cities, and digital data analytics.	*Eastern Journal of European Studies*	To showcase the demand for more cultural amenities in smart cities to provide a broader attractiveness to the city profile	Most studies regarding the evolution of city planning are related to urban land use planning. Most research planning research has been to culturally attractive and sustainable a city is and how it operates.	Smart Cities	AI and cloud computing in the area of Smart governance	Urban analytics and digital research were used to provide a multidimensional research study.	Informs the work of research findings to measure cultural, attractiveness, and sustainability of an area	Further data metrics policies are needed to ensure effective cultural heritage policies are used

(Continued)

TABLE 1.7 (Continued)

Review Summary Table

No	Author	Year	Title	Journal	Aim	Relevance	Application Area	Technologies	Methods	Opportunities	Constraints
45	Boeing, G	2018	Measuring the complexity of urban form and design	*Urban Design International*	To present a framework that	This journal article notes urban data and its city analysis. Complexity is under performing and there is a lack resilience. The framework looks at the network of a city and analyses urban form and a person experience	Urban Form Big Data	AI and cloud computing in the area of Smart surveillance	Systematic Performance Network analysis of urban forms and designs	Metrics enable urban designers to examine and analyse adaptability, resilience, connectedness, and liability	More focus needs to be put on visual, temporal, spatial, connectivity, and scaling measures of the urban form
46	Lofgren, K. & Webster, W.	2020	The value of Big Data in government: The case of 'smart cities'.	*Big Data and Society*	To analyse the evolution of digital governance research	The value chain has been applied in a governmental context to take into account the stages of urban data in a smart city context. The analysis made from this is that different types of values and information can be taken from urban data analytics	Transport Planning Sustainability Big Data Governance	AI and cloud computing in the area of Smart governance	Data was found through the use of sensor to generate decisions and services. Value chain analysis	Studying transportation, public safety and sustainability within a smart city, urban analytics demonstrates that urban analytics and urban data tools are increasingly relevant and important to government bodies.	Issues include urban digital data and the ethics on using this data as has caused issues with quality and reliability

(Continued)

TABLE 1.7 (Continued)
Review Summary Table

No	Author	Year	Title	Journal	Aim	Relevance	Application Area	Technologies	Methods	Opportunities	Constraints
47	Lim et al.	2018	Smart cities with big data: Reference models, challenges, and considerations.	*Cities*	To analyse four reference model to identify challenges relating to smart cities and big data	The journal article found six challenges in the research 1. Data quality management due to the amount of urban data available 2. Data integration 3. Data privacy 4. Understanding of the citizens and residents of the data being used 5. Methods to delivery geographic information The 'design of smart city services that deliver information from urban big data'	Smart City Urban Form Governance	AI and cloud computing in the area of Smart governance	Information and Communication Technologies (ICT) and Latent Dirichlet Allocation (word cloud) were used to collect information and is used as a technique to understand data	Future application-oriented discussions on the use of urban big data	There are privacy and security issues associated with big data collection that need to be improved and managed
48	Clifton et al.	2008	Quantitative analysis of urban form: A multidisciplinary review	*Journal of Urbanism: International Research on Placemaking and Urban Sustainability*	To provide an analysis of urban form.	Analyses urban form into five areas which include landscape ecology, economic structure, surface transportation, community design and urban design Providing a framework for a how urban data literature can be reviewed	Urban Form	AI and cloud computing in the area of Smart grid	Use and analysis of Graphing Information. System Mapping Multidisciplinary Review	Opportunity to use GIS research technology to collect urban analytics	Concern for urban sprawl and its impacts of traffic congestion, property taxes, and loss of urban space

(Continued)

TABLE 1.7 (Continued)

Review Summary Table

No	Author	Year	Title	Journal	Aim	Relevance	Application Area	Technologies	Methods	Opportunities	Constraints
49	Fleischmann et al.	2020	Measuring urban form: Overcoming terminological inconsistencies for a quantitative and comprehensive morphologic analysis of cities	*Environment and Planning B: Urban Analytics and City Science*	To perform an analysis on urban form and urban morphology	Quantitative approaches to urban morphology are needed in order to continually inform future findings. His article also noted that What is needed is future research on quantitative analysis of urban form	Urban Form	AI and cloud computing in the area of Smart grid	Quantitative Analysis measuring urban form	Quantitative approaches are used to uncover limits and potentials of existing measuring methods	Terminological inconsistencies Terminology was very unclear across the numerous literatures reviewed
50	Kitchin, et al.	2015	Knowing and governing cities through urban indicators, city benchmarking, and real-time dashboards	*Regional Studies, Regional Science*	To understand the governance of cities by research indicators, benchmarking, and dashboards	Defines that urban data that relates to indicators, benchmarks, and dashboards have become more used in data collection	Governance	AI and cloud computing in the area of Smart government	Real-time data caught through sensors, social and locative media, and cameras.	Initiatives argue that they advance an epistemology view that reshapes how people come to know and later govern cities. This is taking the city as a visualised fact	Indicators, benchmarks, and dashboards have been used to make urban processes, however, are often overlooked

(Continued)

TABLE 1.7 (Continued)
Review Summary Table

No	Author	Year	Title	Journal	Aim	Relevance	Application Area	Technologies	Methods	Opportunities	Constraints
51	Kourtit et al.	2019	Cultural Heritage Appraisal by Visitors to Global Cities: The Use of Social Media and Urban Analytics in Urban Buzz Research.	*Sustainability*	To present a collection of data that analyses the cultural heritage aspect of a place	Enjoyment of general amenities lead to tourist satisfaction regarding cultural elements. From this, it can be suggested the management of cultural amenities and assets regarding tourism should be heavily considered just as important as urban image and dynamics	Society	Digital information (e.g., trip bookings, travel decisions, tourist site evaluations)	Social Media Collection	The management of cultural amenities and assets regarding tourism should be heavily considered just as important as urban image and dynamics	There is a need for amenities as it increases tourism attractiveness. This is to be used in conjunction with urban infrastructure and landscapes. It was also found that cultural assets only contributed to the attractiveness due to their commodification and integration
52	Osman, A. M. S	2019	A novel big data analytics framework for smart cities	*Future Generation Computer Systems*	To provide evidence on the benefits of using big data analytics for smart cities using a framework	The findings from this journal article noted that big data is an increasing trend that works to provide further analysis to the person	Smart City	AI and cloud computing in the area of Smart governance	ICT collection and analysis	New functionalities being used in smart cities in terms of model management and aggregation	Conversations regarding big data analytics characteristics are further needed

(Continued)

TABLE 1.7 (Continued)

Review Summary Table

No	Author	Year	Title	Journal	Aim	Relevance	Application Area	Technologies	Methods	Opportunities	Constraints
53	Puiu et al.	2012	CityPulse: Large Scale Data Analytics Framework for Smart Cities	*IEEE Access*	To develop a framework to not only analyse data for smart cities, but also the benefits of using this framework across other fields	As cities are beginning to sprawl, they have begun using deploy sensors to make the public feel more at ease. This framework, however, was found to be able to be used in many different scenarios and reduce complexity and time	Smart Cities	IoT Data sensors	A framework was developed to explore and analyse the benefits of using big data. Collected by sensors and general data collection	This framework was found to be able to be used in many different scenarios and reduce complexity and time	Need for more intelligent uses of resources that relate to urbanisation. Needs to be more research done on the collection and visual isolation of datasets
54	Rabari, C., & Storper, M.	2015	The digital skin of cities: Urban theory and research in the age of the sensored and metered city, ubiquitous computing and big data	*Cambridge Journal of Regions, Economy and Society*	To develop a framework to analyse the digital skin of cities	Looking at smart city management systems and governance and participation to distinguish the difference between a 'real' city and a smart city	Smart Cities	IoT Data sensors	Digital Skin – sensored and metered urban development	The difference is past and present and the modes of information collections that have advanced or been introduced	Digital skin is a portfolio of such urban aspects and techniques The data collection process notes that this form needs to be advanced as the findings can be inconsistent and broad
55	Rathore et al.	2018	Exploiting IoT and big data analytics: Defining Smart Digital City using real-time urban data	*Sustainable Cities and Society*	The interconnection of urban smart data, and IoT devices	Collect urban data is exampled in this journal article This system has been proven to be feasible and work to analyse smart cities and smart city sensors	Smart City	IoT Data sensors	Sensors for vehicular networking, smart parking, smart home, surveillance, weather, and water monitoring system	Introduction of world smart city sensors around the world	This system has also proven to be efficient for real-time data processing and scalability

(Continued)

TABLE 1.7 (Continued)
Review Summary Table

No	Author	Year	Title	Journal	Aim	Relevance	Application Area	Technologies	Methods	Opportunities	Constraints
56	Pathiranage et al.	2018	Remote Sensing Data and SLEUTH Urban Growth Model: As Decision Support Tools for Urban Planning	*Chinese Geographical Science*	To analyse reviews and test theories from the SLEUTH framework and journal	After analysis of the urban landforms in the simulation, it was determined that the SLEUTH model was the most useful planning tool for the future urbanisation of cities in Sri Lanka. The SLEUTH model is an automata/cellular based model that is a computer simulation that analyses historical land use and cove, road, hillshade, and slope	Smart City Urban Planning	Data sensors	Sensors SLEUTH model data collection – computer simulation	The SLEUTH model provides a continuous use framework that can be used in many different areas	there is a need for urban plans and improvements to be put in place
57	Cheng. J.	2011	Exploring urban morphology using multi-temporal urban growth data: A case study of Wuhan, China	*Asian Geographer*	To provide research on urban morphology	It was found that urban analytics are typically collected by and/or commercial enterprises and have small survey sample sizes	Smart City	Spatial analysis	Sample surveys to investigate research and mapping	The findings present a lost opportunity in visualising and analysing the amount of available data	Poor interpretation of urban morphology. Using research, mapping, and surveys, collecting urban analytics can be illegible due to the scale of the study

(Continued)

TABLE 1.7 (Continued)

Review Summary Table

No	Author	Year	Title	Journal	Aim	Relevance	Application Area	Technologies	Methods	Opportunities	Constraints
58	Behnisch et al.	2019	Urban big data analytics and morphology.	Urban Analytics and City Science	To perform an analysis on urban morphology and determine trends	On a spatial and temporal scale, the article notes the concept of the burgage cycle and the theory of natural movement, when researching streets, plots and buildings. The journal article also noted a multi-step geoprocessing approach for small-scale urban form analysis that takes into account morphological indicators	Urban Form	Spatial analysis	Geo-referenced data Spatial metrics	After the influence of spatial configuration on human spatial behaviour was analysed, it was found that spatial cognition is actually solely determined by space and not people and that there is further need for this	Noted that attractiveness and accessibility need to be in the approach to form a basis for modelling applications
59	Kaur, H., & Garg, P.	2019	Urban sustainability assessment tools: A review.	Journal of Cleaner Production	To provide a review of urban sustainability assessment tools	The Himalayan hill regions of India were used as a subject area to research Notes that different aspects of different tools were given more importance and do not address all context-specific aspects of the others	Urban Form	AI and cloud computing in the area of Smart city	Performance analysis study in the Himalayan hill, India.	Notes effects on environment. First urban analytic in regard to urban sustainability and form	Some tools are unable to address he relationships between criteria, categories and one's ability perform/carry out tasks

(Continued)

TABLE 1.7 (Continued)
Review Summary Table

No	Author	Year	Title	Journal	Aim	Relevance	Application Area	Technologies	Methods	Opportunities	Constraints
60	Kitchin, R.	2016	The ethics of smart cities and urban science.	*Philosophical Transactions of the Royal Society A: Mathematical, Physical and Engineering Sciences*	The paper aims to investigate the forms, practices, and ethics of smart cities as well as urban science	Further looking into instrumental rationality and realist epistemology; privacy, datafication, dataveillance and geo-surveillance; and data uses, it is argued that initiatives and urban science need to be re-cast to orientate how cities are conceived, reconfigure the underlying epistemology and adopt ethical principles	Society Smart City	AI and cloud computing in the area of Smart city	Data-informed urbanism – dataset analysis from GPS, smartphone data, sensors, cameras, and smart energy grids.	Opportunity to create principles with include both smart city concepts and urban city	Argued that initiatives and urban science needs to be 're-cast' to orientate how cities are conceived, reconfigure the underlying epistemology, and adopt ethical principles

References

Andriole, S.J. (2019). Social media analytics, wearable technology, and the internet-of-things. *IEEE Computer Architecture Letters, 21*(5), 11–15.

Babar, M., & Arif, F. (2017). Smart urban planning using big data analytics to contend with the interoperability in internet of things. *Future Generation Computer Systems, 77*, 65–76.

Babar, M., & Arif, F. (2019). Real-time data processing scheme using big data analytics in internet of things based smart transportation environment. *Journal of Ambient Intelligence and Humanized Computing, 10*(10), 4167–4177.

Behnisch, M., Hecht, R., Herold, H., & Jiang, B. (2019). Urban big data analytics and morphology. *Environment and Planning B: Urban Analytics and City Science*, 1203–1205, https://doi.org/10.1177/2399808319870016.

Bibri, S.E. (2018). The IoT for smart sustainable cities of the future: An analytical framework for sensor-based big data applications for environmental sustainability. *Sustainable Cities and Society, 38*(1), 230–253.

Boeing, G. (2018). Measuring the complexity of urban form and design. *Urban Design International, 23*(4), 281–292.

Boeing, G., Besbris, M., Schachter, A., & Kuk, J. (2021). Housing search in the age of big data: Smarter cities or the same old blind spots? *Housing Policy Debate, 31*(1), 112–126.

Brower, R.L., Jones, T.B., Osborne-Lampkin, L., Hu, S., & Park-Gaghan, T.J. (2019). Big qual: Defining and debating qualitative inquiry for large data sets. *International Journal of Qualitative Methods, 18*, 1609406919880692.

Chen, H., Zheng, Z., & Ceran, Y. (2016). De-biasing the reporting bias in social media analytics. *Production and Operations Management, 25*(5), 849–865.

Cheng, J. (2011). Exploring urban morphology using multi-temporal urban growth data: A case study of Wuhan, China. *Asian Geographer, 28*(2), 85–103.

Clifton, K., Ewing, R., Knaap, G.-J., & Song, Y. (2008). Quantitative analysis of urban form: A multidisciplinary review. *Journal of Urbanism, 1*(1), 17–45.

De Andrade, S.C., Restrepo-Estrada, C., Nunes, L.H., Rodriguez, C.A., Estrella, J.C., Delbem, A.C., & Porto de Albuquerque, J. (2021). A multicriteria optimization framework for the definition of the spatial granularity of urban social media analytics. *International Journal of Geographical Information Science, 35*(1), 43–62.

Dur, F., & Yigitcanlar, T. (2015). Assessing land-use and transport integration via a spatial composite indexing model. *International Journal of Environmental Science and Technology, 12*(3), 803–816.

Fan, J., Han, F., & Liu, H. (2014). Challenges of big data analysis. *National Science Review*, 293–314.

Fan, W., & Yan, X. (2015). Novel applications of social media analytics. *Information & Management, 1*(2), 761–763.

Fiore, S., Elia, D., Pires, C.E., Mestre, D.G., Cappiello, C., Vitali, M., Andrade, N., Braz, T., Lezzi, D., Moraes, R., & Basso, T. (2019). An integrated big and fast data analytics platform for smart urban transportation management. *IEEE Access, 7*(1), 117652–117677.

Fleischmann, M., Romice, O., & Porta, S. (2020). Measuring urban form: Overcoming terminological inconsistencies for a quantitative and comprehensive morphologic analysis of cities. *Environment and Planning. B: Urban Analytics and City Science*, https://doi.org/10.1177/2399808320910444.

Hilbert, M. (2016). Big data for development: A review of promises and challenges. *Development Policy Review, 34*(1), 135–174.

Huang, J.-Y., & Wey, W.-M. (2019). Application of big data and analytic network process for the adaptive reuse strategies of school land. *Social Indicators Research, 142*(3), 1075–1102.

Kandt, J., & Batty, M. (2021). Smart cities, big data and urban policy: Towards urban analytics for the long run. *Cities, 109,* 102992.

Kankanamge, N., Yigitcanlar, T., Goonetilleke, A., & Kamruzzaman, M. (2019). Can volunteer crowdsourcing reduce disaster risk? A systematic review of the literature. *International Journal of Disaster Risk Reduction, 35,* 101097.

Kankanamge, N., Yigitcanlar, T., Goonetilleke, A., & Kamruzzaman, M. (2020a). Determining disaster severity through social media analysis: Testing the methodology with South East Queensland flood tweets. *International Journal of Disaster Risk Reduction, 42,* 101360.

Kankanamge, N., Yigitcanlar, T., & Goonetilleke, A. (2020b). How engaging are disaster management related social media channels? The case of Australian state emergency organisations. *International Journal of Disaster Risk Reduction, 48,* 101571.

Kaur, H., & Garg, P. (2019). Urban sustainability assessment tools: A review. *Journal of Cleaner Production, 210,* 146–158.

Khalifa, S., Elshater, Y., Sundaravarathan, K., Bhat, A., Martin, P., Imam, F., Rope, D., Mcroberts, M., & Statchuk, C. (2016). The six pillars for building big data analytics ecosystems. *ACM Computing Surveys, 49*(2), 1–36.

Kitchin, R. (2016). The ethics of smart cities and urban science. *Philosophical Transactions of the Royal Society A: Mathematical, Physical, and Engineering Sciences, 374*(2083), 20160115.

Kitchin, R., Lauriault, T.P., & McArdle, G. (2015). Knowing and governing cities through urban indicators, city benchmarking and real-time dashboards. *Regional Studies, Regional Science, 2*(1), 6–28.

Kordzadeh, N., & Young, D.K. (2020). How social media analytics can inform content strategies. *The Journal of Computer Information Systems,* 1–13, https://doi.org/10.1080/08874417.2020.1736691.

Kourtit, K. (2019). Cultural heritage, smart cities and digital data analytics. *Eastern Journal of European Studies, 10*(1), 151–159.

Kourtit, K., Nijkamp, P., & Romao, J. (2019). Cultural heritage appraisal by visitors to global cities: The use of social media and urban analytics in urban buzz research. *Sustainability, 11*(12), 3470.

Löfgren, K., & Webster, C.W. (2020). The value of big data in government: The case of 'smart cities'. *Big Data & Society, 7*(1), 2053951720912775.

Laurell, C., Sandström, C., Berthold, A., & Larsson, D. (2019). Exploring barriers to adoption of virtual reality through social media analytics and machine learning – An assessment of technology, network, price and trialability. *Journal of Business Research, 100,* 469–474.

Lim, C., Kim, K.-J., & Maglio, P.P. (2018). Smart cities with big data: Reference models, challenges, and considerations. *Cities, 82,* 86–99.

Lock, O., Bednarz, T., & Pettit, C. (2021). The visual analytics of big, open public transport data – A framework and pipeline for monitoring system performance in greater Sydney. *Big Earth Data, 5*(1), 134–159.

Moe, W.W., & Schweidel, D.A. (2017). Opportunities for innovation in social media analytics. *The Journal of Product Innovation Management, 34*(5), 697–702.

Morgan, C. (2020). Can smart cities be environmentally sustainable? Urban big data analytics and the citizen-driven internet of things. *Geopolitics, History and International Relations, 12*(1), 80–86.

Nanda, P., & Kumar, V. (2019). Social media to social media analytics: Ethical challenges. *International Journal of Technoethics, 10*(2), 57–70.

Nigel, F., Xuguang, R., & Bela, S. (2018). Precomputing architecture for flexible and efficient big data analytics. *Vietnam Journal of Computer Science, 5*(2), 133–142.

Osman, A.M. (2019). A novel big data analytics framework for smart cities. *Future Generation Computer Systems, 91*, 620–633.

Pääkkönen, J., Laaksonen, S.-M., Jauho, M., Lohmeier, C., Pentzold, C., & Kaun, A. (2020). Credibility by automation: Expectations of future knowledge production in social media analytics. *Convergence, 26*(4), 790–807.

Petrescu, M., & Krishen, A.S. (2020). The dilemma of social media algorithms and analytics. *Journal of Marketing Analytics, 8*, 187–188.

Pfeffer, K., Verrest, H., & Poorthuis, A. (2015). Big data for better urban life? - An exploratory study of critical urban issues in two Caribbean cities: Paramaribo (Suriname) And Port of Spain (Trinidad And Tobago). *European Journal of Development Research, 27*(4), 505–522.

Puiu, D., Barnaghi, P., Tönjes, R., Kümper, D., Ali, M.I., Mileo, A., Parreira, J.X., Fischer, M., Kolozali, S., Farajidavar, N., & Gao, F. (2016). CityPulse: Large scale data analytics framework for smart cities. *IEEE Access, 4*, 1086–1108.

Rabari, C., & Storper, M. (2015). The digital skin of cities: Urban theory and research in the age of the sensored and metered city, ubiquitous computing and big data. *Cambridge Journal of Regions, Economy and Society, 8*(1), 27–42.

Rathore, M.M., Ahmad, A., Paul, A., & Rho, S. (2016). Urban planning and building smart cities based on the internet of things using big data analytics. *Computer Networks, 101*, 63–80.

Rathore, M.M., Paul, A., Hong, W.-H., Seo, H., Awan, I., & Saeed, S. (2018). Exploiting IoT and big data analytics: Defining smart digital City using real-time urban data. *Sustainable Cities and Society, 40*, 600–610.

Sarin, P., Kar, A.K., Kewat, K., & Ilavarasan, P.V. (2020). Factors affecting future of work: Insights from social media analytics. *Procedia Computer Science, 167*, 1880–1888.

Sebei, H., Hadj Taieb, M.A., & Ben Aouicha, M. (2018). Review of social media analytics process and big data pipeline. *Social Network Analysis and Mining, 8*(1), 1–28.

Sedkaoui, S., & Khelfaoui, M. (2019). Understand, develop and enhance the learning process with big data. *Information Discovery and Delivery, 47*(1), 2–16.

Serasinghe Pathiranage, I.S., Kantakumar, L.N., & Sundaramoorthy, S. (2018). Remote sensing data and SLEUTH urban growth model: As decision support tools for urban planning. *Chinese Geographical Science, 28*(2), 274–286.

Singh, S.P., Nayyar, A., Kumar, R., & Sharma, A. (2019). Fog computing: From architecture to edge computing and big data processing. *The Journal of Supercomputing, 75*(4), 2070–2105.

Stieglitz, S., Dang-Xuan, L., Shulman, S.W., Datta, A., & Lim, E.-P. (2013). Social media and political communication: A social media analytics framework. *Social Network Analysis and Mining, 3*(4), 1277–1291.

Stieglitz, S., Mirbabaie, M., Ross, B., & Neuberger, C. (2018). Social media analytics – Challenges in topic discovery, data collection, and data preparation. *International Journal of Information Management, 39*, 156–168.

Stiglbauer, M., Kühn, A.-L., & Häußinger, C. (2014). Semantic social media analytics of CSR image: The benefit to know stakeholders' perspective. *Problems and Perspectives in Management, 12*(2), 34–42.

Tang, L., Zhang, Y., Dai, F., Yoon, Y., Song, Y., & Sharma, R.S. (2017). Social media data analytics for the U.S. Construction industry: Preliminary study on Twitter. *Journal of Management in Engineering, 33*(6), 4017038.

Tversky, A., & Kahneman, D. (1981). *Evidential Impact of Base Rates.* Stanford University Press, California.

Wey, W.-M., & Peng, T.-C. (2021). Study on building a smart sustainable city assessment framework using big data and analytic network process. *Journal of Urban Planning and Development, 147*(3), 04021031.

Yang, D., Qu, B., & Cudre-Mauroux, P. (2020). Location-centric social media analytics: Challenges and opportunities for smart cities. *IEEE Intelligent Systems*, https://doi.org/10.1109/MIS.2020.3009438.

Yang, S., & Zeng, X. (2018). Sustainability of government social media: A multi-analytic approach to predict citizens' mobile government microblog continuance. *Sustainability, 10*(12), 4849.

Yao, F., & Wang, Y. (2020). Towards resilient and smart cities: A real-time urban analytical and geo-visual system for social media streaming data. *Sustainable Cities and Society, 63*, 102448.

Ye, C., Zhang, F., Mu, L., Gao, Y., & Liu, Y. (2020). Urban function recognition by integrating social media and street-level imagery. *Environment and Planning B: Urban Analytics and City Science, 48*(6), 1430–1444.

Yigitcanlar, T., Kamruzzaman, M., Buys, L., Ioppolo, G., Sabatini-Marques, J., da Costa, E.M., & Yun, J.J. (2018). Understanding 'smart cities': Intertwining development drivers with desired outcomes in a multidimensional framework. *Cities, 81*, 145–160.

Yigitcanlar, T., Kankanamge, N., & Vella, K. (2021). How are smart city concepts and technologies perceived and utilized? A systematic geo-twitter analysis of smart cities in Australia. *Journal of Urban Technology, 28*(1–2), 135–154.

Zeng, D., Chen, H., Lusch, R., & Li, S. (2010). Social media analytics and intelligence. *IEEE Intelligent Systems, 25*(6), 13–16.

Zha, Z.-J., Mei, T., & El Saddik, A. (2016). Social media analytics and learning. *Neurocomputing, 1*, 1–2.

Zhang, J., Chen, Z., Xu, Z., Du, M., Yang, W., & Guo, L. (2018). A distributed collaborative urban traffic big data system based on cloud computing. *IEEE Intelligent Transportation Systems Magazine, 11*(4), 37–47.

Zhang, C., Yao, W., Yang, Y., Huang, R., & Mostafavi, A. (2020). Semiautomated social media analytics for sensing societal impacts due to community disruptions during disasters. *Computer-Aided Civil and Infrastructure Engineering, 5*(12), 1331–1348.

Zhu, R., Lin, D., Jendryke, M., Zuo, C., Ding, L., & Meng, L. (2018). Geo-tagged social media data-based analytical approach for perceiving impacts of social events. *International Journal of Geo-Information, 8*(1), 15.

2

Volunteer Crowdsourcing and Social Media

2.1 Introduction

People all across the world are exposed to a range of natural disasters. These disasters are referred to as damaging and destructive events that threaten the wellbeing of individuals (Gardoni & Murphy, 2010; O'Sullivan et al., 2013; Aslam Saja et al., 2018). Indian Ocean Tsunami in 2004, Haiti Earthquake in 2010, Tōhoku Earthquake and Tsunami in 2011, Hurricane Sandy in 2012, Mexico Earthquake in 2017, Sierra Leone Floods and Landslides in 2017, Japan Floods and Mudslides in 2018 are some of the devastating natural disasters recorded in recent history. Just in 2015, 574 disaster events killed over 32 thousand people, adversely affected around 108 million people, and caused about US$70 billion in damage (IFRC, 2016). Figure 2.1 illustrates the gradual increase in the frequency of natural disasters, creating significant economic and human loss (CRED, 2018).

In order to avoid catastrophic consequences; attention has focused on reducing the risks associated with the increasing frequency of disasters. Disaster risk reduction (DRR) is the concept and practice adopted for reducing disaster risks through systematic efforts by analysing and managing the consequences. Practitioners have adopted different instruments at different stages of the disaster process, such as increasing community awareness, establishing early warning systems, and disaster forecasting as DRR strategies (Gardoni & Murphy, 2010; Baytiyeh, 2017). Yet, there is no noticeable reduction in disaster risks, when compared to the 90s (CRED, 2018).

Factually, the extant DRR instruments and increasing disaster risks, together, confirm the inadequacy of monopolistic professional-driven DRR approaches developed around disaster authorities. A novel approach to DRR is needed. In recent years, citizen engagement or volunteerism is being increasingly used in DRR (Dror et al., 2015). Although volunteerism is not new to disaster management, the sheer pervasiveness of technology has created the space and the opportunity for a unique type of volunteerism.

Citizen presence in technology-mediated approaches such as social media, mobile applications are often referred to as 'crowdsourcing' or 'participatory sensing'. The term, crowdsourcing was initially coined by Howe (2006) and

DOI: 10.1201/9781003278986-3

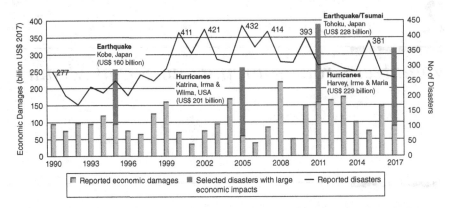

FIGURE 2.1
Annual disaster occurrence and economic damages. (Derived from CRED, 2018.)

since then its applications have been in use in many areas including DRR. While, the crowdsourcing notion implies 'outsourcing', 'crowd power' and 'participation' concepts, these are inadequate to completely define the role of crowdsourcing in the Web 2.0 era (Oliveira et al., 2017). The Web 2.0 era refers to the period that enabled people to customise spatial content, generate map mashups and blend information with multiple sources such as social media, emails, and mobile phones to address information scarcity that occurs during various events and incidents—including disasters (Miller & Goodchild, 2015).

The dissemination of bidirectional Web 2.0 technologies creates an opportunity for the planet—with its seven billion inhabitants (UN, 2017)—to become a place with over seven billion moving sensors (Poblet et al., 2017; Ludwig et al., 2017). This can create eye-witnessed, in-situ, geographical, and geo-tagged information during disasters (Roche et al., 2013; Yigitcanlar, 2016). With this new advancement, emergency managers and cartographic professionals are further supported with timely information to enhance their tasks (Goodchild & Li, 2012; Lue et al., 2014; Hossain & Kauranen, 2016). This also helps in bridging the gap between professionals and non-profession that is referred to as 'neogeography' or 'neocartography' (Turner, 2006).

Web 2.0 technologies along with social media and other smart urban technologies have underpinned a paradigm shift—an increased smartness with the help of smart technology utilisation (Yigitcanlar, 2015; Lara et al., 2016; Yigitcanlar et al., 2018). Twitter, Instagram, Ushahidi, and Sahana are the most cited platforms in the crowdsourcing and disaster literature (Yang et al., 2014; Harrison & Johnson, 2016; Poblet et al., 2017). The volunteer crowdsourcing approach assumes that the aggregated information from many citizens will enhance professional knowledge (Surowiecki, 2004; Deng et al., 2016). Although there is growing popularity of crowdsourcing in the disaster context (Lue et al., 2014; Harrison & Johnson, 2016; Ernst et al., 2017), the compatibility between DRR and volunteer crowdsourcing is an understudied area of research.

Against this backdrop, the study has identified the current knowledge gaps and future research directions, the role of volunteer crowdsourcing, including its key attributes and relevant technologies, in DRR. By addressing the research question, 'whether volunteer crowdsourcing can reduce disaster risk', this study strives to deepen our understanding of crowdsourcing, the generic use of crowdsourced data, and specifically the extent of the application areas of crowdsourced data in DRR. The methodological approach of this research adopts a systematic critical review of the relatively scarce and highly disjointed literature developed over the past decade to address the aforesaid aim.

2.2 Literature Background

2.2.1 Instruments of Disaster Risk Reduction

Instruments of DRR can be defined as techniques, tools, or methods applied to DRR strategies. Different instruments are used to prepare DRR strategies at different phases of the disaster process. Lin Moe and Pathranarakul (2006) identified five disaster management phases: Prediction; Warning; Emergency relief; Rehabilitation; Reconstruction. These are on par with four main activities: Mitigation; Preparedness; Response; Recovery. In broader terms, these phases and activities could be categorised into three-time spans: Pre-disaster; During-disaster; Post-disaster. Adoption of instruments varies based on the disaster risk level at each time span. Disaster risks exist throughout the disaster management phases at different levels. However, all the DRR instruments adopted throughout the five disaster management phases are intended to reduce the disaster risks (Guan & Chen, 2014).

The following DRR strategies are primarily applied during the pre-disaster period: Disaster forecasting (Burston et al., 2015); Increasing disaster awareness including engagement and education (Haworth, 2016; Mojtahedi & Oo, 2017; Lagmay et al., 2017); Evacuation planning (Cova & Johnson, 2002; Kolen & Helsloot, 2014; Cumiskey, 2018). These strategies require instruments such as contingency funding and insurance, weather-stations and software, for modelling (Harrison & Johnson, 2016; Mechler, 2016; Cumiskey et al., 2018), planning (Kolen & Helsloot, 2014), and monitoring (Arthur et al., 2018; Wang et al., 2018).

DRR instruments such as damage assessments and valuation techniques are often used during the post-disaster period (Liu, 2014; Mechler, 2016; Mejri et al., 2017). These instruments are applied by professionals with the requisite expertise. Due to the absence of visual evidence and misplacement of docu-ments, difficulties occur in actual damage assessments. This can create gaps between the actual damages and concessions made.

Emergency warning and rapid emergency relief activities are launched to reduce the disaster risks during the disaster response phase (Mojtahedi & Oo, 2017). Information received through emergency speed dial numbers and direct observations are the key instruments used in this stage (Yuan & Liu, 2018a). However, these instruments are becoming outdated with the emergence of mobile phones, social media, and crowdsourcing techniques (Goodchild, 2007).

Revisiting these instruments is required, as their existence has not resulted in a reduction in the ever-increasing disaster risk (CRED, 2018). For instance, the triple-zero emergency call facility was introduced in the 1960s as a cen-tralised system in Australia. Despite their decades-long contribution to DRR, the system is also attributed with a range of drawbacks. For example, the absence of proper location information about victims and difficulty in shar-ing information via messages and images. In contrast, the governments of the USA and Canada initiate their evaluations by incorporating crowdsource data for DRR (Harrison & Johnson, 2016). Regardless, incorporation of vol-unteer crowdsourcing for state emergency management is still not common.

2.2.2 Characteristics of Volunteer Crowdsourcing

Crowdsourcing, in simple terms, is outsourcing tasks to a group of people. There are many definitions of crowdsourcing in the literature. Table 2.1 lists the commonly used definitions with primary themes of crowdsourcing with the most common being 'crowd power', 'outsourcing', and 'volunteerism'.

The 2010 Haiti Earthquake was the tipping point for realising the value of crowd power, outsourcing, and volunteerism. Haiti is a developing country with limited infrastructure, did not have roadmaps to distribute disaster aid (Liu, 2014). Consequently, 640 volunteers contributed to creating road maps of Haiti in two weeks. Volunteers mapped the roads and humanitarian fea-tures including displaced person camps of Haiti (Liu, 2014). Further, the Haiti government launched a mission, where people could send text requests for shelter, food, and medicines. Later, the tasks of translating, geocoding, and categorising 4,636 messages were outsourced through social media (Liu, 2014). Gurman and Ellenberger (2015) showed the possibility of using social media for disease prevention after a disaster. Factually, the underlined themes of volunteer crowdsourcing play a significant role in reducing disaster risks.

Volunteer crowdsourcing information provides a 'bottom-up' knowl-edge to manage a disaster in terms of monitoring and evaluating the built environment (Wang & Taylor, 2018). Other than the 2010 Haiti Earthquake, 2011 Victoria Floods (Australia), 2014 North Stradbroke Island Bushfires (Australia), and 2015 Houston Flooding (USA), 2016 California Drought and Wildfires (USA), which used the power of volunteers to enforce crowd

TABLE 2.1

Definitions and Primary Themes of Crowdsourcing

Publication	Definition	Theme	Citation
Riccardi (2016)	It uses the power of the internet and social media to virtually harness the power of individuals and brings them together in support of a disaster	Crowd power, social media, technology	4[b]
Estellés and González (2012)	It is a type of participative online activity in which an individual, institution, or company proposes to a group of individuals of varying knowledge, heterogeneity, and number, via a flexible open call voluntary undertaking of a task	Crowd power, outsourcing, volunteerism	509[b]
Vivacqua and Borges (2012)	It is outsourcing a task to the crowd to execute effectively, instead of executing it oneself	Outsourcing, crowd power	43[b]
Boulos et al. (2011)	It is capitalising on the power of the masses or crowds and relying on citizen participation to achieve their goals	Crowd power	192[b]
Doan et al. (2011)	It means distributing a query to several Twitter users to aggregate the results and exploit the wisdom-of-crowds' effect	Crowd power, social media	697[b]
Schenk and Guittard (2011)	It is a compound contraction of crowd and outsourcing, meaning outsourcing to the crowd	Crowd power, outsourcing	431[a]
Whitla (2009)	It is a process of organising labour, where firms parcel out work to some online community, offering payment for anyone within the crowd who completes the task the firm has set	Outsourcing, payments for micro-tasking	363[a]
Brabham (2008)	It is not merely a web 2.0 buzzword but is instead a strategic model to attract an interested, motivated crowd of individuals capable of providing solutions superior in quality and quantity	Crowd power, problem-solving	851[b]
Kleemann et al. (2008)	It is crowdsourcing or the outsourcing of tasks to the general internet public	Outsourcing	682[a]
Howe (2006)	It is the act of taking a job traditionally performed by a designated employee and outsourcing it to an undefined, generally large group of people in the form of an open call	Outsourcing, open-source	587[a]

[a] Google Scholar citations in the absence of Scopus citations.
[b] Scopus citations.

power against the disaster risks (Harrison & Johnson, 2016; McCormick, 2016; Sachdeva et al., 2017). Further, Liu and Xu (2018) proved that the actions taken by the public in response to disasters are far better than the actions of officials, in terms of emotional relief, recovery activities, and acknowledgement of efforts.

Not all crowdsourcing activities are volunteered. For instance, Amazon's Mechanical Turk (www.mturk.com) focuses on micro-tasking. This is a process of taking a large task and outsourcing it into smaller groups. They are conducive to hiring cheap labour to complete a major task (Liu, 2014). That is fundamentally a commercially driven agenda. In contrast, in the Web 2.0 era, it is remarkable to see the way social media has redesigned relationships in communities without any commercial objectives. Brabham (2013) referred to this blend as a bottom-up, open, and creative process with top-down organisational goals. Absence of profit orientation, presence of online communities, involvement of a large group of people, knowledge sharing, and self-governing are the foremost characteristics of volunteer crowdsourcing (Liu, 2014; Ernst et al., 2017; Peng, 2017).

Despite some sporadic use of volunteer crowdsourcing as an instrument, the DRR process mostly relies on traditional instruments. Traditional DRR instruments are mostly professionally driven (Ernst et al., 2017). Nevertheless, the wide applicability of volunteer crowdsourcing in DRR depends on satisfactorily addressing the following questions: (a) How can emerging technologies engage citizens with DRR? (b) How can the attributes of volunteer crowdsourcing support DRR? (c) How can crowdsourcing be conceptualised in the context of DRR? This calls for further investigations on the role of volunteer crowdsourcing, including its key attributes and relevant technologies in DRR.

2.3 Methodology

This study undertook a review of research literature to address the research question based on the approach proposed by Yigitcanlar et al. (2019) as illustrated in Figure 2.2.

Firstly, a research plan involving the research aim, keywords, and a set of inclusion and exclusion criteria was developed. Research aim was framed to identify key characteristics associated with crowdsourcing. As the keywords, it was decided to use 'crowdsourcing' and 'disaster'. Peer-reviewed research articles in the English language were considered as the inclusion criteria. An online search was conducted using an academic search engine that connects to 393 different databases, including ScienceDirect, Scopus, Web of Science, Wiley Online Library, Directory of Open Access Journals. Research excluded edited or authored books, conference proceedings, journal editorials, articles

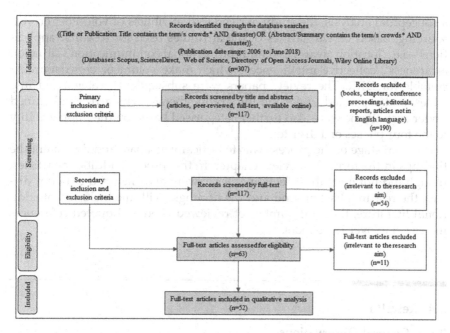

FIGURE 2.2
Article selection procedure.

in languages other than English, grey literature such as government or industry reports, and non-academic research. The search included only peer-reviewed and full-text journal articles available online.

Secondly, the search was conducted in June 2018 for journal articles published between January 2006 and June 2018. January 2006 was used as a milestone, as it was the year which Howe (2006) introduced the word 'crowdsourcing'. The resultant search items were initially checked by reading the abstract, and then by reading the full text to verify the scope against the research questions.

Thirdly, the initial thematic search was conducted using the keywords of 'crowdsourcing' and 'disaster' to identify articles that discussed crowdsourcing within the context of a disaster. The Boolean search line was: ((Title or Publication Title contains the term/s crowds* AND disaster) OR (Abstract/Summary contains the term/s crowds* AND disaster)). Truncation was used in the term crowds* to broaden the search to synonyms such as 'crowdsense', 'crowdsensing', 'crowdsource'. The search initially resulted in 307 papers, which were subsequently reduced to 52 articles after checking their full-texts, to ensure their compatibility with the research scope.

Fourthly, all the 52 articles were reviewed and analysed. Then, they were again categorised under four main themes, based on identifying the similarities or patterns among the research outcomes—i.e., 'geo-technology', 'mobile communication', 'crisis information', 'digital volunteerism'. After conducting a conceptual analysis, the study derived four attributes of volunteer crowd-sourcing, based on similarities of the attributes used for research applications—i.e., 'location awareness', 'multi-directional communication', 'situation awareness', 'collective intelligence'—which make volunteer crowdsourcing suitable for DRR. The review papers were subsequently, categorised into tables, and separated under the initial four themes. The articles identified under each theme were also further categorised based on their applicability to the four phases of a disaster.

The final stage of the process was to critically evaluate and document the findings in the form of a review chapter. In this process, additional articles, though did not meet the selection criteria, were also included to better discuss the research background and the findings. With the inclusion of additional literature, the total number of reviewed cited and quoted references increased to over 130 papers.

2.4 Results

2.4.1 General Observations

The review revealed four main technologies of volunteer crowdsourcing; geo-technology (24 articles), mobile communication (11 articles), digital crisis information (10 articles), digital volunteerism (7 articles). Looking at the distribution of articles, 49% of the articles have a geo-technical focus in developing either a volunteer crowdsourcing platform or an application. It reflects the technical orientation of the extant research. As explained in the methodology section, all 52 articles were classified according to their applicability to each disaster phase; mitigation (11 articles), preparedness (16 articles), response (46 articles), recovery (33 articles). It shows that two-thirds of the publications focus on the disaster response phase.

Volunteer crowdsourcing in the disaster context has been investigated in a few countries, such as Japan, Haiti, Australia, the USA, Israel, and China. While most of the research into policy-level applications of volunteer crowdsourcing originate from USA and Canada, countries such as the Philippines, China, and Japan have focused on developing technical applications and designing mapping platforms for flooding, typhoons, bush fires, tsunami, and earthquakes.

Among all reviewed publications, the earliest publication related to crowdsourcing and disaster dated back to 2011. This demonstrates the research interests in applying crowdsourcing in the context of a disaster that has been initiated after five years after the term, crowdsourcing, was introduced. Between 2006 and 2014, the total number of publications on crowdsourcing and disaster was 15 and this was more than doubled as of the date (37 articles).

2.4.2 Technologies for Volunteer Crowdsourcing

Communication and information sharing is significant for DRR (Gray et al., 2016; Kryvasheyeu et al., 2016). Most of the DRR strategies—such as launching rescue missions, conducting damage assessments, distributing subsidies, and raising funds can become difficult due to information and communication deficiencies. In comparison, volunteer crowdsourcing applications, backed by four different technologies made such tasks efficient (Liu, 2014). The four technologies are Geo-technology; Mobile communication; Digital crisis information; Digital volunteerism.

Using geo-technology, people who live a distance away from the disaster location can map the location-specific information of the victims in need, where subsequently the authorities could use it to provide assistance—e.g., food requests made by the victims after the Haiti Earthquake (Liu, 2014). Volunteer crowdsourcing can make disaster-related information available in the cloud within a few hours after a disaster. For instance, a few hours after the Haiti Earthquake in 2010, nearly 40,000 independent reports were plotted (Yang et al., 2014). Prior to the proliferation of volunteer crowdsourcing, fundraising after a disaster was also a challenging task. With the plurality of digital crisis information, social media, and mobile applications, volunteers are able to launch virtual fund-raising campaigns—e.g., Facebook fundraising facility. Further, Lue et al. (2014) used geo-enabled videos to assess the damage caused by the 2012 Dallas Fort-Worth Tornado. Factually, the information, communication, volunteerism, and technology have not simply resulted in a reduction in disaster risks through volunteer crowdsourcing. In comparison, the four technologies discussed below, allow people to volunteer from a distance to reduce the disaster risks at a distant location.

2.4.2.1 Geo-technology

Among the 52 selected papers, 24 of them have a geo-technical focus (Table 2.2). Two decades ago, the term 'geo-technology' only referred to a technology used in the mining industry or to a complex process of gathering geographic information using remote sensing. The extant geo-technologies, such as social media, ground-based sensor networks, surveillance cameras, vibration sensors backed by mobile and sensor technologies (Burston et al., 2015; Lagmay et al., 2017). Inevitably, this has led citizens to act as moving sensors, reporters, social computers, and micro-taskers (Goodchild, 2007; Liu, 2014; Poblet et al., 2017) to collect geographic information which was later called—Volunteered Geographic Information (VGI) (Goodchild & Li, 2012). These fundamental changes are leading towards a proliferation of georeferenced information. As exemplified by Goetz and Zipf (2013), by 2011, OpenStreetMap (OSM) dataset contained more than 1.25 billion georeferenced nodes and 114 million ways. Miller and Goodchild (2015) elaborated that it is not only about the georeferenced data volume, but the diversity and the speed, with which citizens can capture the georeferenced data is also important.

TABLE 2.2

Literature on Volunteer Crowdsourcing and DRR with Geo-technology Focus

Publication	Applicability				Outcome
	Mitigation	Preparedness	Response	Recovery	
Ahmad et al. (2018)			√	√	A system, JORD, is able to autonomously collect social media data about environmental disasters to link crowdsource data automatically to remote-sensed data
Chu and Chen (2018)	√	√			Data sharing to extract hazardous space-time information through disaster historical disaster photography uploaded to a web photograph album without traditional remote sensing data sources and to declare disaster-prone areas
Feng and Sester (2018)		√	√		Disaster event detection through crowdsourcing social media texts and photos and visualisation in a web map application
Han et al. (2018)			√		Crowdsourcing and internet-of-things (IoT) integration model for disaster relief
Yuan and Liu (2018a)			√	√	New indices—disaster-related ratio and damage related ratio—to assess disaster-related impacts using geo-located twitters
Zhao et al. (2018)			√	√	An urban safety application and a website to collect structural security information during-disaster
Frank et al. (2017)			√	√	Remote sensing-based classifier design for crowdsourcing driven geospatial label noise rectification for damage assessment
Fritz et al. (2017)			√		Replacing high-resolution satellite images with crowdsourcing methods—Google Maps and Bing Maps; OSM or Google MapMaker to collect georeferenced data
Havas et al. (2017)	√	√	√	√	A system architecture for Copernicus Emergency Management Service uses open-source user-generated data

(Continued)

TABLE 2.2 *(Continued)*

Literature on Volunteer Crowdsourcing and DRR with Geo-technology Focus

Publication	Applicability				Outcome
	Mitigation	Preparedness	Response	Recovery	
Ludwig et al. (2017)			✓	✓	A prototype for 'CityShare' mobile application for crisis crowdsourcing—a situated crowdsourcing application encompasses different information sources such as social media
Sachdeva et al. (2017)			✓	✓	Using user-generated social media to measure the particulate pollution from wildfire smoke
Yan et al. (2017)	✓	✓	✓	✓	A scientific workflow and method using geotagged flicker photos for disaster prevention, preparation, and response—a crowdsourcing based qualitative photo analysis
Deng et al. (2016)		✓	✓	✓	A new model based on disaster-related social media data
Juhász et al. (2016)		✓	✓	✓	An open-source web-based pilot application to collected geotagged data for disaster management in line with the open geospatial consortium standards
Kantarci et al. (2016)	✓	✓	✓	✓	Mobile social networks, an open-source library, mobile sensing technology used in Social Network Assisted Trustworthiness Assurance to increase crowdsensing utility
Koswatte et al. (2015)			✓	✓	Using spatial data infrastructures (SDIs) for disaster management—for semantic information analysis to improve spatial data information matching
Lorenzi et al. (2015)			✓	✓	A prototype framework—Public Engagement in Emergency Response—delivers a comprehensive online and mobile crowdsourcing platform for situation reporting and resource volunteering

(Continued)

TABLE 2.2 *(Continued)*

Literature on Volunteer Crowdsourcing and DRR with Geo-technology Focus

Publication	Applicability				Outcome
	Mitigation	Preparedness	Response	Recovery	
Panteras et al. (2015)			√		Use of ubiquitous computing and social media advancements to disseminate geospatial content—Google Map Maker, OSM, WikiMapia GIS to assess the impact area of a disaster
Pitrénaité-Žilienė et al. (2014)	√	√	√	√	ICTs as e-tools, platforms for disaster management—the need for disaster authorities using social technologies for disaster management
Wan et al. (2014)			√	√	An on-demand location-based visualisation, crowdsourcing data collection platform—CyberFlood
Yang et al. (2014)			√		Aa crowdsourcing disaster support platform for relief tasks
Crooks and Wise (2013)			√	√	A model to assess how crowdsourced geospatial data to emulate the behaviour of individuals in a crisis context
Kerle and Hoffman (2013)			√	√	Weaknesses in current collaborative damage mapping approach and propose a collaborative damage mapping, where users can decide on what information is required in the post-recovery period
Boulos et al. (2011)			√	√	Overlapping domains of the sensor web, citizen sensing, and 'human-in-the-loop sensing' and their roles in these domains of crisis/disaster informatics

Based on the geo-technical user platforms, the research has identified three taxonomies: (a) Software and online mapping tools; (b) Networks; (c) Devices. For instance, open-source mapping platforms such as OSM, Google Earth, Google Maps, Bing Maps, and Yahoo Maps are the most commonly cited online mapping tools in the reviewed literature (Boulos et al., 2011; Castillo et al., 2012; Sachdeva et al., 2016). Geographic information systems (GIS) and Quantum GIS (Q-GIS) are prominent software used for geospatial analysis (Yigitcanlar et al., 2007; Goodchild et al., 2007; Liu, 2014; Lorenzi et al., 2015). Additionally, Map-mashups and WebGIS are widely applied to visualise information in a comprehensive map. Victorian Bushfire Map, South California Bushfire Map, Google Australia (Liu & Palen, 2010; Roche et al., 2013; Liu, 2014), Queensland Globe, are the popular map-mashups.

WebGIS plays the role of the end-user interface to share information between experts and non-experts (Baum et al., 2010; Gudes et al., 2010; Pitrénaité-Žilenienè et al., 2014). Geographic positioning systems (GPS), GPS-enabled cameras, mobile devices, videography, vibration sensors, geo-sensors, closed-circuit televisions, and drones act as virtual arenas to collect georeferenced information (Sagun et al., 2009; Havas et al., 2017).

The selection of papers given in Table 2.2, discusses the application of numerous geo-technologies under different phases of the disaster process. Such technologies are rarely developed and adopted in developing countries. Therefore, future research should focus on applying geo-technologies among socially and culturally diverse communities.

2.4.2.2 Mobile Communication

Among the 52 articles reviewed, only 11 had a direct focus on mobile communications (Table 2.3). However, it was noted that all the reviewed publications had at least a few sentences to discuss the significance of mobile communication in DRR, without justifying through systematic research.

Harrison and Johnson (2016) saw volunteer crowdsourcing as a communication platform that can be used during and after a disaster event. Traditional communication modes such as wired telephones, television, and radios frequently crash during-disaster phase. However, social media and mobile applications can often remain intact and provide a reliable means of communication due to their distributed and agile nature. Poblet et al. (2017) ascertained the plurality of mobile communication modes by identifying 38 crowdsourcing applications developed for data collection in emergencies. Especially, the propagation speed and the reaction time of social media has challenged the use of traditional communication modes during-disasters.

Among social media, the most widely used mobile communications are Twitter, Instagram, and Facebook (Maresh-Fuehrer & Smith, 2016; Feng & Sester, 2018; Wang et al., 2018). These include dedicated mobile phone applications such as Flood patrol (Philippines), SIGNALERT (France), mPING (USA),

TABLE 2.3

Literature on Volunteer Crowdsourcing and DRR with Mobile Communication Focus

| Publication | Applicability | | | | | Outcome | Communication Tool |
	Mitigation	Preparedness	Response	Recovery			
Pánek et al. (2017)			√	√		Significance of crisis mapping (Ushahidi) and a list of best practices in deployment	Ushahidi
Poblet et al. (2017)	√	√	√	√		How mobile technologies, web-based platforms, and social media transform the disaster landscape	iCoast, Geofedia, Stormpins, FirstToSee, MyShake, UN-Assign, Pushpin
Dufty (2016)	√	√	√	√		Twitter facilitates communication during disasters and is used for crisis mapping and information sharing	Twitter
Harrison and Johnson (2016)	√	√	√	√		Identify crowdsourcing as an online damage reporting tool and emergency information communication tool between governments and citizens, use of crowdsourcing in all four phases of disaster management with the intervention of government officials	iCoast, Scipionuos, Twitter, Facebook, Ushahidi, GeoCommons, CrowdHelp
Fekete et al. (2015)		√		√		Crowdsourcing information integrated with GIS and remote sensing have capabilities of dispersing information during-disaster at a failure of national critical infrastructure	Twitter
Dailey and Starbird (2014)			√	√		A perspective for characterising the information-sharing activities—human-powered mesh network	Ushahidi, CoverItLive Liveblog, Watershed Post's, Twitter Hurricane Irene Catskills Liveblog, Facebook

(Continued)

TABLE 2.3 *(Continued)*

Literature on Volunteer Crowdsourcing and DRR with Mobile Communication Focus

| Publication | Applicability | | | | | Outcome | Communication Tool |
	Mitigation	Preparedness	Response	Recovery			
Handmer et al. (2014)		√	√			Providing personal warning through mobile devices and social media	Twitter
Liu (2014)			√			A crisis crowdsourcing framework to merge official and informal crisis crowdsourcing communications	Ushahidi, OSM, MapGive, Humanitarian OpenStreetMap Team, Timelapse Vimeo videos, CrowdMap, Did You Feel It? Real-time website, iCoast, USGS Tweet Earthquake Dispatch, Community Internet Intensity Maps
Lue et al. (2014)			√	√		Experience and experience damage assessors delivering similar results in damage assessment	Digital/spatial video technology driving through disaster affected areas having GPS enabled cameras mounted to a car, Map-mashups, GeoWeb for data collection
Vivacqua and Borges (2012)		√	√	√		Individuals' high capacity to respond quickly to emergencies, introducing a framework to use collective knowledge in disaster response	Ushahidi
Kuehn et al. (2011)	√	√	√	√		An architecture for emergency communication and crowdsourcing in emergency prevention and response	Twitter, Wikis

Sina, and Weibo (China) (Le Coz et al., 2016; Sachdeva et al., 2016). Additionally, online reporting, live blogging, geotagged picture messages, micro blogging platforms, mapping applications are the other sources of information. These applications provide 24/7 accessibility to data and information (Harrison & Johnson, 2016).

Table 2.3 lists the mobile applications and social media usage in different phases of the disaster process. Accordingly, the main attention of both, social media and mobile applications is to enhance the peer-to-peer communication flows (Handmer et al., 2014). The ever-growing popularity and the quality of information generated has seriously challenged the conventional disaster warning methods. For instance, warnings are typically announced for larger areas. This has been criticised by emergency management practitioners and morphed the famous Tip O'Neil quote 'all politics is local' into 'all disasters are local' (Perry, 2003), whereas mobile communication and volunteer crowdsourcing together can deliver personalised warnings.

After the catastrophic Haiti Earthquake in 2010, people published numerous texts and photos about their personal experiences during the earthquake via social media sites such as Twitter, Flickr, Facebook, blogs, and videos posted on YouTube (Yang et al., 2014; Wang et al., 2018). Except for Twitter, most of the existing research have failed to use other social media for DRR, forming a future research direction to address, in the field.

2.4.2.3 Digital Crisis Information

Among the reviewed articles (Table 2.4), only 10 had a direct focus on crisis information. From that, four articles discussed about using volunteer crowdsourcing for emergency level policy planning by interviewing emergency managers and competent authorities, three articles discuss developing frameworks based on crisis information, and only three articles focused on the credibility of the crisis information.

Under a bureaucratic agenda, crisis information is generated, managed, updated, and disseminated through a closed process (Roche et al., 2013). Therefore, disasters are marked by high-level of information need and low-level of information availability (Shklovski et al., 2010). More often, crisis information collection has been a manual or a satellite-based method (Kerle & Hoffman, 2013; Pánek et al., 2017). With the emergence of geo-technologies and fingertip mobile communications, crisis information has become available in the Cloud within a short period of time after the disaster (Haworth & Bruce, 2015). For example, in the case of 2012 Hurricane Sandy, the University of Colorado Boulder harvested 26 million publicly available Tweets over a two-week post-period (Palen & Hughes, 2018).

Mejri et al. (2017) emphasised the usefulness of feeding the information to the planning process as lessons learned. Erik Hersman, the co-founder

TABLE 2.4

Literature on Volunteer Crowdsourcing and DRR with Digital Crisis Information Focus

Publication	Applicability				Outcome
	Mitigation	Preparedness	Response	Recovery	
Lin et al. (2018)			✓		A computational method—Artificial and crowd intelligence filter—to evaluate the drawbacks of disaster responses
Ernst et al. (2017)			✓	✓	The ways in which emergency managers are benefitted from volunteers and social network effects and how it can exploit information using crowdsourcing
Mejri et al. (2017)			✓	✓	Application of web-based technologies for crisis data analysis using territorial georeferenced and time referenced data for disaster recovery; how such data could be used as a repository of information in decision-making
Callaghan (2016)			✓		Need of using crowdsourcing information for problem-solving; introduction of problem-solving concept for disaster management; need of advancing disaster management theories with crowdsourcing
Carley et al. (2016)			✓		Limitation of using Twitter as the sole technology for reaching the entire population with information; lack of gender and age information in Twitter; cannot be used to estimate the location of certain at-risk groups; most Twitter users use other social media and possibility to cross communication the information sent to Twitter
McCormick (2016)	✓	✓	✓	✓	Emergency planners lack knowledge in using crowdsourcing data for disaster management; internal policies, staffing, and structures keep using crowdsourcing information away
Mehta et al. (2016)			✓	✓	Models for social media information verification based on trust relationships
Riccardi (2016)			✓	✓	Crowdsourcing—as a mode of information collection—is a tool for disaster response and recovery
Castillo et al. (2012)			✓		Collecting newsworthy and credible information from a during-disaster microblogging platform
Gao et al. (2011)				✓	Using automated disaster reports for social behaviour prediction; geotag determination and report verification as main challenges of crowdsourcing

of Ushahidi, called the overloaded crisis data as 'wasted crisis data' until they become 'actionable information' to be used by emergency managers (Liu, 2014). Crowd-curating was identified as a solution by a number of scholars, to make information actionable. The term 'curating' refers to information processing activities such as filtering, synthesising, and exhibiting. Further, Liu (2014) explained that in an emergency, curating crisis data means finding actionable crisis information and then sharing it in a meaningful way with key stakeholders. Only a limited number of studies have explored credibility assessment methods such as indexing, matrices, ratio (positive/negative) (Yuan & Liu, 2018a), to improve crowd-source information quality (Goodchild & Glennon, 2010; Castillo et al., 2012). Therefore, the development of comprehensive, practical, and user-friendly approaches for credibility assessments, remain as an understudied research area.

2.4.2.4 Digital Volunteerism

From the reviewed publications, only seven have a direct focus on digital volunteerism (Table 2.5). The other publications only discuss volunteerism briefly as volunteerism is a topic and a news item during-disaster. The very limited number of publications on the topic highlights the infancy of scholarly discussions about digital volunteerism in disasters.

Traditionally, volunteer taskforces and rescue forces are the key volunteers engaged during-disasters. However, with the ICT innovations, volunteerism has become more digitally enabled and collaborative (Liu, 2014). Nourbakhsh et al. (2006) and Goodchild (2007) are pioneers, who foresaw volunteer breeding with the emerging technologies. Fostering volunteerism facilitates information sharing about missing people and damaged property. After a disaster, people can be virtually linked to raise funds and to help build back better. The promising results delivered by digital volunteerism have made people devote their time and knowledge without demanding any monetary reward (Goodchild & Glennon, 2010).

According to the publications listed in Table 2.5, digital volunteerism can be interpreted as a grassroots level effort and provide services to meet humanitarian needs (Palen & Hughes, 2018). Nonetheless, the popularity of the concept is limited only to a few countries. It has moved one step ahead enabling people to virtually organise and engage in volunteer activities via initiatives such as Barcamps, CrisisCommons organisation, HumaityRoad global volunteer organisation. However, these still do not have a link with national voluntary or emergency service providers. Therefore, future research should pay their attention to identify new ways to interlink the backchannel communications with formal disaster communication systems, to expand volunteer forces and associated benefits.

TABLE 2.5

Literature on Volunteer Crowdsourcing and DRR with Digital Volunteerism Focus

Publication	Applicability				Outcome
	Mitigation	Preparedness	Response	Recovery	
Ogie et al. (2017)			√		Types of human sensors: Rarely active human sensors, active human sensors, super active human sensors
Peng (2017)		√	√		Web-based ICTs and crowd crisis mapping is replacing the historically dominated disaster management agenda of the government
Sosko and Dalyot (2017)	√				Use volunteers as geo-sensors assures the possibility of using volunteered weather data with the authoritative weather data
Givoni (2016)			√	√	Impossibility of democratising disaster response through ICT and emphasise the emergence of digital humanitarian volunteers—as micro mappers—that serves the dual and potentially incommensurate purposes of resilience
Dror et al. (2015)		√	√	√	Volunteered geographic information to create, share, visualise, and analyse geographic information and knowledge—OSM and Ushahidi as crowdsourcing services, Waze and Moveit follow the wisdom of crowd paradigm
Sievers (2015)			√	√	Crowdsource-problem-crowd-platform-solution model as to decentralise emergency planning through 'whole community' approach
McCormick (2012)			√	√	Lay mapping as a tactic to gain citizen knowledge to gather data on diverse impacts

2.4.3 Attributes of Volunteer Crowdsourcing

2.4.3.1 Multidirectional Communication

Typically, communication between victims and rescue forces are limited to one-way, whilst crowdsourcing fosters two-way communication (Lorenzi et al., 2015). Through this, authorities can receive information from multiple sources and victims can be approached by the closest responders. By introducing an emergency contact number, people are restricted to one mode of communication, e.g., telephone calls (Dailey & Starbird, 2014). In the alternative, volunteer crowdsourcing provides many channels accessible to many people across the world. Volunteer crowdsourcing potentially serves as a megaphone where victims feel like asking help from the entire world (Murthy & Gross, 2017). Therefore, crisis information no longer comes in a top-down workflow, instead, it is transmitted vertically and horizontally among people (Collins et al., 2016). This leads to the transfer of information to on-site rescue forces via remote assistance (Yang et al., 2014). Since communications are occurring in multidirectional ways, it allows people to leverage local knowledge (Ludwig et al., 2017).

Although the successive delivery of multidirectional communication during-disaster is apparent, bridging the relationship between volunteer crowdsourcing and official protocols is a challenge (Handmer et al., 2014). A complex chain of authority backs presents linear communication systems. It needs to change, in order to harvest the full potential of volunteer crowdsourcing. Despite ignoring the legitimacy in disaster communication, volunteer crowdsourcing-driven 'backchannel' communications have become prominent. There are also emerging platforms such as 'Tweak the Tweet', which attempts to develop two-way communication with authorities during-disaster (Starbird & Stamberger, 2010). Jung and Moro (2014) identified three levels of social media communication: micro-level (among individuals); mezzo-level (among local communities); and macro-level (countries, mass media organisations)—where it is possible to establish one-on-one and one-to-many communication.

According to Handmer et al. (2014), messages received through personal, but informal networks are often the key to disseminating the warning alerts and environmental cues among people. This expands people's ability to obtain confirmed and personalised warnings from their associates and provides assurance that their loved ones are safe, which can be termed as interpersonal trust (Mehta et al., 2016). Moreover, they will receive such information in a customised language to aid interpretation (Vivacqua & Borges, 2012). People use the power of crowdsourcing to engage in live news prioritisation to update the status of a situation and meet the victims' needs promptly (Yuan & Liu, 2018a). Based on the feedback, extant emergencies are initially sensed through the 'eyes' of personal mobile cameras and then transmitted via communication platforms to people, rather than reporting to officials (Koswatte et al., 2015). Therefore, it is recommended that future research should study the changing role of emergency managers and information flows, to interlink the back-channel communications with official communication systems.

2.4.3.2 Situation Awareness

The term situation awareness was initially coined by Endsley (1995) in order to develop a theory on situation awareness. According to Endsley (1995), situation awareness is the perception of elements in the environment within time and space, the comprehension of their meaning, and the projection of their status in the future. Initially conceptualised for the military purposes, situation awareness is now becoming more relevant in DRR using crowdsourcing.

Harrison and Johnson (2016) defined situation awareness as the understanding of unfolding events that are impacting many actors and moving parts. It is a critical tool required in ex-post disaster response. Social media and other communication pathways deliver aggregate situation awareness and provide opportunities to assist at an individual level (Gao et al., 2011).

Previous technologies used to gain situational awareness in disaster situations are complex and need a high-level of skills. For instance, radar satellites are employed to penetrate the cloud cover during disasters, helicopters to observe the disaster-prone or disaster-affected areas, and direct observations to identify displaced and trapped people. Geo-temporal gaps in the satellites and atmospheric conditions limit the use of satellites to harvest location-specific data during disasters and observing the victims from a helicopter can fail in identifying trapped victims (Cervone, 2016; Fritz et al., 2017). However, rectifying these issues are time-consuming complex processes and emergency managers encounter difficulties in coordination. On the other hand, collecting location-specific data is critical in a disaster to establish evacuation paths, damage assessments, and accelerate recovery activities (Lu et al., 2018). Therefore, significant research is required to empower location-based information intelligence for proper situation awareness (Ernst et al., 2017).

Volunteer crowdsourcing has the capacity to provide location information without using any advanced instruments. Having geolocation of the sender in a metadata file helps to identify the disaster hotspots and the required responses (Gao et al., 2011; Lorenzi et al., 2015). Without physically observing the context, Japan identified the adversely affected locations and the disaster footprint in the aftermath of the 2011 Tōhoku Earthquake and Tsunami (Japan), using Ushahidi volunteer reports. Moreover, internet-mediated new mapping platforms and applications, so-called geographic worldwide-web (GeoWeb), underpin the increasing popularity of location-specific data (Yigitcanlar, 2005, 2006; Dror et al., 2015). With the advancement of such geo-technologies, it is expected that the volume of location-specific data would increase by 50 folds by 2020 (Dror et al., 2015). These are succinct, accessible, and readable to anyone. With these, live updates about a disaster could improve the response time and resource allocation procedures by emergency managers. Therefore, future research should investigate initiatives to harvest the potential of data-driven cities.

Volunteer crowdsourcing can provide information on badly affected locations, messages, images, videos of the damaged properties and people, voice recordings of the victims, and locations of the evacuation camps (Lorenzi et al., 2015; Kryvasheyeu et al., 2016). Further, Vieweg et al. (2010) identified 13 situational features of volunteer crowdsourcing, which will contribute to increasing the situation awareness in disasters. These features include Warning; Preparatory activity; Evacuation information; Volunteer information; Fire line/hazard location; Weather; Flood level; Wind; Visibility; Road conditions; Advice on how to cope with the emergency, and/or advice on other Twitter users or websites to follow; Animal management; Damage/ injury reports. Inarguably, such information will enhance the situation awareness in a disaster situation.

A range of response measures can be supported with the extracted volunteer crowdsourcing information compared to a situation where location information is unknown such as detecting disaster events, updating the disaster severity, identifying the disaster footprint, personal warnings, disaster relief processes, contingency funding, and damage assessments become efficient and easier, compared to a situation where location information is not fully available (Vieweg et al., 2010; De Albuquerque et al., 2015; Fekete et al., 2015; Gray et al., 2016; Kryvasheyeu et al., 2016; Sosko & Dalyot, 2017; Han et al., 2018). Likewise, Givoni (2016) explained that situation awareness is essential in relief tasks, helping to detect people buried under rubble and linking people in need with people willing to help. To share location information, a person is not required to be present physically. Instead, the virtual volunteer can tag the location using a hashtag.

Real-time mapping of geo-enabled volunteer crowdsourcing messages is a way of disseminating real-time information (Liu, 2014). According to Panteras et al. (2015), except for the precise geotagged Tweets, there are about 40-70% Tweets available with a descriptive toponym. These can help the rescue forces to at least airdrop the necessary provisions, where roads are inaccessible (Han et al., 2018). This highlights the value of the information generated via social media. Therefore, future research should focus on understanding the citizens' responsibilities in information sharing during disasters. However, there is no legal way of using such information to deliver government aid. Future research should investigate how existing disaster-related legal procedures can be enhanced to incorporate technical developments.

2.4.3.3 Collective Intelligence

According to Harrison and Johnson (2016), the crowdsourcing process starts with the first step of collecting information from citizens. Prior to the development of the technology and communication, citizens did not have a media available to participate in decision-making. Today, citizens have an abundance of pathways to express what they see, their opinion, and possible solutions (crowd-voting), which led to the creation of democracy in DRR. Citizens act as the main role player throughout the crowdsourcing process, irrespective of their education and experience level. In support, Sheth (2009) argued that citizens with internet or web-enabled community and Web 2.0 technologies can augment citizens to citizen sensors.

Goodchild (2007) pointed out that citizen sensors are the sensor nodes equipped with a working subset of the five senses and with the intelligence to compile and interpret what they sense and being free to roam around the surface of the earth. It shows that in terms of collective intelligence, a sensor is not basically hardware. With the ramification of citizens acting as sensors, 'amateur citizens' (Duong, 2013) have the opportunity to be involved in professionally driven DRR activities. McCormick (2016) identified 'amateur professionals' as the leaders who contribute to this knowledge-sharing process. Collective knowledge generation leads to the creation of citizen science, where scientific decisions are taken by the aggregated knowledge of the citizens.

Since the crowd is the focal point of crowdsourcing, its services are best coupled with the wisdom of crowds (Surowiecki, 2004; Dror et al., 2015). It is axiomatic, that when a large group works on one theme, they are producing strong and useful knowledge. With the use of social media citizens self-organise and carry out tasks to face the emerging disaster risks (Albris, 2018). Accordingly, volunteer crowdsourcing can be upgraded to a level where, weather data could be collected through citizens (Sosko & Dalyot, 2017) and could be used both, in ex-ante and ex-post DRR. Throughout the past decades, many researchers proved the possibility of deriving high-quality results by harnessing crowd-power (Vivacqua & Borges, 2012). Photo sharing through Flicker, Facebook, and Twitter has granted citizens the role of a journalist, which is referred to as 'citizen journalism'. For instance, a Facebook group called 'Fluthilfe Dresden (Flood Help Dresden)', created during the Elber River Flood 2013 attracted 12,000 followers within 24 hours. That group guided thousands of people to help the people in need (Albris, 2018). Consequently, today social media is no longer being looked at as a simple communication tool.

Factually, citizen presence is grounded and rooted in emergency planning, leading to citizen science or participation of both, experts and non-experts in scientific research. Web 2.0 technologies offer availability, interactivity, and customisability of spatial content (Lue et al., 2014). With the ramification of Web 2.0 technologies, citizens carry sensor-laden devices such as mobile phones wherever they go (Boulos et al., 2011). This enables the crowd to sense the environment and incidents around them. Consequently, information relating to incidents that take place in cities and adjacent areas can be overwhelming in the new age of neogeography (Connors et al., 2012).

Increasing collective intelligence is the main foundation for neogeography. Neogeography is defined as the blurring of the distinctions between producer, communicator, and consumer of geographic information (Goodchild, 2009). Turner (2006), who cemented the term neogeography, defines it as new geography with a set of techniques and tools that fall outside the realm of traditional GIS. Turner (2006) further elucidated that, while professional cartographers use ArcGIS, talk of Mercator versus Mollweide projections, a neogeography uses mapping application programming interfaces (API) such as Google Maps and geotag photos, which are open and simple. As such, the democracy in generating geo-spatial content makes user-generated content qualified for DRR. This is referred to as 'citizen science' (Liu, 2014). Accordingly, to which extent citizens engage in DRR through crowdsourcing, how effective it is, how to motivate citizen engagement in volunteer crowdsourcing, and their reflections require further research.

2.5 Discussion and Conclusion[1]

Despite the growing popularity of volunteer crowdsourcing, there is no consensus on what volunteer crowdsourcing is, and how volunteer crowdsourcing support DRR, despite a wide-range of applications being available. This is attributed to the fact that a range of different disciplinary perspectives is individually applied to crowdsourcing. The four attributes of volunteer crowdsourcing identified through literature include, 'location awareness', 'multi-directional communication', 'situation awareness', 'collective intelligence', all of which emphasise the suitability of applying volunteer crowdsourcing in DRR. To-date, volunteer crowdsourcing has been considered as a random tool, popularised through different mobile applications and social media. Due to the dearth of scholarship and in-depth investigations, authorities are reluctant to make it part of the formal decision-making process in relation to DRR. However, these four attributes, clearly underpin the reliability and potential value of volunteer crowdsourcing in DRR. Therefore, in the face of increasing disaster risk, governments should welcome the skills and knowledge of the citizens and for that volunteer, crowdsourcing could be a promising instrument.

To date, emergency managers identify the disaster response period as a blind period, where victims need to ensure their own safety and security (Givoni, 2016). Conversely, volunteer crowdsourcing shares real-time,

---

[1] This chapter, with permission from the copyright holder, is a reproduced version of the following journal article: Kankanamge, N., Yigitcanlar, T., Goonetilleke, A., & Kamruzzaman, M. (2019). Can volunteer crowdsourcing reduce disaster risk? A systematic review of the literature. *International Journal of Disaster Risk Reduction*, 35, 101097.

time-critical and location-specific information whenever a disaster occurs. This assists the emergency managers to take necessary actions to reduce the disaster risk, increase the real-time awareness and predict the direction in which the disaster is spreading. Consequently, the disaster response phase should no longer be a blind period.

The reviewed literature does not have an agreed definition of volunteer crowdsourcing; whether it is simply a data collection, decision-making, or awareness-raising tool. The literature review findings demonstrate the inappropriateness of crowdsourcing definitions to the Web 2.0 era. Such definitions inhibit the advancement of our understanding of volunteer crowdsourcing since they confine to a few themes such as crowd power, outsourcing, and volunteerism (Table 2.1). The analysis reveals the usage of crowdsourcing as a general term in both, where people use micro-tasking for monetary rewards (Whitla, 2009) and information sharing without any monetary gain (Doan et al., 2011; Riccardi, 2016). This comes as no surprise as it reflects the infancy of the field. Considering this situation, the research results emphasise the significance of using the term 'volunteer crowdsourcing', whenever the crowd volunteers without any financial rewards.

Traditionally, information, communication, volunteerism, and technology were the media used by governments, to interact with people in a disaster. However, due to volunteer crowdsourcing, these channels are being replaced by new technological foundations such as digital crisis information, mobile communication, digital volunteerism, and geo-technology. Furthermore, while most claim the significance of incorporating volunteer crowdsourcing into policy planning and emergency communication, they seem to use volunteer crowdsourcing simply as a data collection tool, whilst claiming them being holistic. This can be quite problematic in nature and highlights a knowledge gap for in-depth investigation. Additionally, almost all the research in this area has neglected to analyse the influence of motivation levels, occupation, education level, cultural backgrounds, towards volunteer crowdsourcing in disasters.

The fast-growing volunteer crowdsourcing literature is heading to identify the causes of disasters using social media data. Identifying the causes for damages informs disaster managers and urban and emergency planners to plan better disaster response activities and DRR activities beforehand. For instance, Yuan and Liu (2018b) analysed the root causes of the damages that occurred during Hurricane Harvey using volunteered crowdsourcing data. Such studies underpin the use of volunteer crowdsourcing data to the principle notion of 'build back better', proposed in the UNISDR's Sendai Framework for DRR (UNISDR, 2015; Yuan & Liu, 2018b). Furthermore, Zheng et al. (2018) attempted to identify the relationships among different disasters through volunteer crowdsourced data which can be used for disaster predictions, e.g., storms and floods.

The attributes and technological foundations identified and discussed so far, contribute to the practices of emergency planning and resilient urban infrastructure planning. This approach highlights the need for moving from professionally driven resilience planning to collaborative resilience planning, where volunteer crowdsourcing could play a critical role. Volunteer crowdsourcing will support the role of professionals in DRR since the citizens also bear the responsibility for acting as sensors through back-channel communication. Therefore, the bureaucratic decision-making processes, DRR guidelines, legal procedures, and resilient urban planning processes need to be reviewed, analysed, and amended accordingly to accommodate volunteer crowdsourcing.

The study has the following limitations: (a) Conference proceedings, book chapters, and white papers were excluded, which may have reduced the research knowledge base reviewed; (b) selected search keywords could have omitted some relevant articles; (c) Authors' unconscious bias could have an influence on the findings; (d) Although this chapter covered neogeography and citizen science topics, the review did not specifically focused on these areas; (e) The methodology was a manual literature review technique and did not include techniques such as bibliometrics, scientometrics, content analysis, cognitive mapping, concept clustering. Despite these limitations, the research results shed light on the way forward for emergency and urban planners to ensure a democratic and participatory planning process by incorporating volunteer crowdsourcing.

References

Ahmad, K., Pogorelov, K., Riegler, M., Conci, N., & Halvorsen, P. (2018). Social media and satellites. *Multimedia Tools and Applications, 1*, 1–39.

Albris, K. (2018). The switchboard mechanism: How social media connected citizens during the 2013 floods in Dresden. *Journal of Contingencies and Crisis Management, 26*, 350–357.

Arthur, R., Boulton, C.A., Shotton, H., & Williams, H.T. (2018). Social sensing of floods in the UK. *Plos One, 13*, 1–18.

Aslam Saja, A.M., Teo, M., Goonetilleke, A., & Ziyath, A.M. (2018). An inclusive and adaptive framework for measuring social resilience to disasters. *International Journal of Disaster Risk Reduction, 28*, 862–873.

Baum, S., Kendall, E., Muenchberger, H., Gudes, O., & Yigitcanlar, T. (2010). Geographical information systems. *Health Information Management Journal, 39*, 28–33.

Baytiyeh, H. (2017). Can disaster risk education reduce the impacts of recurring disasters on developing societies? *Education and Urban Society, 50*, 230–245.

Boulos, M.N., Resch, B., Crowley, D.N., Breslin, J.G., Sohn, G., Burtner, R., Pike, W.A., Jezierski, E., & Chuang, K.Y. (2011). Crowdsourcing, citizen sensing, and sensor web technologies for public and environmental health surveillance and crisis management. *International Journal of Health Geographics, 10*, 67–96.

Brabham, D.C. (2008). Crowdsourcing as a model for problem solving. *Convergence, 14,* 75–90.

Brabham, D.C. (2013). *Crowdsourcing.* MIT Press, Boston.

Burston, J., Ware, D., & Tomlinson, R. (2015). The real-time needs of emergency managers for tropical cyclone storm tide forecasting. *Natural Hazards, 78,* 1653–166.

Callaghan, C. (2016). Disaster management, crowdsourced R&D, and probabilistic innovation theory. *International Journal of Disaster Risk Reduction, 17,* 238–250.

Carley, K.M., Malik, M., Landwehr, P.M., Pfeffer, J., & Kowalchuck, M. (2016). Crowd sourcing disaster management. *Safety Science, 90,* 48–61.

Castillo, C., Mendoza, M., & Poblete, B. (2012). Predicting information credibility in time-sensitive social media. *Internet Research, 23,* 560–588.

Cervone, G., Sava, E., Huang, Q., Schnebele, E., Harrison, J., & Waters, N. (2016). Using Twitter for tasking remote-sensing data collection and damage assessment. *International Journal of Remote Sensing, 37,* 100–124.

Chu, H.J., & Chen, Y.C. (2018). Crowdsourcing photograph locations for debris flow hot spot mapping. *Natural Hazards, 90,* 1259–1276.

Collins, M., Neville, K., Hynes, W., & Madden, M. (2016). Communication in a disaster. *Journal of Decision Systems, 25,* 160–170.

Connors, J., Lei, S., & Kelly, M. (2012). Citizen science in the age of neogeography. *Annals of the Association of American Geographers, 102,* 1267–1289.

Cova, T.J., & Johnson, J.P. (2002). Microsimulation of neighborhood evacuations in the urban-wildland interface. *Environment and Planning A, 34,* 2211–2229.

CRED (2018). *Natural Disasters in 2017.* Centre for Research on Epidemiology of Disasters, Brussels.

Crooks, A.T., & Wise, S. (2013). GIS and agent-based models for humanitarian assistance. *Computers, Environment and Urban Systems, 41,* 100–111.

Cumiskey, L., Priest, S., Valchev, N., Viavattene, C., Costas, S., & Clarke, J. (2018). A framework to include the (inter)dependencies of disaster risk reduction measures in coastal risk assessment. *Coastal Engineering, 134,* 81–92.

Dailey, D., & Starbird, K. (2014). Journalists as crowdsourcers. *Computer Supported Cooperative Work, 23,* 445–481.

De Albuquerque, J.P., Herfort, B., Brenning, A., & Zipf, A. (2015). A geographic approach for combining social media and authoritative data towards identifying useful information for disaster management. *International Journal of Geographical Information Science, 29,* 667–689.

Deng, Q., Liu, Y., Zhang, H., Deng, X., & Ma, Y. (2016). A new crowdsourcing model to assess disaster using microblog data in typhoon Haiyan. *Natural Hazards, 84,* 1241–1256.

Doan, A., Ramakrishnan, R., & Halevy, A.Y. (2011). Crowdsourcing systems on the world-wide web. *Communications of the ACM, 54,* 86–96.

Dror, T., Dalyot, S., & Doytsher, Y. (2015). Quantitative evaluation of volunteered geographic information paradigms. *Survey Review, 47,* 349–362.

Dufty, N. (2016). Twitter turns ten. *Australian Journal of Emergency Management, 31,* 50–54.

Duong, P. (2013). Bloggers unplugged: Amateur citizens, cultural discourse, and the public sphere in Cuba. *Journal of Latin American Cultural Studies, 22,* 375–397.

Endsley, M.R. (1995). Toward a theory of situation awareness in dynamic systems. *Human Factors, 37,* 32–64.

Ernst, C., Mladenow, A., & Strauss, C. (2017). Collaboration and crowdsourcing in emergency management. *International Journal of Pervasive Computing and Communications, 13*, 176–193.

Estellés, A.E., & González, L.G. (2012). Towards an integrated crowdsourcing definition. *Journal of Information Science, 38*, 189–200.

Fekete, A., Tzavella, K., Armas, I., Binner, J., Garschagen, M., Giupponi, C., Mojtahed, V., Pettita, M., Schneiderbauer, S., & Serre, D. (2015). Critical data source: Tool or even infrastructure? *ISPRS International Journal of Geo-Information, 4*, 1848–1870.

Feng, Y., & Sester, M. (2018). Extraction of pluvial flood relevant volunteered geographic information by deep learning from user generated texts and photos. *ISPRS International Journal of Geo-Information, 7*, 39–64.

Frank, J., Rebbapragada, U., Bialas, J., Oommen, T., & Havens, T.C. (2017). Effect of label noise on the machine-learned classification of earthquake damage. *Remote Sensing, 9*, 803–821.

Fritz, S., Fonte, C., & See, L. (2017). The role of citizen science in earth observation. *Remote Sensing, 9*, 357–370.

Gao, H., Barbier, G., Goolsby, R., & Zeng, D. (2011). Harnessing the crowdsourcing power of social media for disaster relief. *IEEE Intelligent Systems, 26*, 1541–1672.

Gardoni, P., & Murphy, C. (2010). Gauging the societal impacts of natural disasters using a capability approach. *Disasters, 34*, 619–636.

Givoni, M. (2016). Between micro mappers and missing maps. *Environment and Planning D, 34*, 1025–1043.

Goetz, M., & Zipf, A. (2013). The evolution of geo-crowdsourcing. In *Crowdsourcing Geographic Knowledge*. Springer, Berlin, pp. 139–159.

Goodchild, M.F. (2007). Citizens as sensors. *GeoJournal, 69*, 211–221.

Goodchild, M.F., Yuan, M., & Cova, T.J. (2007). Towards a general theory of geographic representation in GIS. *International Journal of Geographical Information Science, 21*, 239–260.

Goodchild, M.F. (2009). Neogeography and the nature of geographic expertise. *Journal of Location Based Services, 3*, 82–96.

Goodchild, M.F., & Glennon, J.A. (2010). Crowdsourcing geographic information for disaster response. *International Journal of Digital Earth, 3*, 231–241.

Goodchild, M.F., & Li, L. (2012). Assuring the quality of volunteered geographic information. *Spatial Statistics, 1*, 110–120.

Gray, B.J., Weal, M.J., & Martin, D. (2016). Social media and disasters. *International Journal of Information Systems for Crisis Response and Management, 8*, 41–55, https://doi.org/10.4018/IJISCRAM.2016100103.

Guan, X., & Chen, C. (2014). Using social media data to understand and assess disasters. *Natural Hazards, 74*, 837–850.

Gudes, O., Kendall, E., Yigitcanlar, T., Pathak, V., & Baum, S. (2010). Rethinking health planning. *Health Information Management Journal, 39*, 18–29.

Gurman, T.A., & Ellenberger, N. (2015). Reaching the global community during disasters. *Journal of Health Communication, 20*, 687–696.

Han, S., Huang, H., Luo, Z., & Foropon, C. (2018). Harnessing the power of crowdsourcing and the internet of things in disaster response. *Annals of Operations Research, 26*, 1–16.

Handmer, J., Choy, S., & Kohtake, N. (2014). Updating warning systems for climate hazards. *Australian Journal of Telecommunications and the Digital Economy, 2*, 70–84.

Harrison, S.E., & Johnson, P.A. (2016). Crowdsourcing the disaster management cycle. *International Journal of Infrastructure Systems for Crisis Response Management, 8,* 17–40.

Havas, C., Resch, B., Francalanci, C., Pernici, B., Scalia, G., Fernandez-Marquez, J., Van Achte, T., Zeug, G., Mondardini, M., Grandoni, D., Kirsch, B., Kalas, M., Lorini, V., & Rüping, S. (2017). E2mC. *Sensors, 17,* 2766–2798.

Haworth, B., & Bruce, E. (2015). A review of volunteered geographic information for disaster management. *Geography Compass, 9,* 237–250.

Haworth, B. (2016). Emergency management perspectives on volunteered geographic information. *Computers, Environment and Urban Systems, 57,* 189–198.

Howe, J. (2006). The rise of crowdsourcing. *Wired Magazine, 14,* 1–4.

Hossain, M., & Kauranen, I. (2016). Open innovation in SMEs. *Journal of Strategy and Management, 9,* 58–73.

IFRC (2016). *World Disasters Report.* International Federation of Red Cross and Red Crescent Societies (IFRC), Lyon.

Jung, J.Y., & Moro, M. (2014). Multi-level functionality of social media in the aftermath of the Great East Japan earthquake. *Disasters, 38,* 123–143.

Juhász, L., Podolcsák, Á, & Doleschall, J. (2016). Open source web GIS solutions in disaster management. *Journal of Environmental Geography, 9,* 15–21.

Kantarci, B., Carr, K.G., & Pearsall, C.D. (2016). Social network-assisted trustworthiness assurance in smart city crowdsensing. *International Journal of Distributed Systems and Technologies, 7,* 59–78.

Kerle, N., & Hoffman, R.R. (2013). Collaborative damage mapping for emergency response. *Natural Hazards & Earth System Sciences, 13,* 97–113.

Kleemann, F., Voß, G.G., & Rieder, K. (2008). Un (der) paid innovators. *Science, Technology & Innovation Studies, 4,* 5–26.

Kolen, B., & Helsloot, I. (2014). Decision-making and evacuation planning for flood risk management in the Netherlands. *Disasters, 38,* 610–635.

Koswatte, S., McDougall, K., & Liu, X. (2015). SDI and crowdsourced spatial information management automation for disaster management. *Survey Review, 47,* 307–315.

Kryvasheyeu, Y., Chen, H., Obradovich, N., Moro, E., Van Hentenryck, P., Fowler, J., & Cebrian, M. (2016). Rapid assessment of disaster damage using social media activity. *Science Advances, 2,* 1–11.

Kuehn, A., Kaschewsky, M., Kappeler, A., Spichiger, A., & Riedl, R. (2011). Interoperability and information brokers in public safety. *Journal of Theoretical and Applied Electronic Commerce Research, 6,* 43–60.

Lagmay, A.M., Racoma, B.A., Aracan, K.A., Alconis-Ayco, J., & Saddi, I.L. (2017). Disseminating near-real-time hazards information and flood maps in the Philippines through web-GIS. *Journal of Environmental Sciences, 59,* 13–23.

Lara, A.P., Da Costa, E.M., Furlani, T.Z., & Yigitcanlar, T. (2016). Smartness that matters: Towards a comprehensive and human-centred characterisation of smart cities. *Journal of Open Innovation: Technology, Market, and Complexity, 2,* 8.

Le Coz, J., Patalano, A., Collins, D., Guillén, N.F., García, C.M., Smart, G.M., Bind, J., Chiaverini, A., Le Boursicaud, R., & Dramais, G. (2016). Crowdsourced data for flood hydrology. *Journal of Hydrology, 541,* 766–777.

Lin Moe, T., & Pathranarakul, P. (2006). An integrated approach to natural disaster management. *Disaster Prevention and Management, 15,* 396–413.

Lin, W.Y., Wu, T.H., Tsai, M.H., Hsu, W.C., Chou, Y.T., & Kang, S.C. (2018). Filtering disaster responses using crowdsourcing. *Automation in Construction, 91,* 182–192.

Liu, S.B., & Palen, L. (2010). The new cartographers. *Cartography and Geographic Information Science, 37,* 69–90.

Liu, S.B. (2014). Crisis crowdsourcing framework. *Computer Supported Cooperative Work, 23,* 389–443.

Liu, F., & Xu, D. (2018). Social roles and consequences in using social media in disasters. *Information Systems Frontiers, 20,* 693–711.

Lorenzi, D., Chun, S.A., Vaidya, J., Shafiq, B., Atluri, V., & Adam, N.R. (2015). Peer. *International Journal of E-Planning Research, 4,* 29–46.

Lu, H., Zhu, Y., Shi, K., Lv, Y., Shi, P., & Niu, Z. (2018). Using adverse weather data in social media to assist with city-level traffic situation awareness and alerting. *Applied Sciences, 8,* 1193–1211.

Ludwig, T., Kotthaus, C., Reuter, C., Van Dongen, S., & Pipek, V. (2017). Situated crowdsourcing during disasters. *International Journal of Human-Computer Studies, 102,* 103–121.

Lue, E., Wilson, J.P., & Curtis, A. (2014). Conducting disaster damage assessments with spatial video, experts, and citizens. *Applied Geography, 52,* 46–54.

Maresh-Fuehrer, M.M., & Smith, R. (2016). Social media mapping innovations for crisis prevention, response, and evaluation. *Computers in Human Behavior, 54,* 620–629.

McCormick, S. (2012). After the cap. *Ecology and Society, 17,* 31–41.

McCormick, S. (2016). New tools for emergency managers. *Disasters, 40,* 207–225.

Mechler, R. (2016). Reviewing estimates of the economic efficiency of disaster risk management. *Natural Hazards, 81,* 2121–2147.

Mehta, A., Bruns, A., & Newton, J. (2016). Trust, but verify. *Disasters, 41,* 549–565.

Mejri, O., Menoni, S., Matias, K., & Aminoltaheri, N. (2017). Crisis information to support spatial planning in post disaster recovery. *International Journal of Disaster Risk Reduction, 22,* 46–61.

Miller, H.J., & Goodchild, M.F. (2015). Data-driven geography. *GeoJournal, 80,* 449–461.

Mojtahedi, M., & Oo, B.L. (2017). Critical attributes for proactive engagement of stakeholders in disaster risk management. *International Journal of Disaster Risk Reduction, 21,* 35–43.

Murthy, D., & Gross, A.J. (2017). Social media processes in disasters. *Social Science Research, 63,* 356–370.

Nourbakhsh, I., Sargent, R., Wright, A., Cramer, K., McClendon, B., & Jones, M. (2006). Mapping disaster zones. *Nature, 439,* 787–788.

Ogie, R.I., Forehead, H., Clarke, R.J., & Perez, P. (2017). Participation patterns and reliability of human sensing in crowd-sourced disaster management. *Information Systems Frontiers, 20,* 713–728.

Oliveira, A.C., Botega, L.C., Saran, J.F., Silva, J.N., Melo, J.O., Tavares, M.F., & Neris, V.P. (2017). Crowdsourcing, data and information fusion, and situation awareness for emergency management of forest fires. *Computers, Environment and Urban Systems,* https://doi.org/10.1016/j.compenvurbsys.2017.08.006,

O'Sullivan, T.L., Kuziemsky, C.E., Toal-Sullivan, D., & Corneil, W. (2013). Unraveling the complexities of disaster management. *Social Science & Medicine, 93,* 238–246.

Palen, L., & Hughes, A.L. (2018). Social media in disaster communication. In *Handbook of Disaster Research.* Springer, Berlin, pp. 497–518.

Pánek, J., Marek, L., Pászto, V., & Valůch, J. (2017). The crisis map of the Czech Republic. *Disasters, 41,* 649–671.

Panteras, G., Wise, S., Lu, X., Croitoru, A., Crooks, A., & Stefanidis, A. (2015). Triangulating social multimedia content for event localisation using Flickr and Twitter. *Transactions in GIS, 19,* 694–715.

Peng, L. (2017). Crisis crowdsourcing and China's civic participation in disaster response. *China Information, 31,* 327–348.

Perry, R.W. (2003). Incident management systems in disaster management. *Disaster Prevention and Management, 12,* 405–412.

Pitrėnaitė-Žilienė, B., Carosi, A., & Vallesi, P. (2014). Enhancing societal resilience against disasters. *Social Technologies, 4,* 318–332.

Poblet, M., García-Cuesta, E., & Casanovas, P. (2017). Crowdsourcing roles, methods, and tools for data-intensive disaster management. *Information Systems Frontiers, 1,* 1–17.

Riccardi, M.T. (2016). The power of crowdsourcing in disaster response operations. *International Journal of Disaster Risk Reduction, 20,* 123–128.

Roche, S., Propeck-Zimmermann, E., & Mericskay, B. (2013). GeoWeb and crisis management. *GeoJournal, 78,* 21–40.

Sachdeva, S., McCaffrey, S., & Locke, D. (2017). Social media approaches to modeling wildfire smoke dispersion. *Information, Communication & Society, 20,* 1146–1161.

Sagun, A., Bouchlaghem, D., & Anumba, C.J. (2009). A scenario-based study on information flow and collaboration patterns in disaster management. *Disasters, 33,* 214–238.

Schenk, E., & Guittard, C. (2011). Towards a characterisation of crowdsourcing practices. *Journal of Innovation Economics & Management, 1,* 93–107.

Sheth, A. (2009). Citizen sensing, social signals, and enriching human experience. *IEEE Internet Computing, 4,* 87–92.

Shklovski, I., Burke, M., Kiesler, S., & Kraut, R. (2010). Technology adoption and use in the aftermath of Hurricane Katrina in New Orleans. *American Behavioral Scientist, 53,* 1228–1246.

Sievers, J.A. (2015). Embracing crowdsourcing. *State and Local Government Review, 47,* 57–67.

Sosko, S., & Dalyot, S. (2017). Crowdsourcing user-generated mobile sensor weather data for densifying static geosensor networks. *ISPRS International Journal of Geo-Information, 6,* 61–83.

Starbird, K., & Stamberger, J. (2010). Tweak the tweet. In *Proceedings of the 7th International ISCRAM Conference.* Western Australia.

Surowiecki, J. (2004). *The Wisdom of Crowds.* Doubleday, London.

Turner, A. (2006). *Introduction to Neogeography.* O'Reilly Media, London.

UN (2017). *World Population Prospects.* United Nations (UN), New York.

UNISDR (2015). *Sendai Framework for Disaster Risk Reduction.* United Nations International Strategy for Disaster Reduction (UNISDR), Geneva.

Vieweg, S., Hughes, A.L., Starbird, K., & Palen, L. (2010). Microblogging during two natural hazards events. In: Proceedings of the SIGCHI conference on human factors in computing systems. Georgia.

Vivacqua, A.S., & Borges, M.R. (2012). Taking advantage of collective knowledge in emergency response systems. *Journal of Network and Computer Applications, 35,* 189–198.

Wan, Z., Hong, Y., Khan, S., Gourley, J., Flamig, Z., Kirschbaum, D., & Tang, G. (2014). A cloud-based global flood disaster community cyber-infrastructure. *Environmental Modelling & Software, 58,* 86–94.

Wang, R.Q., Mao, H., Wang, Y., Rae, C., & Shaw, W. (2018). Hyper-resolution monitoring of urban flooding with social media and crowdsourcing data. *Computers & Geosciences, 111,* 139–147.

Wang, Y., & Taylor, J.E. (2018). Coupling sentiment and human mobility in natural disasters. *Natural Hazards, 92,* 907–925.

Whitla, P. (2009). Crowdsourcing and its application in marketing activities. *Contemporary Management Research, 5,* 15–28.

Yan, Y., Eckle, M., Kuo, C.L., Herfort, B., Fan, H., & Zipf, A. (2017). Monitoring and assessing post-disaster tourism recovery using geotagged social media data. *ISPRS International Journal of Geo-Information, 6,* 144–161.

Yang, D., Zhang, D., Frank, K., Robertson, P., Jennings, E., Roddy, M., & Lichtenstern, M. (2014). Providing real-time assistance in disaster relief by leveraging crowdsourcing power. *Personal Ubiquitous Computing, 18,* 2025–2034.

Yigitcanlar, T. (2005). Is Australia ready to move planning to online mode? *Australian Planner, 42,* 42–51.

Yigitcanlar, T. (2006). Australian local governments' practice and prospects with online planning. *URISA Journal, 18,* 7–17.

Yigitcanlar, T., Sipe, N., Evans, R., & Pitot, M. (2007). A GIS-based land use and public transport accessibility indexing model. *Australian Planner, 44,* 30–37.

Yigitcanlar, T. (2015). Smart cities: An effective urban development and management model? *Australian Planner, 52,* 27–34.

Yigitcanlar, T. (2016). *Technology and the city.* Routledge, New York.

Yigitcanlar, T., Kamruzzaman, M., Buys, L., Ioppolo, G., Sabatini-Marques, J., Costa, E., & Yun, J. (2018). Understanding 'smart cities': Intertwining development drivers with desired outcomes in a multidimensional framework. *Cities, 81,* 145–160.

Yigitcanlar, T., Kamruzzaman, M., Foth, M., Sabatini-Marques, J., Costa, E., & Ioppolo, G. (2019). Can cities become smart without being sustainable? A systematic review of the literature. *Sustainable Cities and Society, 45,* 348–365.

Yuan, F., & Liu, R. (2018a). Feasibility study of using crowdsourcing to identify critical affected areas for rapid damage assessment. *International Journal of Disaster Risk Reduction, 28,* 758–767.

Yuan, F., & Liu, R. (2018b). Crowdsourcing for forensic disaster investigations. *Natural Hazards, 93,* 1529–1546.

Zhao, X., Wang, N., Han, R., Xie, B., Yu, Y., Li, M., & Ou, J. (2018). Urban infrastructure safety system based on mobile crowdsensing. *International Journal of Disaster Risk Reduction, 27,* 427–438.

Zheng, L., Wang, F., Zheng, X., & Liu, B. (2018). Discovering the relationship of disasters from big scholar and social media news datasets. *International Journal of Digital Earth, 1,* 1–23.

3

Government Social Media Channels

3.1 Introduction

Disasters were responsible for about 0.1% of the global deaths, and a large amount of damages to infrastructure (Ritchie & Roser, 2014). For example, the 2013 Typhoon Haiyan killed over 10,000 people, and the 2013 European Floods caused over 12 billion Euros in damages (Ludwig et al., 2017). Communication barriers, inability to reach the community/individuals in need, inadequate number of volunteers, scarcity of information, and fund deficiencies can cause significant increases in the disaster risks. Even after a disaster, it takes a considerable time to conduct damage assessments and provide compensation to the affected people (Yuan & Liu, 2018a). This emphasises the need for a more community-centric and efficient approach to collect timely data, recruit more volunteers, and communicate effectively with the affected people in all possible ways.

The recently emerged mobile technologies and social media tools have transformed the landscape of our cities, societies, and also disaster management (Gooodchild, 2007; Goodchild & Glennon, 2010; Yigitcanlar et al., 2019a). There are numerous social media channels available across the world, which allow people to communicate and share their experiences, such as Facebook, Twitter, Instagram, LinkedIn, Snapchat, Pinterest, Reddit, and Tumblr. Irrespective of the physical distances, millions of people network across these social media channels. In early 2019, there were 3.7 billion active social media users in the world, representing 48% of the total world population, and among them, 3.6 billion people accessed social media through their mobile devices (Kemp, 2019). These facts reflect the popularity of social media across the globe and its potential for use by emergency services to enhance community engagement.

At the beginning of the social media age, social media channels were simply used by people to communicate and network with each other. In view of the dispersed use of social media, it has recently received more attention as a volunteer crowdsourcing tool for disaster management (Feng & Sester, 2018; Yuan & Liu, 2018b; Kankanamge et al., 2019). Volunteer crowdsourcing approaches trust the aggregated community knowledge than the elite few

DOI: 10.1201/9781003278986-4

(Surowiecki, 2004; Deng et al., 2016). Accordingly, social media data is currently widely used for research and development (R&D) purposes including in the field of disaster management.

The main applications of social media information within the context of disaster management include the use of: (a) Social media data to accelerate damage assessment (Kerle & Hoffman, 2013; Yuan & Liu, 2018a); (b) Photos shared in social media to investigate disaster severity (Feng & Sester, 2018); (c) Sentiment values in the social media messages to assess disaster severity (Kankanamge et al., 2020a); (d) Social media data to accelerate disaster relief efforts (Vivacqua & Borges, 2012); and (e) Mapping information on social media to identify and prioritise disaster response tasks (Givoni, 2016; Riccardi, 2016).

All of these advanced applications were based on the information generated by the community (Liu, 2014). Thus, a high community engagement with the social media pages dedicated to disaster management activities is deemed essential in order to generate important and time-critical information (Han et al., 2018). Nevertheless, evaluating and identifying ways to enhance community engagement in social media pages dedicated to disaster events is an understudied area of research.

Against this backdrop, the current study evaluates user engagement levels of the messages circulated by the social media pages dedicated to disaster events. Present social media channels (i.e., Twitter, Facebook, and Instagram) allow anyone to create their own pages in any social media channel they prefer—e.g., Facebook and Twitter social media pages of the UN Volunteers. By addressing the research question of 'How engaging are disaster management related social media channels?', the study contributes to an understanding of the possible ways of making social media pages in different social media channels efficient and effective. The methodological approach of this study accommodated five indices, namely, popularity, commitment, virality, engagement, and utilisation, in order to evaluate the community engagement levels of social media channels.

3.2 Literature Background

3.2.1 Community Engagement in Disaster Management at Large

Community engagement in disaster management literature has a long history (Mercer et al., 2008). Identification of 'community' as a central topic in disaster management was initiated around the 1940s with the introduction of the 'dominant paradigm' (White, 1945). The dominant paradigm focused on the integration of the human element by considering community perceptions about natural hazards and the way they dealt with them (Mercer et al., 2008). From that point onwards, the community has become one of the central topics in disaster management literature. Especially with population growth and settlement expansion, disaster impacts have become more severe (Haigh & Sutton, 2012). Considering the nature of the engagement, community engagement methods can be categorised into traditional and contemporary methods.

Since the early 2000s, numerous tools and methods have been developed to increase community engagement in disaster management, which can be categorised as traditional methods where people's presence in person is mandatory to engage with these tools. Disaster toolkits and training workshops (Samaddar et al., 2017), stakeholder meetings to improve skills and attitudes, public meetings, transect walks, participatory mapping (Osti et al., 2008), and community partnerships with government and non-government organisations (Wells et al., 2013; Baybay & Hindmarsh, 2019) can be categorised as traditional disaster management tools and methods. There are two main objectives of these tools. They are to develop community capacities while collecting local community knowledge for future decision-making (Yigitcanlar, 2006; Yigitcanlar & Dur, 2013; Baybay & Hindmarsh, 2019). Although community engagement in disaster management has been identified as an essential fact, aforesaid tools and methods have not proven to be very effective, especially in larger cities where community bonds are loose.

In particular, public gatherings consume time, space, and resources. They have fixed and tight schedules, which the community may not be comfortable at engaging. Even such tools and methods become inadequate with the increasing frequencies of disasters. Increasing number of disasters emphasises the need for community presence throughout the disaster management cycle—i.e., preparedness, response, recovery, and mitigation (Kankanamge et al., 2019). Although through the traditional methods, such as public gatherings, community engagement was activated in mitigation and preparedness phases of disaster management, these methods were not effective in the response and recovery phases (Zhang et al., 2013). While the use of traditional methods provides face-to-face communication, which is particularly helpful in receiving info from authorities, such communication may make the community not easily express or share their situation or views with the authorities (Haigh & Sutton, 2012). Hence, there has been a need for more innovative methods to make people more easily engaged with disaster management practices.

Contemporary technologies can override some of the aforesaid barriers for engaging the community in disaster management. They can make the community further engage in disaster management tasks through technology-mediated approaches such as e-government platforms (Rottz et al., 2019), online gamification tools (Kankanamge et al., 2020b), and online volunteer crowdsourcing (Howe, 2006; Goodchild & Glennon, 2010; Liu, 2014). The relevant community-centric technologies include social media mobile applications such as Ushahidi, iCoast, Stormpins (Poblet et al., 2017), vibration sensors backed by mobile and sensor technologies (Burston et al., 2015; Lagmay et al., 2017), open street mapping (Goetz & Zipf, 2013), and open-source gaming applications

(Poblet et al., 2017). Among them, social media is considered as one of the key drivers of volunteer crowdsourcing applications (Kankanamge et al., 2020a). The 2010 Haiti Earthquake, 2010-2011 Brisbane Floods, and 2011 Christchurch Earthquake were the tipping points of understanding the importance of the use of social media for disaster management (DHS, 2013).

3.2.2 Community Engagement in Disaster Management via Social Media

Social media is becoming an important source of information to better manage disasters (Anikeeva et al., 2016). In using social media, the community can 'like', 'comment', 'share', 'follow', and 'retweet' the posts. Most liked posts receive greater community attention and most commented posts lead to the generation of an in-depth discussion within the social network. By sharing and retweeting, the community can make a post, 'viral'. Higher community engagement in disaster management via social media can enhance the three unique attributes of social media as a volunteer crowdsourcing application. These are: (a) Situation awareness; (b) Collective intelligence, and (c) Multi-directional communication (Poblet et al., 2017; Oki, 2018; Kankanamge et al., 2019).

Situation awareness is the ability to provide a comprehensive understanding of an event that could impact the community. This is critical when it comes to disasters, as a greater understanding of a disaster event provides more confidence to the people to be prepared. If a social media page has adequate followers, awareness-raising, and information sharing through social media will become easier than organising and conducting public meetings (Anikeeva et al., 2016). Thus, people can engage to make posts related to warnings and awareness-raising popular by following and sharing them. By sharing any warning alert, people can contribute to increase awareness-raising within their social network (Kankanamge et al., 2019). Moreover, people can update the disaster conditions about their locality through social media. This will also translate to personalised warnings to their associates (Handmer et al., 2014; Mehta et al., 2016).

The second positive attribute of social media is the ability to collect dispersed community knowledge within a shorter time period—collective intelligence. People can take photos of lost people due to a disaster using their mobile phone cameras. By posting and sharing such messages, people can make these messages viral until the relevant parties see the messages (Koswatte et al., 2015). Social media channels such as Facebook and Twitter allow people to share location-specific information by tagging the location of the incident. For example, without physically observing the disaster, Japan identified the adversely affected areas of the 2011 Tohoku Earthquake and Tsunami (Gao et al., 2011). Similarly, Gao et al. (2011) discussed the significance of community engagement in providing information to social media channels to find the areas which needed a greater disaster relief effort.

The third positive attribute is the ability of social media messages to communicate in multiple directions. The traditional disaster management tools are much bureaucratic, and people find limited opportunities to interact (Sobaci, 2016). Nonetheless, in the case of social media, people do not have any communication barriers. Social media acts as an intermediate channel for authorities and communities to develop a frequent participatory dialogue (Veil et al., 2011; Ernst et al., 2017). Hence, dedicated social media pages for a disaster management authority have become common practice. Authorities can also screen the patterns of emerging dialogue related to environmental changes in social media (Allaire, 2016). Hence, active community engagement in such virtual dialogue help authorities to align their services in line with the community demands (USDHS, 2013).

The difficulty in verifying community engagement with social media during disasters has been the main critique in assessing the value of social media in community engagement. However, there is adequate evidence of the use of social media during a range of disaster events such as the 2016 California Drought and Wildfires (Tang et al., 2015), 2011 Bangkok Floods (Allaire, 2016), 2010-2011 Queensland Floods, and 2014 North Stradbroke Island Bushfires. There are mobile applications such as Situmap and Photosorter, which work as social media mapping applications, which further enhance the efficiency of social media information (Maresh-Fuehrer & Smith, 2016).

During the 2011 Bangkok Flood, about 40% of the flood-related messages were created and circulated through social media channels (Allaire, 2016), and around 50 Facebook groups were formed to share updates and photos with their loved ones. All these approaches were voluntarily done by the people without any intervention from the state authorities (Yigitcanlar, 2016; Ernst et al., 2017). Consequently, authorities need to play an integral role by maintaining social media pages and ensuring adequate community engagement with their social media pages.

Leveraging the use of social media data provides more prospects to manage disasters. Although in general, the use of social media is expanding at a rapid rate, its use in disaster management is not at its optimum. Especially, official social media pages maintained by the state authorities need broader community engagement. This will enable the delivery of reliable and timely information to the people. In its absence, people tend to obtain information from unreliable resources, which in turn can lead to the spreading of rumours and false information (Castillo et al., 2012; Maddock et al., 2015; Harrison & Johnson, 2016).

In this regard, Tapia and Moore (2014) highlighted increased confidence in data coming from trustworthy organisations and authorities—e.g., state emergency services. Accordingly, the absence of a significant relationship between the community and the key authorities might accelerate the spreading of misinformation. In spite, there are cases in which the communities have used social media as a powerful tool to rectify rumours and misinformation circulated in the social media, at the time of poor contributions of state authorities, to rectify false information—e.g., bomb threats in Netherlands and Paris 2015 (Jong & Dückers, 2016). This highlights the significance of establishing a strong connection between the community and the social media pages maintained by the key disaster management authorities.

An increasing number of researchers in the field started to use social media information and analytics to (a) Measure disaster impacts and leverage disaster responses (Firoj et al., 2018; Ueoka et al., 2019; Kiran et al., 2018; Zahra et al., 2018; Kankanamge et al., 2020a); (b) Identify user types of social media during crisis responses (Leon et al. 2018; Purohit & Chan, 2017); (c) Determine efficient uses of social media by interviewing emergency management officials (Shklovski et al., 2008; Grace et al., 2018); (d) Build indices and frameworks (Homberg, 2017); and (e) Develop new applications and technologies to enhance the use of social media information in disaster management (Sakurai & Murayama, 2019)

Nevertheless, not many of these researches have focused on studying the community engagement levels on social media channels, which is a key determinant to identify the efficient use of social media in disaster management. Thus, further studies are required to identify strategies to improve community engagement in social media pages maintained by the credible state disaster management authorities.

3.3 Methodology

3.3.1 Selection of Official Social Media Pages

Australia is one of the prominent countries in the use of social media by the authorities to provide information about disasters, and by the public to voice their experiences and concerns about disaster events (Anikeeva et al., 2016). Australia, due to its vastness and varied climatic conditions, is exposed to many different disasters such as floods, cyclones, earthquakes, heatwaves, bushfires, and droughts. Particularly the states of New South Wales (NSW), Victoria (VIC), and Queensland (QLD) are highly vulnerable to these disasters as they host the majority of the Australian population and economic activities, and the impact of disasters is more significant (DAE, 2017).

Thus, their state authorities actively engage in using social media for disaster management. Due to this popularity, several social media pages in Facebook, Twitter, and Instagram have been operationalised for disaster-related issues—e.g., QLD flood support, NQ flood updates, NSW rural fire service, NSW & QLD fires, and Victoria fire. Henceforth, this study used four criteria to select suitable social media pages to conduct the investigations. These were: (a) Legal background of the social media page owners;

(b) Availability of state-level information; (c) Number of disasters considered in creating/sharing posts; and (d) Number of followers.

In terms of the first criterion—i.e., legal background, the Australian Council of State Emergency Services (ACSES) is responsible for maintaining the State Emergency Services (SES) for each state. SESs are well-established volunteer organisations that are enabled by both, state and local governments (ACSES, 2015). Hence, making SES suitable for this study.

The second criterion concerns the availability of state-level information. All the SES organisations maintain a social media page dedicated to a state or a local government area. Most of such pages stand by the state name, namely VIC State Emergency Service, NSW State Emergency Service. Thus, social media pages maintained by SES were selected for this study. However, QLD SES did not meet the second criteria with regards to the availability of state-level information. Rather than having one page for the QLD state, there were many pages, which provide information related to the local government areas—i.e., QLD SES for Ipswich city-state emergency services unit. Hence, from QLD, the official social media page maintained by the Queensland Fire and Emergency Services (QFES) was selected.

The third criterion considered the number of disasters considered in sharing the posts. At the initial screening process, it was confirmed that all the selected pages—i.e., NSW SES, VIC SES, and QFES on Facebook, Twitter, and Instagram consisted of messages related to natural disasters such as floods, cyclones, and bushfires. Although QFES highlighted 'fire' in its social media page name, it also covered posts related to floods and severe storms during the flood season in the state, which further confirmed the suitability of QFES for this study.

The last criterion concerned the number of followers. It was decided to omit Instagram social media channel due to the inadequate number of followers—i.e., NSW SES (3,604 followers), VIC SES (4,137 followers), QFES (27,108 followers).

The study looked at the last 12 months and collected and analysed 2,332 posts available in NSW SES, VIC SES, and QFES Facebook and Twitter social media channels between October 2018 and September 2019 (Table 3.1).

3.3.2 Measuring Level of Community Engagement

3.3.2.1 Indices

As given in Table 3.2, this study was built on a methodology with four indices, which were originally developed by Bonsón and Ratkai (2013). These are: (a) Popularity; (b) Commitment; (c) Virality; and (d) Engagement. These indices were initially adopted to evaluate stakeholder engagement through digital content analysis. Recently, these indices have become popular in business and marketing management disciplines for evaluating customer engagement (Sigala & Gretzel, 2017). Nonetheless, to the best of our knowledge, past

TABLE 3.1

Analysed Official Social Media Sites

State	Network	Organisation	URL	Posts Collected
NSW	Facebook	New South Wales State Emergency Services (NSW SES)	https://www.facebook.com/NSW.SES	344
	Twitter	NSW SES	https://twitter.com/NSWSES	265
VIC	Facebook	Victoria State Emergency Service (VIC SES)	https://www.facebook.com/vicses	538
	Twitter	VIC SES	https://twitter.com/vicsesnews	477
QLD	Facebook	Queensland Fire and Emergency Services	https://www.facebook.com/QldFireandEmergencyServices	519
	Twitter	QFES	https://twitter.com/QldFES	189

TABLE 3.2

Metrics for Social Media User Engagement

Metrics	Sign	Equation	Explanation
Popularity	P	((Total number of likes/total number of posts)/(number of followers)) *1,000	Measures the attractiveness and notoriety
Commitment	C	((Total number of comments/ total number of posts)/ (number of followers)) 1,000	Measures the deeper level of engagement with fellow users by spending some time to comment and reply to a post.
Virality	V	((Total number of posts shared/total number of posts)/ (number of followers)) *1,000	Measures users' interest in the post's content shared via social media. This reflects the user preference to see the same content in the users' social media profile
Engagement	E	P + C + V	Cumulative results of popularity, commitment, and virality metrics

researchers have not applied these indices to evaluate social media pages dedicated to disaster events.

3.3.2.2 Community Engagement by the Types of Social Media Posts

Social media pages use different media such as images, links, texts, animated images, and videos, and graphic interchange formats (GIF) to communicate with the community. Nevertheless, the community attraction to different media types is not identical in different contexts (Yoo & Lee, 2018). Therefore, an understanding of which media attracts more community attention within the context of disasters helps social media pages to communicate their messages to the community effectively.

Social media pages maintained by non-profit organisations such as SES share sensitive and time valued content-related to disasters. The main objective of such social media pages is to keep the community safe and resilient by keeping them informed and aware. Such social media pages need to ensure that the time-valued messages created and shared by them attract adequate community attention at the right time. Accordingly, the study calculated Popularity (P), CommitmeI (C), Virality (V), and EngagInt (E) indices for different media types. For that, all the 2,332 messages collected were categorised by the type of media used at the time of data collection. Then, the number of likes, comments, and shares received were considered in order to calculate the P, C, V, and E indices.

3.3.2.3 Community Engagement by the Social Media Content

Analysing community engagement levels by social media content consisted of two-steps. The first step was to categorise social media content by adopting a three-step cluster analysis methodology: (a) Parsing text; (b) Identification of concepts/themes; and (c) Clustering (McCulloch, 2004). For this exercise, Leximancer content analysis software was employed. Then, P, C, V, and E indices were calculated per each cluster to identify the content with the maximum community engagement.

The second step was more theoretical as it classified the derived clusters to measure the utilisation of the three attributes of volunteer crowdsourcing for disaster management: (a) Situation awareness; (b) Collective intelligence; and (c) Multi-directional communication (Kankanamge et al., 2019). To make the social media pages efficient, such pages need to ensure that they utilise the aforesaid attributes well in creating and sharing messages. As given in Tables 3.3 and 3.4, clusters were first categorised related to the three attributes by observing the characteristics of the cluster. The literature was referred to and cited while categorising the clusters under the three aforementioned attributes. Accordingly, engagement levels of the suitable clusters were used as a measurement to evaluate the utilisation of each attribute—i.e., utilisation index (U).

TABLE 3.3

Utilisation Index

Metric	Sign	Equation	Explanation
Utilisation	U	Total number of engagements per cluster$_1$ per 1000 users (E_1 of Cluster$_1$) + Total number of engagements per cluster per 1000 users (E_n of Cluster$_n$)	This metric is associated with cluster analysis. Based on the cluster characteristics, clusters could be used to measure the performance of attributes/themes. This examines the utilisation of an attribute/theme based on the derived clusters.

TABLE 3.4

Clusters to Calculate the Utilisation Index

	Facebook				Twitter			
	Followers	P	C	V	E	Followers	P	C	V	E
NSW SES	146,008	0.51	0.11	0.30	0.92	67,500	0.22	0.01	0.16	0.39
VIC SES	104,137	0.30	0.09	0.18	0.57	19,090	0.26	0.02	0.21	0.48
QFES	440,534	0.26	0.10	0.14	0.50	70,086	0.19	0.01	0.13	0.34

These utilisation index values inform the social media pages about the broad areas to improve when creating social media messages. For instance, if a social media page is reflecting low community engagements in the attribute of situation awareness, it is necessary to examine novel ways to attract greater community engagement in order to disseminate time-critical information to the community.

3.4 Results

3.4.1 General Observations

Among Facebook and Twitter SES and QFES social media pages, Facebook was the most widely used social media channel, though the Twitter pages compete with Facebook. While the QFES Facebook page has the highest number of followers, the VIC SES Twitter page has the lowest number of followers (Table 3.5). Among all the six social media pages, Facebook and Twitter pages of VIC SES posted about two messages (1.5) per day. NSW Facebook page posted around one (0.8) message per day. Among all the indices, the overall community engagement level was higher for the index

TABLE 3.5

P, C, V, and E Indices by the Organisations

	Attributes of Volunteer Crowdsourcing in Disaster Management		
Cluster Name	Situation Awareness	Collective Intelligence	Multi-directional Communication
Cluster 1	E1		
Cluster 2	E2		
Cluster 3		E3	
Cluster 4		E4	
Cluster ...			E
Cluster n			En
Utilisation	E1+E2	E3+E4	E5+En

of popularity (P index) than commitment (C index) and virality (V index) indices. This means that the community tends to prefer the post rather than commenting and sharing them unless it creates a real interest for them.

As given in Table 3.5, NSW SES and VIC SES Facebook pages were the most popular social media pages with 0.51 and 0.3 P index values, respectively. Furthermore, NSW SES and QFES Facebook pages were the most committed social media pages with 0.11 and 0.10 C index values. In terms of message virality, Facebook page of NSW SES (V=0.30) and the Twitter page of VIC SES (V=0.21) were the most prominent. This highlights the community interest to share the messages on the NSW SES Facebook page into their personal social media pages. Overall, NSW SES and VIC SES Facebook pages were the best social media pages to share messages, which create immediate community attention.

Among all the Twitter pages analysed, the VIC SES Twitter page is the most popular. However, it has the lowest number of followers. This represented a high level of engagement by a limited number of followers. Although QFES Facebook and Twitter pages have the highest number of followers, they are not much engaged with the messages. Therefore, the social media page organisers should devise new ways to encourage greater community engagement. The NSW SES Facebook page has the highest V index.

3.4.2 Community Engagement by the Types of Social Media Posts

Community engagement of the considered six social media pages have changed significantly based on the media type used. Across the six social media pages, images, external links, videos, maps, and texts are the prominently used media types. According to Figure 3.1, the followers of the three SESs social media pages have different preferences in engaging with social media messages.

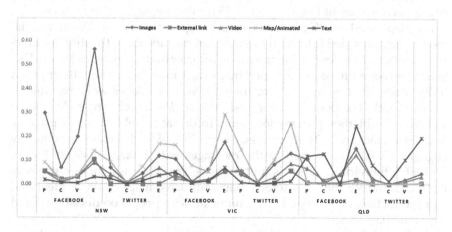

FIGURE 3.1
P, C, V, and E indices by the media type.

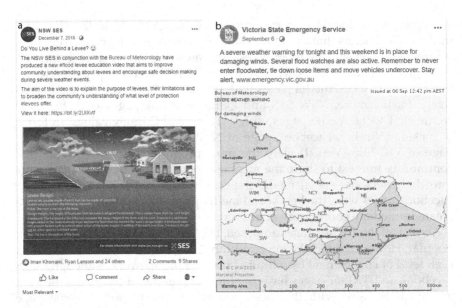

FIGURE 3.2
(a) Awareness-raising through images; (b) use of maps to convey messages.

For instance, NSW SES Facebook messages with images received more community engagement (E=0.56). This means that the NSW SES Facebook messages were highly liked (P=0.30) and shared (V=0.20) by the community. NSW SES used different images ranging from real ground images to attractive posters to reach the community. As illustrated in Figure 3.2(a), the use of informative images has made the NSW SES Facebook page more productive. Even the Facebook pages of VIC SES and QFES recorded the second-highest engagement values of E=0.18 and E=0.15 for the messages with images.

The maps used in VIC SES social media pages and NSW SES Twitter social media page provided information to the community about the disaster moving direction, the extent of the prevailing disaster impact areas, and so on. VIC SES messages with maps/animated maps were more or less equally engaged in Facebook (E=0.29) and Twitter (E=0.25). Such messages were also highly liked in both, Facebook (P=0.16), and Twitter (P=0.14) channels. As shown in Figure 3.2(b), they provide locational information related to the possible disaster impact areas. Twitter messages of NSW SES with maps were highly engaged (E=0.17) compared to the messages with images (E=0.12). Except for QFES, the virality index is high in both, Facebook and Twitter pages of NSW SES and VIC SES. Therefore, maps/animated maps could be identified as a productive media type to communicate with people on disaster-related social media pages.

Unlike NSW SES and VIC SES, text messages circulated in Facebook and Twitter pages of QFES were highly engaged with 0.24 and 0.19 engagement values. QFES used signs and symbols along with the texts as a strategy to attract greater community engagement. The symbols used by QFES in the text messages included, 🔥 (bush fire), ⊘ (warning), 🚌 ☂ ☁ (heavy rain), ⚡ (thunderstorm), ☂ (Cyclone), 👀 (attention), and 👁 (evaluate community perceptions). Such text messages with symbols were also highly commented (C=0.12) on Facebook. These findings provide insights for all six pages to learn from each other's success.

3.4.3 Community Engagement by the Social Media Content

The study used cluster analysis to identify the different content types used across the social media messages. As presented in Figure 3.3, nine clusters were derived through cluster analysis. These clusters were: (a) Warning; (b) Awareness raising; (c) Volunteer recruitment; (d) Update the disaster coltion; (e) Disaster recovery operations; (f) Online polls; (g) Data collection; (h) Fund raising; and (i) Volunteer appreciation. All the messages, which provide warning alerts to the people with regards to any kind of natural disaster, were categorised as 'Warning' (Gardoni & Murphy, 2010; Baytiyeh, 2017). The messages provide people with the relevant information to reduce the risks associated with a disaster such as emergency call contact numbers,

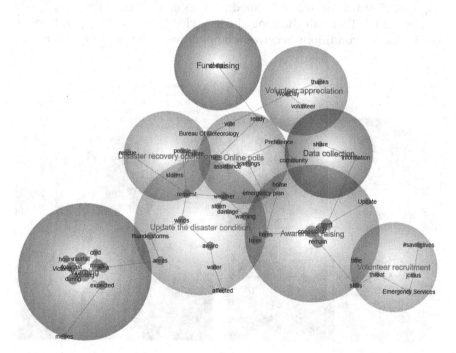

FIGURE 3.3
Clusters determined through the cluster analysis.

arranging sandbags during a heavy rainfall, which were categorised as 'Awareness raising' (Haworth, 2016; Mojtahedi & Oo, 2017; Lagmay et al., 2017). Any message that contains both, information related to warnings and awareness-raising together were categorised based on the content composition related to warning and awareness-raising information.

Messages that invite people to act as volunteers were categorised as messages for 'Volunteer recruitment' (Palen & Hughes, 2018). The messages that update the situation regarding a prevailing disaster was categorised as 'Updating the disaster condition'. All the messages, which provided information related to disaster recovery activities and methods or any messages that requested recovery help, were categorised as 'Disaster recovery operations'. The messages, which canvassed community opinion, were categorised as 'Online polls', such as the evaluation of the level of preparedness of the people or marking safe in safety check polls during disasters. As illustrated in Figure 3.4(a), messages that were created to collect localised information from people—i.e., people as sensors—were categorised as 'Data collection' (Goodchild, 2009). Messages used to collect funds from the people, i.e., virtual fundraising, were categorised as 'Fund raising' (Goodchild & Glennon, 2010). Finally, all the messages, which appreciated the hard work of volunteers, were categorised as 'Volunteer appreciation' (Figure 3.4b).

Figure 3.5 ranks the six social media pages according to the P, C, V, and E index values. From all the nine clusters, clusters of warning and updating of disaster conditions received comparatively the highest community

FIGURE 3.4
(a) Data collection through social media; (b) volunteer appreciation.

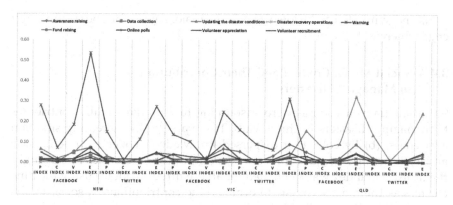

FIGURE 3.5
P, C, V, and E indices by the clusters.

engagement. Warning messages received from the NSW SES Facebook page was the most engaged (E=0.53) and the most viral (V=0.19) social media messages. 64% of these Facebook warning messages were circulated with an image. Moreover, most of the messages with warnings were also highly re-tweeted (0.11). The VIC SES Facebook and Twitter social media warning messages were also highly engaged with 0.15 and 0.17 index values, respectively, where 43% of the messages contained maps or images. These findings further confirm that the messages with images, maps, and symbols receive high community engagement compared to messages with simple text.

QFES Facebook messages which updated disaster conditions have the highest engagement value (E=0.32). 92% of such messages contained either symbols or images related to the disaster condition. The Facebook page of NSW SES had the second-highest engagement value (E=0.13) for the cluster consisting of updating disaster conditions. Nevertheless, none of the social media pages received high engagement values for messages with content to increase awareness-raising. NSW SES Facebook messages for awareness-raising were the least engaged.

Except for NSW SES Facebook, none of the social media pages received a high engagement in order to raise funds (E=0.07) for people in need during disaster situations. However, none of these messages, which looked to raise funds, used the Facebook fundraiser option. Instead, they were built around posters, which requested donations for people in need. Furthermore, volunteer recruitment, online polls, information related to disaster recovery operations, and data collection clusters were poorly engaged. All the messages related to volunteer recruitment were requests for people to be on-site volunteers. None of these messages discussed the possibilities of being a virtual volunteer (Goodchild & Glennon, 2010). Due to the limited number of messages shared, for example, only two online polls exist in the VIC SES, and not using popular media approaches such as, images and texts with signs and symbols, can be identified as the major causes for poor community engagement of these posts.

3.4.4 Social Media Content and Their Contribution to Managing Disasters

Social media as a volunteer crowdsourcing tool fundamentally contributes to managing disasters in three ways. These are: (a) By increasing situation awareness; (b) By collecting dispersed knowledge—collective intelligence; and (c) By acting as a multi-directional communication channel. Accordingly, the utilisation index was calculated for all the three attributes using the nine clusters as the measurements to evaluate the contributions of social media for managing disasters (Table 3.6).

These three attributes were discussed in many different publications individually (Goodchild & Glennon, 2010; Gao et al., 2011; Alexander, 2014; Deng et al., 2016; Dufty, 2016; Harrison & Johnson, 2016; Palen & Hughes, 2018). However, Kankanamge et al. (2019) derived the aforesaid three attributes of volunteer crowdsourcing after systematically reviewing over 130 publications including 52 refereed journal articles. Nonetheless, these attributes might need to be revisited in the future due to the rapid expansion of the literature on the use of social media in disaster management.

Using the relevant literature, the nine clusters were categorised under the three attributes as discussed above. For instance, the engagement (E index) values for 'awareness raising', 'updating the disaster conditions' and 'warning',

TABLE 3.6

Categorised Clusters to Measure the Utilisation of Attributes of Volunteer Crowdsourcing

| Cluster Name | Attributes of Volunteer Crowdsourcing in Disaster Management | | |
	Situation Awareness	Collective Intelligence	Multi-directional Communication
Awareness-raising	E1		
Update the disaster condition	E2		
Warning	E3		
Data collection		E4	
Volunteer appreciation		E5	
Online polls		E6	
Disaster recovery operations/requests			E7
Fund raising			E8
Volunteer recruitment			E9
Utilisation	E1+E3	E4+E6	E7+E9

inform the community about a disaster situation, which could impact people. Such information creates an opportunity for people to prepare themselves for a potential disaster situation (Vivacqua & Borges, 2012). Thus, the aforesaid three clusters were used to evaluate the utilisation of the attribute of situation awareness (Lagmay et al., 2017; Kankanamge et al., 2019). 'Data collection', 'volunteer appreciation', and 'online polls' represent the dispersed community knowledge. Especially, by collecting data through people, and evaluating community perceptions through online polling methods help authorities to provide more community-centric services (Sobaci, 2015; Palen & Hughes, 2018; Kankanamge et al., 2019).

Clusters of 'disaster recovery operations/requests', 'fund raising', and 'volunteer recruitments', engage in communicating with many people at a time. Such social media messages advertise and motivate people to be a volunteer (Goodchild & Glennon, 2010; Alexander, 2014; Tang et al., 2015; Kankanamge et al., 2019). Albeit, recruiting volunteers is a time-consuming process without social media channels. Figure 3.6 presents the final utilisation index calculated based on the engagement values of the clusters.

Accordingly, all the social media pages in both, Facebook and Twitter channels contribute to managing disasters by increasing the disaster situation awareness. Nevertheless, none of the other two attributes—collective intelligence and multi-directional communication are well utilised to manage disasters. Possibility of using collective intelligence to manage disasters is one of the foremost advantages of using social media for disaster management. Countries, such as the UK and the US, already collect weather data and people's experiences of changing weather conditions via digital crisis information (Sosko & Dalyot, 2017).

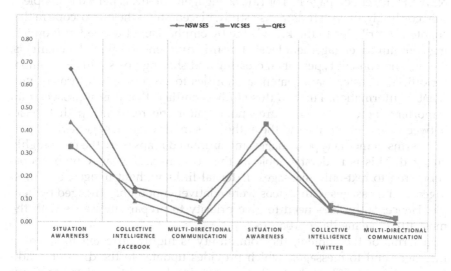

FIGURE 3.6
Attributes of volunteer crowdsourcing.

Moreover, social media channels create an opportunity for authorities to communicate with millions of people at a time. Consequently, fundraising, disseminating warnings, updating disaster conditions, and volunteer recruitment activities are far easier than ever before, which helps in reducing the disaster risks as well. Accordingly, a higher level of community engagement in social media will deliver adequate time-critical information related to disasters and volunteer support to the public. In return, this will increase the community preparedness towards possible disaster events. Albeit, the prospects of using social media channels to manage disasters and to reduce disaster risks are not yet well utilised in the investigated social media channels from Australia.

3.5 Discussion

3.5.1 How Effectively Do People Engage in Social Media in Relation to Disaster Management?

Disasters are becoming increasingly damaging and thus, an effective method to make people aware and safe is essential. Enabled by ubiquitous communication techniques, social media has substantially altered the traditional and bureaucratic forms of organisations, communities, and ways of communicating (Velev & Zlateva, 2012). However, in general, the overall community engagement with the NSW SES, VIC SES, and QFES social media pages were not highly satisfactory. For instance, the highest engagement level of the NSW SES Facebook page has only 0.92 engagement levels per 1,000 people.

Accordingly, the Australian case study, placed under the microscope in this chapter, contributes to the knowledge by emphasising the need of monitoring community engagement levels towards different social media channels, media, and content types when creating and sharing posts. This is essential for official disaster management authorities to keep people informed with reliable information. Further, this study identified that this approach is an important indicator to measure and monitor the relationship that exists between the community and the authorities in disaster management.

In terms of media types, images and animated maps were the most highly engaged. This is understandable as they communicate easily with people compared to text-only messages. External links without images, text messages, and messages with videos were relatively not highly engaged by people. Hence, authorities need to give priority to prepare messages with the most attractive media approaches.

In terms of the content, the community is highly attracted to warning messages and to messages, which provides updates to the disaster conditions. Moreover, 56% of the total messages circulated either related to warnings or to update the disaster conditions. The messages related to warning and disaster conditions invariably help to increase the situation awareness among people. While acknowledging the higher utilisation of social media to increase situation awareness, this study emphasises the possibility of utilising social media to also harvest the dispersed community knowledge. The V index was comparatively low in all the social media pages analysed. This confirmed the poor utilisation of the social media pages.

The use of social media in disasters is generally widespread (Liu, 2014). However, community engagement towards the 'official social media pages' maintained by the authorities is poor. Hence, this could result in large volumes of misinformation being circulated. For example, the New Orleans Mayor's official Twitter account was used to rectify numerous misinformation being circulated during the 2012 Hurricane Isaac (DHS, 2013). This emphasised the need to maintain and enforce official social media pages to attract greater community engagement to official social media pages.

3.5.2 How Does Social Media Contribute to Disaster Management?

Social media helps authorities to manage disasters by enabling initiatives such as launching fund raising campaigns, data collection, linking social media pages with popular blogs, introducing online databases. Although none of the three social media pages analysed have used the above services to their full potential, there are encouraging examples from around the world, where official social media pages have been used very effectively to manage disasters.

For instance, some of the social media pages maintained by Fairfax (Virginia) launched an online disaster damage database system as a reporting tool to collect eye-witnessed photos and videos from people (DHS, 2013). Additionally, official social media pages need to actively respond to community messages. For instance, the average response time of the QFES Facebook page is a few hours, which can be considered a good performance. Most of the time, emergency call numbers can be overwhelmed due to the large numbers of calls received. Therefore, authorities can make social media pages more active in order to respond to people in need. For instance, the City of New Orleans official Twitter account used @NOLAready to respond to the community inquiries during the 2012 Hurricane Isaac.

Fostering volunteerism is an essential part of disaster management. Social media can foster two types of volunteerism. Firstly, to find volunteers who are skilled and well-trained to manage a disaster by being on location. The other type of volunteers is those who are virtually linked with the social media network—i.e., digital volunteers. They could help to locate missing people and identify damage to properties through virtual campaigns. Examples include Barcamps, and CrisiCommons (Goodchild, 2009; Crooks & Wise, 2013; Liu, 2014; Han et al., 2018).

Harvesting time-critical information from the community, e.g., collective intelligence, is a proven contribution of social media. After the 2012 Typhoon

Bopha/Pablo, an organisation for crowdsourcing, Digital Humanitarian Networks (DHN), requested the digital volunteers to collect social media data posted during the typhoon. Such data was used to geo-locate the posts and estimate the damage caused by the typhoon (Liu, 2014). Accordingly, from the 2010 Haiti Earthquake, social media has started to play a significant role in contributing to managing disasters across the globe.

3.6 Conclusion[1]

In the anthropogenic climate change-induced disaster era (Sotto et al., 2019; Yigitcanlar et al., 2019b), that is upon us, benefiting from the novel and afford-able technology solutions has become a promising method in preparing for and protecting communities from disasters (Yigitcanlar et al., 2019c). Social media is one of these promising technologies (Houston et al., 2015). This study concentrated on investigating, in the case of Australian official emergency services, how engaging disaster management-related social media channels are.

Firstly, the study findings confirmed that community engagement towards the Twitter social media channel is comparatively low. However, Twitter social media has been widely used across the world to analyse social media data related to disasters (Boulos et al., 2011; Sievers, 2015; Kantarci et al., 2016; Ludwig et al., 2017; Kankanamge et al., 2020a). Twitter allows researchers and practitioners to use the Application Programming Interface (API) to down-load data based on their interests, which has made it more appropriate for analysis compared to other social media. Therefore, promoting community engagement towards official Twitter pages maintained by various disaster management authorities will help to deliver more productive and reliable information to be circulated via social media networks.

Secondly, the study emphasises the need for rapid responses by authorities to avoid spreading any misinformation in the social media. The community engages in social media individually or by creating informal groups. However, the newsworthiness and credibility of such information can some-times be questionable (Castillo et al., 2012). For instance, around 10,000 tweets circulated during the 2012 Hurricane Sandy were identified as fake. Among them, 86% of tweets, which spread fake information were re-tweeted. Hence, there were only relatively very few original tweets (Dufty, 2016). This empha-sises the need for a prominent social media page, which can officially and efficiently deliver and monitor reliable information delivery to the community while overriding the backchannel communications. Although this study highlighted the credibility issue in relation to social media information, it

---

[1] This chapter, with permission from the copyright holder, is a reproduced version of the following journal article: Kankanamge, N., Yigitcanlar, T., & Goonetilleke, A. (2020). How engaging are disaster management related social media channels? The case of Australian state emergency organisations. *International Journal of Disaster Risk Reduction, 48,* 101571.

also acknowledges the highly accurate, validated, and innovative approaches adopted to derive important knowledge from social media information.

Next, it is important to underline the need to provide adequate legal safeguards to protect the users of social media to manage disasters. Canada and the US have already initiated encouraging the use of social media with adequate legal provisions, which is rare in most of the other countries across the world (Harrison & Johnson, 2016). Enforcing the use of social media within legal frameworks will help relevant organisations to maximise its use, especially in the case of financial matters such as donations (Kuehn et al., 2011).

Lastly, this study has the following limitations: (a) It only considered three official social media pages related to disaster management; (b) Selecting clusters to measure the utilisation of three attributes of volunteer crowdsourcing was done by considering the characteristics of the clusters; and (c) The study only considered social media messages over the last 12 months. Despite these limitations, the research revealed insights that shed light on the way forward for authorities to create data-intensive disaster management practices.

References

ACSES (2015). *The worst in nature the best in us*. Australian Council of State Emergency Services. Accessed on 12 December 2019 from http://www.ses.org.au/4.html?0.

Alexander, D.E. (2014). Social media in disaster risk reduction and crisis management. *Science and Engineering Ethics, 20,* 717–733.

Allaire, M.C. (2016). Disaster loss and social media: Can online information increase flood resilience? *Water Resources Research, 52,* 7408–7423.

Anikeeva, O., Steenkamp, M., & Arbon, P. (2016). The future of social media use during emergencies in Australia: Insights from the 2014 Australian and New Zealand disaster and emergency management conference social media workshop. In *Effective Communication During Disasters* (pp. 151–162). Apple Academic Press.

Baybay, C.S., & Hindmarsh, R. (2019). Resilience in the Philippines through effective community engagement. *Australian Journal of Emergency Management, 34,* 65–81.

Baytiyeh, H. (2017). Can disaster risk education reduce the impacts of recurring disasters on developing societies? *Education and Urban Society, 50,* 230–245.

Bonsón, E., & Ratkai, M. (2013). A set of metrics to assess stakeholder engagement and social legitimacy on a corporate Facebook page. *Online Information Review, 37,* 787–803.

Boulos, M.N., Resch, B., Crowley, D.N., Breslin, J.G., Sohn, G., Burtner, R., Pike, W.A., Jezierski, E., & Chuang, K.Y. (2011). Crowdsourcing, citizen sensing, and sensor web technologies for public and environmental health surveillance and crisis management. *International Journal of Health Geographics, 10,* 67–96.

Burston, J., Ware, D., & Tomlinson, R. (2015). The real-time needs of emergency managers for tropical cyclone storm tide forecasting. *Natural Hazards, 78,* 1653–1668.

Castillo, C., Mendoza, M., & Poblete, B. (2012). Predicting information credibility in time-sensitive social media. *Internet Research, 23,* 560–588.

Crooks, A.T., & Wise, S. (2013). GIS and agent-based models for humanitarian assistance. *Computers, Environment and Urban Systems, 41*, 100–111.

DAE (2017). *Building Resilience to Natural Disasters in Our States and Territories*. Deloitte Access Economics, Sydney.

Deng, Q., Liu, Y., Zhang, H., Deng, X., & Ma, Y. (2016). A new crowdsourcing model to assess disaster using microblog data in typhoon Haiyan. *Natural Hazards, 84,* 1241–1256.

Dufty, N. (2016). Twitter turns ten. *Australian Journal of Emergency Management, 31,* 50–54.

Ernst, C., Mladenow, A., & Strauss, C. (2017). Collaboration and crowdsourcing in emergency management. *International Journal of Pervasive Computing and Communications, 13,* 176–193.

Feng, Y., & Sester, M. (2018). Extraction of pluvial flood relevant volunteered geographic information by deep learning from user generated texts and photos. *ISPRS International Journal of Geo-Information, 7,* 39–64.

Firoj, A., Ferda, O., Muhammad, I., & Michael, A. (2018). A Twitter tale of three Hurricanes. In: *Proceedings of the 15th ISCRAM Conference*, New York, 553–572.

Gao, H., Barbier, G., Goolsby, R., & Zeng, D. (2011). Harnessing the crowdsourcing power of social media for disaster relief. *IEEE Intelligent Systems, 26,* 1541–1672.

Gardoni, P., & Murphy, C. (2010). Gauging the societal impacts of natural disasters using a capability approach. *Disasters, 34,* 619–636.

Givoni, M. (2016). Between micro mappers and missing maps. *Environment and Planning D, 34,* 1025–1043.

Goetz, M., & Zipf, A. (2013). The evolution of geo-crowdsourcing. In: *Crowdsourcing Geographic Knowledge*. Springer, Berlin, pp. 139–159.

Goodchild, M.F. (2007). Citizens as sensors. *GeoJournal, 69,* 211–221.

Goodchild, M.F. (2009). Neogeography and the nature of geographic expertise. *Journal of Location-Based Services, 3,* 82–96.

Goodchild, M.F., & Glennon, J.A. (2010). Crowdsourcing geographic information for disaster response. *International Journal of Digital Earth, 3,* 231–241.

Grace, R., Kropczynski, J., & Tapia, A. (2018). Community coordination. In: *Proceedings of the 15th ISCRAM Conference*, New York, 609–620.

Haigh, R., & Sutton, R. (2012). Strategies for the effective engagement of multi-national construction enterprises in post-disaster building and infrastructure projects. *International Journal of Disaster Resilience in the Built Environment, 3,* 270–282.

Han, S., Huang, H., Luo, Z., & Foropon, C. (2018). Harnessing the power of crowdsourcing and the internet of things in disaster response. *Annals of Operations Research, 26,* 1–16.

Handmer, J., Choy, S., & Kohtake, N. (2014). Updating warning systems for climate hazards. *Australian Journal of Telecommunications and the Digital Economy, 2,* 70–84.

Harrison, S.E., & Johnson, P.A. (2016). Crowdsourcing the disaster management cycle. *International Journal of Infrastructure Systems for Crisis Response Management, 8,* 17–40.

Haworth, B. (2016). Emergency management perspectives on volunteered geographic information. *Computers, Environment and Urban Systems, 57,* 189–198.

Homberg, M.V.D. (2017). Toward a Balkans' data for disaster management collaborative? In *Implications of climate Change and disasters on Military Activities* (pp. 11–18). Springer, Dordrecht.

Houston, J.B., Hawthorne, J., Perreault, M.F., Park, E.H., Goldstein Hode, M., Halliwell, M.R., & Griffith, S.A. (2015). Social media and disasters: A functional framework for social media use in disaster planning, response, and research. *Disasters, 39,* 1–22.

Howe, J. (2006). The rise of crowdsourcing. *Wired Magazine, 14*, 1–4.

Jong, W., & Dückers, M.L. (2016). Self-correcting mechanisms and echo-effects in social media: An analysis of the "gunman in the newsroom" crisis. *Computers in Human Behavior, 59*, 334–341.

Kankanamge, N., Yigitcanlar, T., Goonetilleke, A., & Kamruzzaman, M. (2019). Can volunteer crowdsourcing reduce disaster risk? A systematic review of the literature. *International Journal of Disaster Risk Reduction*, 101097.

Kankanamge, N., Yigitcanlar, T., Goonetilleke, A., & Kamruzzaman, M. (2020a). Determining disaster severity through social media analysis: Testing the methodology with South East Queensland Flood tweets. *International Journal of Disaster Risk Reduction, 42*, 101360.

Kankanamge, N., Yigitcanlar, T., Goonetilleke, A., & Kamruzzaman, M. (2020b). How can gamification be incorporated into disaster emergency planning? A systematic review of the literature. *International Journal of Disaster Resilience in the Built Environment*, https://doi.org/10.1016/10.1108/IJDRBE-08-2019-0054.

Kantarci, B., Carr, K.G., & Pearsall, C.D. (2016). Social network-assisted trustworthiness assurance in smart city crowdsensing. *International Journal of Distributed Systems and Technologies, 7*, 59–78.

Kemp, S. (2019). *Digital 2019*. Datareportal, Accessed on 12 December 2019 from https://datareportal.com/reports/digital-2019-q4-global-digital-statshot.

Kerle, N., & Hoffman, R.R. (2013). Collaborative damage mapping for emergency response. *Natural Hazards & Earth System Sciences, 13*, 97–113.

Koswatte, S., McDougall, K., & Liu, X. (2015). SDI and crowdsourced spatial information management automation for disaster management. *Survey Review, 47*, 307–315.

Kuehn, A., Kaschewsky, M., Kappeler, A., Spichiger, A., & Riedl, R. (2011). Interoperability and information brokers in public safety. *Journal of Theoretical and Applied Electronic Commerce Research, 6*, 43–60.

Lagmay, A.M., Racoma, B.A., Aracan, K.A., Alconis-Ayco, J., & Saddi, I.L. (2017). Disseminating near-real-time hazards information and flood maps in the Philippines through web-GIS. *Journal of Environmental Sciences, 59*, 13–23.

Leon, D., Meesters, K., Bontcheva, K., & Maynard, D. (2018). Helping crisis responders find the informative needle in the Tweet haystack. In: *Proceedings of the 15th ISCRAM Conference*, New York, 649–662.

Liu, S.B. (2014). Crisis crowdsourcing framework. *Computer Supported Cooperative Work, 23*, 389–443.

Ludwig, T., Kotthaus, C., Reuter, C., Van Dongen, S., & Pipek, V. (2017). Situated crowdsourcing during disasters. *International Journal of Human-Computer Studies, 102*, 103–121.

Maddock, J., Starbird, K., Al-Hassani, H.J., Sandoval, D.E., Orand, M., & Mason, R.M. (2015). Characterizing online rumoring behavior using multi-dimensional signatures. In: *Proceedings of the 18th ACM Conference on Computer Supported Cooperative Work & Social Computing*, Vancouver, 228–241.

Maresh-Fuehrer, M.M., & Smith, R. (2016). Social media mapping innovations for crisis prevention, response, and evaluation. *Computers in Human Behavior, 54*, 620–629.

McCulloch, G. (2004). *Documentary Research: In Education, History and the Social Sciences*. Routledge.

Mehta, A., Bruns, A., & Newton, J. (2016). Trust, but verify. *Disasters, 41*, 549–565.

Mercer, J., Kelman, I., Lloyd, K., & Suchet-Pearson, S. (2008). Reflections on use of participatory research for disaster risk reduction. *Area, 40*, 172–183.

Mojtahedi, M., & Oo, B.L. (2017). Critical attributes for proactive engagement of stakeholders in disaster risk management. *International Journal of Disaster Risk Reduction, 21*, 35–43.

Oki, T. (2018). Possibility of using Tweets to detect crowd congestion. In: *Proceeding of the 15th ISCRAM Conference*, New York, 584–608.

Osti, R., Tanaka, S., & Tokioka, T. (2008). Flood hazard mapping in developing countries: Problems and prospects. *Disaster Prevention and Management: An International Journal, 17*, 104–113.

Palen, L., & Hughes, A.L. (2018). Social media in disaster communication. In: *Handbook of Disaster Research*. Springer, Berlin, pp. 497–518.

Poblet, M., García-Cuesta, E., & Casanovas, P. (2017). Crowdsourcing roles, methods, and tools for data-intensive disaster management. *Information Systems Frontiers, 1*, 1–17.

Purohit, H., & Chan, J. (2017). Classifying user types on social media to inform who-what-where coordination during crisis response. In: *Proceedings of the 14th ISCRAM Conference*, Albi, France, 656–665.

Riccardi, M.T. (2016). The power of crowdsourcing in disaster response operations. *International Journal of Disaster Risk Reduction, 20*, 123–128.

Ritchie, H., & Roser, M. (2014). Natural disasters. *Our World in Data*.

Rottz, M., Sell, D., Pacheco, R., & Yigitcanlar, T. (2019). Digital commons and citizen coproduction in smart cities: Assessment of Brazilian municipal e-government platforms. *Energies, 12*, 2813.

Sakurai, M., & Murayama, Y. (2019). Information technologies and disaster management–Benefits and issues. *Progress in Disaster Science, 2*, 100012.

Samaddar, S., Okada, N., Choi, J., & Tatano, H. (2017). What constitutes successful participatory disaster risk management? Insights from post-earthquake reconstruction work in rural Gujarat, India. *Natural Hazards, 85*, 111–138.

Shklovski, I., Palen, L., & Sutton, J. (2008). Finding community through information and communication technology in disaster response. In: *Proceedings of the 2008 ACM Conference on Computer Supported Cooperative Work*, New York, 127–136.

Sievers, J.A. (2015). Embracing crowdsourcing. *State and Local Government Review, 47*, 57–67.

Sigala, M., & Gretzel, U. (2017). *Advances in Social media for Travel, Tourism, and Hospitality: New Perspectives, Practice, and Cases*. Routledge.

Sobaci, M.Z. (2015). *Social Media and Local Governments: Theory and Practice* (Vol. 15). Springer.

Sobaci, M.Z. (2016). Social media and local governments: An overview. In *Social Media and Local Governments* (pp. 3–21).

Sosko, S., & Dalyot, S. (2017). Crowdsourcing user-generated mobile sensor weather data for densifying static geosensor networks. *ISPRS International Journal of Geo-Information, 6*, 61–83.

Sotto, D., Philippi, A., Yigitcanlar, T., & Kamruzzaman, M. (2019). Aligning urban policy with climate action in the global south: Are Brazilian cities considering climate emergency in local planning practice? *Energies, 12*, 3418.

Surowiecki, J. (2004). *The Wisdom of Crowds*. Doubleday, London.

Tang, Z., Zhang, L., Xu, F., & Vo, H. (2015). Examining the role of social media in California's drought risk management in 2014. *Natural Hazards, 79*, 171–193.

Tapia, A.H., & Moore, K. (2014). Good enough is good enough: Overcoming disaster response organisations' slow social media data adoption. *Computer Supported Cooperative Work, 23,* 483–512.

Ueoka, T., Ishii, A., & Kawahata, Y. (2019). A study of trends in the effects of TV ratings and social media (Twitter)--Case study 1. *arXiv preprint arXiv:1909.01078.*

USDHS (2013). *Innovative Users of Social media in Emergency Management.* United States Department of Homeland Security, USA.

Veil, S.R., Buehner, T., & Palenchar, M.J. (2011). A work-in-process literature review: Incorporating social media in risk and crisis communication. *Journal of Contingencies and Crisis Management, 19,* 110–122.

Velev, D., & Zlateva, P. (2012). Use of social media in natural disaster management. *International Proceedings of Economic Development and Research, 39,* 41–45.

Vivacqua, A.S., & Borges, M.R. (2012). Taking advantage of collective knowledge in emergency response systems. *Journal of Network and Computer Applications, 35,* 189–198.

Wells, K.B., Springgate, B.F., Lizaola, E., Jones, F., & Plough, A. (2013). Community engagement in disaster preparedness and recovery: A tale of two cities–Los Angeles and New Orleans. *Psychiatric Clinics, 36,* 451–466.

White, G.B. (1945). *Human Adjustment to Floods,* The University of Chicago.

Yigitcanlar, T. (2006). Australian Local governments' practice and prospects with online planning. *URISA Journal, 18,* 7–17.

Yigitcanlar, T. (2016). *Technology and the city: Systems, Applications, and Implications.* Routledge, New York.

Yigitcanlar, T., & Dur, F. (2013). Making space and place for knowledge communities: Lessons for Australian practice. *Australasian Journal of Regional Studies, 19*(1), 36–63.

Yigitcanlar, T., Wilson, M., & Kamruzzaman, M. (2019a). Disruptive impacts of automated driving systems on the built environment and land use: An urban planner's perspective. *Journal of Open Innovation: Technology, Market, and Complexity, 5,* 24.

Yigitcanlar, T., Foth, M., & Kamruzzaman, M. (2019b). Towards post-anthropocentric cities: Reconceptualising smart cities to evade urban ecocide. *Journal of Urban Technology, 26,* 147–152.

Yigitcanlar, T., Kamruzzaman, M., Foth, M., Sabatini-Marques, J., Costa, E., & Ioppolo, G. (2019c). Can cities become smart without being sustainable? A systematic review of the literature. *Sustainable Cities and Society, 45,* 348–365.

Yoo, K. H., & Lee, W. (2018). Facebook marketing by hotel groups: Impacts of post content and media type on fan engagement. In *Advances in Social Media for Travel, Tourism and Hospitality* (pp. 131–146). Routledge.

Yuan, F., & Liu, R. (2018a). Crowdsourcing for forensic disaster investigations. *Natural Hazards,* 1–18.

Yuan, F., & Liu, R. (2018b). Feasibility study of using crowdsourcing to identify critical affected areas for rapid damage assessment. *International Journal of Disaster Risk Reduction, 28,* 758–767.

Zahra, K., Imran, M., & Ostermann, F.O. (2018). Understanding eyewitness reports on Twitter during disasters. In: *Proceedings of the 15th ISCRAM Conference,* New York, 687–695.

Zhang, X., Yi, L., & Zhao, D. (2013). Community-based disaster management: A review of progress in China. *Natural Hazards, 65,* 2215–2239.

Part II

Applications

This part of the book concentrates on providing application examples of urban analytics with social media data. These examples include social media analytics for determining disaster severity, social media analytics for assisting authorities in pandemic policy, social media analytics for capturing public perceptions on smart cities, and social media analytics for capturing public perceptions on artificial intelligence.

DOI: 10.1201/9781003278986-5

4

Social Media Analytics in Disaster Policy

4.1 Introduction

People across the world are confronted with destructive natural disasters. For instance, the 2004 Indian Ocean Tsunami killed over 230,000 people across 14 countries, 2013 Typhoon Haiyan caused the loss of around 10,000 lives, and 2013 European Floods led to damages of over 12 billion Euros (Ludwig et al., 2017). Such disasters degrade the capabilities of disaster response systems in any country (Aslam-Saja et al., 2018). This has made it challenging to coordinate disasters with a limited number of trained professionals (Ludwig et al., 2017). The uncertainty of disasters limits the provision of relevant information to the affected population. Consequently, emergency management agencies, world-wide, have identified the significance of harvesting real-time information through a range of sources—rather than solely relying on conventional disaster forecasts (Zhang et al., 2010; Yang et al., 2014).

At the onset of a disaster, real-time information is critical in order to respond in time (Yang et al., 2014). Location-specific, timely information is particularly needed in order to identify the locations where food, water, shelter, and medical care are most urgently required (Gao et al., 2011; Harrison & Johnson, 2016). Inadequate, outdated, and/or paucity of information can hamper the disaster recovery efforts. Nevertheless, recent technological advancements have made it increasingly possible to compensate for any prevailing lack of information (Crooks & Wise, 2013).

The timely dissemination of relevant information increases the ability of the population to face a disaster more prepared (Gardoni & Murphy, 2010). Among many technological advancements, social media applications act as a citizen-centric technology which helps to propagate information. People contribute to disaster relief efforts by generating information, sharing images of their experiences, and updating their status on social media using a range of applications (Feng & Sester, 2018). This practice of distributing conversations in which individuals collectively respond is referred to as 'ambient journalism'. Social media information does not act 'itself', but it is 'acted upon' (Hermida, 2010). However, there is no widely accepted methodological approach to incorporate such timely valued information in order to expedite the disaster recovery efforts.

DOI: 10.1201/9781003278986-6

In recent years, with the proliferation of social media, different tasks are entrusted to people, to work as volunteers for different purposes during disasters. This is referred to as 'volunteer crowdsourcing' (Howe, 2006; Brabham, 2008; Kankanamge et al., 2019; Estellés & González, 2012). Volunteer crowdsourcing uses the power of the internet and social media to virtually harness the power of individuals to support disaster management (Riccardi, 2016). Santa Barbara (Goodchild & Glennon, 2010) and Haiti earthquakes (Liu, 2014) are some of the earliest examples where volunteer crowdsourcing has been used to contribute to disaster management. In these cases, volunteer crowdsourcing operations rapidly sprang into action in contrast to the professional bodies. Such operations contributed to save lives and resources (Riccardi, 2016). All such volunteering activities were random, and there was no established mechanism to obtain information from social media platforms.

Social media in a disaster context carries real-time crisis information such as the status of communication channels, the status of roads, needs of the evacuation camps, and other important knowledge (Yang et al., 2014; Dror et al., 2015; Riccardi, 2016). Accordingly, volunteer crowdsourcing information has three unique attributes, which qualify it to be used in disaster management—i.e., collective intelligence, multi-directional communication, and situation awareness (Kankanamge et al., 2019). Such attributes establish the strength of social media as a promising volunteer crowdsourcing tool to be used in disaster management (Kankanamge et al., 2019). Although there is a growing popularity of using social media to contribute to managing disasters, the development of a robust approach for extracting important disaster-related information from social media is an understudied area of research.

Against this backdrop, this chapter presents the outcomes of an analysis using innovative methodology and focusing on the 2010-2011 South East Queensland Floods—as a case study to highlight how disaster severity can be assessed using social media messages. Accordingly, the objectives of this study are to (a) Explore the effectiveness of utilising social media data during- and post-disaster management activities, and (b) Determine the disaster severity through a social media data analysis.

4.2 Literature Review

4.2.1 Existing Technologies in Disaster Management

Technology has been proven to contribute to making disaster management approaches more efficient. Geographic information and global positioning systems (Yigitcanlar, 2009), remote sensing technologies (Michel et al., 2012), aerospace technology (Verstappen, 1995), static sensor networks, modelling, and prediction (Sosko & Daylot, 2017) are commonly used technologies in disaster management. However, these technologies have significant limitations. For instance, due to high cloud cover, remote sensing technologies can fail to capture images with a high resolution during a flood disaster (Havas et al., 2017). Additionally, disaster predictions through advanced modellings require considerable time and resources and then become problematic to use in unpredictable and extreme weather conditions.

Furthermore, they are high-cost technologies and require highly skilled personnel, which hitherto has been a significant constraint to their wide adoption by many countries and organisations (Havas et al., 2017). In recent years, fostered by the internet and corresponding technological advancements, disaster information generated through social media, smart devices, and mobile applications have gained significant attention (Gao et al., 2011; Ludwig et al., 2017; Yigitcanlar & Kamruzzaman, 2018). Consequently, crowd-sensing social technologies are making significant advances and widespread adoption (Kantarci et al., 2016). This has led to a disruption of the conventional sender/receiver model commonly operated during disasters (Xiao et al., 2015).

Contemporary technologies for disaster management can be categorised under three taxonomies: (a) Software and online mapping tools; (b) Networks, and (c) Devices (Kankanamge et al., 2019). Open-source mapping platforms such as OSM, Google Earth, Google Maps, Bing Maps, and Yahoo Maps are the commonly cited online mapping tools in the literature (Boulos et al., 2011; Roche et al., 2013; Ludwig et al., 2017). Geographic information systems (GIS) and Quantum GIS (Q-GIS) are the prominent software used for geospatial analysis (Crooks & Wise, 2013). People who voluntarily contribute to generating geospatial data through social media mapping during crises are referred to as micro-mappers (Givoni, 2016).

In addition, Map-mashups and WebGIS are widely applied to visualise information in one comprehensive map (Baum et al., 2010; Gudes et al., 2010; Roche et al., 2013). Victorian Bushfire Map, South California Bushfire Map, Google Australia (Liu & Palen, 2010; Goodchild, 2012; Liu, 2014), and Queensland Globe are some of the popular map-mashups. In the case of devices, global positioning systems (GPS), GPS-enabled cameras, mobile spectrometers, videography, vibration sensors, geo-sensors, closed-circuit television, drones, and mobile applications act as mobile sensor devices that generate in-situ critical information (Crooks & Wise, 2013; Burston et al., 2015; Haworth & Bruce, 2015; Lagmay et al., 2017).

There is a clear gap between traditional technologies and the contemporary technologies used for disaster management. The traditional technologies are driven by professionals and involve low citizen engagement (Haworth & Bruce, 2015). Conversely, contemporary practices enable people to customise spatial content, generate maps, and blend information with several sources such as mobile devices, social media, and email messages (Miller & Goodchild, 2015).

Such open-source technology-driven approaches bridge the gaps between experts and non-experts (Pitrėnaitė-Žilienienė et al., 2014; Poblet et al., 2017). Contemporary technologies trust the aggregated information power of many citizens rather than an elite few—so-called 'wisdom of crowds' (Surowiecki, 2004; Brabham, 2013; Deng et al., 2016). Consequently, extant technologies for disaster management have become more integrated as a big data-driven approach with shared responsibilities.

4.2.2 Social Media as a New Technology for Disaster Management

Social media usage is growing at an exponential rate (Asur et al., 2011). Facebook, Twitter, Flickr, wikis, blogs, and YouTube channels are the most popular social media platforms today. All such social media information is considered as volunteer crowdsourcing information (Estellés et al., 2012; Kankanamge et al., 2019). In 2014, more than 500 million tweets were posted daily (Twitter, 2014). By 2015, 65% of the US adult population used social media, and that is nearly a 10-fold increase from the past decade (Perrin, 2015). According to the March 2019 Australian social media statistics, 15 million Australians (~60%) were active in Facebook, and 4.7 million Australians (~19%) used Twitter (Cowling, 2019). The knowledge generated by the so-called social media users can be used effectively for different contexts, and disaster management is not an exception (Haworth, 2016).

When a technology is developed as a product that fulfils a particular requirement of society. This will eventually transform technology into a solution (Grover et al., 2018). Decades ago, social media was a technology for social networking, and now it is being used as a solution tool rather than a sole technology. For instance, after the 2010 Haiti Earthquakes, citizens used social media to transmit requests for food from evacuation centres (Gao et al., 2011). During the 2007 Southern California Wildfires, people used social media information to assess the disaster events, gather real-time information, and disseminate information, as they did not receive adequate and timely information from official channels about the specific areas that experienced devastation (Sutton et al., 2008; Neubaum et al., 2014).

Analysis of social media content to extract disaster-related knowledge for disaster management purposes have surged during the last decade (Panteras et al., 2015; Xiao et al., 2015). Since then, all the social media applications could be operated using handheld devices. Therefore, people produce location-specific data in many ways even without knowing that they are doing so—e.g., automated GPS traces and GPS locations (Granell & Ostermann, 2016). Such user-generated information associated with location information (e.g., name/location) is referred to as 'volunteered geographic information' (VGI) (Goodchild, 2007). Generation of VGI through social media addresses the geospatial data scarcity in disaster management (Goetz & Zipf, 2013). According to Dror et al. (2015), by 2020, the volume of existing volunteer crowdsourcing data streams will increase by 50-fold, with a substantial volume of VGI. Yet, there are no robust and validated methods developed to harvest the best from VGI generated through social media platforms (Goodchild & Glennon, 2010; Feng & Sester, 2018).

Using social media information for disaster management can incorporate local knowledge into professional practices (Poblet et al., 2017; Sagun et al., 2009). Social media is used in disaster management for communication, disaster monitoring, education and awareness-raising, public engagement, and behavioural trajectories (Callaghan, 2016; Han et al., 2018). Table 4.1 further elaborates the uses of social media applications in disaster management.

TABLE 4.1

Applications and Impacts of Social Media for Disaster Management

Applications	Literature Evidence	Impact
Communication	Handmer et al. (2014) Callaghan (2016) McCormick (2016) Riccardi (2016)	a. Personalised warning alerts receive from personal networks (back-channel communication) b. Ability to verify and share the images/videos c. Notify the safety status of individuals and areas d. Finding lost people/pets or goods
Disaster monitoring system	Lue et al. (2014) Handmer et al. (2014) Haworth and Bruce (2015) Yuan and Liu (2018)	a. Disasters event detection b. Disaster monitoring through disaster dedicated mobile applications i.e., spectrometer, geo-enabled videography c. Identify food, water demands by locations i.e., Haiti earthquake d. Acceleration of disaster evacuation efforts e. Fund raising and volunteer services
Disaster education and awareness	Shklovski et al. (2010) Ernst et al. (2017) Han et al. (2018) Ludwig et al. (2017) Gray et al. (2016) Sagun et al. (2017)	a. Knowledge sharing about the new updates b. Awareness raising about hazards, disasters, mitigation strategies. c. Seek to inform and support existing disaster management strategies d. Seek and provide national and regional disaster warnings
Public engagement and behavioural trajectories	Havas et al. (2017) Givoni (2016) Wan et al. (2014) Panteras et al. (2015) Han et al. (2018)	a. Digitising, mapping, and location-based information visualisation i.e., CyberFlood, Google map maker, Open-source mapping b. Re-connect communities c. Launching virtual fund-raising campaigns d. To seek emotional support e. To check in with family and friends f. Derive an overall picture about the disaster and the reflections of the community

Prior application of social media information shows potential to support all the four phases of the disaster management cycle—mitigation, preparedness, response, and recovery. The mitigation and preparedness phases focus on reducing the disaster risk and vulnerability. During these phases, social media platforms establish multi-directional communication to increase community awareness about the upcoming risks.

Compared to other phases, disaster response and recovery phases are much more sensitive. The main focus of these two phases is to launch rescue efforts and to provide basic humanitarian needs. Crowdsourcing platforms such as Ushahidi, Red Cross app, and GeoCommons engage in collecting and disseminating data generated through social media and open-source applications. This is to accelerate disaster response and rescue efforts (Harrison & Johnson, 2016). These recent applications also use social media information for post-disaster damage assessments i.e., Hurricane Matthew, Florida; Typhoon Haiyan, China (Deng et al., 2016; Athanasia & Stavros, 2015).

Knowledge directly gained through social media, however, is not comprehensive enough to derive the 'big picture' of a disaster event. Even though people can generate a vast multitude of social media data throughout a disaster (Chang, 2015), limitations in data processing, analysis, and interpretation (Ragini et al., 2018) still exists. Even the extant literature limits their focus to descriptive studies, rather than integrating the advantages of location reference social media data into practice. Accordingly, this study utilises the potential of harnessing geo-located community emotions through social media data content to determine the disaster severity using the 2010-2011 South East Queensland Floods as the testbed.

4.3 Case Study

South East Queensland (SEQ) has a long history of flooding (Van Den Honert & McAneney, 2011). Since the European settlement of Australia, floods in 1893, 1974, and 2010–2011 are recorded as among the most destructive events. During the period of November 2010 and January 2011, SEQ received a total rainfall between 600 and 1200 mm. This created two major flood events over the period of 25 December 2010 to 25 January 2011. As shown in Figure 4.1, several towns such as Dalby, Oakey, Ipswich, Yeronga, Yeerongpilly, Woolloongabba, Westlake, West-End, Gatton, and many other towns were inundated. Other towns located away from SEQ, such as Chinchilla and Bundaberg, were also affected by this flood.

Unlike the previous flood events, community response to assist the flood victims was significantly high during the 2010-2011 SEQ Floods (Van Den Honert & McAneney, 2011; Shaw et al., 2013). High social media usage enabled a distributed conversation about the collective responses and information

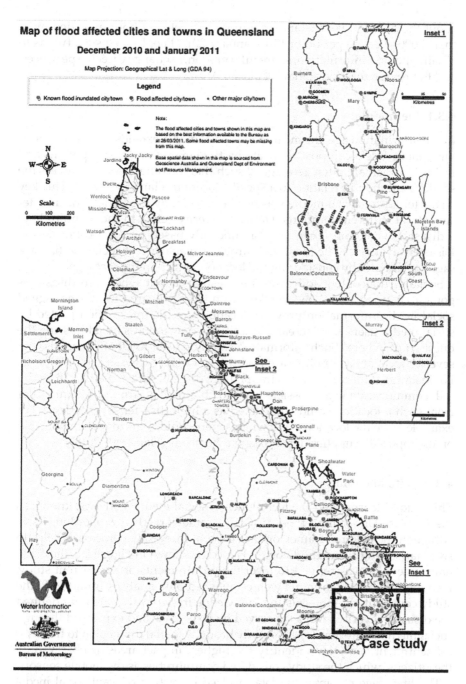

FIGURE 4.1
Location of the case study. (Courtesy of BoM, 2012.)

about the disaster. For instance, #qldfloods tweets per hour exceeded more than 1,000 over the period of 10-16 January 2011. People used such tweets to obtain updated information, share information, exchange direct experiences, and to provide reactions (Shaw et al., 2013).

4.3.1 Methodology

In the information age, the meaning of social media extends beyond connecting people. Users can post blogs at any time expressing their opinions and feelings, which are often geo-tagged such that the other users can assess the sender's emotion in relation to a specific location (Han et al., 2018). This key characteristic of social media was used in this study to evaluate the disaster severity at different locations. Disaster severity refers to the magnitude of a disaster event, and it can vary significantly based on the location factor. Disaster severity can be identified through an analysis of social media message content and by considering the location tagged in the message.

Social media content addresses the questions about 'when' this disaster is going to happen, and 'how' to take action to be prepared for it. Geo-tagged social media information provides location-specific information posted by social media users and increases the situation awareness by addressing the question of 'where'. Such information could be used to identify the disaster severity level at each point based on the emotions expressed in blog posts. For instance, if there is a victim trapped in a disaster-affected area, the victim will communicate in all possible ways to obtain help. Around 1-2 km buffer from such a location could be denoted as a high disaster severity level. For example, once the location is known, rescuers could come to that person's aid or airdrop relief supplies depending on the needs (Han et al., 2018).

4.3.2 Data and Tools

This study incorporated the techniques of social media analytics, known as the Capture-Understand-Present (CUP) framework (Fan & Gordon, 2014). Although the original framework is a general three-stage process, it helps to summarise lengthy methodologies. Hence, as shown in Figure 4.2, the original framework was refined to meet the requirements of the current study. By applying and extending a well-established data analysis framework; the study contributed to the existing knowledge in two ways: (a) Study defined the disaster severity level as observed by lay people and expressed through social media platforms; (b) This study brought spatial dimension to the typical sentiment analysis to identify the highest impact areas as observed by the citizens, which the study considered communities as the mobile sensors.

The first stage of capturing data involved extracting relevant social media information. Among many social media platforms, this study used Twitter to extract relevant information based on the following justification: (a) Since its inception in 2006 as a microblogging service, Twitter has become the fastest

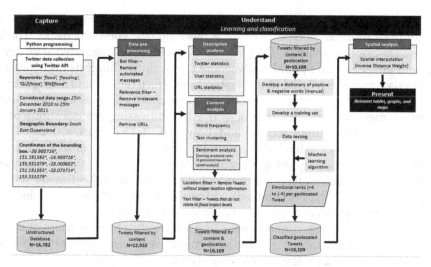

FIGURE 4.2
Social media analysis framework. (Derived from Fan & Gordon, 2014.)

growing social media platform; (b) Twitter offers Application Programming Interface (API) to researchers and practitioners to conduct analysis based on their interests (Twitter, 2013); (c) Compared to Facebook, Twitter data is considered as 'open data', which provides succinct real-time data to the public (Dufty, 2016); (d) Searching and streaming APIs of Twitter allows researchers to write queries and download information using certain keywords (Guan & Chen, 2014).

The capture stage involves downloading Twitter data including its meta-data file starts with the identification of keywords, hashtags, and the use of Twitter API. This study downloaded Twitter messages (referred to as 'tweets') with the keywords of 'flood', 'flooding', 'QLDflood', 'BNEflood', posted from 25 December 2010 to 25 January 2011 within the SEQ Region of Australia. Analysis of the raw data is challenging as it is not well structured. Thus, the five-step data cleaning process introduced by Arthur et al. (2018) was adopted—time zone filter, date filter, bot filter, relevance filter, and text filter.

Among them, the first two filtering steps—time zone filter, and date filter—were done at the time of downloading the data through the Twitter API. The other two filtering steps—bot filter (removal of automated messages), and relevance filter (removal of irrelevant meanings)—were applied later. In total, 16,782 geotagged tweets were downloaded, of which 12,910 cleaned tweets were used for descriptive and content analysis. From the cleaned tweets, 10,109 were only attributed with their exact location and disaster impact levels, which were used for the spatial analysis. Twitter data contains numerous information such as the tweet 'creation_date', 'user-screen name', 'text', 'user-location', 'longitude', 'latitude', 'place', and 'retweeted'. From these, user names, geographic location, date, time, and content attributes were used in this study.

The understanding stage consists of three types of analysis to extract knowledge from multiple perspectives for a more holistic comprehension. These were: Descriptive analysis (DA); Content analysis (CA) integrated with sentiment analysis, and Spatial analysis (SA). Descriptive analysis and content analysis were widely used to understand the effectiveness of utilising social media in disaster management activities. These two analyses together were used to meet the first research objective by addressing the questions of—when to do/take (things/actions) and, how to do/take (things/actions). This study methodology extended the popular descriptive and content analyses into a new direction by integrating sentiment analysis and spatial analysis techniques. Spatial analysis was conducted to understand the disaster severity in each town/city. This analysis addressed the second research objective by addressing the questions of—what to do, and to where.

The presentation stage contains revealing the results of the abovementioned analyses. Relevant tables, graphs, and maps were used as appropriate to present the findings of the aforesaid analyses.

4.3.3 Descriptive Analysis

Descriptive analysis (DA) was conducted to understand the trending topics among the people within the considered time period. Though there are many descriptive metrics that are certainly possible to be used in this study, only three metrics—Twitter statistics, user analysis, and weblink (URL) analysis were used in the DA as these met the required secondary data needs to minimise potential confusion and complexities. Such descriptive statistics are widely used in disaster management studies to derive a broader picture about the incident/disaster. DA acted as the basis for many other analyses as well. Especially by identifying the prominent hashtags, the number of tweets, keywords, and URLs to different photographs and websites delivered a holistic picture about the event. This also helped to progress towards the online analysis such as content analysis and sentiment analysis. Accordingly, DA aspired to emphasise basic, but crucial information about the dataset (Chae, 2015).

4.3.4 Content Analysis

Content analysis (CA) was adopted to examine the community behaviour and community artefacts such as idioms, pictures, audios, and videos. CA was used to create replicable and meaningful content from the text to the contexts of their use (Krippendorff, 2009). Generally, tweets are informal and primarily reflect the characteristics of lay language. Thus, data cleaning was a prerequisite before proceeding to detailed analysis. Tweets are not simply texts. They might be opinions, observations, or abstracts (Fritz et al., 2017). Therefore, advanced text mining techniques such as sentiment analysis were used in extracting knowledge from tweets.

Machine learning algorithms, lexicons, and text mining methods have been applied in transforming unstructured texts into more structured texts. Consequently, this study adopted decision tree machine learning algorithm for text classification. After cleaning the dataset, it could be used for word frequency analysis, text clustering, and sentiment analysis. Word frequency analysis exposed frequently discussed hot topics during the selected period. As disasters are uncertain events, it is critical to understand the changes in the dominant themes across the prescribed 30-day time duration. This helped to understand the changes in the disaster risk levels across the pre-, during-, and post-disaster recovery phases of the disaster.

Secondly, text clustering was adopted to categorise the fields of interests or the pressing needs—i.e., food demands, evacuations. Finally, sentiment analysis was conducted to label an emotional rank to each and every tweet. The objective of conducting sentiment analysis was to categorise the negative, positive, and neutral tweets as reflected by the words of the Twitter message content. To do so, a dictionary of positive and negative words was developed especially considering the tweets downloaded for this study. Accordingly, a value ranging between (-4) to +4 was given to each tweet. The study used Weka 2.0 open-source machine learning software to conduct the sentiment analysis using the decision tree algorithm. Decision tree algorithm is the most commonly applied machine learning algorithm for text classification (Ahmad et al., 2018; Koswatte et al., 2015).

4.3.5 Spatial Analysis

Geotagged data generated by the social media users are referred to as 'volunteered geographic information' (VGI). It acts as the prominent source of information to conduct spatial analysis (De Albuquerque et al., 2015; Panteras et al., 2015). Spatial analysis enables us to gain situation awareness and to understand how the impacts of a disaster are spatially distributed. Without a doubt, a spatial map which reflects community knowledge about the disaster severity in each area will make the relief efforts efficient (Zhang et al., 2013). Geo-located tweets that described the situation at different locations were filtered out in performing this analysis. Exiting studies mostly use spatial and temporal characteristics of social media information to assist disaster managers. Albeit, giving a spatial dimension to the rich public sentiments in disaster-related social media content is challenging and there is only limited research in this area (Han & Wang, 2019).

The study used 'inverse distance weighted' (IDW) interpolation method to identify the distribution of disaster impact levels based on observed location data and related descriptions (ArcMap, 2016). IDW spatial analysis tool assumes that the influence of a mapped variable decreases with the distance (ArcMap, 2016). In order to calculate the IDW, each point was weighted with a Z value which described the disaster magnitude level at each point. The study considered the sentiment values derived for each point as the Z value to calculate the IDW.

4.4 Results

4.4.1 Descriptive Analysis

The descriptive analysis provided an in-depth understanding of the devastating impacts of the flood. The study adopted text mining methods and statistical techniques to develop and visualise the content of Twitter messages—i.e., tweets.

4.4.1.1 Twitter Statistics

Among the 16,782 tweets collected, 8,727 (52%) of them were original, and 8,055 (48%) had been retweeted. It reflected the highly interactive nature of the users. Yet, there was no high diversity in the hashtags used. All the discussions were developed around 20 hashtags. The most commonly used hashtags were: #bnestorm, #rain, #QLDflood, #bneflood, #brisfloods, #qldweather, #GranthomFloodSupport, #prayAUS, #prayforaustralia, #thebigwet, #LegalClinic #VolunteeringQLD, #brisbanecityQLD, #riverlife, #teamwork, #glutenfreegoodies, #bakedrelief #donate, #AUdonate, and #corporateresponsibility.

Over 8,000 tweets contained at least one hashtag. Hashtag usage substantially changed with the change of disaster risk levels. For instance, from 1 to 7 January 2011, the frequently used hashtags were the #rain, #bnestorm, which show the signs of a potential flood event. From 10 to 15 January 2011, #bneflood, #qldflood, #the bigwet were the most used hashtags, which reflected the occurrence of the flood event. From 16 January onwards, hashtags such as #AUdonate, #glutenfreegoodies, #donate, and #corporateresponsibility were the most significant. This provides an indication of the different demands that were created during different time spans.

4.4.1.2 User Analysis

In total 1,074 users contributed to create the dataset with 16,782 tweets. Accordingly, on average one user has posted 16 tweets (15.62) within the selected 30 days of time. However, the contribution of all the users is not uniform. Figure 4.3 shows the most active users and the number of tweets they contributed.

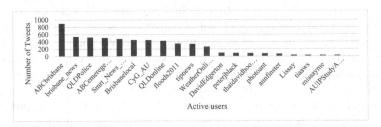

FIGURE 4.3
Most active users during the flooding.

Among the most active users, the first 10 users fall into the categories of either news channels (e.g., ABCbrisbane, brisbane_news), or communities (e.g., CyG_AU, floods2011). In the total dataset considered, 34% was contributed by 20 users. The other 1,054 users sent around 9-10 tweets during the 30-day period. This confirmed the dynamic use of Twitter during the 2010-2011 SEQ Floods.

4.4.1.3 URL Analysis

Although URLs are generally popular in Twitter, many URLs were not found in the dataset. Only 318 (1.8%) of the tweets contain a URL and they are directed to images and videos that described the incident well. Among these, 179 (1.06%) URLs linked to news websites or quoted breaking news.

Figures 4.4 and 4.5 illustrate the disaster magnitude around Brisbane, the capital city of Queensland State, Australia—and central city of SEQ. People have used images to express their suffering and feelings regarding the disaster.

There are certain URLs that were tweeted by many users. These were: https://www.youtube.com/watch?v=kYUpkPTcqPY; https://www.youtube.com/watch?v=Dzuyw6aruhY&feature=youtube_gdata_player; and http://bit.ly/euFTKa.

Tweets with URLs have received at least one retweet as a response. The limited number of tweets with URLs reflected the fact that the majority of the people have used Twitter to express their own views and conditions during the disaster period—rather than using Twitter to share content generated by others.

4.4.2 Content Analysis

Twitter, as a social media tool, often forms a communication channel during disasters, not only within the affected areas but also between the affected areas. This led to the generation of interpersonal alerts to warn other people or seek help. There were tweets from SEQ, which described the flooding of towns

FIGURE 4.4
This photo of a flood scene was posted Dec. 28, 2010 by Twitter user @bieberific_abi: " I don't find It very nice: / I'M FLOODED!! My state is underwater!! That is my backyard".

FIGURE 4.5
This photo a flood scene was posted Jan. 12, 2011 by Twitter user; "Guess my daughter's interview Thursday is off??? We are going to suffer for a long time☹".

located away from SEQ. For instance, Bundaberg, Emerald, and Rockhampton are locations far away from SEQ, but there were tweets generated within SEQ about the floods in these distant localities. Hence, all cleaned tweets (in total 12,910) were categorised by the town/city name based on the tweet content. The content analysis was two-fold. The first one focused on the towns located away from SEQ. The other contained the towns and cities within SEQ. As given in Table 4.2, a total of 9,474 tweets were filtered with at least one city/town name. The remaining 3,436 tweets also contained references to the SEQ Floods, but without any locality name mentioned in their content.

The number of tweets is proportionate to the population living in a particular area. Accordingly, as shown in Table 4.3, all tweets were weighted by the population of each city or town.

TABLE 4.2

Tweet Numbers by Location

Location	Number of Tweets
Brisbane	3,379
Ipswich	2,193
Toowoomba	1,692
Rockhampton	583
Bundaberg	482
Emerald	324
Dalby	299
Chinchilla	149
Goodna	128
Gatton	123
Helidon	22

TABLE 4.3

Population Weighted Tweets in Percentage

City/Town Date		Western Down and Central Highlands Region						South Brisbane				
		Chinchilla	Bundaberg	Emerald	Rockhampton	Dalby	Toowoomba	Helidon	Gatton	Ipswich	Goodna	Brisbane
2010-12-26	A	0.03	0.02	0.00	0.00	0.00	0.00	0.00	0.00	0.00	0.00	0.00
2010-12-27		0.77	0.01	0.02	0.01	0.05	0.01	0.00	0.00	0.01	0.00	0.00
2010-12-28		0.25	0.02	0.08	0.01	0.21	0.00	0.00	0.00	0.00	0.00	0.00
2010-12-29		0.15	0.09	0.47	0.00	0.22	0.00	0.00	0.00	0.00	0.00	0.00
2010-12-30		0.02	0.07	0.35	0.00	0.00	0.00	0.00	0.00	0.00	0.00	0.00
2011-01-01		0.02	0.04	0.13	0.01	0.01	0.00	0.00	0.01	0.00	0.00	0.01
2011-01-02		0.05	0.02	0.20	0.00	0.05	0.00	0.00	0.03	0.00	0.00	0.00
2011-01-03		0.02	0.01	0.23	0.03	0.06	0.00	0.00	0.01	0.00	0.00	0.00
2011-01-04		0.03	0.01	0.11	0.03	0.00	0.00	0.00	0.00	0.00	0.00	0.00
2011-01-05		0.02	0.01	0.16	0.07	0.02	0.00	0.00	0.00	0.00	0.00	0.01
2011-01-06		0.02	0.01	0.08	0.16	0.32	0.01	0.00	0.01	0.00	0.00	0.01
2011-01-07		0.02	0.01	0.08	0.12	0.09	0.01	0.00	0.00	0.01	0.00	0.01
2011-01-08	B	0.02	0.00	0.03	0.09	0.02	0.00	0.00	0.00	0.00	0.00	0.01
2011-01-09		0.03	0.01	0.10	0.04	0.48	0.01	0.00	0.00	0.01	0.09	0.00
2011-01-10		0.48	0.01	0.05	0.05	0.61	0.34	0.70	0.75	0.33	0.30	0.00
2011-01-11		0.18	0.03	0.08	0.03	0.25	0.28	0.30	0.53	0.44	0.29	0.04
2011-01-12		0.28	0.06	0.05	0.03	0.11	0.34	0.20	0.22	0.27	0.41	0.07
2011-01-13		0.02	0.06	0.07	0.03	0.00	0.18	0.30	0.09	0.11	0.29	0.03
2011-01-14		0.02	0.01	0.05	0.03	0.02	0.08	0.00	0.09	0.11	0.08	0.05
2011-01-15		0.02	0.00	0.01	0.00	0.00	0.05	0.30	0.00	0.01	0.25	0.01
2011-01-16		0.00	0.00	0.02	0.00	0.00	0.05	0.00	0.00	0.02	0.00	0.00
2011-01-17		0.00	0.01	0.02	0.00	0.00	0.05	0.00	0.00	0.04	0.00	0.01

(Continued)

TABLE 4.3 *(Continued)*

Population Weighted Tweets in Percentage

City/Town Date	Western Down and Central Highlands Region						South Brisbane				
	Chinchilla	Bundaberg	Emerald	Rockhampton	Dalby	Toowoomba	Helidon	Gatton	Ipswich	Goodna	Brisbane
2011-01-18	0.03	0.00	0.08	0.00	0.00	0.08	0.20	0.00	0.01	0.00	0.00
2011-01-19	0.02	0.01	0.01	0.00	0.00	0.06	0.00	0.00	0.09	0.00	0.00
2011-01-20	0.00	0.01	0.01	0.00	0.00	0.06	0.00	0.00	0.05	0.00	0.00
2011-01-21	0.00	0.00	0.02	0.00	0.00	0.02	0.00	0.00	0.02	0.00	0.00
2011-01-22	0.00	0.00	0.02	0.00	0.00	0.02	0.00	0.00	0.01	0.00	0.01
2011-01-23	0.00	0.00	0.05	0.00	0.00	0.02	0.20	0.00	0.01	0.00	0.01
2011-01-24	0.00	0.00	0.13	0.00	0.00	0.01	0.00	0.06	0.01	0.00	0.03
2011-01-25	0.00	0.00	0.02	0.00	0.00	0.01	0.00	0.00	0.02	0.00	0.01
2011-01-26	0.00	0.00	0.00	0.00	0.00	0.00	0.00	0.00	0.00	0.00	0.01

A—Flood flow line 1

B—Flood flow line 2

Table 4.3 presents the analysis of tweets (weighted by the population of each city/town) circulated each day within the considered 30-day flood period in 2010–2011. The analysis assumed that the number of flood-related tweets have a positive relationship with the disaster impact levels. Hence, flood flow lines were developed joining Twitter message peaks of each city/town. As presented in Table 4.3, there are two flood flow lines which adjoined the flood-related Twitter peaks over the selected one-month period.

The flow line A (Table 4.3) started on 27 December 2010 from Chinchilla, which is a small town in the Western Downs region of Queensland, with a 5,877 population (ABS, 2011). Chinchilla was totally evacuated during December 2010. The flow line A ended in Brisbane around 14 January 2011, and according to the BoM, 2012) report, Brisbane city experienced flooding on 15 January 2011. According to flow line A, the number of tweets on Dalby flooding increased on 8 January 2011, which was the first town flooded closer to SEQ. Then onwards, tweets about flooding in SEQ towns and cities such as Toowoomba, Ipswich, Goodna, and Brisbane started to increase on 9 January 2010. These reflections of the Twitter behaviour have significant compatibility with the records of the BoM, 2012) report. For instance, Twitter analysis marked 10-15 January 2011 as the most devastating period of the SEQ Floods. Similarly, from 10 to 15 January 2011 flood warnings were issued for 57 cities and towns. Among them, 32 cities/towns experienced inundation above floor level or near levee overtopping (BoM, 2012).

The flow line B (see Table 4.3) shows the second flood peak at Chinchilla on 10 January 2011. Although these two flow lines reflect the Twitter behaviour, they do not deviate from the real flood behaviour patterns. For instance, BoM, 2012) has also recorded 28 December 2010 and 12 January 2011 as the flood-affected dates for Chinchilla. Accordingly, tweets carry time-critical information, which could assist the disaster relief works by addressing the questions of (a) When (to take actions), and (b) How (to take actions). However, this study equally accredits the significance of using aerial imageries and flood modelling technologies for disaster management. Still, adopting social media as an information-rich innovative approach for disaster management is essential (Kankanamge et al., 2019).

Figure 4.6 depicts a comparison between the Twitter peaks and Brisbane flood peaks (station number 540198). As illustrated in Figure 4.7, the flood-related tweets increased for one or two days (P2) before the actual flood peak in the Brisbane River City gauge (G_1) (station number 540198). It confirms that people were much aware and have extensively discussed about the potential of increasing flood levels. There is a transition period of two days between the main Twitter peak (P2) and the actual Brisbane River City gauge (G1). This delivered informal warnings to the people and the authorities for deciding when to take action. Therefore, any notification of an unusual rise in tweets around a particular topic will deliver authorities an informal warning to be prepared. In many instances, people who live far away from the impacted areas are better informed through social media (Goodchild & Glennon, 2010).

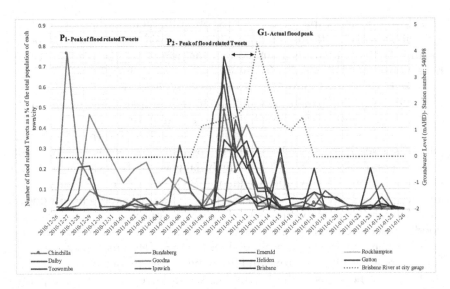

FIGURE 4.6
Relationship between behaviour of tweets and flood levels/impact.

With the decline in flood levels in the Brisbane City gauge, Twitter posts related to disaster relief tasks became popular. Launching fund raising campaigns—virtual fundraising—were in operation through Twitter during the 2010-2011 SEQ Floods—i.e., RT @mayshars: open: http://www.ppia-qld.org/ and Donate (provided as exemplar tweets). Know any flood-affected families

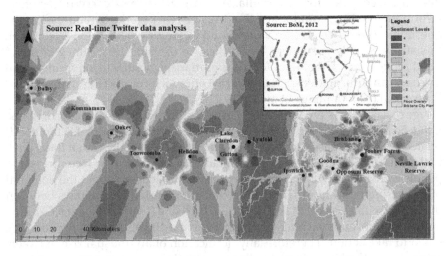

FIGURE 4.7
Disaster severity map derived from VGI analysis.

in need of one? Let me know! #bneflood. Accordingly, social media developed a new path to address mostly unaddressed questions of 'how (to help/to approach the victims)'.

Virtual volunteers—virtual volunteerism—can analyse tweets related to a disaster event and derive real-time assistance demanded. For instance, there were many geo-located tweets with the words 'trap' and 'blocked'—i.e., Water is on my doorstep, and Heavy raining and wondering what to do (exemplar tweets). Tweets play a complementary role to traditional disaster relief and rescue efforts (Ragini et al., 2018). This was particularly salient in the SEQ Floods, as Twitter unveiled the food and other basic demands of the flood victims by cities/towns. For instance, the evacuation centres at Ipswich requested baked foods and Bundaberg requested blankets. Such information helped authorities to meet the real-time demands, which led to an increase in efficiency and the efficacy of the disaster management procedures. The analysis confirmed the significance of social media usage in disaster management for communication, disaster monitoring, disaster education, and awareness-raising among the public.

4.4.3 Spatial Analysis

The immediacy of accurate location-specific information is invaluable to derive locational conclusions (Goodchild & Li, 2012; Haworth & Bruce, 2015). Spatial analysis could reflect the community sentiments by the geolocation. VGI or tweets with geolocations (10,109) were used for the spatial analysis.

Initially, the emotional value/sentiment value of all the geo-located tweets were identified by training the dataset using the decision tree algorithm through the Weka 2.0 software. Prior to the data training exercise, two-word bags were developed with positive and negative words as given in Table 4.4. This was used as the data dictionary for data training and testing exercises.

TABLE 4.4

Two-word Bags Developed Based on the Downloaded Tweets

Sentiments	Words
Negative	afraid, bad, bigwet, blocked, boats, cry, curse, cursed, damage, damaged, deluge, dying, dead, disaster, downpour, drown, drowning, evacuate, evacuated, evacuating, expose, exposure, fear, flash, flood, flooded, flooding, flush, help, helpless, inundate, inundated, lost, mourn, mourning, peak, pray, need, rain, raining, risk, risky, sad, scary, severe, severely, storm, submerge, trap, trapped, underwater, unfortunate, upset, victim, unfortunately, vulnerable, warn, warned, warning, wash, washed, water, worried, worry, worrying, worst
Positive	best, blessed, fortunate, fortunately, free, good, happy, lucky, luckily, safe, safer, strong, thanks

Accordingly, data training was done under eight parameters ranging from (–4) to +4, where +4 denoted the extreme positive sentiments and (–4), the extreme negative sentiments. Higher the existence of negative words in a Twitter message, higher the possibility of classifying the tweet as an extreme negative sentiment. Lower the existence of negative words higher the possibility of classifying the tweet as a positive sentiment.

The quality of the dataset was finally evaluated using the precision and 'root mean square error' (RMSE) values. Precision addressed the question of— from all tweets labelled as positive/negative/neutral, how many were actually positive/negative/neutral. The precision value of 0. 82 (>0.5) reflected the low occurrence of possible random errors. RMSE is the standard deviation of the prediction errors. RMSE of 0.18 depicted the high accuracy of the dataset. Sample of geo-located tweets and the calculated sentiment values are exemplified in Table 4.5.

Sentiment values, listed in Table 4.4, were derived through a data training exercise and the results were used for the IDW spatial analysis. The sentiment values of geo-located tweets were used to calculate the disaster severity by locations. Under the IDW method, closer features are weighted more heavily than the features which exist further away. This analysis provided a spatial interpretation for the location-specific community knowledge shared or expressed in a form of a Twitter message. All these Twitter messages discuss about disaster impact levels about their localities/towns.

Figure 4.7 represents real-time observations and insights of people/Twitter users. When compared to the small towns—e.g., Dalby, Oakey—Ipswich, Brisbane, and Toowoomba had larger flood footprints. The areas shown in green or positive sentiment values show the areas with low disaster impacts. Most of the areas with positive sentiment values referred to hilly areas— i.e., Seven Hills bushland reserve—or farmlands and low-density areas—i.e., Kentville, Lynford, Lake Claredon. Tweets generated in such areas had positive sentiments which appreciated their presence in such areas during the flood. Tweets generated in high-impact areas with more negative sentiment values provided information about the flood depth and observed rainfalls. The sentiment analysis reflected the citizen knowledge stored in tweets, but not the information gained through surveys or advanced modelling techniques. Hence, the reflections illustrated in Figure 4.7 need to be justified through a ground-truthing process to evaluate the credibility of the methodology adopted (Sachdeva et al., 2017).

The aforementioned findings can be justified through the actual statistics of the SEQ Floods. The flood-affected area map (Figure 4.1), produced by BoM, 2012), shares a number of similarities with the results of the sentiment analysis. Accordingly, both the maps have identified Toowoomba, Helidon, Gatton, Ipswich, and Brisbane as severely affected cities/towns. Henceforth, the spatial analysis conducted through VGI has prioritised the locations with high disaster impact levels, which addressed the question of 'where (to provide assistance immediately)'.

TABLE 4.5

Time-Critical Information Sent by Users

No	Applications/ Impact	Latitudes/ Longitudes	Date and Time	User Screen Name	Text	Sentiment Value
1	Disaster education and awareness	−27.181994°, 151.259816°	Tue Jan 11 11:37:20 +0000 2011	sascharundle	Dalby Mayor: Chinchilla prediction for 7 m peaks, 2nd flood there in weeks after 210 mls rain in 72 hrs #qldfloods	Ignored. (Sender is from Dalby and explained about Chinchilla)
2	Disaster monitoring	−27.580414°, 151.932473°	Mon Jan 10 02:39:30 +0000 2011	RedMoHaircutter	We are severely flooded from every corner. Need more boats #Harristown #Toowoomba	−3 (Negative)
3	Disaster monitoring	−27.599880°, 152.768553°	Tue Jan 11 23:46:42 +0000 2011	editormum75	Ipswich is going under water, higher than the flood expected. Condamine was completely evacuated again. #qldfloods	−4 (Negative)
4	Disaster monitoring	−27.481229°, 152.418925°	Thu Jan 13 23:40:57 +0000 2011	benhamilton	Good that we moved to Kentville. No flooding here. All good and happy	+4 (Positive)

4.5 Discussion

This study elaborated the Capture-Understand-Present (CUP) framework to better understand the applicability of social media data to determine disaster severity using the 2010-2011 SEQ Floods as a testbed. Key findings generated from this study and their implications for research and policy are discussed in the subsections below.

4.5.1 Ways That Social Media Can Be Utilised for Better Managing Disaster Stages

The use of social media data has considerably changed the disaster management practices from primary professional domains to extended social technologies (Goodchild, 2009; Goodchild & Glennon, 2010;). Further, social media is considered as a Findable-Accessible-Interoperable-Reusable (FAIR) big data category with significant scientific and societal potential (Wilkinson et al., 2016). Nevertheless, there is limited knowledge and understanding for adopting social media data for disaster management. In order to bridge this gap, the study employed the aforesaid modified CUP framework to evaluate the applicability of social media data for disaster management. The study disclosed several ways of using social media throughout the disaster management cycle under the following areas: (a) When to do/take (things/actions); (b) Where to do (things/actions) and (c) How to do/take (things/actions). They are elaborated below.

Disaster management strategies could be divided into three phases—pre-, during-, and post-disaster stages. These stages do not demand the same services from disaster management authorities. They demand preparedness, rescue, and recovery activities, respectively. Disaster management authorities are inevitably stretched thin during sudden disasters such as flash floods and earthquakes (Goodchild & Glennon, 2010). Limited numbers of staff and the inability to acquire ground information cause disadvantages to the authorities to a considerable extent during a disaster. Hence, a precise understanding of *'when to do (things/actions)?'* helps everyone to manage the disaster in a better way. During the SEQ Floods, authorities sent alerts to people using television and radio messages. Further, such information was released on a river basin scale (BoM, 2012).

Albeit, the circulation of such information through social media in a timely and continuous manner encourages awareness among people. For instance, the word count analysis of the flood-related tweets prominently highlighted the circulation of words such as 'emergency (376)', 'fear' (178), 'threat' (97) 'prepare' (51), and 'alert' (43) during 1-8 January 2011. These words attract the attention of people and help them to prepare, and evacuate from vulnerable areas.

Moreover, by 12 January, Goodna and Brisbane went through power cuts. The terms, 'evacuation' (1095), 'peak' (155), 'damage' (126), and '000' (32), were highly used during that period. Conversely, while the areas outside of SEQ, such as Emerald and Rockhampton were in the disaster recovery stage, SEQ experienced the disaster response stage with severe floods. Therefore, the authorities could exert greater effort towards SEQ than the towns such as Emerald and Rockhampton (Figure 4.1) from central highlands. Accordingly, knowing when to do the appropriate thing to where enhance the efficiency of resource utilisation during a disaster.

Accurate information on where to provide assistance first is critical— providing a precise understanding of *'where to do (things/actions)?'* The analysis of geo-located tweets addressed this question by identifying the locations by disaster severity. Although collecting geo-located information immediately after a disaster is challenging, better management of VGI makes the task easy and convenient. Deriving a clear understanding of the inundated areas helps authorities to identify their priorities. Accordingly, all the riverine cities/towns were warned, whilst people in vulnerable areas in Toowoomba and Brisbane (Figure 4.7) were informed where to evacuate and avoid driving, walking, or riding through floodwaters. Advanced remote sensing technologies also could be used to harvest locational information. Incorporating VGI with such technologies will enhance the data quality.

Among many questions unaddressed during an emergency, the third question is about *'how to do/take (things/actions)'*. Especially, lack of sound, real-time information, and inability to use dispersed community knowledge, will make recruiting volunteers, fund raising, dispelling rumours, and gathering information problematic. With the use of social media, people can observe and will be empowered with the ability to geolocate their observations (Goodchild & Glennon, 2010; Fritz et al., 2017). This opens up new pathways to increase disaster recovery activities for fund raising and volunteering.

Unlike social media, disaster management authorities are hierarchical and driven by predetermined formal agendas. For instance, Queensland flood events are monitored by the Bureau of Meteorology, Flood Warning Centre, Regional Forecasting Centre, and Tropical Cyclone Warning Centre, and many more other institutions (BoM, 2012). They have their own scope to play in a disaster period which sometimes limits their efficiency. Consequently, authorities in the US and Canada already use social media to gather and disseminate information and to dispel rumours that could jeopardise public safety (Harrison & Johnson, 2016).

4.5.2 Myths and Facts About Using Social Media Data for Disaster Management

While social media has received substantial attention as a promising tool to increase the efficiency of disaster management, there are certain arguments that caution about using social media for disaster management. Among these, the most critical and valid arguments are: (a) Social inequality in the usage of social media—digital divide; (b) Low information accuracy, and (c) Limited information from severely damaged areas—spatial heterogeneity (Xiao et al., 2015). Due to these facts, many government agencies are reluctant to incorporate social media information for disaster management-related decision-making (Harrison & Johnson, 2016).

Despite the evidence of the value of social media to those experiencing a disaster and those who are seeking disaster-related information, the discussion on—'digital divide'—argues about the unequal access to information technology (Yigitcanlar, 2005, 2006; Ngamassi et al., 2020). The validity of this argument is substantially decreasing over time. There were 3.4 billion social media users by 2019 January and it is growing at an increasing rate (Hootsuite, 2019). Additionally, many towns and cities are becoming part of the online planning and smart city movement (Yigitcanlar, 2016). For instance, nowadays most of the cities provide Wi-Fi connections within city limits and social media have almost become an open-source technology that allows anyone to use it without spending nothing or little (Pitrénaité-Žilenienė et al., 2014; Yigitcanlar, 2015). This argument was valid to a majority of the people many years ago, but now the majority of the people do have access to many social media platforms.

The 2010–2011 SEQ Floods is a case study, where at that time social media was not as popular as it is today. However, the data harvested during the floods has delivered promising results that enlightens interested parties to use social media for disaster management. Although towns such as Gatton, Oakey, and Dalby are located far away from Brisbane, there were geo-located tweets that expressed the situation information. Hence, rather than arguing about the inequality of technology distribution, extant population expectations motivated by social media have risen to an extent where people expect personal warnings either to their social media accounts or to their handheld smart devices (Handmer et al., 2014).

Low information accuracy is the second critical argument raised against using social media in disaster management. Sharing false information, sharing rumours, and generating hypothetical information could reduce the accuracy of the information generated in social media. Due to the high usage of social media during disasters, there are specific methods that have been adopted by authorities to limit the spreading of misinformation. Maintaining social media pages and distributing validated information to the community is one of the common methods adopted to provide guaranteed information to the people (Harrison & Johnson, 2016).

The accuracy of the locations tagged in tweets may not be perfect (Gao et al., 2011). Among many social media, Twitter is the prominent social media that provide geotagged information for research purposes. Sometimes tagged location may not represent the exact location information of the sender. This is a possible drawback in using geotagged social media data for disaster management. Nonetheless, this is becoming an outdated fact as social media platforms allow people to tag distant locations. Consequently, any person can tag any location which relates to the content discussed in the message. There are geotagged images and videos circulated in social media that provide location-specific, trustworthy information than text messages (Ernst et al., 2017). This opens a new research arena for future studies to evaluate the accuracy of geotagged tweets.

Spatial heterogeneity is one of the critical arguments that are hard to address. With the warning alerts, people can be evacuated from risky areas. Nevertheless, disaster occurrences and their severities are unpredictable in nature. For instance, the study collected geo-located tweets, and the analysis provided location-specific details about the disaster severity (QFCI, 2012). Besides, there is a high possibility of receiving more tweets from the areas with more people. Henceforth, interpreting disaster severity by the number of tweets generated in each area cannot be justified. Albeit, this study contributes to the current knowledge by considering the sentiment values of the geo-tagged tweets, rather than solely depending on the number of disaster-related tweets.

The study faced two main challenges in analysing Twitter data, which need to be addressed in prospective research. The first one is downloading geo-tagged tweets and classifying the texts for sentiment analysis. Twitter messages can be retrieved through an API or a commercial data provider. Capturing tweets through a Twitter API has certain limitations as the Twitter API method only provides access to 1% of publicly available Twitter data. Although Twitter data is available through data providers—i.e., DataSift, with 100% access, it is costly. Furthermore, Facebook has a strong data privacy policy which is time-consuming and costly to comply with (Guan & Chen, 2014).

The second one is that the study used decision tree algorithm to conduct the sentiment analysis as the highly cited machine learning algorithm for text classification. However, there are several other machine learning algorithms such as 'naïve bayes', and 'random forest' (Castillo et al., 2012; Feng & Sester, 2018) that could be used for sentiment analysis. Thus, future research should focus on proposing a suitable machine learning algorithm for sentiment analysis for those who conduct disaster-related tweet analysis.

4.6 Conclusion[1]

The study reported in this chapter contributes to the deepening of our understanding of the systematic application of volunteer crowdsourcing data for enhancing disaster management practices. The analysis of disaster-related tweets of the 2010-2011 SEQ Floods, through the lens of the social media analysis framework, generated invaluable insights.

---

[1] This chapter, with permission from the copyright holder, is a reproduced version of the following journal article: Kankanamge, N., Yigitcanlar, T., Goonetilleke, A., & Kamruzzaman, M. (2020). Determining disaster severity through social media analysis: Testing the methodology with South East Queensland Flood tweets. *International Journal of Disaster Risk Reduction*, 42, 101360.

First of all, the findings of the case study analysis reflected the significance of using social media information for disaster management. Social media analysis forms a collective analysis of the emotive and evaluative experiences and views of people, who experience and feel the impacts of disasters. As confirmed by the study findings, social media information simply does not generate new information. Instead, social media information is user-centric, geo-located, and responsive to the emerging information gaps. Accordingly, this study establishes the value of utilising social media information for multilateral collaborations among disaster management authorities, the community, and community-based organisations through the social media space.

Secondly, the study identified the significance of understanding disaster-related tweets across different periods. As disclosed in this chapter, a close analysis of such tweets will deliver an overarching image of pressing demands of different areas at different time-lapses. Having a better knowledge of the severity of the disaster, what to deliver, when to deliver, and where to deliver will help authorities to better plan their resources, and actions, and to make prompt and effective decisions to save lives.

Lastly, the study validated the applicability of geo-located tweets to identify disaster severities. Inequality of geo-located tweets is a highly stressed constraint so far, for using this method. Nevertheless, as the methodology adopted in the study considered both, sentiment values and locations of tweets, this limitation was addressed to a certain extent. Despite this limitation, the research findings shed light on new possibilities/opportunities for emergency managers and urban planners to incorporate volunteer crowdsourcing (through social media analysis and campaigns) to realise a more people-centric and effective disaster management practice.

References

ABS (2011). *2011 Census quick stats,* Australian Bureau of Statistics, https://quickstats. censusdata.abs.gov.au/census_services/getproduct/census/2011/quickstat/ 3001?opendocument.

ABS (2016). *2016 Census quick stats,* Australian Bureau of Statistics, https://quickstats. censusdata.abs.gov.au/census_services/getproduct/census/2016/quickstat/ UCL314009?opendocument.

Ahmad, K., Pogorelov, K., Riegler, M., Conci, N., & Halvorsen, P. (2018). Social media and satellites. *Multimedia Tools and Applications, 1,* 1–39.

Athanasia, N., & Stavros, P. T. (2015). Twitter as an instrument for crisis response: The Typhoon Haiyan case study. In *The 12th International Conference on Information Systems for Crisis Response and Management.*

ArcMap (2016). *How IDW works,* http://desktop.arcgis.com/en/arcmap/10.3/tools/3d-analyst-toolbox/how-idw-works.htm.

Arthur, R., Boulton, C.A., Shotton, H., & Williams, H.T. (2018). Social sensing of floods in the UK. *Plos One, 13,* 1–18.

Aslam-Saja, A.M., Teo, M., Goonetilleke, A., & Ziyath, A.M. (2018). An inclusive and adaptive framework for measuring social resilience to disasters. *International Journal of Disaster Risk Reduction, 28,* 862–873.

Asur, S., Huberman, B.A., Szabo, G., & Wang, C. (2011). Trends in social media, In *Proceedings of the fifth international AAAI conference on weblogs and social media.*

Baum, S., Kendall, E., Muenchberger, H., Gudes, O., & Yigitcanlar, T. (2010). Geographical information systems: An effective planning And decision-making platform for community health coalitions in Australia. *Health Information Management Journal, 39,* 28–33.

BoM (2012). *Report to Queensland Floods Commission of Inquiry,* Bureau of Meteorology.

Boulos, M.N., Resch, B., Crowley, D.N., Breslin, J.G., Sohn, G., Burtner, R., Pike, W.A., Jezierski, E., & Chuang, K.Y. (2011). Crowdsourcing, citizen sensing, and sensor web technologies for public and environmental health surveillance and crisis management. *International Journal of Health Geographics, 10,* 67–96.

Brabham, D.C. (2008). Crowdsourcing as a model for problem solving. *Convergence, 14,* 75–90.

Brabham, D.C. (2013). *Crowdsourcing.* MIT Press, Boston.

Burston, J., Ware, D., & Tomlinson, R. (2015). The real-time needs of emergency managers for tropical cyclone storm tide forecasting. *Natural Hazards, 78,* 1653–1668.

Callaghan, C. (2016). Disaster management, crowdsourced R&D, and probabilistic innovation theory. *International Journal of Disaster Risk Reduction, 17,* 238–250.

Castillo, C., Mendoza, M., & Poblete, B. (2012). Predicting information credibility in time-sensitive social media. *Internet Research, 23,* 560–588.

Chae, B. K. (2015). Insights from hashtag# supplychain and Twitter analytics: Considering Twitter and Twitter data for supply chain practice and research. *International Journal of Production Economics, 165,* 247–259.

Chang, V. (2015). Towards a big data system disaster recovery in a private cloud. *Ad Hoc Networks, 35,* 65–82.

Cowling, D. (2019) *Social Media Statistics Australia–March 2019,* Social media news, https://www.socialmedianews.com.au/social-media-statistics-australia-march-2019/

Crooks, A.T., & Wise, S. (2013). GIS and agent-based models for humanitarian assistance. *Computers, Environment and Urban Systems, 41,* 100–111.

De Albuquerque, J.P., Herfort, B., Brenning, A., & Zipf, A. (2015). A geographic approach for combining social media and authoritative data towards identifying useful information for disaster management. *International Journal of Geographical Information Science, 29,* 667–689.

Deng, Q., Liu, Y., Zhang, H., Deng, X., & Ma, Y. (2016). A new crowdsourcing model to assess disaster using microblog data in typhoon Haiyan. *Natural Hazards, 84,* 1241–1256.

Dror, T., Dalyot, S., & Doytsher, Y. (2015). Quantitative evaluation of volunteered geographic information paradigms. *Survey Review, 47,* 349–362.

Dufty, N. (2016). Twitter turns ten: Its use to date in disaster management. *Australian Journal of Emergency Management, 31,* 50–54.

Ernst, C., Mladenow, A., & Strauss, C. (2017). Collaboration and crowdsourcing in emergency management. *International Journal of Pervasive Computing and Communications, 13,* 176–193.

Estellés, A.E., & González, L.G. (2012). Towards an integrated crowdsourcing definition. *Journal of Information Science, 38,* 189–200.

Fan, W., & Gordon, M.D. (2014). The power of social media analytics. *Communications of the ACM, 57,* 74–81.

Feng, Y., & Sester, M. (2018). Extraction of pluvial flood relevant volunteered geographic information by deep learning from user generated texts and photos. *ISPRS International Journal of Geo-Information, 7,* 39–64.

Fritz, S., Fonte, C., & See, L. (2017). The role of citizen science in earth observation. *Remote Sensing, 9,* 357–370.

Gao, H., Barbier, G., Goolsby, R., & Zeng, D. (2011). Harnessing the crowdsourcing power of social media for disaster relief. *IEEE Intelligent Systems, 26,* 1541–1672.

Gardoni, P., & Murphy, C. (2010). Gauging the societal impacts of natural disasters using a capability approach. *Disasters, 34,* 619–636.

Givoni, M. (2016). Between micro mappers and missing maps. *Environment and Planning D, 34,* 1025–1043.

Goetz, M., & Zipf, A. (2013). The evolution of geo-crowdsourcing. In: *Crowdsourcing Geographic Knowledge.* Springer, Berlin, pp.139–159.

Goodchild, M.F. (2007). Citizens as sensors. *GeoJournal, 69,* 211–221.

Goodchild, M.F., Yuan, M., & Cova, T.J. (2007). Towards a general theory of geographic representation in GIS. *International Journal of Geographical Information Science, 21,* 239–260.

Goodchild, M.F. (2009). Neogeography and the nature of geographic expertise. *Journal of Location Based Services, 3,* 82–96.

Goodchild, M.F., & Glennon, J.A. (2010). Crowdsourcing geographic information for disaster response. *International Journal of Digital Earth, 3,* 231–241.

Goodchild, M.F., & Li, L. (2012). Assuring the quality of volunteered geographic information. *Spatial Statistics, 1,* 110–120.

Granell, C., & Ostermann, F.O. (2016). Beyond data collection. *Computers, Environment and Urban Systems, 59,* 231–243.

Gray, B.J., Weal, M.J., & Martin, D. (2016). Social media and disasters. *International Journal of Information Systems for Crisis Response and Management, 8,* 41–55.

Grover, P., Kar, A.K., & Davies, G. (2018). Technology enabled health. *International Journal of Information Management, 43,* 85–97.

Guan, X., & Chen, C. (2014). Using social media data to understand and assess disasters. *Natural Hazards, 74,* 837–850.

Gudes, O., Kendall, E., Yigitcanlar, T., Pathak, V., & Baum, S. (2010). Rethinking health planning: A framework for organising information to underpin collaborative health planning. *Health Information Management Journal, 39*(2), 18–29.

Han, S., Huang, H., Luo, Z., & Foropon, C. (2018). Harnessing the power of crowdsourcing and internet of things in disaster response. *Annals of Operations Research, 26,* 1–16.

Han, X., & Wang, J. (2019). Using social media to mine and analyse public sentiment during a disaster. *ISPRS International Journal of Geo-Information, 8,* 185–201.

Handmer, J., Choy, S., & Kohtake, N. (2014). Updating warning systems for climate hazards. *Australian Journal of Telecommunications and the Digital Economy, 2,* 70–84.

Harrison, S.E., & Johnson, P.A. (2016). Crowdsourcing the disaster management cycle. *International Journal of Infrastructure Systems for Crisis Response Management, 8,* 17–40.

Havas, C., Resch, B., Francalanci, C., Pernici, B., Scalia, G., Fernandez-Marquez, J., Van Achte, T., Zeug, G., Mondardini, M., Grandoni, D., Kirsch, B., Kalas, M., Lorini, V., & Rüping, S. (2017). E2mC. *Sensors*, *17*, 2766–2798.

Haworth, B., & Bruce, E. (2015). A review of volunteered geographic information for disaster management. *Geography Compass*, *9*, 237–250.

Haworth, B. (2016). Emergency management perspectives on volunteered geographic information. *Computers, Environment and Urban Systems*, *57*, 189–198.

Hermida, A. (2010). From TV to Twitter: How ambient news became ambient journalism. *Media/Culture Journal*, *2*, 1–6.

Hootsuite (2019). *Digital 2019*, Hootsuite, Canada, https://p.widencdn.net/kqy7ii/Digital2019-Report-en.

Howe, J. (2006). The rise of crowdsourcing. *Wired Magazine*, *14*, 1–4.

Kankanamge, N., Yigitcanlar, T., Goonetilleke, A., & Kamruzzaman, M. (2019). Can volunteer crowdsourcing reduce disaster risk? A systematic review of the literature. *International Journal of Disaster Risk Reduction*, *35*, 2212–2224.

Kantarci, B., Carr, K.G., & Pearsall, C.D. (2016). Social network assisted trustworthiness assurance in smart city crowdsensing. *International Journal of Distributed Systems and Technologies*, *7*, 59–78.

Koswatte, S., McDougall, K., & Liu, X. (2015). SDI and crowdsourced spatial information management automation for disaster management. *Survey Review*, *47*, 307–315.

Krippendorff, K. (2009). *The Content Analysis Reader*. SAGE.

Lagmay, A.M., Racoma, B.A., Aracan, K.A., Alconis-Ayco, J., & Saddi, I.L. (2017). Disseminating near-real-time hazards information and flood maps in the Philippines through web-GIS. *Journal of Environmental Sciences*, *59*, 13–23.

Liu, S.B., & Palen, L. (2010). The new cartographers. *Cartography and Geographic Information Science*, *37*, 69–90.

Liu, S.B. (2014). Crisis crowdsourcing framework. *Computer Supported Cooperative Work*, *23*, 389–443.

Ludwig, T., Kotthaus, C., Reuter, C., Van Dongen, S., & Pipek, V. (2017). Situated crowdsourcing during disasters. *International Journal of Human-Computer Studies*, *102*, 103–121.

Lue, E., Wilson, J. P., & Curtis, A. (2014). Conducting disaster damage assessments with Spatial Video, experts, and citizens. *Applied Geography*, *52*, 46–54.

McCormick, S. (2016). New tools for emergency managers. *Disasters*, *40*, 207–225.

Michel, U., Thunig, H., & Reinartz, P. (2012). Rapid change detection algorithm for disaster management. In: *Proceedings of the ISPRS Annals of the Photogrammetry, Remote Sensing and Spatial Information Sciences*, Melbourne.

Miller, H.J., & Goodchild, M.F. (2015). Data-driven geography. *GeoJournal*, *80*, 449–461.

Neubaum, G., Rösner, L., Rosenthal-von der Pütten, A.M., & Krämer, N.C. (2014). Psychosocial functions of social media usage in a disaster situation. *Computers in Human Behavior*, *34*, 28–38.

Ngamassi, L., Ramakrishnan, T., & Rahman, S. (2020). Investigating the use of social media by underserved communities for disaster management. In *Proceedings of the 17th International Conference on Information Systems for Crisis Response and Management (ISCRAM)*, pp. 490–496.

Perrin, A. (2015). *Social Media Usage*. Pew Research Centre.

Panteras, G., Wise, S., Lu, X., Croitoru, A., Crooks, A., & Stefanidis, A. (2015). Triangulating social multimedia content for event localisation using Flickr and Twitter. *Transactions in GIS*, *19*, 694–715.

Pitrėnaitė-Žilenienė, B., Carosi, A., & Vallesi, P. (2014). Enhancing societal resilience against disasters. *Social Technologies, 4*, 318–332.

Poblet, M., García-Cuesta, E., & Casanovas, P. (2017). Crowdsourcing roles, methods, and tools for data-intensive disaster management. *Information Systems Frontiers, 1*, 1–17.

QFCI (2012). *Final Report.* Queensland Floods Commission of Inquiry, Queensland.

Ragini, J.R., Anand, P.R., & Bhaskar, V. (2018). Big data analytics for disaster response and recovery through sentiment analysis. *International Journal of Information Management, 42*, 13–24.

Riccardi, M.T. (2016). The power of crowdsourcing in disaster response operations. *International Journal of Disaster Risk Reduction, 20*, 123–128.

Roche, S., Propeck-Zimmermann, E., & Mericskay, B. (2013). GeoWeb and crisis management. *GeoJournal, 78*, 21–40.

Sachdeva, S., McCaffrey, S., & Locke, D. (2017). Social media approaches to modeling wildfire smoke dispersion. *Information, Communication & Society, 20*, 1146–1161.

Sagun, A., Bouchlaghem, D., & Anumba, C.J. (2009). A scenario-based study on information flow and collaboration patterns in disaster management. *Disasters, 33*, 214–238.

Shaw, F., Burgess, J., Crawford, K., & Bruns, A. (2013). Sharing news, making sense, saying thanks: Patterns of talk on twitter during the Queensland floods. *Australian Journal of Communication, 1*, 23–40.

Shklovski, I., Burke, M., Kiesler, S., & Kraut, R. (2010). Technology adoption and use in the aftermath of Hurricane Katrina in New Orleans. *American Behavioral Scientist, 53*, 1228–1246.

Sosko, S., & Dalyot, S. (2017). Crowdsourcing user-generated mobile sensor weather data for densifying static geosensor networks. *ISPRS International Journal of Geo-Information, 6*, 61–83.

Surowiecki, J. (2004). *The Wisdom of Crowds.* Doubleday, London.

Twitter (2013). *The year on Twitter,* https://blog.twitter.com/en_gb/a/en-gb/2013/2013-the-year-on-twitter.html.

Twitter (2014). *The year on Twitter,* https://blog.twitter.com/en_gb/a/en-gb/2014/2014-the-year-on-twitter.html.

Van Den Honert, R.C., & McAneney, J. (2011). The 2011 Brisbane floods. *Water, 3*, 1149–1173.

Verstappen, H.T. (1995). Aerospace technology and natural disaster reduction. *Advances in Space Research, 15*, 3–15.

Wan, Z., Hong, Y., Khan, S., Gourley, J., Flamig, Z., Kirschbaum, D., & Tang, G. (2014). A cloud-based global flood disaster community cyber-infrastructure. *Environmental Modelling & Software, 58*, 86–94.

Wilkinson, M.D., Dumontier, M., Aalbersberg, I.J., Appleton, G., Axton, M., Baak, A., Blomberg, N., Boiten, J.W., da Silva Santos, L.B., Bourne, P.E., & Bouwman, J. (2016). The FAIR guiding principles for scientific data management and stewardship. *Scientific Data, 3*, 1–9.

Xiao, Y., Huang, Q., & Wu, K. (2015). Understanding social media data for disaster management. *Natural Hazards, 79*, 1663–1679.

Yang, D., Zhang, D., Frank, K., Robertson, P., Jennings, E., Roddy, M., & Lichtenstern, M. (2014). Providing real-time assistance in disaster relief by leveraging crowdsourcing power. *Personal Ubiquitous Computing, 18*, 2025–2034.

Yuan, F., & Liu, R. (2018). Crowdsourcing for forensic disaster investigations. *Natural Hazards, 93*, 1–18.

Yigitcanlar, T. (2005). Is Australia ready to move planning to online mode? *Australian Planner, 42*, 42–51.

Yigitcanlar, T. (2006). Australian local governments' practice and prospects with online planning. *URISA Journal, 18*, 7–17.

Yigitcanlar, T. (2009). Planning for smart urban ecosystems: Information technology applications for capacity building in environmental decision making. *Theoretical and Empirical Researches in Urban Management, 4*, 5–21.

Yigitcanlar, T. (2015). Smart cities: An effective urban development and management model? *Australian Planner, 52*, 27–34.

Yigitcanlar, T. (2016). *Technology and the city: Systems, Applications, and Implications.* Routledge, New York.

Yigitcanlar, T., & Kamruzzaman, M. (2018). Does smart city policy lead to sustainability of cities? *Land Use Policy, 73*, 49–58.

Zhang, C., Zhao, T., & Li, W. (2010). Automatic search of geospatial features for disaster and emergency management. *International Journal of Applied Earth Observation and Geoinformation, 12*, 409–418.

Zhang, X., Yi, L., & Zhao, D. (2013). Community-based disaster management: A review of progress in China. *Natural Hazards, 65*, 2215–2239.

5

Social Media Analytics in Pandemic Policy

5.1 Introduction

Human beings have witnessed many pandemic events with catastrophic impacts on their health and socioeconomic wellbeing (Qiu et al., 2017; Reshadat et al., 2019a). Yellow fever outbreak, cholera, plague, tuberculosis, Spanish flu, Ebola, AIDS, influenza, and West Nile disease are among some notable examples of pandemics (Saunders-Hastings & Krewski, 2016).

Since the 80s, the globalisation process of the world has increased the threat of diseases as well as accelerated the spread of novel viruses (Tumpey et al., 2005). The latest one, the novel coronavirus (SARS-CoV-2) has been spreading globally since its outbreak and rapid transmission in late 2019 in Wuhan, China. World Health Organization (WHO) termed the infection as COVID-19 and declared the outbreak as a pandemic in March 2020 (WHO, 2020)

As of 1 July 2020, the global COVID-19 cases have reached up to 10,574,637 infected people, and 513,144 deaths (Worldometer, 2020). Besides the global health implications (Zhang et al., 2020), the COVID-19 outbreak has also had global socioeconomical and behavioural impacts. The pandemic has influenced human behaviour in a way that results in panic, overbuying, and non-compliance with government restrictions (Ling & Chyong Ho, 2020). On the other hand, the economic impact of COVID-19 is also immense as many national economies are in recession, this will likely lead to a global financial crisis down the track (Daneshpour, 2020).

In efforts to curb the pandemic, numerous scientific clinical trials and medical research have been undertaken, including the development of vaccines to treat the disease. Non-clinical measures—mainly the government interventions, e.g., social distancing policies, self-isolation, quarantines, movement control, travel restrictions, and lockdowns—are also adopted to control the further spread of COVID-19 (Honey-Roses et al., 2020).

The outbreak of COVID-19 has had a profound impact on urban transport and mobility, where restrictions on travel and social gatherings have been announced to limit the spread (Newman, 2020). For instance, as of 21 April 2020, the average mobility via public transit, on-foot, bike, and personal vehicles decreased to less than 10% in Vienna, London, New York, Madrid, Moscow, Singapore, and Milan

DOI: 10.1201/9781003278986-7

(Statista, 2020). In addition, home-based office and online education became other salient features of the global pandemic period (Jones et al., 2020). This has turned our homes into a mixed-use place with home schooling space for the kids and work from home space for adults (Shenker, 2020).

Meanwhile, the lockdown also exhibited an extraordinary demand for e-commerce for daily necessities and activities—e.g., groceries, medicines, clothes, and ready foods. This has triggered an increased use of digital technologies and platforms, including social media, by the public. The increased data, via social media channels, generates an opportunity for authorities to benefit from crowd-sourced information to capture public perception in order to make well-informed decisions.

Especially over the past decade, social media has become one of the major data sources for academic research (Alzahrani, 2016; Brooker et al., 2016), government departments, private and not-for-profit organisations, and individuals (Sebei et al., 2018). Besides, social media analytics can also benefit government authorities by capturing public opinions on and extracting relevant messages regarding the COVID-19 pandemic.

This chapter aims to generate insights into how social media analytics can assist authorities in pandemic-related policy decisions that are needed to ease or control pandemics. To achieve the research purpose, this study undertakes a social media analysis of geotagged tweets originated from Australian states and territories between 1 January 2020 and 4 May 2020.

5.2 Literature Background

5.2.1 Epidemic and Pandemic

An epidemic is an outbreak of a disease that is not anticipated but spreads quickly and affects many people. It may particularly have a bigger toll on the underprivileged population (Reshadat et al., 2019b). An example of epidemic would be the 2013–2016 Western African Ebola virus epidemic that took about 11,310 lives (Chowell et al., 2015). An outbreak can occur in a community, geographical area or several countries. In an epidemic, symptomatic cases are the predominant focus of treatment and usually represent the bulk of reported cases. Nonetheless, infected individuals who are asymptomatic yet infectious can be a critical factor in the spread of some pathogens (Fraser et al., 2004).

A pandemic is a type of epidemic that relates to geographic spread and describes a disease—e.g., COVID-19—that affects an entire country, continent or most parts of the world. An epidemic becomes a pandemic when it spreads over significant geographical areas and affects a large proportion of the population. A pandemic: (a) Affects a wider geographical area, and often worldwide; (b) Infects a larger number of people; (c) Is often caused by a new virus or a new strain of virus that has not circulated within people for a long time; (d) Is where people have little to no immunity against the virus and it spreads quickly; (e) Causes more deaths; and (f) Often creates social disruption and economic loss. Examples of past pandemics include the Flu pandemic of 1968, HIV/AIDS pandemic, and Bubonic plague. The terms pandemic and epidemic are not used to indicate the severity of the disease, they only indicate the degree at which the disease is spreading (Rochester Regional Health, 2020)

5.2.2 Stages of a Pandemic Spread

5.2.2.1 Pre-concave

The first stage (Stage 1) of the spread of a pandemic disease, e.g., COVID-19, is the pre-concave stage. This is when infected people travelled from affected countries into other countries. In Stage 1, only those who have travelled abroad test positive for the disease. The disease does not spread locally at this stage (Bharat, 2020).

Some of the interventions at this stage, in the case of COVID-19, include: (a) Activating border measures; (b) Contact tracing; (c) Cancel mass gatherings of people; (d) Staying at home if sick and have the symptoms; (e) Intensive testing for the virus; and (e) Physical distancing encouragement (Wade, 2020).

5.2.2.2 Concave-Up

The second stage (Stage 2) in the spread of a pandemic disease is the concave-up stage. This is the stage when local transmission occurs and its sources—e.g., originally infected patients who possibly had travel history to other already affected countries, are known and can be located. They would have come in close contact with the patients in situations such as family get-togethers or occasions, where many people gather like in weddings and parties (Bharat, 2020). At this stage the virus might be contained, but the risk of community transmission still grows, and the number of new cases show increase.

Some of the interventions at this stage, in the case of COVID-19, include: (a) Maximising entry border measures; (b) Further restrictions on mass gatherings; (c) Physical distancing on public transport; (d) Limiting non-essential travel around the country; (e) Employers begin alternative ways of working—e.g., working from home, shifts, and so on; (f) Activating business contingency plans; and (g) Remaining at home for people—particularly high risk groups (Wade, 2020).

5.2.2.3 Linear

The third stage (Stage 3) of the spread of a pandemic disease is the linear stage. At this stage, transmission rate of the disease has become stable—in other words, the number of new cases stay the same or change in a smaller variation in the linear stage.

Some of the interventions at this stage, in the case of COVID-19, include: (a) Traveling in areas of community transmission is limited; (b) Affected educational facilities closed; (c) Mass ways of working required and non-essential businesses are closed; (d) Non-face-to-face primary consultations; (e) Elective surgeries and procedures deferred; and (f) Healthcare staff are reprioritised (Wade, 2020).

5.2.2.4 Concave-Down

The fourth stage (Stage 4) of the spread of a pandemic disease is the concave-down stage. At this stage, the transmission rate of the disease shows a decline—in other words, the number of new cases decrease.

Some of the interventions at this stage, in the case of COVID-19, include: (a) Staying at home; (b) Closing educational facilities; (c) Closing all non-essential businesses; (d) Rationing of supplies and requisitioning of facilities; (e) Severe travel restrictions; and (f) Major reprioritisation of healthcare services (Wade, 2020).

5.2.3 Global Suppression Measures

5.2.3.1 Flattening the Curve

During a pandemic situation, a tall and skinny curve of infected people to date is highly undesired (Figure 5.1). This means a lot of people will get infected at once in a short period of time, because inadequate actions have been undertaken to prevent the disease from spreading. While most people might not get sick enough to be hospitalised, those who do could easily overwhelm the number of beds, equipment and healthcare staff available (Gavin, 2020).

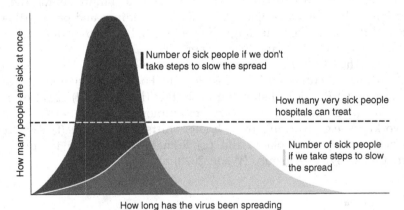

FIGURE 5.1
Flattening the curve function. (Derived from Gavin, 2020.)

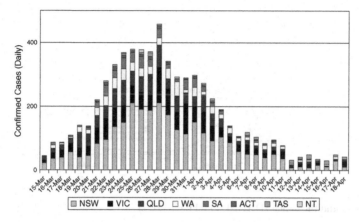

FIGURE 5.2
The flattened COVID-19 curve in Australia. (Derived from Wargent, 2020.)

For instance, in the case of COVID-19, to this point, Australia has been highly successful in flattening the curve. The number of daily new COVID-19 cases in Australia is comparatively low (Figure 5.2). This means, thus far, the spread of COVID-19 has been slowed down and Australia has the capacity in the healthcare system to manage the impact of SARS-CoV-2. Nevertheless, the ultimate success depends on following government directives and maintaining the new community norm—e.g., social distancing, good hygiene practices, and using the COVIDSafe app (Hu, 2020). As for the businesses, this also means taking the time to prepare and develop a plan to operate in a COVID-19 safe way to protect customers and employees (DoH, 2020a).

5.2.3.2 Hammer and Dance

The hammer; in a pandemic situation, it is crucial to act quickly and aggressively. Hammering a pandemic, e.g., COVID-19, within a few weeks means it is controlled, and authorities are in a much better shape to address its disruption. Applying a heavy hammer with strict social distancing measures can help immensely in controlling the outbreak within weeks (Pueyo, 2020).

The dance, according to Pueyo's (2020) graph, during the dance and in the case of COVID-19, it is crucial to go through the isolation and social distancing, ban large gatherings, test people properly, and also tighten up restrictions when needed.

The dance R, some countries/cities/regions can experience outbreaks again, others may not for long periods of time. Depending on how cases evolve, it is needed to tighten up or relax social distancing measures. That is called the 'Dance of R', which is a dance of measures between getting our lives back on track and spreading the disease—e.g., balancing economic, health measures, and outcomes (Figure 5.3). During the hammer, the goal is to get R as close

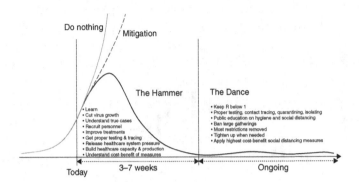

FIGURE 5.3
The hammer and the dance. (Derived from Pueyo, 2020.)

to zero, as fast as possible, to quench the pandemic. Once it moves into the dance, it is not needed to be done anymore. The goal is to bring down the R value below 1 (Pueyo, 2020).

5.2.4 Social Media Analytics

Social media analytics are started to be used in the health sector these days. During the past decades, social media has redesigned the relationships in communities without any commercial objectives (Kankanamge et al., 2019). People become more expressive in social media than face to face direct discussions. Hence, the use of social media data for opinion mining, topic modelling, and sentiment analysis could benefit policy- and decision-makers to understand true public interest about health-related issues (Kankanamge et al., 2020a).

For instance, social media analytics were used to increase the efficiency of the health sector in different ways (Paul & Dredze, 2014). Some of the examples include: (a) Predictions-related to non-contagious diseases, e.g., heart disease mortality using psychological language used in tweets (Eichstaedt et al., 2015); (b) Predictions-related to contagious diseases, e.g., the use of tweets to evaluate the disease activity and the US public perceptions during the influenza H1N1 pandemic (Signorini et al., 2011); (c) Governance in health, e.g., adapting social media in local health departments (Harris et al., 2013); (d) Awareness raising, e.g., health information dissemination through social networks (Scanfeld et al., 2010); (e) Study on non-healthy addictions, e.g., college student's addiction to alcohol using Facebook and Twitter posts (Moreno et al., 2016); (f) Student education in the health sector, e.g., importance in introducing social media analytics to nursing curriculum (Jones et al., 2016); and (g) Healthcare professionals-related issues, e.g., women in the health sector (Devi, 2015). Nevertheless, the use of social media analytics to increase the efficiency of community centric policy decisions during a pandemic is still an understudied area of research.

5.3 Research Design

An empirical investigation is undertaken to answer the research question—How can social media analytics assist authorities in pandemic-related policy decisions? This investigation will help in understanding the behavioural tendencies of Australia's states and territories during the COVID-19 pandemic. The research steps include determining the case study, identifying the methodological approach, collection of data, and execution of the analysis.

5.3.1 Case Study

Australia is a suitable country to investigate the research question empirically for the following reasons. Australia is an advanced nation with a diverse culture that adapts the technological trends of the world, with the largest being, social media (Cowling, 2020). In 2018, 79% of Australian's used social media and the average number of internet-enabled devices owned is 3.5 (Sensis, 2018). Like the rest of the world, Australia has been facing the COVID-19 disruption across all states and territories, adapting to social distancing restrictions, and altered ways of life to stop the spread. Between 1 January 2020 and 4 May 2020, Australia had a total of 6,849 confirmed cases of COVID-19 and 96 related deaths (AG, 2020)—as of 1 July 2020 these figures have reached to 7,836 and 104 respectively. The states and territories with the most infections are coherent with population numbers, descending from NSW to VIC, QLD, WA, SA, TAS, ACT, and NT. Outbreaks have occurred in each state and territory in different ways, mostly relating to overseas travel/visitors. The largest outbreak occurred on the Ruby Princess cruise ship, which docked in Sydney allowing its passengers to leave (NSW Government, 2020).

5.3.2 Methodological Approach

In the digital age, that is upon us, local community perceptions and suggestions about the changes happen in and around their environment are well reflected through social media messages (Faasse & Newby, 2020). A thorough analysis of such social media data will help to understand the community demands, issues, and reflections (Yigitcanlar et al., 2020a). Accordingly, this study analysed geotagged Twitter social media messages circulated by the general public related to COVID-19 in Australia. Twitter has become the fastest growing social media platform source in the world. It also offers an Application Programming Interface (API) to researchers and practitioners to conduct analysis—such as the one undertaken in this study.

5.3.3 Data and Tools

An ethical approval was obtained to obtain and analyse the social media posts of the Australian public. The first step, after the ethics clearance, in the

TABLE 5.1

List of Keywords

Keywords
1 meter distance, 1.5 meter distance, 2 meters distance, Auslaw, australialockdown, BigGovVirus, bleed, boarder/s, bored, boredinhouse, chest pain, china virus, ChinaLiedPeopleDied, chinese virus, clammy, cold, corona, corona virus, CoronaAU, coronaAUS, coronaaustralia, coronagoaway, CoronaSpread, CoronaVillains, coronavirus, coronavirusapp, coronavirusaustralia, CoronavirusLiar, CoronavirusOutbreak, CoronavirusPandemic, CoronaVirusUpdate, CoronaWarriorsAu, cough, coughing, cover mouth, cover nose, Covid, Covid – 19, Covid 2019, Covid 2020, Covid_19australia, COVID19au, COVID19Aus, Covid-19australia, Covid19Outbreak, COVIDIOTS, cruise, cruise staff, DontTouch, DontTradeWithChina, drowsy, elbow cough, facemask, facial drooping, false, fatigue, fever, FightCoronaWithPositivity, flu, hand sanitiser, health workers, HealthForAll, HerdImmunity, homeschool, homeschooling, hotspot, immunity, isolation, ISOLife, jobless, lockdown, N95 mask, new virus, OneWorldTogetherAtHome, online education, online learning, online teaching, outbreak, pale, pandemic, panicbuying, panicbuyingau, panicshopping, passengers, PCR, PrayForHeros, quarantine, quarantinelife, realheros, remotelearning, RemoteWorking, Ruby Princess, salute, sars-cov-2, SatyAtHomeSaveLives, schoolclosure, scomovirus, seizure, selfdistancing, selfisolation, shortness of breath, shutdown, social distancing, SocialDistancing2020, socialdistancingfail, sore throat, stay safe, stayhome, StayHomeAustralia, StopTheSpread, StopTheSpreadOfCorona, SupportAustralians, surgical masks, symptoms, temperature, test, urgent, use mask, vaccination, vaccine, virus, vuhan virus, WashYourHands, WHO, WorkFromHome, WorkingFromHomeTips, Wuhan virus, Wuhanvirus

methodology was a document survey to identify the actions taken by the Australian Governments (federal and state/territory) in response to the COVID-19 pandemic. This involved a collection of official government health department documents on COVID-19 in Australia—e.g., Pandemic Health Intelligence Plan at the federal level, and the Queensland Whole-of-Government Pandemic Plan at the state level. Such official documents were screened to identify 128 keywords (Table 5.1) to obtain/download related Twitter posts (a.k.a. tweets).

The second stage of the data collection involved the extraction of relevant Twitter information in the form of tweets. This is considered 'open data' and is publicly available to anyone. Tweets were extracted from the Digital Observatory of the Queensland University of Technology (QUT) (www.qut. edu.au/institute-for-future-environments/facilities/digital-observatory). Only the geotagged tweets were obtained as the locations of these posts were important for the analysis/study. Initially 96,666 geotagged tweets were collected using over pre-identified keywords related to COVID-19 symptoms, behaviours, precautions, and services. Some of the examples of symptom-related keywords include the text such as fever, flu, fatigue, cough and, temperature. Examples of behaviour-related keywords include the text such as social distancing, isolation, quarantine, bored, and working from home. Examples of precaution-related keywords include the text such as facemask, hand sanitiser, and cover mouth. Examples of service-related keywords include the text such as health workers, salute, and real heroes.

The third step is to clean the data. This procedure began with a data pre-processing stage, involving the removal of automated messages, irrelevant messages, and URLs. The removal of these items was conducted using Arthur et al.'s (2018) process. The first of these was to remove automated messages with bot filtering, which discarded automated Twitter accounts that produced a high volume of tweets, affecting the data. The second step was relevance filtering, removing irrelevant tweets that contained keywords from the word bag (e.g., "the temperature is very high today"). The last was to remove URLs, which separated the URLs from the tweets so that a further analysis on the content of the URLs could be conducted. Excel software was used for the data cleaning processes. After filtering, 35,969 geotagged tweets were selected to conduct the sentiment analysis. For this analysis, an open access software for machine learning and data mining, known as WEKA, was employed—a software with a collection of visualisation tools. The Random Forest algorithm was used for data analysis and predictive modelling (Kankanamge et al., 2020b).

The fourth step in this process was to create a word bag to identify the community sentiments based on the filtered tweets. Accordingly, words such as dying/dead were classified as negative and the words, which express positive emotions such as enjoy and happy were classified as positive sentiments. In total, 1,183 words were used for this analysis; 588 of them with positive and 595 with negative sentiments. In determining the word bags, the study used the following steps. Firstly, a random sample of 1,000 tweets were inspected to identify the initial pool of word bags. Secondly, around 60% of total tweets (about 20,000 tweets) were screened to see the representation of the initial pool. Additional words were included in the word bags pool as a result of this screening. Thirdly, a randomised check of 500 tweets is conducted to confirm the words assigned in each sentiment category—i.e., positive and negative sentiments. Lastly, the list of 1,183 words were finalised (588 positive, 595 negative). Examples of the word bags developed based on the analysed tweets are listed in Table 5.2.

TABLE 5.2

Word Bag Examples

Word Bag	Example
Positive	Adapt, best, better, cure, defeat, distance, discharge, exercise, facemask, fight, fun, handwash, healing, help, homedelivery, good, glad, great, hope, immunity, informative, joy, love, prepare, productive, protect, recover, release, safe, safety-first, stable, save, security, stay-home, support, survive, saving, treat, thank, vaccine, wash, well, welfare, win, wish, wonderful.
Negative	Abuse, apocalypse, angry, anxiety, bad, catastrophic, contract, cough, crisis, danger, dead, death, delay, die, disgusted, disease, ebola, emergency, fail, fever, fighting, fired, hazard, homeless, hurt, infect, kill, outbreak, pain, problem, recession, respiratory, resist, regret, scare, sick, stress, stupid, violence, victim, vulnerable, waste, worry, wtf.

The final step is to identify the frequently used words in each sentiment category. Accordingly, the frequently used words were identified by each state by each sentiment category. For this NVivo software was utilised—a qualitative data analysis software package.

5.4 Results

5.4.1 General Observations

Out of 35,969 geotagged tweets analysed, about 63% were negatively classified, and almost 37% were positively classified. Most of the negatively classified tweets were posted during the pre-concave stage (70%). About 63% of the tweets circulated within the concave-up and linear stages carried negative sentiments. The concave-down stage had the least percentage of negatively classified tweets (62%). Majority of the negatively classified tweets were tweeted from NSW, VIC, WA, and ACT people. Accordingly, in these states and territories, there were 9,885 more negatively classified tweets than the positively classified tweets.

The concave-up stage is the most critical period of a pandemic curve. During this period the number of confirmed cases rapidly increase within a shorter time period. Nonetheless, the Australian government developed 14 major responses to control the dispersion of COVID-19. Accordingly, on average, the concave-up stage of Australia lasted only for around 16 days and 29% of the total tweets were circulated within this shorter time period.

5.4.2 Suppression Measures

Transmission of COVID-19 can be categorised into (a) Small chains of transmission, and (b) Large chains resulting in extensive spread. Countries such as Sri Lanka and New Zealand took strong measures at the earliest, and ended up in small chains of transmission. The countries that have not taken strong measures at the earliest ended up in large chains of transmission such as USA and Brazil (Anderson et al., 2020).

Australia took strong actions to fight with this new pandemic. On 25th January 2020, the first COVID-19 patient was confirmed, who had flown to Melbourne from Guangdong Province of China on 19 January 2020 (DoH, 2020b). On 1 February 2020, Australian government blocked China arrivals to the country. Since then, until 4 May 2020, Australian government has developed 14 major responses—so-called pandemic responses—to control spreading the COVID-19 in Australia, and another 7 major responses—so-called economic responses—to address the economic downturn (AG, 2020). These 21 major governmental responses are listed in Table 5.3, and also marked in Figures 5.4–5.12.

TABLE 5.3

Major Responses Undertaken by the Australian Government to Combat COVID-19

No	Date	Response
1	01/02/2020	Blocked China arrivals[a]
2	29/02/2020	Blocked Iran arrivals[a]
3	05/03/2020	Blocked South Korea arrivals[a]
4	11/03/2020	Blocked Italy arrivals[a]
5	13/03/2020	Outdoor gatherings limited to 500 persons[a]
6	16/03/2020	Self-isolation for overseas travellers, cruise ships blocked for 30 days[a]
7	18/03/2020	Indoor gatherings limited to 100 persons[a]
8	19/03/2020	Borders closed to non-citizens and residents[a]
9	20/03/2020	Started to pay JobSeeker payments[b]
10	23/03/2020	Pubs/clubs closed, restaurants take-away only[a]
11	24/03/2020	Ban on Australians travelling overseas[a]
12	25/03/2020	Temporarily reduced minimum drawdown rated for superannuation[b]
13	26/03/2020	Expanded testing criteria[a]
14	28/03/2020	Mandatory isolation in hotels for all travellers[a]
15	30/03/2020	Outdoor/indoor gatherings two persons only[a]
16	31/03/2020	Provided payments of $750 to social security, veteran and other income support recipients[b]
17	26/04/2020	The COVIDSafe App is released[a]
18	27/04/2020	Expanded eligibility to income support payments[b]
19	27/04/2020	Paid the time restricted COVID-19 supplement of $500 which paid per fortnight[b]
20	01/05/2020	Increased transfer payments from reduced deeming rates[b]
21	04/05/2020	Started to pay JobKeeper payments[b]

[a] Health response
[b] Economic response

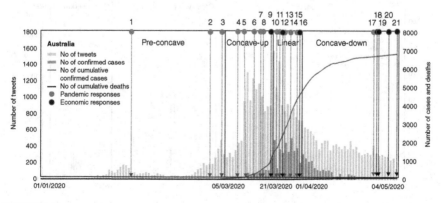

FIGURE 5.4
Distribution of tweets and confirmed COVID-19 cases in Australia.

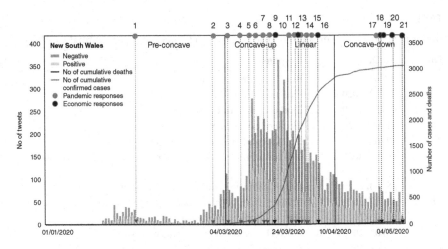

FIGURE 5.5
Distribution of tweets by the public perceptions in NSW.

Figure 5.4 shows the dispersion of confirmed COVID-19 cases, deaths, the tweets circulated in Australia and the responses undertaken by the Australian government to stop the spreading of COVID-19. As shown in Figure 5.4, the number of tweets and the number of confirmed cases have a positive relationship with a statistical correlation of 0.72 at 0.05 significance level. This shows that the number of tweets changed according to the number of confirmed cases. Furthermore, Figure 5.4 emphasised that 21 major governmental responses (14 health and 7 economic) to the pandemic undoubtedly have led to the flattening of the COVID-19 pandemic curve of Australia.

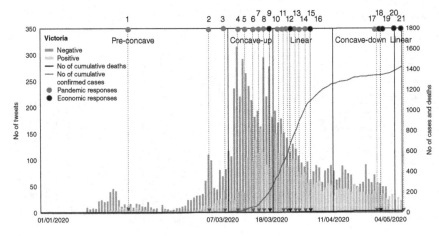

FIGURE 5.6
Distribution of tweets by the public perceptions in VIC.

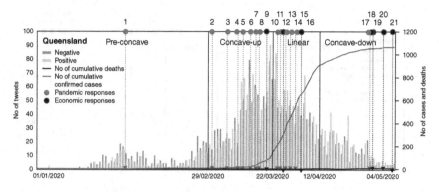

FIGURE 5.7
Distribution of tweets by the public perceptions in QLD.

When governments respond to a pandemic, their economy also get affected. Hence, taking strong economic responses simultaneously with pandemic responses is important to battle a pandemic effectively (ABS, 2018). Among such responses, community welfare needs to be given priority as people go out of jobs due to unprecedented pandemic responses such as social distancing, self-isolation, and restriction to mass gatherings. As listed Table 5.3, Australian government introduced 7 major economic responses within the study period. They were oriented towards delivering funds to the financially struggling people, and unemployed (Australian Government, 2020a, b). Additionally, the federal government decided to reduce social security deeming rates. Accordingly, on 1 May 2020, the upper and lower deeming rates were 2.25% and 0.25% respectively. These reductions created a low interest

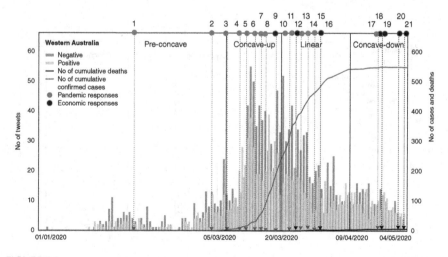

FIGURE 5.8
Distribution of tweets by the community perceptions in WA.

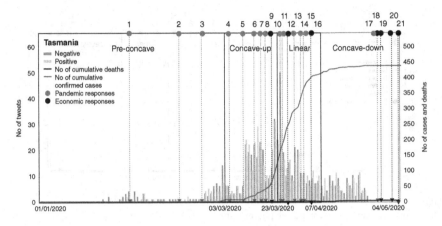

FIGURE 5.9
Distribution of tweets by the public perceptions in SA.

environment, which benefitted around 900,000 income support recipients, and around 565,000 pensioners.

Albeit, the community perceptions towards such 'radical' and 'unprecedented' measures need to be reviewed closely and thoroughly. Most significantly, during pandemic situations, where social distancing is a must, social media analytics can help policy- and decision-makers to screen community behaviours without reaching the community directly. Table 5.4 contains the most frequent used across all the four stages. In all of the phases, the words such as coronavirus, covid, COVID-19, covidaus, pandemic, virus, and outbreak were used and repeated extensively. For that reason, such words were not included in Table 5.4.

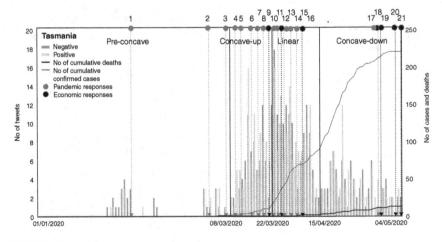

FIGURE 5.10
Distribution of tweets by the public perceptions in TAS.

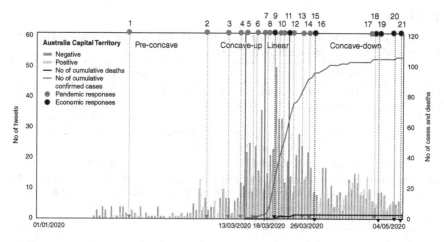

FIGURE 5.11
Distribution of tweets by the public perceptions in ACT.

Figures 5.5–5.12 illustrate the distribution of positively and negatively classified tweets in all Australian states and territories—along with the number of infection cases and deaths. In Australia, the only state/territory that did not experienced the COVID-19 concave-up stage was NT (Figure 5.12). This is due to successful execution of health responses in line with the hammer and dance approach (presented in the literature background section). In the case of VIC, the last week of the analysis (27 April to 04 May 2020) has shown an increase in the confirmed cases. Hence, that week was registered as the second linear stage (Figure 5.5). This is an example of pandemics not having a consistent pattern. Without the right responses and interventions, a second wave could be experienced.

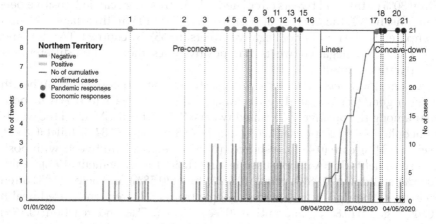

FIGURE 5.12
Distribution of tweets by the public perceptions in NT.

TABLE 5.4

The Most Frequent Positive and Negative Words of Pre-concave, Concave-Up, Linear, and Concave-Down Stages in All States

	Positive	Negative
Pre-concave	People (0.89%), health (0.63%), test (0.49%), government (0.47%), care (0.46%)	People (0.87%), cases (0.74%), travel (0.69%), death (0.55%), outbreak (0.5%), spread (0.4%)
Concave-up	People (0.81%), good (0.63%), help (0.53%), stay (0.47%), support (0.4%)	People (0.41%), cases (0.45%)
Linear	People (0.75%), test (0.43%), home (0.43%)	People (0.78%), home (0.4%)
Concave down	Safe (0.97%), start (0.8%), people (0.67%), work (0.66%), test (0.58%), days (0.56%), support (0.52%), stay (0.46%), health (0.42%), government (0.41%)	People (0.69%), deaths (0.45%), suffer (0.42%), work (0.4%), home (0.4%)

In all figures presented, there was a small twitter peak in the pre-concave stage, when there was no significant number of confirmed cases. Such unusual twitter peaks provide an indication of a possible disaster, an unusual behaviour in the environment, or a special community demand (Castillo et al., 2013; Feng & Sester, 2018; Kankanamge et al., 2020c). Thus, mining the perceptions of the general public via social media platforms during a pandemic is essential for policy- and decision-makers to take people-centric decisions, while adhering to the regulations of social distancing and so on.

5.4.3 Positive Community Perceptions

5.4.3.1 Pre-concave

Only 30% of the total tweets circulated within this stage carried positive perceptions. In NT, the number of positive tweets (n=105) in this stage was high compared to the number of negative tweets (n=65). By contrast, TAS, SA, and QLD had more negative tweets than positive ones, though their difference is comparatively small.

Among the tweets circulated in NT, the words of people (0.73%), health (0.55%), good (0.55%), family, government (0.45%), and learn (0.41%) were popular among the positively classified tweets. People from TAS used the words of people (2.09%), response (1.26%), masks (0.84%), save (0.84%), toilet (0.84%), paper (0.84%), care (0.42%), resources (0.42%) frequently in tweets with positive sentiments. In SA people used testing (1.09%), management (0.9%), health (0.81%), shutdown (0.98%), people (0.65%), toilet (0.58%), and help (0.45%) often to express their positive attitudes. People from QLD frequently used health (0.91%), good (0.88%), quarantine (0.84%), test (0.7%) and reaction (0.46%) words to express their positive ideas. Table 5.5 shows the example tweets circulated related to the abovementioned words.

TABLE 5.5

Example Tweets with Positive Sentiments Circulated Within Pre-concave Stage

Date and Time	State	Keyword	Exemplar Tweet
18/04/2020 05:31	SA	Health	Deloitte develops digital accelerator healthcare systems for communities to address covid19 crisis #exphealthcare
30/03/2020 13:27	VIC	Family	Coronavirus wedding, Melbourne family allowed to celebrate!
16/03/2020 08:07	SA	Shutdown	The Australian arts and events sector MUST be supported during the coronavirus shutdown
23/01/2020 22:46	QLD	Tests	Here in Queensland to date we've already tested 4 people all 4 came back negative 2 waiting on results
07/03/2020 14:27	TAS	Resources	At work we've put together some coronavirus info & resources to support people living with disability. Please feel free to share with anyone it may help

NSW, VIC, WA and ACT had comparatively much fewer tweets with positive sentiments. Nevertheless, in general the words such as survive, health, good, young, support, protect, care, and family were frequent among the positively classified tweets circulated within the aforesaid states/territories.

5.4.3.2 Concave-Up

Around 37% of the total tweets circulated within this stage carried positive sentiments. TAS, SA, and QLD had more positive tweets compared to other states and territories. NT did not go through the concave-up stage due to the low number of confirmed COVID-19 cases mainly because NT practiced the hammer and dance successfully, where the identified small COVID-19 patient clusters were strictly hammered by the enacted measures.

People from TAS repeatedly used the words of positive sentiments such as good (0.92%), block (0.74%), immediate (0.65%), health (0.63%), care (0.56%), ban (0.51%), support (0.42%), and prepare (0.41%). The tweets circulated within SA with positive sentiments mostly carried the words of health (0.99%), shutdown (0.98%), people (0.65%), expect (0.57%), distance (0.57%), enjoy (0.53%), isolate (0.45%), and help (0.45%). The words such as people (0.78%), practice (0.75%), health (0.57%), care (0.41%), stay (0.41), and expect (0.4%) were popular among the tweets with positive sentiments circulated in QLD. Table 5.6 shows the example tweets circulated related to the abovementioned words.

NSW, VIC, WA, and ACT had lesser tweets with positive sentiments during this stage compared to the other states/territories. Nevertheless, the words such as people, health, good, motivate, care and help were plural in the limited number of positively classified tweets in the abovementioned states/territories.

TABLE 5.6

Example Tweets with Positive Sentiments Circulated Within Concave-Up Stage

Date and Time	State	Keyword	Exemplar Tweet
17/03/2020 04:47	TAS	Shut	PM lockdowns the country Australian shut turn weeks actions managed essential services supply chains protected coronavirus impact for months #auspol
05/04/2020 07:16	SA	Distance	Day thirteen covid isolation keeping distance. casual Thursday catch covid19 create with every breath custom we make it #supportsmallbusiness #sunstatejewellers #sunstate# jewellers
09/02/2020 06:46	QLD	Enjoy	Enjoying Netflix series pandemic moment interesting watch reiterated fact antivaxxers insane #quickdetector
14/03/2020 12:09	TAS	Practice	Support promoting positive mental health wellbeing practices pandemic news climate greatly appreciated
21/03/2020 21:44	SA	Health	Patients declared, corona virus south Australia declared safe released #hospital #happy #response #senseurgency #australian #healthcare #industry

5.4.3.3 Linear

About 37% of the total tweets circulated in this stage were classified as tweets with positive sentiments. This is the period, when the number of daily reported cases gradually increase at an equal/slower rate than in the concave-up stage. Consequently, more positive tweets can be expected from this stage. Similarly, QLD, SA, TAS, and NT had more tweets with positive sentiments than other regions.

The most frequently used words in QLD were, lives (0.95%), prevent (0.72%), online (0.72%), distance (0.6%), support (0.54%), advice (0.48%), and family (0.48%). Tweets with positive sentiment values circulated in SA included more words such as people (1.1%), lives (0.79%), advantage (0.71%), health (0.65%), government (0.52%), stay (0.46%), quarantine (0.43%), family (0.42%), and care (0.4%). People form TAS had more tweets in this phase related to the words of people (0.78%), health (0.59%), check (0.44%). NT community used the words of crisis (0.95%), days (0.72%), distance (0.6%), government (0.48%), and people (0.48%). Table 5.7 displays the example tweets related to the abovementioned words.

Although NSW, VIC, WA and ACT had more negative tweets in this stage, the words such as help, good, safe, family, global, study, and health were popular among the positively classified tweets.

5.4.3.4 Concave-Down

About 38% of the total tweets circulated within this stage carried positive sentiment values. QLD, NT, TAS, and SA had a few more tweets with

TABLE 5.7

Example Tweets with Positive Sentiments Circulated Within Linear Stage

Date and Time	State	Keyword	Exemplar Tweet
29/02/2020 21:19	QLD	Online	Social media teachers deliver classes online, countries covid focus appears delivery content students demonstrating evidence learning keen hear thoughts
28/03/2020 09:20	SA	Family	Kind positive happy message family quarantine #stayhome positive kind happy documentary covid19 coronavirus #SA australia #adelaide #adelaide #australia
15/03/2020 00:01	QLD	Prevent	Maths extensive social distancing read quarantine preventative purposes waiting sick effective strategy flatten covid19 curve
14/04/2020 01:00	NT	Government	Australian government launches coronavirus publicity blitz country runs testing kits
27/03/2020 08:20	TAS	Check	Remember folks, libraries closed free ebooks library check library's website

positive sentiment values than those with negative sentiment values. People (0.74%), safe (0.71%), test (0.66%), fund (0.64%), support (0.64%), app (0.43%), invest (0.41%), care (0.4%), and isolate (0.4%) were the mostly used words in the positively classified word category in QLD. Positively classified tweets circulated within this period in NT carried words such as approach (4.76%), good (4.76%), herd (4.76%), and immunity (2%). People from TAS used government (0.86%), attitude (0.74%), app (0.72%), family (0.58%), distance (0.43%), vaccine (0.43%), and safe (0.41%). SA people used the words such as good (0.92%), app (0.61%), track (0.6%), normal (0.57%), vaccine (0.54%), claim (0.5%), and days (0.46%) often in the tweets with positive sentiments. Sample tweets circulated related to the frequently used positive sentiments are given in Table 5.8.

NSW, VIC, WA, and ACT also had comparatively a low number of positively classified tweets related to this stage. Among them, the words such as tests, stay, support, health, learn, people, help, good and school were popular.

5.4.4 Negative Community Perceptions

5.4.4.1 Pre-concave

Almost 70% of the total tweets circulated within this stage carried negative sentiments. VIC, NSW, ACT, and WA had more negative tweets than positive ones (Figure 5.7). VIC confirmed the first Australian COVID-19 patient on 25 January 2020 (DoH, 2020c). Since then, confirmed cases emerged across the state. The words such as arrival (1.16%), immediate (0.72%), cases (0.67%), paper (0.62%), catch (0.5%), toilet (0.5%), commodities (0.5%), dead (0.8%), and spread (0.43%) were plural among the negatively classified tweets in VIC.

TABLE 5.8

Example Tweets with Positive Sentiments Circulated Within Concave-Down Stage

Date and Time	State	Keyword	Exemplar Tweet
24/04/2020 06:36	TAS	App	Fully understand downloading covidsafe app doesn't automatically prevent virus, but it's a good initiative
12/04/2020 14:40	SA	Normal	Covid19 permanently normalise virtual technologies judging zoom meetings
23/04/2020 22:41	TAS	Vaccine	AAMRIS members projects progress relating covid19 covering vaccines drug trials diagnostics screening tests mental health indigenous health
11/04/2020 15:46	QLD	Fund	Scott Morrison pressed abc730 virgin australia's request 14b loan bailout pm suggests industry superannuation funds to super fund step fed govt #abcnews #twuaus #coronavirus #virginaustralia
29/04/2020 04:48	NT	Immunity	Pretty great idea herd immunity approach controlling spread virus

NSW community used the words related to suffer (0.94%), fail (0.73%), cases (0.67%), and death (0.47%) frequently in the tweets shared. Tweets classified as negative in ACT included words such as die (1.06%), cases (0.81%), arrive (0.69%), and days (0.52%). The words such as hard (1.56%), contract (1.51%), die (0.93%), buy (0.67%), work (0.59%), affect (0.46%), panic (0.4%) were often used in WA. Sample tweets circulated related to the frequently used negative sentiments are given in Table 5.9.

TABLE 5.9

Example Tweets with Negative Sentiments Circulated Within Pre-concave Stage

Date and Time	State	Keyword	Exemplar Tweet
02/03/2020 02:12	VIC	Fail	Making sickening joke of Morrisons plan he has on potential carriers of coronavirus looking tends be part of widespread failure of LNP While AFP are looking all wrong places auspol
29/01/2020 08:58	NSW	Suffer	Interesting. Last heard some people had virus were reinfected afterwards Apparently did not develop an immunity 2 virus Inoculate supposed trigger the effect yet hears sufferers developed any type immunity reinfect may wrong
30/03/2020 00:06	VIC	Arrival	Need to assure that the community evacuees from diamond princess cruise be heavily screened before their arrival
28/02/2020 02:45	ACT	Dead/die	Media bull shit Corona Get Common cold die FFS peoples together think percentages not raw numbers wealthy worry does homelessness poverty pure desperation fellow countrymen not move more
25/01/2020 05:53	WA	Hard	Moneys come hard during pandemic

Although QLD, SA, TAS, and NT had more positive tweets than negative ones in this stage, the words such as spread, risk, infect, flu, work, China, business, death, and panic were common among the negatively classified tweets.

5.4.4.2 Concave-Up

During this phase the number of tweets with negative sentiments (63%) were significantly high compared to the number of positive tweets. For instance, the number of negatively classified tweets in NSW and VIC were almost the twice of the positively classified tweets. Besides, both ACT and WA had more negative tweets than positively classified tweets circulated within this stage.

Most of the negatively classified tweets circulated within NSW carried the words such as cause (1.26%), work (1%), fail (0.76%), travel (0.76%), immediate (0.68%), hard (0.64%), cases (0.57%), control (0.48%), collapse (0.42%), and death (0.4%). Within the tweets from VIC, arrival (1.41%), travel (0.87%), immediate (0.7%), cases (0.49%), and lives (0.41%) were the most popular. People from ACT used more words such as die (1.39%), affect (0.51%), mortgage (0.43%), and suffer (0.42%). The words such as die (1.18%), work (0.77%), hard (0.72%), check (0.65%), suffer (0.5%) and cases (0.42%) were used frequently in the tweets circulated within WA. Table 5.10 lists the example tweets circulated related to the abovementioned words. These tweets showed economic challenges experienced by the local community such as unemployment and difficulty in paying mortgages.

The negatively classified tweets circulated within QLD, SA, and TAS included the words such as employment, spread, panic, confirm, business, risk, fear, anxious and cuts frequently.

TABLE 5.10

Example Tweets with Negative Sentiments Circulated Within Concave-Up Stage

Date and Time	State	Keyword	Exemplar Tweets
06/03/2020 14:28	WA	Die	15 MILL people will die best-case coronavirus scenario
15/03/2020 04:12	VIC	Arrival	Advice on how self-isolate on arrival Australia please see their Dept of Health's guide COVID which covers this. Don't create take risk
03/03/2020 08:20	NSW	Work	Can't stop COVID19 without protecting our health workers he said prices surgical masks increased sixfold while cost ventilators had tripled he added
17/03/2020 21:06	ACT	Mortgage	Wouldn't nice Aussie government absorb rent mortgages during hard times COVID-au
4/03/2020 07:46	NSW	Cause	Who think coronavirus would cause toilet paper apocalypse

5.4.4.3 Linear

Similar to the concave-up stage, 63% of total tweets circulated within this stage were negative. NSW, VIC, WA, and ACT had more tweets with negative sentiments.

The words such as lives (0.97%), national (0.53%), contract (0.48%), offices (0.44%), stop (0.43%), positive (0.44%), prevent (0.42%) and employer (0.4%) were popular among the tweets circulated in NSW in this phase. Tweets circulated within VIC carried more words such as arrival (1.18%), immediate (0.89%), employment (0.73%), die (0.6%), check (0.56%), positive (0.5%), cases (0.45%), and days (0.44%). The words such as suffer (1.2%), arrival (1%), hard (0.71%), work (0.66%), and dead (0.47%) were frequently used in the tweets circulated within WA. Tweets collected from ACT had more words such as work (0.96%), causes (0.84%), cases (0.57%), government (0.42%), and spread (0.41%). Example tweets related to the abovementioned words are given in Table 5.11.

Although QLD, SA, TAS and NT did not have more negatively classified tweets related to this stage, the words such as employment, death, issue, work, cuts, and businesses were popular among the negatively classified tweets.

5.4.4.4 Concave-Down

Australia did not experience high infection cases and resulting deaths compared to other countries such as USA, Brazil, UK, and Italy. Within a shorter time period Australia was able to control the pandemic situation. Soon after,

TABLE 5.11

Example Tweets with Negative Sentiments Circulated Within Linear Stage

Date and Time	State	Keyword	Exemplar Tweet
27/03/2020 02:33	NSW	Arrival	Face masked ship crew arrive Sydney amid coronavirus warnings
19/03/2020 09:53	VIC	Employment	Really You don't think shutting down schools and keeping kids home won't make them stressed How about when there's mass unemployment and Great Depression kids be stressed then There's longer game here then just virus
20/03/2020 07:25	WA	Suffer	Watching Simpsons ep Bart tricks everyone cruise ship the world suffering virus they stay quarantined How often they predict future
18/03/2020 08:25	ACT	Work	People own business works themselves markets shows losing job no help coronavirus
11/03/2020 07:03	NSW	Lives	Scott Morrison MP Greg Hunt MP please before become China/Italy stop mass gatherings lock down few weeks could make huge difference how many Aussies become ill coronavirusaustralia you will be saving lives pandemic

the gap between negatively and positively classified tweets was narrowed down. However, still, 62% of the total tweets circulated within this phase were negative. NSW, VIC, ACT and WA had more negative tweets than positive ones. The tweets generated from the aforementioned states and territories in this stage either showed the reflections of the community about the life they experienced during the past days or the issues and problems they have to face in the upcoming new normal era.

Most of the tweets from NSW were generated around the words of employment (0.84%), dead (0.55%), cases (0.53%), contract (0.53%), days (0.51%), novel (0.48%), direction (0.46%), experience (0.46%), and cautious (0.4%). Tweets from VIC had more words related to suffer (1.28%), die (0.66%), positive (0.53%), cases (0.53%), care (0.5%) and days (0.47%). Tweets from ACT mostly carried the words such as days (0.62%), check (0.54%), die (0.5%), and cases (0.4%). The words such as employment (0.7%), days (0.59%), check (0.57%), people (0.55%), backward (0.53%), cases (0.48%), hard (0.47%), and miss (0.45%) were the most popular in WA. Sample tweets circulated related to the frequently used words are given in Table 5.12.

Compared to other states and territories, the numbers of negatively classified tweets were slightly low in QLD, SA, and TAS. Nevertheless, the words such as employment, business, people, cases, spread, suffer, and industry were popular among the negatively classified tweets in QLD, SA, TAS, and NT.

TABLE 5.12

Example of Tweets with Negative Sentiments Circulated Within Concave-Down Stage

Date and Time	State	Keyword	Exemplar Tweets
22/03/2020 23:54	WA	Employment	Surely you can better your employees Armguard COVID19 NO masks NO gloves NO antibacterial wipes ATMs would hive spreading germs well notes misinformation too responsibility the project
24/04/2020 06:45	VIC	Suffer	Proud Daniel Andrews MP not giving populist attitude demands sticking restrictions coronavirus crisis Another week doesn't hurt anyone even though suffer financially etc
27/03/2020 04:33	ACT	Days	Australia records highest single day increase coronavirus cases
03/04/2020 20:35	NSW	Employment	Impact vast International student's university school employment Coronavirus COVID-AU
18/04/2020 02:23	NSW	Dead	Nearly lost Two people laughed me told couldn't use fitting rooms virus exactly funny deadly virus killing people over world

5.5 Discussion

The use of general public knowledge for public health policy and decision-making is becoming an important part of good governance practice (Baum et al., 2010; Gudes et al., 2010; Vaeztavakoli et al., 2018; Yigitcanlar et al., 2020c). Community juries (Degeling et al., 2017), stakeholder meetings, community-based organisations (Israel et al., 2010), and non-government organisation feedbacks were often used by governments to aid the decision-making process (Smith, 1977). Nonetheless, these cannot be used in pandemic situations, where social distancing is a compulsory rule. With the challenges of social distancing and travel restrictions, appropriate and community centric decisions need to be taken at the right time to tackle a pandemic situation successfully.

In the digital age, the use of social media data can help governments to capture community perceptions within a shorter time period without reaching the people directly/physically (Kankanamge et al., 2020b). This attribute of social media analytics make it qualified to be used to make community friendly decisions during pandemic situations. For instance, the findings of this study can assist policy- and decision-makers in two ways: (a) To review community perceptions about the pandemic situation, and (b) To identify the key requirements of the community to cope up with the pandemic situation.

The analysis has shown that Australian public was not happy at the early stage of the pandemic curve—i.e., pre-concave stage—as they seemed to believe that the Australian government was not responding to this global disaster appropriately. Accordingly, people were in a panic mode, and tried to prepare to face the pandemic at their capacity. The words, toilet/paper were very common in Twitter in all states/territories during the pre-concave stage. This was because consumer panic buying patterns took place in Australia, where people tried to stock toilet papers, hand sanitisers, food and other commodities. This indicated how Australian people act when the government does not provide confidence.

From February 2020 onwards, the Australian government started to add travel restrictions to combat COVID-19. This made people started to build trust in the government. The popular words among positively classified tweets showed that the people were generally happy about the actions taken by the government to combat the virus dispersion in Australia. Frequently used words, such as testing, resources, shutdown, and reaction, showed the awareness level of the community to face an upcoming disaster. For instance, the tweets circulated in QLD emphasised the significance of expending the number of testings per day at the early stage to stop spreading the virus rapidly. Furthermore, most of the tweets discussed about the importance of wearing masks.

Especially, people looked satisfied about the decisions made to expand the testing to reduce spreading SARS-CoV-2. For instance, the Australian government conducted more than two million tests in Australia by the end of

May 2020. The majority of these tests were conducted in the following states: NSW (n=725,817), VIC (n=660,801), QLD (n=274,688), and SA (n=137,290) (DoH, 2020d). The action of expanding the testing was taken during the late March 2020. Yet, it was also well demanded in the tweets circulated during the beginning of March 2020.

Most of the tweets reflected positive sentiments about the policy decisions to limit travelling such as closing state borders to non-citizens and residents, blocking Iran, South Korea and Italy arrivals, contract tracing and limiting outdoor and indoor gatherings. Furthermore, the Australian government introduced two mobile applications: (a) Coronavirus Australia App and (b) COVIDSafe App. They were ranked over four out of five points in both Apple and Android app stores. While such apps are immensely useful, effective use of government social media channels are also required to help the public follow the introduced measures/restrictions. Previous studies have shown the limitations of the government agencies in effective use of social media channels in Australia (Yigitcanlar et al., 2020b).

These applications provided timely demanded information package to the people such as the reported cases by state, advices, symptom checker, location information related to general practitioner respiratory clinics, register to self-isolate, mental health advices, special advices to the age care sector, health information contact number and so on (Ho et al., 2020). The COVIDSafe app is designed to help the Australian government to find close contacts of COVID-19 infected people. This app allows state and territory health officials to quickly contact people that may have been infected with the virus. Factually, people looked satisfied and happy about the decisions took by the Australian government to slow down the spread of the virus. While people were sending tweets related to the policies taken, there were more words related to the economy in the negatively classified tweets. The tweets shared related to financial issues got three forms: (a) Panic buying-related issues; (b) Mortgage-related issues; and (c) Employment-related issues.

The very first economy-related issue faced by Australians was the stock outrage due to the consumer 'panic buying'. As a result, the supply of toilet papers and other commodities were significantly low in NSW, VIC and WA. This situation made supermarkets to limit the number of items per transaction/per customer. Some supermarkets announced plans to give priority to elderly and disabled people when selling their goods. As COVID-19 started to hit Australia after the bushfire, the situation become dire with the consumer panic buying patterns. Moreover, the discussions about the positive relationship between elderly population and the fatality rates increased the death fear of Australians from COVID-19 (Holt et al., 2020).

The words such as businesses, employments, salary cuts, investments, and industries were the first plural cluster of words among the tweets with negative sentiments. Especially, these words were very popular among the tweets generated from NSW, VIC, and ACT. It was estimated that around one million Australians lost their jobs due to the pandemic. This was more significant in VIC, TAS, and SA (ABC, 2020a, b). Although SA had more positive perceptions, the word of employment (1.54%) was common among the negatively classified tweets. These facts showed the financial stress of the community during the pandemic, to which government needs to respond immediately.

The second issue was related to the 'mortgage' payments, which was the second popular word cluster within the negatively classified tweets. The COVID-19 pandemic left 1.4 million Australian in mortgage stress (Cassells & Duncan, 2020). According to Australian Bureau of Statistics (2018), NSW ($462,100), VIC ($400,400), and ACT ($404,200) owned the highest average mortgage sizes among the other states/territories. Thus, people from these states/territories undergo severe financial issues at a time, when they may not be engaging in paid work/employment.

The third issue was related to 'employment'. While the Australian government's JobSeeker and JobKeeper programs are helpful to a degree (ABC, 2020a, b), the uncertainty of these programs generates an anxiety among the people who either lost or might be losing their jobs. It highlights the fact that after controlling the pandemic in a successful way the next challenge waiting for the Australian government is to stimulate the downturn economy of Australia—that is already in recession—due to the COVID-19 pandemic (Australian Government, 2020a). Along with this, the post-COVID-19 era might subject to a prolonged state of psychological fear, worries, and confusion against any small to large scale physical gathering (He et al., 2021). A timely and sound government response, hence, is needed.

5.6 Conclusion[1]

The unpredictable, sudden and rapid emergence and transmission of COVID-19, during the last few months, has triggered significant public health emergencies and concern across both national as well as the global nature. Considering limited availability of clinically proven interventions and the infectious nature of the SARS-CoV-2's transmission, there created a global emergency in the form of a pandemic, resulting in implementations of lockdowns and restrictions in movement for citizens throughout the world. The resultant limitations have, thus, sparked a surge in the usage of online resources by the public, such as the usage of social media as well as the public's reliance on e-commerce services for the purpose of obtaining essential commodities.

[1] This chapter, with permission from the copyright holder, is a reproduced version of the following journal article: Yigitcanlar, T., Kankanamge, N., Preston, A., Gill, P. S., Rezayee, M., Ostadnia, M., ... & Ioppolo, G. (2020). How can social media analytics assist authorities in pandemic-related policy decisions? Insights from Australian states and territories. *Health Information Science and Systems*, 8(1), 1–21.

Considering the increasing influence of social media across the public, especially during the time of restricted movement like the existing lockdown, this chapter examined the potential role of crowdsourced data drawn from social media in informing the government policy- and decision-making process during a pandemic. The dearth of existing evidence, implemented specifically in the Australian context, further prompted the execution of this research. Accordingly, for the purpose of expounding upon the role of social media analytics in influencing governmental policy- and decision-making during a pandemic, a social media analysis approach was adopted by this research, comprising of a systematic and geographical analysis of 35,969 geo-tagged tweets of individuals residing in Australian states/territories.

The findings revealed the prevalence of negatively classified tweets (63%), compared with positively classified ones (37%). The highest prevalence of negatively classified tweets was reported during the pre-concave stage, while the lowest prevalence of 62% was observed during the concave-down stage. The highest prevalence of negatively classified tweets was observed from such territories and states as NSW, VIC, WA, and ACT, where additional 9,885 negative tweets, reflecting the prevalence of concerns regarding a pandemic from the public during stages before transmission of the virus.

Indeed, the concave-up stage or the period of rapid disease transmission was characterised as a relatively short period in Australia, along with the implementation of 21 major governmental responses (14 health and 7 economic responses) to mitigate the impacts of COVID-19. Such data on governmental actions can be well correlated with the reporting of the smallest number of negative tweets during this period by the public. Additionally, the findings also demonstrated the prevalent financial issues faced by the public during the pandemic. Issues related to financial crisis were observed in the negative tweets where the public primarily shared concerns related to: (a) Bulk purchasing due to panic; (b) Inability or difficulty to pay mortgages; and (c) Loss or risk of employment. Such findings, thus, depicted the financial issues faced by the public during national emergency situations like a pandemic, which the government must act upon immediately along with disease prevention.

The overall study findings reveal that: (a) Social media analytics is an efficient approach to capture the attitudes and perceptions of the public during a pandemic; (b) Crowdsourced social media data can guide interventions and decisions of the authorities during a pandemic; and (c) Effective use of government social media channels can help the public to follow the introduced measures/restrictions.

These findings, thus, demonstrate the effectiveness of social media analytics in depicting the public's expectations in response to a national emergency or crisis situation, especially when the governments cannot reach the general public directly/physically. The findings of this research, thus, proved to be useful in recommending and evaluating the potential effectiveness of crowdsourced data from the public's social media activities in informing governmental authorities on possible strategies to implement during a pandemic. To conclude, the findings of this research, hence, recommend governmental authorities to: (a) Conduct social media analytics to capture public perceptions and act accordingly, and (b) Actively utilise social media channels to enhance public health education and awareness concerning social distancing restrictions to be maintained during COVID-19 or other future pandemics.

Lastly, the following limitations of the study should be considered when interpreting the findings. First, the study only covered the period between 1 January and 4 May 2020, when the COVID-19 pandemic still prevailed in Australia at different degrees after this period. Second, as the case of VIC indicated, the four stages of pandemic may repeat again with the identification of newly infected clusters—this was the case for Melbourne on the first week of July 2020 (i.e., Victorian government's lockdown of nine public housing towers in Melbourne, and the lockdown was expanded to the Melbourne metropolitan area in the next days). Third, this study only analysed Twitter data, while other social media channels were not considered. Finally, there might be bias involved in the selection of the word bags and also when supervising the machine learning tool in the used software—i.e., WEKA.

References

ABC (2020a). *Coronavirus recession leaves 1.4m Australians in mortgage stress, almost 100,000 could default after JobKeeper ends. ABC News.* Accessed on 25 June 2020 from https://www.abc.net.au/news/2020-06-04/covid-recession-mortgage-stress-default-home-loans-jobkeeper/12318274.

ABC (2020b). *Almost a million Australians out of work due to coronavirus; RBA tips economy to take 10pc hit. ABC News.* Accessed on 25 June 2020 from https://www.abc.net.au/news/2020-05-05/almost-one-million-australians-lose-jobs-due-to-coronavirus/12215494.

Alzahrani, H. (2016). Social media analytics using data mining. *Global Journal of Computer Science and Technology, 16*(4), 16–19.

Anderson, R.M., Heesterbeek, H., Klinkenberg, D., & Hollingsworth, T.D. (2020). How will country-based mitigation measures influence the course of the COVID-19 epidemic? *The Lancet, 395*(10228), 931–934.

Arthur, R., Boulton, C.A., Shotton, H., & Williams, H.T. (2018). Social sensing of floods in the UK. *PloS One, 13*(1), e0189327.

Australian Bureau of Statistics (2018). *Housing finance, Australia, November 2018,* Australian Bureau of Statistics (ABS), Accessed on 3 July 2020 from https://www.abs.gov.au/ausstats/abs@.nsf/e8ae5488b598839cca25682000131612/d672cf4ebe195f15ca256e910077d9c2!OpenDocument.

Australian Government (2020a). *Economic response to the coronavirus,* Australian Government (AG), Accessed on 23 June 2020 from https://treasury.gov.au/sites/default/files/2020-05/Overview-Economic_Response_to_the_Coronavirus_3.pdf.

Australian Government. (2020b). *Coronavirus (COVID-19) current situation and case numbers,* Australian Government (AG), Accessed on 25 June 2020 from https://www. health.gov.au/news/health-alerts/novel-coronavirus-2019-ncov-health-alert/ coronavirus-covid-19-current-situation-and-case-numbers.

Baum, S., Kendall, E., Muenchberger, H., Gudes, O., & Yigitcanlar, T. (2010). Geographical information systems: An effective planning and decision-making platform for community health coalitions in Australia? *Health Information Management Journal, 39*(3), 28–33.

Bharat, D. (2020). COVID-19: *The Four Stages of Disease Transmission Explained.* Accessed on 25 June 2020 from https://www.netmeds.com/health-library/post/covid-19-the-4-stages-of-disease-transmission-explained.

Brooker, P., Barnett, J., & Cribbin, T. (2016). Doing social media analytics. *Big Data & Society, 3*(2), 2053951716658060.

Cassells, R., & Duncan, A. (2020). JobKeepers and JobSeekers: *How many workers will lose and how many will gain?* Accessed on 1 July 2020 from https://bcec. edu.au/assets/2020/03/BCEC-COVID19-Brief-3-Job-Seekers-and-Keepers_ FINAL.pdf.

Castillo, C., Mendoza, M., & Poblete, B. (2013). Predicting information credibility in time-sensitive social media. *Internet Research, 23*(5), 560–588.

Chowell, G., Viboud, C., Hyman, J.M., & Simonsen, L. (2015). The Western Africa Ebola virus disease epidemic exhibits both global exponential and local polynomial growth rates. *PLoS Currents, 7,* 3261.

Cowling, D. (2020). *SocialMediaNews.com.au. Social Media Statistics Australia–January 2020.* Accessed on 25 June 2020 from https://www.socialmedianews.com.au/ social-media-statistics-australia-january-2020.

Daneshpour, Z.A. (2020). *Out of the coronavirus crisis, a new kind of urban planning must be born.* Accessed on 30 June 2020 from https://novinshahrsaz.ir/wp-content/ uploads/2020/04/Out_of_the_coronavirus_crisis_a_new_kind_of_urban_ planning_must.pdf.

Degeling, C., Rychetnik, L., Street, J., Thomas, R., & Carter, S.M. (2017). Influencing health policy through public deliberation: Lessons learned from two decades of Citizens'/community juries. *Social Science & Medicine, 179,* 166–171.

Department of Health (DoH) (2020a). *Coronavirus (COVID-19) at a glance – 5 May 2020,* Department of Health (DoH), Australian Government. Accessed on 28 June 2020 from https://www.health.gov.au/resources/publications/coronavirus-covid-19-at-a-glance-5-may-2020.

Department of Health (DoH) (2020b). *Coronavirus (COVID-19) current situation and case numbers,* Department of Health (DoH), Australian Government. Accessed on 28 June 2020 from https://www.health.gov.au/news/health-alerts/novel-coronavirus-2019-ncov-health-alert/coronavirus-covid-19-current-situation-and-case-numbers#tests-conducted-and-results.

Department of Health (DoH) (2020c). *Easing of Coronavirus (COVID-19) Restrictions.* Department of Health (DoH), Accessed on 25 June 2020 from https://www. health.gov.au/news/health-alerts/novel-coronavirus-2019-ncov-health-alert/ coronavirus-covid-19-restrictions/easing-of-coronavirus-covid-19-restrictions.

Department of Health (DoH) (2020d). *First confirmed case of novel coronavirus in Australia,* Department of Health (DoH), Australian Government. Accessed on 22 June 2020 from https://www.health.gov.au/ministers/the-hon-greg-hunt-mp/ media/first-confirmed-case-of-novel-coronavirus-in-australia.

Devi, S. (2015). Twitter campaign highlights top women in global health. *The Lancet, 385*(9965), 318.

Eichstaedt, J.C., Schwartz, H.A., Kern, M.L., Park, G., Labarthe, D.R., Merchant, R.M., & Weeg, C. (2015). Psychological language on twitter predicts county-level heart disease mortality. *Psychological Science, 26*(2), 159–169.

Faasse, K., & Newby, J.M. (2020). Public perceptions of COVID-19 in Australia: perceived risk, knowledge, health-protective behaviours, and vaccine intentions. *medRxiv*, https://doi.org/10.1101/2020.04.25.20079996.

Feng, Y., & Sester, M. (2018). Extraction of pluvial flood relevant volunteered geographic information (VGI) by deep learning from user generated texts and photos. *ISPRS International Journal of Geo-Information, 7*(2), 39.

Fraser, C., Riley, S., Anderson, R.M., & Ferguson, N.M. (2004). *Factors that make an infectious disease outbreak controllable. Proceedings of the National Academy of Sciences, 101*(16), 6146–6151.

Gavin, K. (2020). *Flattening the Curve for COVID-19: What Does It Mean and How Can You Help?* Accessed on 25 June 2020 from https://healthblog.uofmhealth.org/wellness-prevention/flattening-curve-for-covid-19-what-does-it-mean-and-how-can-you-help.

Gudes, O., Kendall, E., Yigitcanlar, T., Pathak, V., & Baum, S. (2010). Rethinking health planning: A framework for organising information to underpin collaborative health planning. *Health Information Management Journal, 39*(2), 18–29.

Harris, J.K., Mueller, N.L., & Snider, D. (2013). Social media adoption in local health departments nationwide. *American Journal of Public Health, 103*(9), 1700–1707.

He, M., Xian, Y., Lv, X., He, J., & Ren, Y. (2021). Changes in body weight, physical activity, and lifestyle during the semi-lockdown period after the outbreak of COVID-19 in China: an online survey. Disaster *Medicine* and *Public Health Preparedness, 15*(2), e23–e28.

Ho, C.S., Chee, C.Y., & Ho, R.C. (2020). Mental health strategies to combat the psychological impact of COVID-19 beyond paranoia and panic. *Annals, Academy of Medicine Singapore, 49*(1), 1–3.

Holt, N.R., Neumann, J.T., McNeil, J.J., Cheng, A.C., Unit, H.E., & Prahan, V. (2020). *Implications of COVID-19 in an ageing population. The Medical Journal of Australia.* Accessed on 30 June 2020 from https://www.mja.com.au/system/files/2020-05/Holt%20mja20.00649%20-%206%20May%202020.pdf.

Honey-Roses, J.H., Anguelovski, I., Bohigas, J., Chireh, V., Daher, C., Konijnendijk, C., Litt, J., Mawani, J., McCall, M., Orellana, A., Oscilowicz, E., Sanchez, U., Senbe, M., Tan, X., Villagomez, E., Zapata, O., & Nieuwenhuijsen, M. (2020). *The Impact of COVID-19 on Public Space: A Review of the Emerging Questions.* Accessed on 25 June 2020 from https://doi.org/10.31219/osf.io/rf7xa.

Hu, R. (2020). *Reinventing community in COVID-19: a case in Canberra, Australia. Socio-Ecological Practice Research*, https://doi.org/10.1007/s42532-020-00055-2.

Israel, B.A., Coombe, C.M., Cheezum, R.R., Schulz, A.J., McGranaghan, R.J., Lichtenstein, R., & Burris, A. (2010). Community-based participatory research: A capacity-building approach for policy advocacy aimed at eliminating health disparities. *American Journal of Public Health, 100*(11), 2094–2102.

Jones, C.J., Philippon, T., & Venkateswaran, V. (2020). *Optimal mitigation policies in a pandemic: Social distancing and working from home.* Accessed on 1 July 2020 from https://www.nber.org/papers/w26984.

Jones, R., Kelsey, J., Nelmes, P., Chinn, N., Chinn, T., & Proctor-Childs, T. (2016). Introducing twitter as an assessed component of the undergraduate nursing curriculum: Case study. *Journal of Advanced Nursing, 72*(7), 1638–1653.

Kankanamge, N., Yigitcanlar, T., Goonetilleke, A., & Kamruzzaman, M. (2019). Can volunteer crowdsourcing reduce disaster risk? A systematic review of the literature. *International Journal of Disaster Risk Reduction, 35*, 101097.

Kankanamge, N., Yigitcanlar, T., & Goonetilleke, A. (2020a). How engaging are disaster management related social media channels? The case of Australian state emergency organisations. *International Journal of Disaster Risk Reduction, 48*(1), 101571.

Kankanamge, N., Yigitcanlar, T., Goonetilleke, A., & Kamruzzaman, M. (2020b). How can gamification be incorporated into disaster emergency planning? A systematic review of the literature. *International Journal of Disaster Resilience in the Built Environment, 11*(4), 481–506.

Kankanamge, N., Yigitcanlar, T., Goonetilleke, A., & Kamruzzaman, M. (2020c). Determining disaster severity through social media analysis: Testing the methodology with South East Queensland Flood Tweets. *International Journal of Disaster Risk Reduction, 42*(1), 101360.

Ling, G.H., & Chyong Ho, C.M. (2020). Effects of the coronavirus (COVID-19) pandemic on social behaviors: From a social dilemma perspective. *Technium Social Sciences Journal, 7*, 312–320.

Moreno, M.A., Arseniev-Koehler, A., Litt, D., & Christakis, D. (2016). Evaluating college students' displayed alcohol references on Facebook and Twitter. *Journal of Adolescent Health, 58*(5), 527–532.

Newman, P. (2020). Covid, cities and climate: Historical precedents and potential transitions for the new economy. *Urban Science, 4*(3), 32.

NSW Government (2020). *The Special Commission of Inquiry into the Ruby Princess.* New South Wales Government (NSWG), Accessed on 25 June 2020 from https://www.rubyprincessinquiry.nsw.gov.au.

Paul, M.J., & Dredze, M. (2014). Discovering health topics in social media using topic models. *PloS One, 9*(8), e103408.

Pueyo, T., (2020). *Coronavirus: The Hammer and the Dance.* Accessed on 25 June 2020 from https://medium.com/@tomaspueyo/coronavirus-the-hammer-and-the-dance-be9337092b56.

Qiu, W., Rutherford, S., Mao, A., & Chu, C. (2017). The pandemic and its impacts. *Health, Culture and Society, 9*, 1–11.

Reshadat, S., Zangeneh, A., Saeidi, S., Teimouri, R., & Yigitcanlar, T. (2019a). Measures of spatial accessibility to health centers: Investigating urban and rural disparities in Kermanshah, Iran. *Journal of Public Health, 27*(1), 519–529.

Reshadat, S., Tohidi, M., Ghasemi, M., Zangeneh, A., Saeidi, S., Teimouri, R., & Yigitcanlar, T. (2019b). Interrelationship between underprivileged neighborhoods and health promotion lifestyles: Insights from Kermanshah, Iran. *Journal of Public Health*, https://doi.org/10.1007/s10389-019-01086-0.

Rochester Regional Health (2020). *Pandemic vs Epidemic: What's the difference?* Rochester Regional Health (RRH), Accessed on 25 June 2020 from https://www.rochester-regional.org/news/2020/03/pandemic-vs-epidemic.

Saunders-Hastings, P.R., & Krewski, D. (2016). Reviewing the history of pandemic influenza: Understanding patterns of emergence and transmission. *Pathogens, 5*(4), 66.

Scanfeld, D., Scanfeld, V., & Larson, E.L. (2010). Dissemination of health information through social networks: Twitter and antibiotics. *American Journal of Infection Control, 38*(3), 182–188.

Sebei, H., Taieb, M.A., & Aouicha, M.B. (2018). Review of social media analytics process and big data pipeline. *Social Network Analysis and Mining, 8*(1), 30.

Sensis. (2018). *Yellow Social Media Report 2018. Part One: Consumers.* Accessed on 25 June 2020 from https://www.yellow.com.au/wp-content/uploads/2018/06/Yellow-Social-Media-Report-2018-Consumer.pdf.

Shenker, J. (2020). *Cities After Coronavirus: How COVID-19 Could Radically Alter Urban Life.* Accessed on 25 June 2020 from https://www.theguardian.com/world/2020/mar/26/life-after-coronavirus-pandemic-change-world.

Signorini, A., Segre, A.M., & Polgreen, P.M. (2011). The use of twitter to track levels of disease activity and public concern in the US during the influenza a H1N1 pandemic. *PloS One, 6*(5), e19467.

Smith, B.L. (1977). The non-governmental policy analysis organization. *Public Administration Review,* 253–258.

Statista (2020). *Mobility in cities amid coronavirus crisis 2020.* Accessed on 25 June 2020 from https://www.statista.com/statistics/1106798/change-in-traffic-volume-amid-coronaviruscrisis-selected-cities.

Tumpey, T.M., Basler, C.F., Aguilar, P.V., Zeng, H., Solórzano, A., Swayne, D.E., & Garcia-Sastre, A. (2005). Characterization of the reconstructed 1918 Spanish influenza pandemic virus. *Science, 310*(5745), 77–80.

Vaeztavakoli, A., Lak, A., & Yigitcanlar, T. (2018). Blue and green spaces as therapeutic landscapes: Health effects of urban water canal areas of Isfahan. *Sustainability, 10*(11), 4010.

Wade, A. (2020). *COVID -19 coronavirus alert level 2: NZ lockdown debate, more help for firms as global deaths soar past 13,500.* Accessed on 2 July 2020 from https://www.nzherald.co.nz/nz/news/article.cfm?c_id=1&objectid=12318890.

Wargent, P., (2020). *Miraculous improvement in COVID-19 Cases.* Accessed on 25 June 2020 from https://www.propertyobserver.com.au/pete-wargent/112767-miraculous-improvement-in-covid-19-cases-pete-wargent.html.

WHO (2020). *Strengthening and adjusting public health measures throughout the COVID-19 transition phases: policy considerations for the World Health Organization European Region,* World Health Organization (WHO). Regional Office for Europe.

Worldometer (2020). COVID-19 Coronavirus pandemic. Accessed on 1 July 2020 from https://www.worldometers.info/coronavirus.

Yigitcanlar, T., Goonetilleke, A., & Kankanamge, N., (2020a). *Disasters expose gaps in emergency services' social media use.* Accessed on 5 July 2020 from https://theconversation.com/disasters-expose-gaps-in-emergency-services-socialmedia-use-134912.

Yigitcanlar, T., Kamruzzaman, M., Teimouri, R., Degirmenci, K., & Aghnayi, F. (2020b). Association between park visits and mental health in a developing county context: The case of Tabriz, Iran. *Landscape and Urban Planning, 199*(1), 103805.

Yigitcanlar, T., Kankanamge, N., & Vella, K. (2020c). How are the smart city concepts and technologies perceived and utilized? A systematic geo-twitter analysis of smart cities in Australia. *Journal of Urban Technology, 23*(1–2), 135–154. https://doi.org/10.1080/10630732.2020.1753483.

Zhang, Y., Xiao, M., Zhang, S., Xia, P., Cao, W., Jiang, W., & Wang, C. (2020). Coagulopathy and antiphospholipid antibodies in patients with Covid-19. *New England Journal of Medicine, 382*(17), e38.

6

Social Media Analytics in Capturing Perceptions

6.1 Introduction

At the dawn of global socioeconomic and environmental crises, the utilisation of smart city technologies is seen by many city administrations as a popular avenue to achieve desired urbanisation outcomes (Albino et al., 2015; Komninos, 2016). A smart city can be described as an urban locality that employs digital data and technology to create efficiencies for boosting economic development, enhancing the quality of life, and improving the sustainability of the city (Bibri, 2019). Today, many cities are developing sound smart city strategies and turning them into official local policies (Townsend, 2013). Successful approaches and practices are emerging in London, San Francisco, Singapore, Stockholm, Toronto, Vienna, and in a few other cities (Yigitcanlar & Kamruzzaman, 2018).

Despite the emergence of good smart city policy practices, our knowledge and understanding about how smart city concepts and technologies are perceived and utilised in cities are very limited (Mah et al., 2012). For instance, the literature does not provide clear answers to the following questions: Which smart city concepts and technologies are currently trending? What are the relationships between popular smart city concepts and technologies? What are the official smart city policies that influence the perception and utilisation of smart city concepts and technologies? The answers to these questions will inform policymakers and planners in shaping their future policy agendas—e.g., improving the quality and implementation of smart city policies.

In order to address this gap in the literature, this chapter evaluates 'how relevant smart city concepts and technologies are perceived and utilised' in cities. This investigation is undertaken through a case study analysis. Australian cities are selected as the testbed—as they are among the early and successful adopters of smart city technologies (Pettit et al., 2018). The study provides a snapshot of community perceptions on smart city concepts and technologies with the objective to inform smart city policymaking.

DOI: 10.1201/9781003278986-8

The methodological approach adopted in this study utilises a novel approach—instead of traditional survey and interview techniques. Thanks to the proliferation of social media platforms, capturing and evaluating community perceptions has become much easier (Williamson & Ruming, 2019). Social media motivates people to express their thoughts, criticisms, reflections in the form of social media posts (Kankanamge et al., 2020). By commenting, sharing, and responding to such posts, people create trending topics in social media networks—and some go viral (Dufty, 2016). Thus, in this study, trending smart city concepts and technologies are identified and analysed through the social media analysis of geo-Twitter messages (tweets).

There are two different types of locations associated with a tweet: (a) Geo-tagged tweets that give the exact longitude and latitude information of the sender; (b) Geo-located tweets that give the area name of the sender's location—e.g., Sydney. As the numbers of the geo-tagged tweets downloaded were marginal in this study, we used a combined set of geo-tagged (n=64) and geo-located (n=3,009) tweets—and we referred to them as 'geo-tweets' (n=3,073). These geo-tweets either contain a latitude/longitude coordinate or can be identified by a city or neighbourhood name. The systematic geo-Twitter analytics method—containing descriptive, content, policy, and spatial analyses—is used to harvest community perceptions expressed as tweets on smart city-related concepts and technologies.

6.2 Literature Background

The urbanisation rate across the globe has been growing exponentially (Arbolino et al., 2017). Urbanisation, when practised as densification, can have positive consequences in making the urban footprint smaller. Nonetheless, when urbanisation is coupled with overpopulation, excessive consumerism, and fossil fuel energy dependency, its consequences become catastrophic for the natural systems (Mysterud, 2017; Arbolino et al., 2018). If these issues are not addressed, the challenges of greenhouse gas emissions, climate change, resource scarcity, housing affordability, and food security will become even more acute, threatening our existence on the planet (Zhang et al., 2013; Yigitcanlar et al., 2019b).

Along with sustainability issues, high urbanisation levels put heightened pressures on urban infrastructure, amenity and service delivery, and governance of cities (Grossi & Pianezzi, 2017; Mora et al., 2017). Housing large populations in cities—particularly in megacities of over 10 million residents—adds further to the already significant challenges facing urban administrations (Ersoy, 2017). This has led city authorities to search for innovative methods and mechanisms, such as smart and sustainable infrastructures to deliver urban services with increased efficiency (Mora et al., 2019).

In recent years, urban policymakers and technocrats have been adopting technology-centric solutions (such as autonomous vehicles, internet-of-things, artificial intelligence, smart poles, digital twins, blockchain, big data, robotics, open data) to urban development and management more than ever (Söderström et al., 2014; Faisal et al., 2019; Yigitcanlar et al., 2019d). Technocentric urban management approaches, which are a part of the 'smart cities' agenda, have become mainstream in many local governments (Caragliu et al., 2011; Praharaj et al., 2018). The digital data and technology utilisation aspect of smart cities is widely recognised as their distinctive characteristic in boosting economic growth, enriching living conditions, and maintaining environmental sustainability (Winden & Buuse, 2017; Joss et al., 2019).

The popularity of smart cities has increased rapidly due to their offerings of the digitalisation of cities (Yigitcanlar, 2009; Aina, 2017). Paradoxically, the extreme reliance on technology has also created drawbacks. Scholars argue that this dependency on technology solutions could become a threat in the near future. According to Kunzmann (2014, p.9), "there is a darker side of smart city that is not much the access to this technology, but rather the extreme dependency on technology, and on corporations dominating technology and related services".

There are various conceptual smart city frameworks developed so far. For instance, Giffinger and Pichler-Milanović's (2007) put together the following key dimensions in a smart city framework comprising smart environment, people, economy, living, mobility, and governance. This framework was adopted by the European Union. There are few other smart city frameworks. The most notable ones are developed by Errichiello and Marasco (2014), Fernandez-Anez et al. (2018), and Yigitcanlar (2018). These frameworks are aimed at providing a clearer view of how the smart city idea can be best operationalised to deliver desired outcomes.

In general, smart city frameworks can be grouped under two categories. The first category is the conceptual frameworks that encompass theories, typologies, features, and strategies for understanding smart cities. They provide the big picture view (De-Jong et al., 2015). The second category is the practical frameworks that contain processes, planning mechanisms, and performance evaluation tools for transforming cities into smart cities. They provide sectoral, specific application areas or practical perspectives (Aina, 2017).

There is not any widely accepted generic smart city framework—either conceptual or practical (Deakin & Reid, 2018). An increasing number of local governments have also developed their own smart policy frameworks. To name a few, the following cities have fully-fledged official smart city government policies: Belfast, Brussels, Greenwich, London, Newcastle, Nottingham, Ottawa, San Francisco, San Jose, Singapore, Stockholm, Toronto, Vienna, and Western Sydney (Yigitcanlar et al., 2019c).

Each of these official smart city strategies has their own unique features, and their common elements. Some of them adopted smart city frameworks developed by scholars. For instance, Giffinger and Pichler-Milanović's (2007) framework was adopted in the smart city policy of the City of Newcastle (Australia). Some others formed their own—e.g., Vienna. Despite the popularity of smart cities policy/practice; how relevant concepts and technologies are being perceived and utilised is still an understudied area of research (Alizadeh, 2015; Komninos et al., 2019).

6.3 Research Design

6.3.1 Case Study

The research selected Australian cities as the case study context. Table 6.1 shows the 2016 population of Australian states and territories—for the sake of simplification, territories will also be referred to as states in the rest of this chapter. The case selection was done due to the following reasons: (a) Australian cities are among the early adopters of smart city technologies (Yigitcanlar, 2018; Yigitcanlar & Kamruzzaman, 2019); (b) Australian cities are listed among the reputable global smart cities (Anthopoulos, 2017); (c) Australian Government introduced a smart city policy in 2016; (d) At present, more than 50 large scale smart city projects across the country are in progress—e.g., Parramatta City Council's smart warning system for flooded roads; Logan City Council's smart urban irrigation system; Cairns Regional Council's smart climate-responsive neighbourhoods; and Monash City Council's i-Sense Oakleigh smart connected precinct.

6.3.2 Data

In recent years, social media channels have been frequently used as key data sources in academic studies. The following can be given as examples: (a) Determining post-disaster damage levels in smart cities (Kankanamge et al., 2020); (b) Evaluating community perceptions, through opinion mining,

TABLE 6.1

Australian State and Territory Populations

State/Territory	Population
New South Wales (NSW)	7,480,228
Victoria (VIC)	5,926,624
Queensland (QLD)	4,703,193
Western Australia (WA)	2,474,410
South Australia (SA)	1,676,653
Tasmania (TAS)	509,965
Australian Capital Territory (ACT)	397,397
Northern Territory (NT)	228,833

on smart city projects (Alizadeh et al., 2019); (c) Calculating home-work travel metrics as smart urban mobility measure (Osorio-Arjona et al., 2019); (d) Assessing the impact of smart tourism policies (Brandt et al., 2017). Despite the increasing number of studies, the use of social media content and analytic techniques in relation to smart city concepts and technologies is still an understudied area of research.

This research adopted an analysis framework introduced by Fan and Gordon (2014) to conduct social media data analysis. Social media has altered our modes of work and life, has received attention from multiple fields (Kane, 2017), and there is also an increasing trend towards social media as a source of big data in urban research (Ciuccarelli et al., 2014). The systematic geo-Twitter analysis framework the study used contains three analysis stages— i.e., 'capture', 'understand', and 'present' (Figure 6.1).

The first stage of the framework involves 'capturing' social media information. This study selected Twitter as a potential social media platform. Nonetheless, Twitter has certain merits and limitations. The main merits include: (a) Twitter is the fastest growing social media microblogging service; (b) Researchers and practitioners can use a free Twitter 'application programming interface' (API) to conduct analysis based on their interests; (c) As opposed to Facebook and Instagram, Twitter data is considered as 'open data', which provides succinct real-time data to public (Dufty, 2016); (d) Search and streaming APIs of Twitter allow researchers to write queries and download information under certain keywords and/or hashtags (Guan & Chen, 2014); (e) Analysing Twitter data is a novel method of harvesting dispersed community knowledge (Kankanamge et al., 2019).

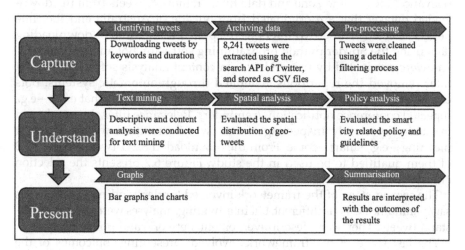

FIGURE 6.1
Systematic geo-Twitter analysis framework. (Derived from Fan & Gordon, 2014.)

The main limitation is the restricted API-based data accessibility, where APIs provide access to only 1% of publicly available Twitter data. From this sample, only around 10% is either geo-located or geo-tagged (Cebeillac & Rault, 2016). Even from geo-located and geo-tagged tweets, geo-tagged tweets are becoming further hard to collect. This is due to not sharing personal mobile location information and ethical barriers as such information consists of the exact latitude and longitude information of the people.

For instance, from the collected data for this analysis, only 64 tweets consisted of geo-tagged information. Therefore, geo-tagged information is often collected through data providers—i.e., DataSift, with 100% access, which is a costly approach, or geo-tagged tweets become often during crisis periods (Kankanamge et al., 2020). As another limitation, Lin and Cromley (2015) highlighted the biased age group of the Twitter data. Despite these limitations, there is an increasing number of studies that use tweets as the main data source (Brandt et al., 2017; Yuan & Liu, 2018).

In this study, Twitter data was collected for the most recent full-year—i.e., 2018. The data capturing process started with the identification of keywords. Accordingly, the study downloaded tweets with the keywords 'smart', 'city', and 'cities' circulated in 2018—between 1 January and 31 December 2018—within Australia. The study did not use the hashtag #smartcity to download the data as it would limit the retrieved number of tweets. These tweets are already picked up by our abovementioned search keywords. Data was downloaded through APIs obtained from the developers of Twitter. In total, 8,241 tweets were obtained. This dataset was not structured; it included duplicates and incomplete or unusable tweets. The study adopted the four-step data cleaning process, introduced by Arthur et al. (2018) to clean the data.

The four-step data cleaning process consists of time zone, date, bot, and relevance filters. Time zone and date filters removed tweets from the downloaded dataset that are originated from outside of Australia and the time period selected. These two filters were applied at the time of downloading data using the Spyder python programming software. Bot and relevance filters were conducted by using Nvivo—a content analysis software. The Bot filter removed the repetitions generated through automatic systems. Bots can be easily recognised through the number of repetitions that exist—e.g., repeated conference notifications/reminders. Relevance filter was conducted manually by closely inspecting tweets, which are used with a different meaning—e.g., smart people. From the downloaded 8,241 tweets, only 3,073 of them qualified to be used in the study. Figure 6.2 presents the selection criteria and types of analyses.

The second stage of the framework involved 'understanding' what tweets say/communicate. Four different, but intertwining, analyses were used to understand tweets. They were descriptive, content, network, and policy analyses.

The last stage of the framework involved 'presenting' outcomes of the abovementioned analyses. It adopted appropriate visualising techniques such as graphs, maps for an easy communication of the results.

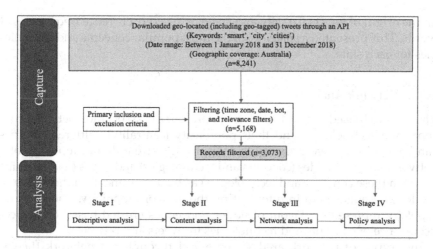

FIGURE 6.2
Tweet selection criteria for analysis.

6.3.3 Descriptive Analysis

Twitter data contains various information, such as 'created_date', 'user-screen name', 'user-name', 'text', 'photo/video', and 'user-location'. The study used a descriptive analysis (DA) to deliver a broader view of the captured data. This study focused on three descriptive statistics namely Twitter statistics, user analysis, and web-link (URL) analysis. Identifying prominent hashtags are especially useful for urban planners as tweets reflect the emotive and evaluative perceptions of the citizens. Twitter statistics provided information about the number of active users, the number of retweets and the number of hashtags used. The study considered all 'retweets' as new tweets with the related location of the retweet sender. This information acted as a gateway for many other inline analyses, such as content analysis and spatial analysis.

6.3.4 Content Analysis

Tweets are informal in nature, and consist of lay language, acronyms, URLs, photos, videos, and ideograms. They also contain people's opinions. Analysing tweets is a sensitive and significant task. Word frequency analysis was the initial point for the content analysis. Word frequency analysis identified the popular concepts and technologies, and then the co-occurrence of words helped in determining the linkages among the concepts and technologies. Popular concepts and technologies reflect both hidden and dispersed community knowledge around smart cities.

The study also conducted a spatial analysis to complement the content analysis. For the analysis, we used the location information collected in tweets to categorise the main themes of the analysis by their locations. We categorised the most popular concepts and technologies into themes based on the origin of tweets (i.e., city and state) using co-occurrence frequencies of words. This presented a snapshot of the most popular concepts and technologies for each state.

6.3.5 Network Analysis

This research used network analysis to present the association between concepts and technologies and their popularity (centrality). Different metrics can be used in network theory to interpret the strength and topology of a network. We used nodes (concepts and technologies) and edges (relationships between these concepts and technologies) as the key elements of the network. Nodes and edges help in interpreting the network topology. The network topology represents a layout of nodes and edges created based on the co-occurrence of concepts and technologies in tweets and retweets.

Two types of network analysis emerged through the network theory. These analyses were centrality and community-level analyses. First, centrality analysis considered the significance of each node compared to adjacent nodes. Second, community-level analysis explored network-level characteristics such as density. This represents all the possible connections between all the nodes. This study used centrality analysis to identify the association between popular concepts and technologies.

6.3.6 Policy Analysis

Through policy analysis, this study evaluated prevailing smart city strategies and planning policies. This aimed to understand processes behind the development of planning policies and the role of strategies in developing the concepts that were identified through descriptive and content analyses. This analysis connects social media data with numerous smart city policies developed and introduced in Australia. It helps in better comprehension of how smart city policies are perceived by the public, and how these policies influenced public perceptions. Exploring both policy and perception dimensions provides policymakers with essential information for consolidating existing policies or developing new effective, efficient, and feasible ones.

6.4 Results

6.4.1 What are the Trending Smart City Concepts and Technologies?

Of the 3,073 usable tweets, 1,179 (38%) were original, and 1,894 (62%) were retweeted, reflecting the highly interactive nature of users. All Twitter discussions developed in total 28 hashtags. The hashtag analysis identified (excluding #smartcities and #smartcity) 16 key hashtags among them as the most strongly associated ones with the smart city domain. These were: #autonomousvehicle; #transport; #5G; #sustainability; #mobility; #internet-of-things; #energy; #innovation; #governance; #artificialintelligence; #blockchain; #bigdata; #robotics; #opendata; #waste; #startups.

Trending hashtags were: #IoT, #AI, #opendata, #robotics, #bigdata, #autonomous, #automation, #automative, #autonomousvehicle, #driverless, #self-driving, #5G, #blockchain. Tweets with these hashtags captured views on incorporating novel, innovative, and advanced technologies to shape smart cities. Other popular hashtags were: #cybersecurity, #android, #traffic, #software, #digitalbuiltaustralia, #austech, #sustainability, #ausbiz. Tweets with these hashtags concentrated on smart city strategies with an economy and mobility focus. The temporal variation of hashtag usage is significant to the study. For instance, tweet numbers increased substantially between September and October 2018 due to the Smart Cities Week Australia 2018 event in Sydney. The event hashtags such as #SCW and #SCWAus were frequently circulated during this period.

In total, 1,090 users contributed to create the dataset of 3,073 tweets. 69% of the tweets were circulated by individual users, and 31% by institutions. However, 75% of the top-20 most active users were institutional users. These organisations include technology firms, research centres, not-for-profit organisations, and conference organisers. The number of tweets of the most active users ranged between 20 and 150 tweets per year. In terms of followers, these organisations had more followers than individuals, meaning they naturally had wider outreach. Yet, it would not be correct to interpret this as their dominance in communicating opinions, as individual user tweets were more than double in quantity than institutional ones.

There were 176 tweets with informative URLs in the dataset. Most of them contained links to blogs, discussion sites, articles, and conference websites that talk about the smart city movement in Australia and overseas. Hot topics discussed include Melbourne's high-tech vision; driverless cars and national autonomous vehicle law; cyber security; smarter irrigation management solutions; and smart waste management systems.

6.4.2 What Are the Relationships Between Smart City Concepts and Technologies?

Tweets obtained from each state were categorised separately (Figure 6.3). The states with the highest number of smart city tweets were NSW (1,372), VIC (710), QLD (432), ACT (371), and SA (103). WA (60), and TAS (25) had the lowest number of tweets. The national capital Canberra is located in the Australian Capital Territory (ACT). The city houses almost all of the Federal authorities, and naturally, the key national policy issues, including smart cities and technologies, are widely discussed in the city. Interestingly, most of the analysed tweets consist of scholarly discussions that evaluate the smart city notion

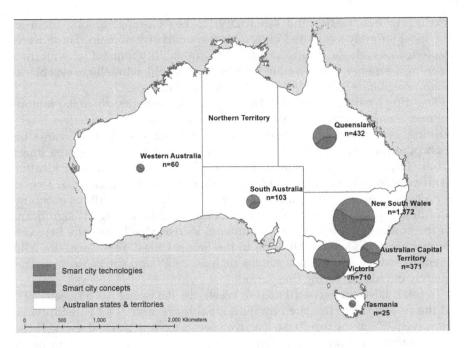

FIGURE 6.3
Spatial distribution of tweets.

under different concepts and technologies. Tweets discussed: Launching robotics roadmaps for automation adoption; Lake Macquarie smart city network project; Tesla's power wall batteries project for smart energy management systems. Twitter provided a user-centric online media/platform to express individual and institutional views on the aforementioned projects. Institutional tweets on policies and projects helped the information circulate widely. This, in return, motivated or provoked individuals to reflect on their responses. For instance, 28 individuals have retweeted posts related to Lake Macquarie Smart City Network with their own comments included. This has ultimately developed a thought-provoking discussion thread related to the project by individuals expressing their concerns or endorsements.

To evaluate the intellectual value of such tweets, the study conducted a word count analysis to identify the frequently used concepts and technologies. When the tweets consisted of more concepts such as innovation and sustainability, they were classified as 'tweets on smart city concepts', and when the tweets discussed about technologies such as AI and IoT, they were classified as 'tweets on smart city technologies'. In a situation, where tweets equally discussed about both concepts and technologies, they were classified under both categories. Further, tweets which generally comment on smart cities without referring to any technology or concept—i.e., Enjoying the life in a smart city of Australia, were ignored.

TABLE 6.2

Smart City Technology Tweets by States

States \ Technologies	IoT	AI	AV	Big data	5G	Robotics	Open data	Blockchain
ACT	27	15	27	11	9	6	9	6
NSW	162	88	71	54	58	45	32	0
QLD	67	41	39	27	6	21	22	11
SA	21	18	12	12	4	5	8	4
TAS	9	0	1	1	0	0	1	1
VIC	103	66	68	44	47	45	34	30
WA	3	3	2	3	2	1	2	1
AUSTRALIA	392	231	220	152	126	123	108	53

Finally, the study identified 16 themes that acted as the basis for most tweets. Across Australia the most referred-to technologies were: Internet-of-Things (IoT) (392); Artificial intelligence (AI) (231); Autonomous vehicle (AV) (220); Big data (152); 5G (126); Robotics (123); Open data (108); and Blockchain (53). These technologies were discussed in relation to key concepts such as: Innovation (423); Sustainability (413); Start-ups (269); Governance (255); Mobility (97); Waste (82); Energy (19); and Transport (13). However, as shown in Table 6.2, the attention paid to each concept and technology varied significantly from state to state.

Australian states have different foci when it comes to adopting novel, innovative and advanced technologies for making their cities smart (Table 6.2). The main exposure technologies of interest in NSW were concentrated around the IoT (162), AI (88), and AV (71); and interest in blockchain was low (0). Conversely, citizens from VIC, QLD, ACT, and SA have a dispersed interest in diversified technologies for smart cities. Although ACT has a comparatively lower number of residents, it performs well with a considerable number of tweets. This reflects the extensive interest, knowledge, and awareness of ACT residents on the smart city concepts and technologies. WA and TAS also have a dispersed interest in technologies, but the lower number of tweets made them insignificant/unreliable. The results displayed that motivation and awareness exist among the local communities of each state in making their cities smarter.

As well as technologies, there were engaging concepts. As given in Table 6.3, eight popular concepts were identified from tweets scrutinised through a word frequency analysis.

Innovation (213), start-ups (145), sustainability (140), and governance (e-governance) (125) were the most popular concepts in NSW. However, compared to the number of tweets, sustainability is much more popular in VIC (207 tweets) as a concept than in NSW. QLD and ACT were interested in smart city agendas to encourage sustainability in their cities through novel innovations and e-governance practices. Accordingly, Twitter users seem to be extensively interested in making their cities smart in transport, governance, innovative economy (e.g., start-ups), and waste management areas.

TABLE 6.3

Smart City Concept Tweets by States

Concepts / States	Innovation	Sustainability	Start-ups	Governance	Mobility	Waste	Energy	Transport
ACT	54	40	14	23	10	12	10	12
NSW	213	140	145	125	44	46	2	4
QLD	30	50	17	31	15	11	2	2
SA	16	6	4	14	5	2	2	0
TAS	5	5	2	7	0	0	0	0
VIC	82	207	88	60	28	19	7	0
WA	11	1	5	6	3	0	1	3
AUSTRALIA	423	413	269	255	97	82	19	13

Table 6.4 demonstrates that Twitter users from the capital cities of Australian states were highly active in using social media to discuss concepts and technologies—i.e., Sydney, Melbourne, Brisbane, Canberra, Adelaide, Perth, Hobart. Top-10 Twitter active cities on smart city discussions also include some locations outside the capital cities—i.e., Sunshine Coast, Gold Coast, Ipswich from QLD. Table 6.4 provides a population-weighted rank of the most active locations in terms of smart city discussion. While the top-10 locations do not change, their order does.

Although Tables 6.1 and 6.2 reflect the trending concepts and technologies, they did not reflect the relationships among popular concepts and technologies. Neither did they reflect the popularity of each concept and technology (when all concepts and technologies are considered). Hence, we conducted a network analysis.

Figure 6.4 presents the layout of network topology, which disclosed the relationships between popular concepts and technologies. Square nodes depict concepts, and circular nodes depict technologies. The widths of the

TABLE 6.4

Most Active (Top-10) Cities in Smart City Tweets

City	Number of Tweets and Retweets	Population Weighted Rank
Sydney (NSW)	1,339	1
Melbourne (VIC)	696	3
Brisbane (QLD)	379	7
Canberra (ACT)	371	4
Adelaide (SA)	103	2
Perth (WA)	52	5
Sunshine Coast (QLD)	29	8
Hobart (TAS)	25	6
Gold Coast (QLD)	14	10
Ipswich (QLD)	10	9

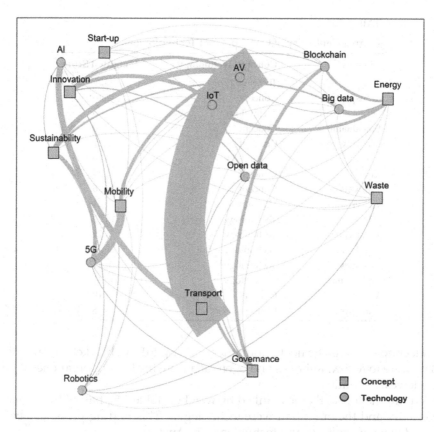

FIGURE 6.4
Relationships between popular concepts and technologies.

edges show the strength of the relationship that exists in between nodes. The strength of the relationships among nodes were calculated through the co-occurrence of concepts and technologies in the tweets and retweets analysed.

Then, the study calculated the centrality (popularity) level of each node. We used weighted degree centrality—a measure to identify the nodes' connectedness with the other nodes in the network—to quantify the perceived levels/ degrees of the aforesaid concepts and technologies. For instance, a node with five links has a higher degree of centrality than a node with two links. The number of co-occurrences were used to create/weigh the links among the nodes.

As per Table 6.5, transport (can be merged with mobility) was by far the most central concept. Sustainability was the second most popular concept. Energy, innovation and governance concepts followed. Waste and start-ups (can be merged with innovation) were other concepts gaining popularity.

Among the technologies, AV was by far the most popular one (by weight) (Table 6.5), and had a strong relationship first with transport, and then with the other concepts such as sustainability, mobility, energy, and innovation (Figure 6.4).

TABLE 6.5

Degree Centrality of Concepts and Technologies

Themes	Concept/Technology	Weighted Score
AV	Technology	129
Transport	Concept	116
5G	Technology	35
Sustainability	Concept	34
Mobility	Concept	32
IoT	Technology	30
Energy	Concept	29
Innovation	Concept	26
Governance	Concept	24
AI	Technology	22
Block chain	Technology	21
Big data	Technology	20
Robotics	Technology	11
Open data	Technology	11
Waste	Concept	10
Start-ups	Concept	8

5G technology was the next popular technology. IoT, AI, blockchain, and big data were to follow. Robotics and open data were the least popular ones with the lowest centrality.

Within the top-16 themes ranked by weights (Table 6.5), half of them were concepts, and the other half were technologies. This finding presents a balanced view of concepts and technologies in Australia.

6.4.3 What Are the Official Smart City Policies That Influence Perception and Utilisation of Smart City Concepts and Technologies?

In general, Australian states perceived concepts and technologies differently. This is most likely due to the varying degree of externalities of smart city policies on local communities in each state. The more community feel the impacts of such policies (positive or negative), the more they will discuss, appreciate or criticise them. Sound and well communicated policies receive higher support from the public; the opposite is also true.

Australia is rich in urban policy with numerous government policies focusing on smart cities (Yigitcanlar et al., 2020). Prominent national-level authorities that have prepared and launched smart city policies, funds and projects include the Smart Cities Council of Australia and New Zealand, the Australian Department of Infrastructure, Transport, Cities and Regional Development, and the Department of the Prime Minister and Cabinet. NSW, VIC, SA and QLD also have state-level smart city policies. At the local level, smart city policies are also gaining prominence. Table 6.6 lists cities with smart city strategy.

TABLE 6.6

Local Government Areas with Smart City Strategy

State	City	Title	URL
QLD	Brisbane	Smart, Connected Brisbane	https://www.brisbane.qld.gov.au/about-council/governance-and-strategy/vision-and-strategy/smart-connected-brisbane
	Sunshine Coast	Smart City Framework	https://www.sunshinecoast.qld.gov.au/Council/Planning-and-Projects/Major-Regional-Projects/Smart-Cities/Smart-City-Implementation-Program
	Townsville	Smart Townsville	https://www.townsville.qld.gov.au/about-council/news-and-publications/city-update-online/smart-townsville
NSW	Canada Bay	Smart City Draft Plan	https://collaborate.canadabay.nsw.gov.au/smartcity
	Goulburn Mulwaree	Smart City Strategy	https://yoursay.goulburn.nsw.gov.au/smart-city-action-plan
	Lake Macquarie	Smart Council Digital Economy Strategy	https://www.lakemac.com.au/city/smart-city-smart-council
	Newcastle	Draft Smart City Strategy	http://newcastle.nsw.gov.au/Community/Get-Involved/Completed-Consultation-Projects/Community-Planning/Smart-City-Strategy-2017-2021
	Paramatta	Smart City Masterplan	https://www.cityofparramatta.nsw.gov.au/smart-city
	Randwick	Draft Smart City Strategy	https://www.yoursay.randwick.nsw.gov.au/smartcities
	Western Sydney	Smart Cities Plan	https://citydeals.infrastructure.gov.au/western-sydney
NT	Darwin	Smart City Plan	https://citydeals.infrastructure.gov.au/darwin
SA	Adelaide	Smart Cities Plan	https://citydeals.infrastructure.gov.au/adelaide
	Charles Sturt	Smart City Plan	https://www.charlessturt.sa.gov.au/SmartCity
TAS	Hobart	Connected Hobart Smart Cities Action Plan	https://yoursay.hobartcity.com.au/smart-city
	Launceston	Smart Cities Plan	https://www.launceston.tas.gov.au/Launceston-City-Deal/City-Deal-Implementation
VIC	Geelong	Smart Cities Plan	https://citydeals.infrastructure.gov.au/geelong
	Wyndham	Smart City Strategy	https://theloop.wyndham.vic.gov.au/smart-city

Smart city policies are categorised into four themes, transport-, energy-, economy- and governance-related policies. All state capitals except WA and NT have clear policies in these areas. There are also smart city projects in progress across all states. NSW has 13 smart city projects, while VIC, QLD, WA, SA have 10, 9, 7, 6, and 2 projects respectively, and NT has one project.

Transport-related policies are the most prominent. This might be something to do with transport being a major challenge for Australian populations and cities that rely heavily on private motor vehicles. The key smart city strategies in operation that refer to legislative issues for smart cities include: Future Transport Strategy of NSW; Connected and Automated Vehicle Plan; Greater Sydney Service and Infrastructure Plan; National Smart Cities Plan. Policy discussions focusing on new and forthcoming legislation include: AV trial guidelines; New transport rules and regulations; Study lessons learned from the US and Singapore; Changing the sign boards; Changing property and other infrastructure-related guidelines for compliance with automated vehicles; Defining vehicle automation levels, designing trial paths; and Establishing a standby setting date to end analogue cars; and smart airports. AV projects and policy for smart transport planning under discussion include: Automated traffic management of Fraser Coast, QLD; Driverless shuttle service of Sydney; Semi-automated port operations in port Botany; Australia posts footpath-based delivery through drones.

Energy-related policies of Australia are concerned about balancing energy supply and energy demand reduction through smart energy use (Strengers, 2013). Australian policies on energy have already identified the significance of smart energy usage to cut energy bills and reduce environmental impacts. A number of smart city projects are already in operation. These include: Resilient energy and water systems of Fremantle, WA; Energy efficient housing of South East Perth, WA; Energy data for smart decision-making in Sydney; Smart grid trials in the Greater Newcastle and Sydney CBD. In addition, government policies on increasing infrastructure for electric vehicle users and increasing awareness about solar and battery storage technologies have also contributed towards the smart energy movement.

Economy-related policies received considerably less attention across Australia, even though the economy has weakened in recent years. Cities are only starting to consider the economic growth dimensions of smart policies. NSW has embraced investors to help Sydney on its mission to achieve 2021 goals. New start-ups, namely Nomad restaurants, Swill house group, Jolly Swagman Backpackers Sydney, Sydney Science Park, and Smart Innovation Centre are some businesses supporting the Smart Green Business Program of Sydney. It was awarded with the NSW Green Globe Award in 2013. Innovation districts are being developed all across the eastern coast of Australia—Sydney, Melbourne, Brisbane (Esmaeilpoorarabi et al., 2018; Pancholi et al., 2019). However, most of these are not directly linked with the smart city initiatives of their host cities. The national innovation district policy is also divorced from smart cities policy. The only exception is in Queensland. In QLD innovation districts were originally designed as part of the former Smart State Strategy of QLD (Hortz, 2016). However, to address this Australia wide limitation, in late 2018, a national policy was released. 'Principles for Australian Innovation Precincts' is prepared by the Federal Department of Industry, Innovation and Science emphasises the connection between innovation districts and smart cities.

Governance-related policies are gaining momentum. Australia is a global leader in the digitalisation of government services. Today, most government services are delivered virtually across many Australian authorities—e.g., tax, development assessment applications. Extensive online services also attract hackers. On cyber security, the Australian Strategic Policy Institute (ASPI) develops strategies to protect the privacy of data and information. Introducing a digital identity, to recognise receipt of a digital signature and secure data exchange mechanisms are the foci of the APSI policy.

Our policy analysis reflects the existence of, but limitations in or the inadequacy of the smart city initiatives at the national level. For instance, in 2017, more than 170 local governments applied for a share in AU$50 million smart cities Federal Government funding. This indicates the limitation of the funds for smart city projects in Australia. Some Australian states, such as TAS and NT do not have strong smart city policies. Instead, they have certain relevant projects implemented on demand. Although this is useful, having a sound national- and state-level policy for smart cities will help advance smart urbanism practices in Australia.

6.5 Discussion and Conclusion[1]

Smart cities have already become a promising approach to create a sustainable and livable urban future (Yigitcanlar et al., 2019a). Smart city discussions and awareness are especially high within the Australian professional and business communities. Smart cities are also highly popular in urban policy circles around the globe. Local, regional, and national governments have been working to transform their cities into smart ones through strategies, plans and projects involving the substantial engagement of technology solutions. Still, expectations from smart cities are highly unrealistic as they are full of speculations (Luque-Ayala & Marvin, 2015; Wiig, 2015). There is limited knowledge and understanding about: trending concepts and technologies, relationships between popular concepts and technologies, policies that influence perception, and use of concepts and technologies.

---

[1] This chapter, with permission from the copyright holder, is a reproduced version of the following journal article: Yigitcanlar, T., Kankanamge, N., & Vella, K. (2021). How are smart city concepts and technologies perceived and utilized? A systematic geo-Twitter analysis of smart cities in Australia. *Journal of Urban Technology, 28*(1–2), 135–154.

In order to bridge the aforementioned knowledge gap, this study employed systematic geo-Twitter analysis to scrutinise discourse and policy in Australia. The research particularly focused on addressing the question of: How are the smart city concepts and technologies are perceived and utilised in Australian cities? The study findings provide a clear snapshot of community perceptions, and disclose the following insights that inform smart city policymaking.

First, the results of the analysis showed that innovation, also including start-ups (with 692 of 3,073 tweets—23%), sustainability (413 tweets—13%), and governance (with 255—8%) were the most popular concepts in Twitter discourse across in Australia. When the degree of centrality of concepts is considered, the top-three concepts were transport (includes mobility), sustainability, and energy. This was followed by innovation and governance.

The ranking of the top-three concepts (i.e., innovation, sustainability, governance) in NSW and ACT were the same as for Australia. In VIC and QLD, sustainability took the first place (followed by innovation and governance), whereas, in TAS, it moved to the third place (following innovation and governance). In SA and WA, governance moved to the second place (after innovation and before sustainability). The variations between the states are an indication of local contextual differences in policy and planning priorities and conceptualisations of the smart city notion.

Second, the findings revealed that IoT (with 392 of 3,073 tweets—13%), AI (231 tweets—8%), and AV (220 tweets—7%) were the most popular technologies based on Twitter trends. When the degree centrality of concepts is considered the top-three ranking was as follows: AV, 5G, and IoT respectively (followed by AI). No tweets were found from NSW mentioning the blockchain technology. Though, throughout Australia, blockchain has been widely discussed in relation to energy and governance-related issues (Figure 6.4). The heightened interest in blockchain in VIC is mainly due to the Blockchain Association of Australia being located in Melbourne, VIC. Similarly, in QLD, the University of Queensland has a Blockchain Club, and Brisbane, QLD hosts the Blockchain Australia National Meetup Roadshows.

The three technologies (i.e., IoT, AI, AV) were in the top-three in all states besides TAS. Additionally, in some states, big data and open data were also shared the top-three position with AV. This finding indicates a degree of consistency across the states. The ranking of the top-three technologies in NSW and QLD were the same as for Australia. In VIC, AV moved one step up (following IoT and followed by AI). In ACT and SA, the first position is shared by IoT and AV (followed by AI). In WA, the third place was shared by AV and big data (following IoT and AI). In TAS, the second place was shared by AV, big data, and open data (following IoT). Similar to concepts, technologies also showed minor variations across the states. This is an indication of differences in technology adoption and prioritisation, and local smart city plans and projects.

Third, the study disclosed that Sydney, Melbourne, and Brisbane as major Australian cities—also their greater city-regions as the leading Australian metropolitan areas—have a higher interest in concepts and technologies. Nevertheless, different policy interventions and priorities of cities cause the increase/decrease of the popularity of aforesaid concepts and technologies among the public. For instance, although Brisbane's Smart Connected Brisbane Policy was only released in 2017, Brisbane has been benefiting from the Smart State Strategy legacy of the state government dating back to 1998. Similarly, Melbourne's relatively new smart city strategy is the rebranding of knowledge city (Millar & Ju-Choi, 2010; Yigitcanlar, 2014) policy of the city dating back to the early 2000s. In other words, Sydney, Melbourne, and Brisbane benefit from their path-dependency. Furthermore, these greater city-regions recently received lucrative funds for their smart city endeavours/ transformation—as part of the Commonwealth Government's Smart Cities Plan. For instance, Western Sydney City Deal in NSW, Geelong City Deal in VIC, and South East Queensland City Deal in QLD are among them— funding is envisaged to stimulate an increase of the economy by improving the productivity and competitiveness of the region.

Fourth, the network analysis findings pointed out a balanced view on the importance of concepts and technologies to achieve smart urbanism or smart city transformation—perhaps this is the Australian way of realising the smart city dream. This is a critical finding as only with such a balanced view— seeing technology as a means to a goal rather than fully relying on it as the panacea—we can address urban developmental problems (Yigitcanlar, 2006). One of the possible reasons for the balanced concept and technology view on smart cities in Australia are the advancing government policy frameworks. Currently, more than a dozen sound smart city policy frameworks are available (Table 6.6) at the local government level, and this number is expected to exponentially increase in the near future.

Fifth, the study proved that systematic geo-Twitter analysis is a useful methodological approach for investigating perceptions and utilisation of concepts and technologies. The social media analytics methodology—the capture-understand-present framework (Fan & Gordon, 2014)—was previously applied to other research areas—e.g., business, and tourism and hospitality (Amadio & Procaccino, 2016). This chapter showcases its application in another field—i.e., smart city concepts and technologies.

Next, this study provides a big picture view of the Twitter user perspectives on the smart city concepts and technologies in Australian cities. It also showcases the usefulness of social media analysis as a complementary method to the studies government agencies, not-for-profit organisations and consultancy firms have been undertaking to follow the latest developments in the field and understand the perceptions of authorities, experts and the public at large. The findings are informative and encourage authorities to adopt social media analytics in their routine data collection mechanisms to make more informed decisions.

Lastly, in interpreting the study findings the following limitations should be considered: (a) Twitter is used as a social media channel to capture the views shared in Australia; (b) The study presents a snapshot in time by analysing tweets from 2018; (c) The study does not involve a time-series analysis; (d) 8,241 tweets were obtained and of these 3,073 qualified for analysis; (e) Different categorisations of smart city concepts and technologies might have an impact of the results; (f) There might be a degree of unconscious bias in the interpretation of the findings. Our prospective studies will concentrate on addressing these limitations.

References

Aina, Y. (2017). Achieving smart sustainable cities with GeoICT support. *Cities, 71,* 49–58.

Albino, V., Berardi, U., & Dangelico, R. (2015). Smart cities. *Journal of Urban Technology, 22,* 3–21.

Alizadeh, T. (2015). A policy analysis of digital strategies. *International Journal of Knowledge-Based Development, 6,* 85–103.

Alizadeh, T., Sarkar, S., & Burgoyne, S. (2019). Capturing citizen voice online. *Cities, 95,* 2751–2761.

Amadio, W., & Procaccino, J. (2016). Competitive analysis of online reviews using exploratory text mining. *Tourism and Hospitality Management, 22,* 193–210.

Anthopoulos, L. (2017). Smart utopia vs smart reality. *Cities, 63,* 128–148.

Arbolino, R., Carlucci, F., Cirà, A., Ioppolo, G., & Yigitcanlar, T. (2017). Efficiency of the EU regulation on greenhouse gas emissions in Italy. *Ecological Indicators, 81,* 115–123.

Arbolino, R., De Simone, L., Carlucci, F., Yigitcanlar, T., & Ioppolo, G. (2018). Towards a sustainable industrial ecology. *Journal of Cleaner Production, 178,* 220–236.

Arthur, R., Boulton, C., Shotton, H., & Williams, H. (2018). Social sensing of floods in the UK. *Plos One, 13,* 1–18.

Bibri, S. (2019). On the sustainability of smart and smarter cities in the era of big data. *Journal of Big Data, 6,* 25.

Brandt, T., Bendler, J., & Neumann, D. (2017). Social media analytics and value creation in urban smart tourism ecosystems. *Information & Management, 54,* 703–713.

Caragliu, A., Del Bo, C., & Nijkamp, P. (2011). Smart cities in Europe. *Journal of Urban Technology, 18,* 65–82.

Cebeillac, A., & Rault, Y.M. (2016). Contribution of geotagged twitter data in the study of a social Group's activity space. *Netcom. Réseaux, Communication Et Territoires, 30,* 231–248.

Ciuccarelli, P., Lupi, G., & Simeone, L., (2014). *Visualizing the Data City,* Springer, Berlin.

De-Jong, M., Joss, S., Schraven, D., Zhan, C., & Weijnen, M. (2015). Sustainable–smart–resilient–low carbon–eco–knowledge cities. *Journal of Cleaner Production, 109,* 25–38.

Deakin, M., & Reid, A. (2018). Smart cities. *Journal of Cleaner Production, 173,* 39–48.

Dufty, N. (2016). Twitter turns ten. *Australian Journal of Emergency Management, 31,* 50–54.

Errichiello, L., & Marasco, A. (2014). Open service innovation in smart cities. *Advanced Engineering Forum, 11,* 115–124.

Ersoy, A. (2017). Smart cities as a mechanism towards a broader understanding of infrastructure interdependencies. *Regional Studies, Regional Science, 4,* 26–31.

Esmaeilpoorarabi, N., Yigitcanlar, T., Guaralda, M., & Kamruzzaman, M. (2018). Does place quality matter for innovation districts? *Land Use Policy, 79,* 734–747.

Faisal, A., Yigitcanlar, T., Kamruzzaman, M., & Currie, G. (2019). Understanding autonomous vehicles. *Journal of Transport and Land Use, 12,* 45–72.

Fan, W., & Gordon, M. (2014). The power of social media analytics. *Communications of the ACM, 57,* 74–81.

Fernandez-Anez, V., Fernández-Güell, J., & Giffinger, R. (2018). Smart City implementation and discourses. *Cities, 78,* 4–16.

Giffinger, R., & Pichler-Milanović, N., (2007). *Smart Cities,* Vienna: Vienna University of Technology.

Grossi, G., & Pianezzi, D. (2017). Smart cities. *Cities, 69,* 79–85.

Guan, X., & Chen, C. (2014). Using social media data to understand and assess disasters. *Natural Hazards, 74,* 837–850.

Hortz, T. (2016). The smart state test. *International Journal of Knowledge-Based Development, 7,* 75–101.

Joss, S., Sengers, F., Schraven, D., Caprotti, F., & Dayot, Y. (2019). The smart City as global discourse. *Journal of Urban Technology, 26,* 3–34.

Kankanamge, N., Yigitcanlar, T., Goonetilleke, A., & Kamruzzaman, M. (2019). Can volunteer crowdsourcing reduce disaster risk? A systematic review of the literature. *International Journal of Disaster Risk Reduction, 35,* 101097.

Kankanamge, N., Yigitcanlar, T., Goonetilleke, A., & Kamruzzaman, M. (2020). Determining disaster severity through social media analysis. *International Journal of Disaster Risk Reduction, 42,* 101360.

Komninos, N. (2016). Smart environments and smart growth. *International Journal of Knowledge-Based Development, 7,* 240–263.

Komninos, N., Kakderi, C., Panori, A., & Tsarchopoulos, P. (2019). Smart City planning from an evolutionary perspective. *Journal of Urban Technology, 26,* 3–20.

Kane, G. (2017). The evolutionary implications of social media for organizational knowledge management. *Information and Organization, 27,* 37–46.

Kunzmann, K. (2014). Smart cities. *Crios, 4,* 9–20.

Lin, J., & Cromley, R.G. (2015). Evaluating geo-located twitter data as a control layer for areal interpolation of population. *Applied Geography, 58,* 41–47.

Luque-Ayala, A., & Marvin, S. (2015). Developing a critical understanding of smart urbanism? *Urban Studies, 52,* 2105–2116.

Mah, D., Vleuten, J., Hills, P., & Tao, J. (2012). Consumer perceptions of smart grid development. *Energy Policy, 49,* 204–216.

Millar, C., & Ju-Choi, C. (2010). Development and knowledge resources. *Journal of Knowledge Management, 14,* 759–776.

Mora, L., Bolici, R., & Deakin, M. (2017). The first two decades of smart-City research. *Journal of Urban Technology, 24,* 3–27.

Mora, L., Deakin, M., & Reid, A. (2019). Strategic principles for smart City development. *Technological Forecasting and Social Change, 142,* 70–97.

Mysterud, A., (2017). *Evolutionary Perspectives on Environmental Problems,* Routledge, New York.

Osorio-Arjona, A., & García-Palomares, J. (2019). Social media and urban mobility. *Cities, 89,* 268–280.

Pancholi, S., Yigitcanlar, T., & Guaralda, M. (2019). Place making in knowledge and innovation spaces. *Technological Forecasting and Social Change, 146*, 616–625.

Pettit, C., Bakelmun, A., Lieske, S.N., Glackin, S., Thomson, G., Shearer, H., & Newman, P. (2018). Planning support systems for smart cities. *City, Culture and Society, 12*, 13–24.

Praharaj, S., Han, H., & Hawken, S. (2018). Urban innovation through policy integration. *City, Culture and Society, 12*, 35–43.

Söderström, O., Paasche, T., & Klauser, F. (2014). Smart cities as corporate storytelling. *City, 18*, 307–320.

Strengers, Y. (2013). *Smart Energy Technologies in Everyday Life*, Springer, Melbourne.

Townsend, A. (2013). *Smart Cities*, W.W.Norton, New York.

Winden, W., & Buuse, D. (2017). Smart City pilot projects. *Journal of Urban Technology, 24*, 51–72.

Wiig, A. (2015). IBM's smart City as techno-utopian policy mobility. *City, 19*, 258–273.

Williamson, W., & Ruming, K. (2019). Can social media support large scale public participation in urban planning? *International Planning Studies*, https://doi.org/10.1080/13563475.2019.1626221.

Yigitcanlar, T. (2006). Australian Local Governments' practice and prospects with online planning. *URISA Journal, 18*, 7–17.

Yigitcanlar, T., Fabian, & Coiacetto, E. (2008). Challenges to urban transport sustainability and smart transport in a tourist City. *The Open Transportation Journal, 2*, 29–46.

Yigitcanlar, T. (2009). Planning for smart urban ecosystems. *Theoretical and Empirical Researches in Urban Management, 4*, 5–21.

Yigitcanlar, T. (2014). *Position Paper, Expert Systems with Applications*, 41, 5549–5559.

Yigitcanlar, T. (2018). Smart City policies revisited. *World Technopolis Review, 7*, 97–112.

Yigitcanlar, T., & Kamruzzaman, M. (2018). Does smart City policy lead to sustainability of cities? *Land Use Policy, 73*, 49–58.

Yigitcanlar, T., Kamruzzaman, M., Buys, L., Ioppolo, G., Sabatini-Marques, J., Costa, J., & Yun, J. (2018). Understanding 'Smart Cities'. *Cities, 81*, 145–160.

Yigitcanlar, T., & Kamruzzaman, M. (2019). Smart cities and mobility. *Journal of Urban Technology, 2*, 21–46.

Yigitcanlar, T., Kamruzzaman, M., Foth, M., Sabatini-Marques, M., Costa, J.E., & Ioppolo, G. (2019a). Can cities become smart without being sustainable? *Sustainable Cities and Society, 45*, 348–365.

Yigitcanlar, T., Foth, M., & Kamruzzaman, M. (2019b). Towards post-anthropocentric cities. *Journal of Urban Technology, 26*, 147–152.

Yigitcanlar, T., Han, H., Kamruzzaman, M., Ioppolo, G., & Sabatini-Marques, J. (2019c). The making of smart cities. *Land Use Policy, 88*, 104187.

Yigitcanlar, T., Wilson, M., & Kamruzzaman, M. (2019d). Disruptive impacts of automated driving systems on the built environment and land use. *Journal of Open Innovation, 5*, 24.

Yigitcanlar, T., Kankanamge, N., Butler, L., Vella, K., & Desouza, K. (2020). *Smart Cities Down Under* (Brisbane: Queensland University of Technology, 2020) <https://eprints.qut.edu.au/136873/> Accessed on February 20, 2020.

Yuan, F., & Liu, R. (2018). Feasibility study of using crowdsourcing to identify critical affected areas for rapid damage assessment. *International Journal of Disaster Risk Reduction, 28*, 758–767.

Zhang, A., Huang, T., Zhu, Y., & Qiu, M. (2013). A case study of sensor data collection and analysis in smart City. *International Journal of Distributed Sensor Networks, 9*, 382132.

7

Social Media Analytics in Analysing Perceptions

7.1 Introduction

Cities provide tangible and intangible infrastructures and platforms from which individuals are able to self-actualise, and consequently create goods and services that further enhance the standards of living of the broader population (Dyer et al., 2019). The city, therefore, has an overarching responsibility for the impact that its hard and soft attributes have on its inhabitants; rendering it an institution that must guarantee the efficiency and reliability of its urban matrix (Liu, 2020). As part of the constant necessity to boost development and economic growth, cities are leveraging the benefits of technological advancements and implementing the latest artificial intelligence (AI) technologies; the aim is to exponentially increase sustainability through the efficient use of energy and resources (Arbolino et al., 2017; Abduljabbar et al., 2019; Yigitcanlar et al., 2020).

Technologies that leverage AI are currently being utilised in many cities across the globe, for example in Amsterdam, London, San Francisco, Stockholm, Singapore, Hong Kong, Vienna, and Toronto, to optimise their urban functionality and service efficiency (Kassens-Noor et al., 2020; Kirwan et al., 2020). For instance, the smart grid initiative acts as one of the foundations for the utilisation of AI in cities; it facilitates spatial navigation in the form of interactive and automated systems that use data processing technology to reveal the dynamics of the urban grid. In this way, digitalisation has enabled cities to identify specific needs, leading to increased productivity and economic performance (Liu, 2020). Subsequently, AI offers an opportunity for enhanced city governance (Ortega-Fernández et al., 2020). AI concepts and technologies can influence and improve the manner in which the city serves its citizens and provide everyone with the desired and responsible urban futures (Zhang et al., 2018; Yigitcanlar et al., 2020).

One of the most outstanding factors that have led cities to become smart is an inherent necessity to adapt to environmentally friendly initiatives

DOI: 10.1201/9781003278986-9

(Mah et al., 2012). The unprecedented reality of global warming has made it necessary to restructure the use of resources, where smart technologies are required to assist in the homogenous distribution of resources; resulting in the reduction in the carbon footprint of cities (Chang et al., 2018; Quan et al., 2019). Accordingly, smart environment technologies are applied in cities, they are generally AI-driven systems, which come in the form of smart traffic lights, noise prediction, air quality prediction, foot traffic as well as car traffic prediction faculties. All this is made possible thanks to big data technology, which facilitates data capture (Liu, 2020). This results in hyper-accurate urban data, which permits for highly productive interventions, enabling cities to use their resources sustainably.

It is evident that cities, so far, have been reaping significant benefits from utilising AI to design and implement city management strategies (Zhou et al., 2020). Nevertheless, it is estimated that a knowledge gap remains, specifically, in the manner in which the public perceives the implementa-tion of those technologies, and how they feel about the extensive applica-tion of AI in their cities (Adhikari et al., 2020; Kankanamge et al., 2020c). A solid understanding of the public's perceptions about AI concepts and technologies in their cities would inform policymakers of the general pub-lic sentiment regarding the different aspects of AI (Fast et al., 2020; Neri et al., 2019). Consequently, governing bodies would be better prepared to respond to the public's demands and to adopt urban AI technology and applications (Wirtz et al., 2019). It is, hence, necessary to explore the ways in which AI directly interacts with individuals and to dissect the manner in which the different AI instruments can potentially benefit or impair an individual or community.

The discourse on AI has become prevalent in Australia in recent times (Abbot et al., 2019: Rahmati et al., 2020). Abbot Particularly, the arrival of autonomous vehicles (AV), robotics, machine learning (ML), internet-of-things (IoT), blockchain, augmented reality (AR), and virtual reality (VR) technologies have resulted in a widespread debate on the future of AI in Australian cities; the citizens have begun to contemplate how big data, 5G, surveillance, and cybersecurity will impact their daily life. This chapter, thus, focuses on the public's perception of AI concepts and technologies in urban planning and development, in the context of Australian cities. The methodological approach of this study employs the social media analytics method and conducts sentiment and content analyses of location-based Twitter messages from Australia.

Following this introduction, Section 7.2 provides a literature background on the topic of investigation. Then, Section 7.3 introduces the methodological approach of the study. Next, Section 7.4 presents the results of the analysis. Afterwards, Section 7.5 discusses the study findings and generated insights. Lastly, Section 7.6 concludes this chapter with the study highlights, final remarks, and future research directions.

7.2 Literature Background

7.2.1 Artificial Intelligence

AI is one of the most disruptive technologies of our time (Yigitcanlar & Cugurullo, 2020). AI can be defined as machines or computers that mimic cognitive functions that humans associate with the human mind, such as learning and problem solving (Schalkoff, 1990; Adikari & Alahakoon, 2020). AI is a branch of computer science that perceives its environment and acts to maximise its chances of success. Furthermore, AI is capable of learning from past experiences, making reasoned decisions, and responding rapidly (Jackson, 2019). The scientific goal of AI researchers, hence, is to understand intelligence by building computer programs that exhibit symbolic inference or reasoning. For instance, according to (Wah et al., 1993), the four main components of AI are:

1. *Expert system:* Handles the situation under examination as an expert and yields the desired or expected performance.
2. *Heuristic problem solving:* Consists in evaluating a small range of solutions and may involve some guesswork to find near-optimal solutions.
3. *Natural language processing:* Enables communication between humans and machines in natural language.
4. *Computer vision:* Generates the ability to recognise shapes and features automatically.

AI is already being used in today's society in numerous areas, including but not limited to marketing, finance, agriculture, healthcare, security, robotics, transport, and artificial creativity and manufacturing (Yunn et al., 2016; Kankanamge et al., 2020). In recent years, AI has become an integral part of urban services as it offers efficient and effective platforms and smart governance opportunities (Rathore et al., 2016; Paulin, 2018; Williams, 2019; Caprotti & Liu, 2020). There are several types of AI hardware (e.g., machines/robots) and software (e.g., algorithms) that each have different capabilities at different levels of development (Bach, 2020). These levels are illustrated in Figure 7.1 and described below.

Level 1 refers to 'Reactive machines', which are programmed to undertake a single task and carry it out perfectly. However, this type of machine cannot learn further as it reacts to human input, rather than planning and pursuing its own original agenda (Girasa, 2020). Level 2 is the 'Independent AI' as human actions do not dictate all of the software actions; after some human lead, AI learns and improves its own ability to perform a given task. AI levels 1 and 2 are referred to as 'artificially narrow intelligence',

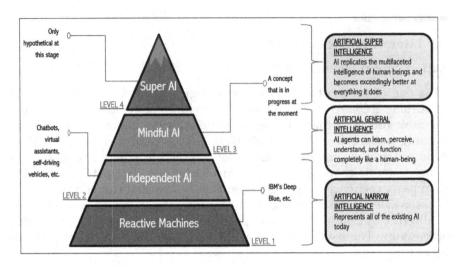

FIGURE 7.1
Levels of artificial intelligence. (Derived from Hengstler et al., 2016.)

they are currently being used in practice and are commonly applied in urban planning and development. Level 3 AI is called 'Mindful AI' and is capable of thinking thanks to a consciousness of its own and multiple domains of knowledge. This level of AI is currently at the stage of conceptual progress. Lastly, Level 4 is called 'Super AI' as it does anything and everything better than humans do (Pueyo, 2018). This level of AI is currently at the hypothetical stage.

7.2.2 Artificial Intelligence Technologies

The market for AI technologies is growing as large corporations are beginning to increase their investment in AI solutions. According to IDC (IDC, 2020), the AI market is expected to grow from $8 billion in 2016 to $57.6 billion by 2021. A study conducted by Cearley et al. (2018) has identified the AI technologies with the most growth so far:

- *Augmented reality:* Designers enhance parts of a user's physical world with computer-generated input that ranges from sound, video, and graphics to GPS overlay.
- *Automation:* Software that follows the instructions or workflows established by individuals for simple and repetitive tasks.
- *Big data:* Structured and unstructured data that is collected by an organisation and can be mined for information extraction and used in machine learning projects, predictive modelling, and other advanced analytical applications.

- *Biometrics:* It enables natural interactions between humans and machines through image, touch recognition, speech and body language.
- *Blockchain:* This is a public electronic ledger that can openly share information with many disparate users to create an unalterable record of transactions.
- *Deep learning platforms:* These are machine learning systems that consist of artificial networks with multiple layers, deep learning is capable of recognising and classifying patterns.
- *Digital twins:* These are digital representations that simulate a real-life object through the law of physics, material properties, virtualised sensors, and causality.
- *Machine learning platforms:* These provide algorithms, application programming interfaces (APIs), development, and training toolkits.
- *Natural language generation:* It produces text from computer data and it is currently being used in customer service, report generation, and summarising business intelligence insights.
- *Robotics:* This refers to the use of machines to perform tasks that are traditionally completed by humans.
- *Virtual agents:* These are advanced systems that can network with humans.

Thanks to the extensive research and advances in the field of AI, it is expected that by the end of 2035 our society and cities will transition from the current AI with complex machine language towards AI that will likely be fully understood by humans (Press, 2020).

7.2.3 Artificial Intelligence Application Areas in Urban Planning and Development

The urban planning environment is increasingly turning to specialised technologies to address uses related to sustainability, society, security, transportation, infrastructure, and governance (Audirac, 2002). The term urban artificial intelligence refers to AI that is embodied in urban spaces and infrastructure. These technologies are turning cities into autonomous entities that operate in an unsupervised manner (Cugurullo, 2020). The emerging concept of smart cities has promoted the development of IoT and through it the incorporation of sensors and big data (Vilajosana et al., 2013). The surge in data brings new possibilities to the design, management and the economy. Furthermore, IoT supports increased connectivity that leads to the generation of data and its subsequent capture, analysis and distribution, contributing to better smart city development (Batty, 2018; Ullah et al., 2020).

AI can significantly contribute to planning by binding frameworks that encompass key dimensions, such as culture, metabolism, and governance, ensuring their achievement. Data can now be sourced from numerous neighbourhoods to gain a more holistic understanding of the urban fabric. This allows planners and policymakers to shift from closed systems (interlinked urban elements) to open, fragmented, peri-urban fabric that has tangible impacts on density fragmentation, cohesion, and compactness (Batty, 2018).

AI-based data processing can help offer better prevision of liveability, through the creation of a clean, healthy, and conducive environment for people to live and work in, overcoming the urban challenges of pollution and congestion (Allam et al., 2019). Additionally, urban areas that leverage AI are enabling infrastructures that attract higher economic returns by offering connectivity, energy, and computing capabilities that support globally competitive jobs, as well as talented and knowledgeable workers (Davenport, 2018).

7.3 Research Design

7.3.1 Case Study

This research chapter follows a case study approach. The conducted case study has focused on the current status of AI and on the identification of AI applications in urban planning and development activities in Australian cities. The reasons behind this selection include: (a) Some of Australia's major cities are considered to be among the leading smart cities in the world. These cities are successfully adopting smart urban technologies that also include AI-related technologies and applications (Yigitcanlar et al., 2020); (b) Australia is among the countries that developed a national AI strategy and roadmap, meaning that AI uptake in cities is planned rather than done on an ad hoc basis (CSIRO, 2020); and (c) Social media use is highly popular in the country, making it a source of first-hand information regarding the Australian society, including its perception of urban technologies. About 66% of Australian internet users use social media daily and around 34% use social media more than five times a day (Yellow, 2018). Among the 66%, 19% of them have accessed Twitter and one-third of them tweet daily (BQ, 2020); (d) Although large amounts of social media data are available regarding AI in Australia, very few studies have been conducted to draw conclusions from this big data. For instance, Yigitcanlar et al. (2020) performed social media analytics on Twitter data to evaluate smart city concepts and technologies across Australia, such as AI, big data, 5G, IoT, AVs, and robotics. However, further investigations are required to capture and evaluate the public's perception of AI and its urban and social implications in Australia.

7.3.2 Methodology

Instead of using a traditional data collection method, the methodological approach applied in this study employs a contemporary method—i.e., social media analysis. As social media are ever-evolving platforms, where people can share thoughts and opinions. They have become a new source of qualitative data (Kankanamge et al., 2019). This data collection method has started to be used as the main data source in a large number of studies. Social media have offered an opportunity to engage with larger groups of people, in an unbiased setting (Kankanamge et al., 2020a). In addition, researchers can engage with people from broader geographic areas with the help of the location of social media users, which is tagged in their posts (Kankanamge et al., 2020b).

A geo-Twitter analysis has proven to be a very successful data collection method (Fan & Gordon, 2014); hence this method has been used in this study. A geo-Twitter analysis increases efficiency in analysing a large amount of shared thoughts and opinions (Gu et al., 2016), and real-time information on ongoing social issues (Gu et al., 2016). For instance, social media analytics has contributed to safeguarding Australian cities and their residents from the coronavirus outbreak (COVID-19) in 2020 (Yigitcanlar et al., 2020).

Initially, sentiment and content analyses were completed for the total number of location-based Twitter messages—a.k.a. tweets. To do this, the original dataset obtained (from the QUT Digital Observatory—https://www.qut.edu.au/institute-for-future-environments/facilities/digital-observatory/digital-observatory-databank) with 98,534 tweets was filtered down to 11,236 tweets. This was done using five data filtering processes, which included frequency analysis, location, date, bot, and relevance filters.

Firstly, we selected the most recent one-year period for the analysis, hence, all tweets outside of Australia and not within the 10 June 2019 to 10 June 2020-time period were removed from this dataset. The reason for only selecting a one-year period was two-fold. The first one is to capture the latest trends, as in the technology domain the development is fast and public perceptions change rather rapidly. The second is easing the analysis tasks as there have been around 50,000 to 100,000 tweets on AI shared annually in Australia during the last five years. The bot filter removed tweet repetitions with the program 'NVivo'—a content analysis automatic software system. In regard to identifying the tweets on themes associated with AI applications in urban planning and development, NVivo has also been used.

Secondly, a word frequency analysis has been conducted using NVivo, with the aim of identifying popular themes, concepts, and technologies.

Next, a word co-occurrence analysis identified the tweets that discussed both AI technologies and urban planning and development related concepts (or AI application areas) in a single Twitter message. For this analysis Nvivo software was employed.

Fourthly, spatial analysis has been conducted to complement the content analysis, which included the tweets being separated by location and collected to help categorise themes, concepts, and technologies based on these locations. This created an overview of the most popular themes, concepts, and technologies for each state/territory in Australia. ArcGIS Pro software was used for visualising spatial information.

Then, the relevance filter has been completed manually and has been used to identify tweets that were related to or discussed AI technologies and urban planning and development related concepts, noting key sentiment words. These words were then classified on a scale of one to three, to measure the sensitivity. This scale read to be: 1 = Positive sentiment, 2 = Negative sentiment, and 3 = Neutral sentiment. These words were then pre-processed in the program 'Weka', which created a dataset that further analysed the word content. The sensitivity of these specific words was showcased in a 'Random tree' classification type.

Finally, network analysis has been created to present the relationships between AI themes, concepts, and technologies, presenting the most popular relationships more centrally. In this analysis, nodes (themes, concepts, and technologies) and edges (relationships between these themes, concepts, and technologies) were used as the key elements of the network. These assist in understanding the network typology, which represents the arrangement of nodes and edges on the basis of the co-occurrence of the themes, concepts, and technologies found in the tweets. For this analysis, Gephi software was employed.

7.4 Results

7.4.1 General Observations

From the final dataset of 11, 262 tweets, 52% (n=5,850) were from NSW, 15% (n=1,704) were from VIC, 12% (n=1,349) were from SA, 10% (n=1,124) were from WA, 7% (n=787) were from QLD, 2% (n=260) were from TAS, and 1% (n=133) was from ACT (Figure 7.2). Compared to the other states and territories the number of tweets received from NT was recorded as 55, which represented a negligible percentage of 0%. This reveals the low interests among the NT community regarding AI-related applications. A wide-range of hashtags were used in the circulated tweets. Among them, hashtags such as #AI, #IoT, #digital, #robotics, #future, # technology, #automation, #big-data, # VR, #AR, #crypto, #bitcoin, #machine learning, #ML were the most popular ones.

7.4.2 Community Sentiments

Out of the analysed 11,262 tweets, 66% (n=7,475) of them carried positive sentiments related to AI technologies and applications within the context

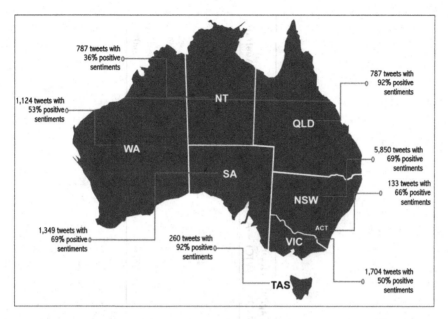

FIGURE 7.2
Tweet numbers and positive sentiment percentages by states and territories.

of urban planning and development. About 17% (n=1,935) had negative sentiments towards AI technologies. Around 16% (n=1,852) of the tweets had neutral sentiments, whereas such tweets have used only a set of hashtags to express their ideas rather than elaborative comments (Table 7.1).

From the tweets originating from NSW and SA, n=5,850 and 1,349 respectively, 69% of them contained positive sentiments—4,022 and 932 tweets from NSW and SA were positive in nature. While, 14% of tweets were negative in NSW, this figure was only 4% in SA. Out of 133, tweets originated from ACT, 66% (n=88) were positive, and 17% (n=22) were negative. VIC had the second-highest number of tweets (n=1,704), and among them 50% (n=854) were positive and 42% (n=715) were negative. From the 1,124 tweets originated from WA, 53% (n=599) were positive and 22% (n=251) were negative in nature. NT had the least number of tweets related to AI; among them 36% (n=20) were positive and only 11% (n=6) were negative. Significantly, 53% (n=29) of tweets from NT were neutral. Example tweets for each sentiment category are given in Table 7.2.

7.4.3 Artificial Intelligence Technologies

Using a word frequency analysis technique, 15 key AI-related technologies were derived from the collected tweets (Figure 7.3 and Table 7.3). These technologies are 'robotics' (n=3,055), 'drones' (n=1,943), 'automation' (n=717), 'digital twins' (n=337), 'block chain' (n=263), 'machine learning' (n=236),

TABLE 7.1

Tweet Sentiments in Percentages per State/Territory

	Queensland (QLD)	Tasmania (TAS)	New South Wales (NSW)	South Australia (SA)	Australian Capital Territory (ACT)	Victoria (VIC)	Western Australia (WA)	Northern Territory (NT)	Australia
Positive Sentiments	92%	92%	69%	69%	66%	50%	53%	36%	66%
Negative Sentiments	5%	3%	14%	4%	17%	42%	23%	11%	15%
Neutral Sentiments	3%	5%	17%	27%	17%	8%	24%	53%	19%
Total	100%	100%	100%	100%	100%	100%	100%	100%	100%

TABLE 7.2

Example Tweets for Three Sentiment Categories

Date and Time	State	Tweet	Sentiment
12/08/2019 21:03	NSW	#drones are changing the meaning of "many hands make light work" for these farmers. The farm of the future will be technology-enabled. We should be happy with that.	Positive
23/07/2019 8:01	VIC	In other words, just move to a city or large town. People are losing their jobs daily. Robots and technology aren't consumers of goods and services.	Negative
15/03/2019 9:42	QLD	Automation has much to offer #IoT #AutonomousVehicles #IoT #SmartCity #smartgrid #Healthcare, but also much to take away from us #Cyberecurity #jobloss #Disruption	Neutral

'digital networks' (n=207), 'digital currency' (n=192), '5G technology' (n=178), 'big data' (n=154), 'augmented reality' (n=124), '3D printing' (n=101), 'virtual reality' (n=86), 'telephony' (n=13), and 'chatbots' (n=11).

Nonetheless, the popularity of each technology differs from one state or territory to another. For instance, in VIC there are more tweets about 'automation' (n=317) compared to the NSW state (n=180). Albeit, 'robotics' is around seven times more popular (n=2,328) in NSW than in VIC (n=340).

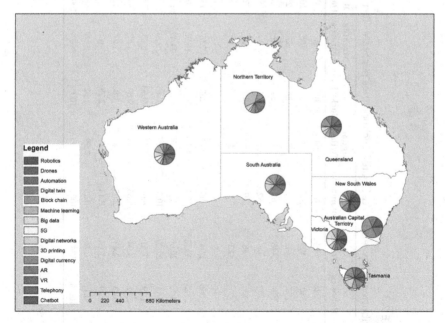

FIGURE 7.3
Distribution of tweets by AI-related technologies per state/territory.

TABLE 7.3

Distribution of Tweets by AI-Related Technologies per State/Territory

	Robotics	Drones	Automation	Digital Twins	BlockChain	Machine Learning	Big Data	5G	Digital Networks	3D Printing	Digital Currency	AR	VR	Telephony	Chatbot
NSW	2,328	694	180	164	104	40	0	54	63	63	116	18	14	8	9
VIC	340	499	317	72	31	105	107	104	65	21	36	40	34	3	2
WA	157	433	74	40	28	55	25	20	24	6	5	16	19	2	0
SA	128	146	62	26	54	19	11	0	38	4	2	43	11	0	0
QLD	77	96	62	24	26	3	8	0	8	5	21	3	5	0	0
TAS	13	48	19	5	10	3	2	0	8	2	6	1	1	0	0
ACT	9	22	1	4	6	0	0	0	0	0	4	2	0	0	0
NT	3	5	2	2	4	11	1	0	1	0	2	1	2	0	0
Total	3,055	1,943	717	337	263	236	154	178	207	101	192	124	86	13	11
NSW	76.2	35.72	25.1	48.66	39.54	16.95	0	30.34	30.43	62.38	60.42	14.52	16.28	61.54	81.82
VIC	11.13	25.68	44.21	21.36	11.79	44.49	69.48	58.43	31.42	20.79	18.75	32.26	39.53	23.08	18.18
WA	5.14	22.29	10.32	11.87	10.65	23.31	16.23	11.23	11.59	5.94	2.6	12.89	22.09	15.38	0
SA	4.19	7.51	8.65	7.72	20.53	8.05	7.15	0	18.36	3.96	1.04	34.68	12.79	0	0
QLD	2.52	4.94	8.65	7.13	9.89	1.27	5.19	0	3.86	4.95	10.94	2.42	5.82	0	0
TAS	0.43	2.47	2.65	1.48	3.8	1.27	1.3	0	3.86	1.98	3.13	0.81	1.16	0	0
ACT	0.29	1.13	0.14	1.19	2.28	0	0	0	0	0	2.08	1.61	0	0	0
NT	0.1	0.26	0.28	0.59	1.52	4.66	0.65	0	0.48	0	1.04	0.81	2.33	0	0
Total	100%	100%	100%	100%	100%	100%	100%	100%	100%	100%	100%	100%	100%	100%	100%

Likewise, tweets from different states and territories had more tweets related to different AI-related technologies. 'Robotics' (n=2,348) was the most tweeted AI technology in NSW. In contrast, 'drones' were the most tweeted technology in VIC (n=499), WA (n=433), SA (n=146), QLD (n=96), TAS (n=48), and ACT (n=22). 'Machine learning' (n=11) was comparatively high among the tweets circulated in NT. Table 7.4 provides exemplar tweets related to each technology.

7.4.4 Artificial Intelligence Related Urban Planning and Development Concepts

On the basis of a word frequency analysis, 16 key urban planning and development related concepts were derived from the AI-related tweets (Figure 7.4 and Table 7.5). These concepts are 'sustainability' (n=774), 'cybersecurity' (n=741), 'innovation' (n=734), 'construction' (n=644), 'governance' (n=585), 'transportation' (n=275), 'health' (n=263), 'communication' (n=241), 'digital transformation' (n=203), 'mobility' (n=190), 'energy' (n=184), 'infrastructure' (n=156), 'waste' (n=144), 'economy' (n=124), 'environment' (n=118), and 'tourism' (n=20).

Sustainability was the most commonly discussed urban planning and development concept, but its usability differed from one state/territory to another. While 'sustainability' (n=418) was the most commonly tweeted urban planning and development concept in NSW, 'innovation' was most popular in VIC (n=182), WA (n=122), and SA (n=110). The use of AI-related technologies in 'governance' was the most popular concept in QLD (n=29) and ACT (n=10). Tweets from TAS had more discussions related to use of AI in 'construction' (n=20). Although there was a lower number of tweets in NT, most of them were related to the use of AI for 'sustainability' (n=9).

As shown in Table 7.5, the use of AI technologies in relation to transportation, health, communication, and digital transformation were also some of the frequently used concepts (or AI application areas). Furthermore, concepts such as 'mobility', 'energy', 'waste', 'economy', 'environment' and 'tourism' did not receive much attention, thus they can be identified as emerging topics within the research contexts of novel AI applications. Table 7.6 provides exemplar tweets related to each urban planning and development concept.

7.4.5 Relationships Between Artificial Intelligence Technologies and Urban Planning and Development Concepts

The objective has been to understand AI-related technologies and the public perception of their application in the urban context. To this end, the study conducted a word co-occurrence analysis, which identified the number of tweets that mentioned both technology and the urban planning and development concepts (Table 7.7).

TABLE 7.4

Example Tweets for AI-Related Technologies

Technology	Data and Time	State	Tweet	Sentiment
Robotics	18/06/2020 2:14 PM	NSW	Boston Dynamics starts selling its Spot robot your own pet robot dog for $74,500 #Robotics #ArtificialIntelligence #robotpetdog #exciting	Positive
Drones	10/01/2020 7:22 PM	QLD	These drones plant thousands of trees ôŸŒ³ every day. Shooting the seeds into the ground. Huge opportunity for massive global tree planting!	Positive
Automation	18/12/2019 9:18 PM	VIC	As automation technology becomes more ingrained into the workplace, employee training becomes critical to direct employees' time towards higher-value work. The results of this survey are fascinating #SkillsGap #DigitalSkills	Positive
Digital twins	5/02/2020 1:38 PM	VIC	See my virtual replica. Experience the difference and the excitements #digitaltwin	Positive
Block chain	16/07/2019 8:35 PM	TAS	A place with abundant renewable generation such as wind, pumped hydro and cool climate would be perfect. #TAS and @HydroTasmania has all three, combined with a blockchain-based electricity marketplace and we can use the exist #futuristic #sustainableworld	Positive
Machine learning	5/02/2020 11:03 AM	ACT	Really excited for this one - our contribution to the discussion on predicting performances based on training load. Plus, an extra section using machine learning to combine the data from multiple athletes to predict outcomes for one. All done using #rstats h	Positive
Network	22/01/2019 5:34 AM	SA	A Hacker-Proof Quantum Network Is Hiding In This City Tunnel. We all are at a big risk	Negative
Digital currency	9/01/2020 11:49 AM	NSW	The latest The Bitcoin Profits Daily! https://t.co/qTJJaBkGEo Thanks to @ EllenDibble @linasantinijos #cryptocurrency #cryptocurrency #enjoytheprofit	Positive
5G technology	9/12/2019 2:27 AM	TAS	What has #5G got to do with helping reduce road traffic accidents? #EmergingTech #AI #ML #IoT #SelfDrivingCars #SmartCities #SelfDriving #Driverless #AutonomousVehicles #SelfDrivingCars #autonomousdriving #Automotive #selfDrivingCar #4IR #safercities	Positive

(Continued)

TABLE 7.4 (*Continued*)

Example Tweets for AI-Related Technologies

Technology	Data and Time	State	Tweet	Sentiment
Big data	2/04/2019 11:09 AM	WA	Training doctors while using #AugmentedReality via @futurism	#AR #VR #Healthcare #InternetofThings #IoT #SmartCity #SmartPhones #ArtificialIntelligence #AI #BigData #DataAnalytics #Data #Video	Positive
Augmented reality	17/01/2019 10:08 AM	WA	The AR market today is similar to where the IoT market was in 2010. AR's capacity to visualise, instruct, and interact can transform the way we work with data #success #newtech	Positive
3D printing	17/01/2019 12:33 AM	WA	Did my first 3D printing? It's amazing super-duper excited to share it with you	Positive
Virtual reality	29/03/2019 8:34 AM	SA	How exciting to see what is possible when AI meets virtual reality in the treatment of mental health conditions	Positive
Telephony	29/08/2019 5:12 PM	NT	Telephony technology has evolved rapidly keeping people distant emotionally and physically	Negative
Chatbots	19/06/2020 3:26 AM	NSW	How can I find screenshots or scripts from the CyberLover chatbot (the bot used to flirt with people in order to steal their data)? I would like to see some of the conversations it held. #wrongexamples	Negative

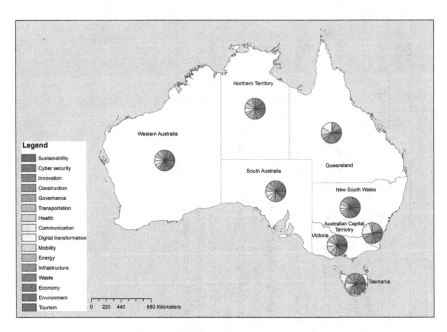

FIGURE 7.4
Distribution of tweets by urban planning and development concepts per state/territory.

Figure 7.5 represents the network topology, developed on the basis of the word co-occurrence analysis. This network typology is initially generated by using the Gephi software. Nonetheless, due to the crowdedness of the original figure—shown in the lower left side of Figure 7.5—a less complex version is recreated by only showing the stronger relationships that occurred between AI technologies and urban planning and development concepts. For that, we have identified connections less than 50 as weak or mid-strength and removed them from the figure. Connection counts between 50 and 99 are determined as semi-strong, connections between 100 and 199 are categorised as strong, and connections over 200 are labelled as very strong. Figure 7.5 illustrates these connections; where only the prominent connections are shown in the main part of the figure, where the full connections are given at the lower left side of the figure.

As shown in Figure 7.5, robotics has a close relationship with urban planning and development concepts such as 'innovation' (n=337), 'sustainability' (n=450), 'cybersecurity' (n=376), 'construction' (n=242), 'governance' (n=139), and 'waste management' (n=121). Secondly, the relationships between 'drone' technology and 'sustainability' (n=178), 'cybersecurity' (n=161) and 'construction' (n=138) were very pronounced. The third popular relationship was the use of 'autonomation' in 'cybersecurity' (n=72), 'construction' (n=63), 'innovation' (n=61), and 'transportation' (n=48). Fourthly, the relationship among 'big data' and 'governance' (n=51), and 'cybersecurity' (n=42) was visible.

TABLE 7.5

Distribution of Tweets by Urban Planning and Development Concepts per State/Territory

	Sustainability	Cybersecurity	Innovation	Construction	Governance	Transportation	Health	Communication	Digital Transformation	Mobility	Energy	Infrastructure	Waste	Economy	Environment	Tourism
NSW	418	358	285	324	264	78	115	116	63	54	79	48	72	61	37	13
VIC	119	173	182	123	101	78	76	35	61	82	67	42	30	24	38	2
WA	115	86	122	72	66	55	30	36	29	24	13	20	12	20	15	5
SA	101	89	110	97	93	47	33	46	26	19	13	35	11	6	21	0
QLD	3	13	11	1	29	6	2	0	16	10	6	4	12	8	1	0
TAS	9	18	16	20	18	7	3	8	2	0	2	4	4	3	4	0
ACT	0	1	1	2	10	0	1	0	4	0	1	2	1	1	1	0
NT	9	3	7	5	4	4	3	0	2	1	3	1	2	1	1	0
Total	774	741	734	644	585	275	263	241	203	190	184	156	144	124	118	20
NSW	54.01	48.31	38.83	50.31	45.13	28.36	43.73	48.13	31.03	28.42	42.93	30.77	50.01	49.19	31.36	65
VIC	15.37	23.35	24.79	19.09	17.26	28.36	28.89	14.52	30.05	43.16	36.41	26.92	20.83	19.35	32.19	10
WA	14.86	11.61	16.62	11.18	11.28	20.01	11.41	14.94	14.29	12.63	7.07	12.82	8.33	16.13	12.71	25
SA	13.05	12.01	14.99	15.06	15.9	17.09	12.55	19.09	12.81	10	7.07	22.44	7.64	4.84	17.8	0
QLD	0.39	1.75	1.5	0.16	4.96	2.18	0.76	0	7.88	5.26	3.26	2.56	8.33	6.45	0.85	0
TAS	1.16	2.43	2.18	3.11	3.08	2.55	1.14	3.32	0.99	0	1.09	2.56	2.78	2.42	3.39	0
ACT	0	0.13	0.14	0.31	1.71	0	0.38	0	1.97	0	0.54	1.28	0.69	0.81	0.85	0
NT	1.16	0.41	0.95	0.78	0.68	1.45	1.14	0	0.98	0.53	1.63	0.65	1.39	0.81	0.85	0
Total	100%	100%	100%	100%	100%	100%	100%	100%	100%	100%	100%	100%	100%	100%	100%	100%

TABLE 7.6

Example Tweets for Urban Planning and Development Concepts

Concepts	Data and Time	State	Tweet	Sentiment
Sustainability	17/06/2020 5:26 AM	NSW	3Ai Director @feraldata and @anucecs Dean @profElanor join the world-first Global Partnership on Artificial Intelligence. An exciting opportunity for Australia to contribute to global work on AI and to shape a safe, responsible, and sustainable future.	Positive
Cybersecurity	18/06/2020 10:07 AM	NSW	Digital human rights issues such as data privacy, cybersecurity, and social impacts of AI can pose risks to companies, and protection of digital human rights take on new considerations in the post-COVID-19 era, according to @ Robeco https://t.co/9zvXiVIDdJ	Negative
Innovation	9/01/2020 10:29 PM	QLD	We are thrilled to be featured in an @AllianceQQ Mag Dec/Jan issue article focusing on new #technology impacting #mining. "The industry is now seeing a second wave of technological #innovation based on #digitization and #IoT"	Positive
Construction	4/02/2020 2:17 PM	SA	I'm working on some amazing #hightech projects with the awesome team. #IOT #industrialiot #meshnetworks #smartmine #miningsolutions #miningtechnology #agriculture #agritech #agribusiness #construction #smartcity	Positive
Governance	29/10/2019 2:14 PM	ACT	How can governments earn trust in the next generation of AI; bot powered digital services? @piawaugh introduces our new fave term Citizen's Ledger in this A+ read on trust infrastructure for the future of democratic government #fake&fraud	Negative
Transportation	29/05/2019 10:13 AM		One of my favourite PBLs that my Ts do is #smartreynoldsburg. Based on what Ss learn about our city's past; the future of transportation; energy, Ss create a 3D model of what Reynoldsburg will look like in 50 yrs, complete with an autonomous car. #teachingland	Positive
Health	16/06/2020 5:56 PM	NSW	Big day today – I have now performed more than 300 transoral robotic surgeries on the da Vinci platform. Thank you to my surgical team and @SVHSydney for the cake! #TORS #HNC #HeadandNeckCancer #roboticsurgery @device_ robotics https://t.co/KNhGvlYF4n	Positive

(Continued)

TABLE 7.6 (Continued)

Example Tweets for Urban Planning and Development Concepts

Concepts	Data and Time	State	Tweet	Sentiment
Communication	3/09/2019 11:50 AM	SA	We are excited to announce the new research initiative: Information, Communication the Data Society. ICDS is an interdisciplinary research initiative on the way AI and algorithms affect the role, impact, and regulation of information	Positive
Digital transformation	1/04/2019 5:29 AM	NSW	What is the #InternetOfThings? Why is it so important? #IoT #DigitalTransformation #Automation #SmartCity #AutonomousVehicles #Driverless #SmartCars #SmartHome #CyberSecurity #SmartTech	Neutral
Mobility	31/03/2019 4:51 PM	SA	Should the AIUS SA focus on the Future of Mobility such as driverless shuttles and other autonomous vehicles? Let us know by completing our 5 minute survey!	Neutral
Energy	20/08/2019 6:27 AM	WA	Australian @PowerLedger_io successfully trialled its blockchain platform's use in P2P trading of renewable electricity in Japan	Positive
Infrastructure	16/04/2020 1:38 PM	QLD	#Virtual presence for physical one could have taken at least a generation #Coronivrus #Covid19 did it in months To #sustain it with #reliability #security & #capacity strong #Telecom infrastructure like #5G is important than ever #ICT #VR #AR #AI #Cloud #Data #IoT #CyberSecurity #safercities	Positive
Waste	17/06/2020 5:43 AM	NSW	As part of a new partnership with @Microsoft, we're using artificial intelligence (AI) and other digital technologies to boost farming and tackle global challenges including illegal fishing and plastic waste	Positive
Economy	1/05/2020 2:08 AM	TAS	Excited to introduce the AI Economist: Extends ideas from Reinforcement Learning for tackling inequality through learned tax policy design. The framework optimises productivity and equality.	Positive
Environment	10/09/2019 6:57 PM	TAS	Going digital will save the environment. Go digital!!!	Positive
Tourism	25/06/2019 7:00 AM	QLD	Autonomous regions, have been well prepared for the peak #tourism season #easytravel #easyapps	Positive

TABLE 7.7

Technology-Concept Relationship Word Co-Occurrence Analysis

	Digital transformation	Sustainability	Health	Environment	Economy	Transportation	Innovation	Communication	Construction	Tourism	Infrastructure	Energy	Cybersecurity	Mobility	Waste	Governance	Total
Robotics	69	450	59	13	22	40	337	110	242	2	14	16	376	44	121	139	2054
Drones	10	178	64	37	17	105	96	61	138	2	29	16	161	13	26	123	1076
Automation	28	48	8	0	18	16	61	26	63	2	4	12	72	8	9	53	428
Big data	11	2	13	12	6	12	25	19	33	0	10	14	42	6	2	51	258
Digital twin	28	23	12	2	8	6	26	4	20	0	12	9	15	6	6	28	205
Network	28	23	12	2	0	8	16	10	23	0	11	20	22	4	2	17	198
Machine learning	4	12	2	2	2	4	16	41	2	0	0	6	6	0	0	8	105
3D printing	2	19	4	0	0	2	13	0	14	0	8	6	6	2	2	6	84
5G	5	14	4	0	2	4	15	2	13	0	2	2	2	8	0	4	77
Block chain	4	10	5	2	0	2	10	6	0	0	0	0	11	2	4	2	58
AR	10	10	2	2	2	2	10	0	7	0	2	2	3	6	0	0	58
VR	11	9	0	0	4	2	13	0	4	0	0	4	0	4	0	4	55
Digital currency	2	10	2	0	0	5	9	0	2	0	0	3	5	0	0	8	46
Chatbot	0	0	0	0	0	0	0	4	6	0	0	0	1	0	0	2	13
Telephony	0	0	0	0	0	0	0	6	0	0	0	0	0	0	0	0	6
Total	212	808	187	72	81	208	647	289	567	6	92	110	722	103	172	445	4721

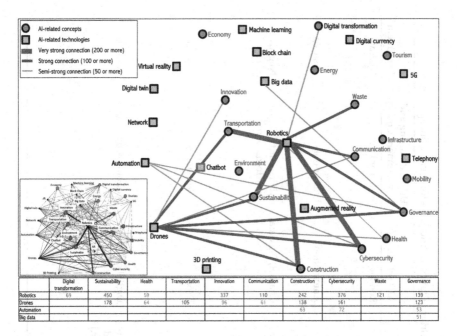

	Digital transformation	Sustainability	Health	Transportation	Innovation	Communication	Construction	Cybersecurity	Waste	Governance
Robotics	69	450	59		337	110	242	376	121	139
Drones		178	64	105	96	61	138	161		123
Automation							63	72		53
Big data										51

FIGURE 7.5
Relationships between AI technologies and urban planning and development concepts.

Although the relationships among the AI-related technologies such as 'digital twin', 'digital networking', 'machine learning', '3D printing' and '5G' were not as frequently used in relation to the derived urban planning and development concepts, they can be identified as emerging discussions within the Twitter hemisphere. The existence of tweets related to the 'digital twin' and 'governance' (n=28), 'digital transformation' (n=28) and 'innovation' (n=26) highlighted the increasing importance of 'digital twin' technology in our society—both public and private sectors. Nevertheless, tweets related to technologies such as 'block chain', 'AR', 'VR', 'digital currency', 'chatbot', and 'telephony' were comparatively low. Table 7.8 shows the example tweets, which discuss AI technologies in the derived urban planning and development concepts (or in other words AI application areas).

7.5 Discussion

AI is a widely used technology in Australia across many urban planning and development areas including, but not limited to, health, safety, environment, energy, infrastructure, transport, education and urban services (AG, 2020). Nonetheless, public perceptions regarding the use of AI are an understudied

TABLE 7.8

Example Tweets Showing the Relationship between AI Technologies and Urban Planning and Development Concepts

Data and Time	State	Tweet	AI Technology	Urban Planning and Development Concept	Sentiment
14/11/2019 5:57 PM	VIC	Great to see @cserAdelaide Lending Library #sphero kit in action with classes designing and building a Sustainable City and then coding robots through the streets of the city.	Robotics	Sustainability	Positive
3/01/2019 7:26 AM	NSW	Building #Sustainable #transport platforms will provide a more efficient #smartcity and cheaper than autonomous and electric vehicles	Automation	Transportation	Positive
17/06/2019 10:36 AM	QLD	City Loses $500,000 to Phishing Attack #CyberSecurity #Databreach #Ransomware #Hackers #infosec @reach2ratan #AI #bots #malware #DDoS #Digitaltransformation #Fintech #Blockchain #Chatbots #Bigdata #datascience #Digital	Chatbot, Big data	Cybersecurity, Digital transformation	Negative
8/08/2019 11:35 AM	TAS	@UTAS_ @DeformedEarth @CityByrne @homehillwines Drone video of @homehillwines landslide and @UTAS_ #UTAS_GSS student at work collecting 3D spatial data. Thanks, @homehillwines for your fantastic hospitality!	Drone	Environment	Positive
5/08/2019 4:24 PM	NSW	Humanity must now accept that a digital economy implemented by global governance w/ AI world systems for ppl and the planet is the way forward from 2020 #bitcoins	Digital currency	Economy, Governance	Positive
29/03/2019 8:34 AM	SA	How exciting to see what is possible when AI meets virtual reality in the treatment of mental health conditions	VR	Health	Positive

line of research (Gao et al., 2020). The study at hand has focused on addressing this limitation. Accordingly, the community's positive perceptions regarding the use of AI are evident in the presented findings. This is to say, overall, the Australian public has a positive perception of AI and its use to make cities more sustainable, innovative, accessible, healthy, and liveable (Yigitcanlar, 2010; Yigitcanlar & Kamruzzaman, 2015).

Nonetheless, in the analysed tweets, the public has also raised concerns about the use of AI, particularly in terms of cybersecurity breaches. Especially during the pandemic, a large part of Australian society was intended to move towards digital transformation. Due to the cyber-attack boom in 2020 in Australia, the discussions on cybersecurity and the ethical concerns associated with using AI technology become highly prominent (Taddeo et al., 2019; Webb & Dayal, 2020). Australian researchers have also highlighted the importance of understanding the loopholes in the present AI systems (Chanthadavong, 2020). Furthermore, the digital transformation has had a negative impact on the elderly population, as they need more assistance to use the technology (Datta et al., 2018; Hu, 2020).

The Australian government has already drafted an 'AI Action Plan' for all Australians, and is currently seeking feedback from the wider community (AG, 2020a). Through this plan, the Australian government has attempted to address the issue of cybersecurity by preparing and publishing an 'AI Ethics Framework'. This framework addresses the following issues: (a) Human, social and environmental wellbeing; (b) Human-centred values; (c) Fairness; (d) Privacy protection and security; (e) Reliability and safety; (f) Transparency and explainability; (g) Contestability; and (h) Accountability (AG, 2020b). Moreover, the Australian government has identified the importance of using AI in the ageing and disability sector to reduce costs while making quality care accessible to adult Australians (CSIRO, 2020). Nevertheless, it is important to pay attention to the user-friendliness and affordability of AI technologies, particularly concerning the disadvantaged populations (Lutz, 2019).

In 2019, the Australian government released an AI roadmap that recognises the current global shift towards smart cities and smart urban infrastructure (CSIRO, 2020). The roadmap suggests that government institutions should work with private organisations to develop, advance, and deploy AI solutions that will improve the urban environment and will help shape sustainable urban futures.

The roadmap has pointed to the potential benefits of AI, such as economic growth (Australia could become a key player on the global AI market in 2030, reaching a value of AU\$22.17 trillion), improved quality of life, environmental sustainability, and solution of the problems experienced by the ageing society (CSIRO, 2020). The roadmap involves the use of AI to decrease the costs and improve the effectiveness of built infrastructure planning, design, construction, operation, and maintenance. This is significant in the built environment as there is a shortcoming of built infrastructure as it is already impacting the operations of towns and cities around Australia (CSIRO, 2020). The following are urban planning and development concepts that were mentioned in the roadmap:

- *Improve the digital infrastructure* (for data transmission storage, analysis, and acquisition) so that AI can safely and effectively be used across Australian cities.
- *Develop AI for better towns, cities and infrastructure*, to improve the safety, efficiency, cost-effectiveness, and quality of the built environment.
- *Improve design, planning, construction, operation, and maintenance* of infrastructure and building with AI.
- *Utilise AI to improve the efficiency and safety* of transportation, electricity, and water services throughout the urban environment.
- *Improve AI technology* that reduces high construction costs and unplanned cost overruns as it is limiting the ability to improve cities and infrastructure.

Since 2010, The Australian Research Council has awarded over AU$243 million on research towards AI and data processing. Significant investment went towards blockchain, AR/VR, robotic process automation (RPA), natural language processing (NLP), and computer vision. These technologies represent the functionality of a digital co-worker as it encompasses both rule-based activities and judgement-based activities (Chaudhry & Dhawan, 2020). The following are the key concepts that were developed in the funded research and have influenced the perception of AI-related urban planning and development:

- *Data analytics:* Real-time or historical data that can provide insights into an urban environment. A key example is intelligent traffic lights that use data analytics to coordinate and make time-based changes in the traffic lights.
- *Machine learning:* Computer vision techniques to collect and annotate datasets. The model can be applied to predict the roads that will undergo more 'Wear and Tear', allowing maintenance crews to focus their energy on repairing potholes, instead of looking for them.
- *Deep learning:* Complex algorithm that analyses large datasets to give planners a predictive insight into data. This provides urban planners with an insight into the nature of traffic, management of traffic flows, and the design of new public transportation.

Perhaps the most important digital infrastructure in the future would be to provide distributed AI services to support the development and operations of ubiquitous urban, rural, industrial, and other applications (Janbi et al., 2020). The 5G networks that promise us unprecedented mobile internet speed have started to appear around the world. However, AI infrastructure requires more than mere fast networks. The work on the sixth-generation (6G) networks has begun. The 6G networks are expected to support extreme-scale ubiquitous AI services through next-generation softwarisation, platformisation, heterogeneity, and configurability of networks (Janbi et al., 2020). This is a technology that will likely have unimaginable impacts on urban planning and development (Allam & Jones, 2021).

7.6 Conclusion[1]

AI is undoubtfully a powerful technology and has already started to reshape and disrupt our economy, society, cities, and urban management systems (Thirgood & Johal, 2017; Panda et al., 2019). Today, there is limited understanding of the trending AI technologies and their application areas—or concepts—in the urban planning and development fields (Wu & Silva, 2010). Moreover, there is a knowledge gap in how the public perceives AI technologies, their application areas, and the AI-related policies and practices of our cities (Hengstler et al., 2016; Musikanski et al., 2020). Hence, the study at hand aimed at advancing our understanding of the relationship between the key AI technologies and their key application areas in urban planning and development.

The social media analytics undertaken in this study has important findings. Overall, the location-based twitter analysis throughout this study has identified that: (a) 'Sustainability' (n=774 tweets); (b) 'Cybersecurity' (n=741); (c) 'Innovation' (n=734); and (d) 'Construction' (n=644) are generally the most discussed urban planning and development concepts across entire Australia, although the popularity differs by states and territories. To accomplish the listed concepts, the following AI-related technologies are the most popularly discussed ones: (a) 'Robotics' (n=3,055 out of 11,262, 27%); (b) 'Drones' (n=1,943, 17%); and (c) 'Automation' (n=717, 23%). The sentiment analysis has also defined that the degree of satisfaction across Australian communities is relatively high. It has been demonstrated that 'robotics', 'drones', and 'automation' are the AI fields that have a close relationship with the urban planning and development concepts of 'sustainability', 'cybersecurity', 'innovation', and 'construction'.

---

[1] This chapter, with permission from the copyright holder, is a reproduced version of the following journal article: Yigitcanlar, T., Kankanamge, N., Regona, M., Ruiz Maldonado, A., Rowan, B., Ryu, A., ... & Li, R. Y. M. (2020). Artificial intelligence technologies and related urban planning and development concepts: How are they perceived and utilized in Australia? *Journal of Open Innovation: Technology, Market, and Complexity*, 6(4), 187.

This study has also disclosed that QLD and TAS have the highest degree of satisfaction (92% of positive sentiments) among the other states and territories. In contrast, given that most states and territories gained dominant positive sentiments, NT has had the lowest degree of satisfaction, as demonstrated by a higher level of neutral sentiments (53%), as well as low interest in sharing their views on social media channels (i.e., Twitter) slightly over 0%. Meanwhile, NSW and VIC, to which the highest percentage of the total tweets belonged, had a lower degree of satisfaction than QLD and TAS. However, their degrees of satisfaction are also relatively high. The close relationship between popular technologies and concepts was also justified in a number of analysis procedures—i.e., sentiment and content analyses, frequency analysis, content analysis, co-occurrence analysis, and spatial analysis.

In addition, concepts and technologies that have received less attention on Twitter are considered to be emerging topics and thus deemed important to keep track of. This study also addressed the significance of improving all of the identified AI-related technologies for their safety, effectiveness, efficiency, and affordances throughout the Australian AI Roadmap. Further empirical studies and analyses are needed to make concerted consolidations of AI across Australia to better understand the public perceptions with improved ethics, regulation, design, planning, construction, operation, and maintenance towards better Australian towns, cities, infrastructure, and buildings. In these prospective researches, a particular attention should also be paid to further consolidate the understanding and relation between AI and responsible urban innovation (Nagenborg, 2018; Alami et al., 2020; Theodorou & Dignum, 2020).

References

Abbot, J., & Marohasy, J. (2019). Application of artificial neural networks to rainfall forecasting in Queensland, Australia. *Advances in Atmospheric Sciences, 29*(4), 717–730.

Abduljabbar, R., Dia, H., Liyanage, S., & Bagloee, S.A. (2019). Applications of artificial intelligence in transport: An overview. *Sustainability, 11*(1), 189.

Adikari, A., & Alahakoon, D. (2020). Understanding citizens emotional pulse in a smart city using artificial intelligence. *IEEE Transactions on Industrial Informatics,* https://doi.org/10.1109/TII.2020.3009277.

Adhikari, A., Yuan, X., Côté, M.A., Zelinka, M., Rondeau, M.A., Laroche, R., ... & Hamilton, W. (2020). Learning dynamic belief graphs to generalize on text-based games. Advances in Neural Information Processing Systems, 33, 3045–3057.

AG. (2020). Artificial intelligence. *Australian Government.* Accessed on 15 November 2020 from https://www.industry.gov.au/policies-and-initiatives/artificial-intelligence.

AG. (2020a). Australia's AI Action Plan. *Australian Government,* Accessed on 15 November 2020 from https://www.industry.gov.au/news/australias-ai-action-plan-have-your-say.

AG. (2020b). AI ethics principles. *Australian Government,* Accessed on 15 November 2020 from https://www.industry.gov.au/data-and-publications/building-australias-artificial-intelligence-capability/ai-ethics-framework/ai-ethics-principles.

Alami, H., Rivard, L., Lehoux, P., Hoffman, S.J., Cadeddu, S.B., Savoldelli, M., & Fortin, J.P. (2020). Artificial intelligence in health care: Laying the foundation for responsible, sustainable, and inclusive innovation in low-and middle-income countries. *Globalization and Health, 16(1),* 52.

Allam, Z., & Dhunny, Z. (2019). On big data, artificial intelligence and smart cities. *Cities, 89,* 80–91.

Allam, Z., & Jones, D.S. (2021). (Future (post-COVID) digital, smart and sustainable cities in the wake of 6G: Digital twins, immersive realities and new urban economies. *Land Use Policy, 101,* 105201.

Alomari, E., Katib, I., & Mehmood, R. (2020). Iktishaf: A big data road-traffic event detection tool using twitter and spark machine learning. *Mobile Networks and Applications,* https://doi.org/10.1007/s11036-020-01635-y.

Arbolino, R., Carlucci, F., Cirà, A., Ioppolo, G., & Yigitcanlar, T. (2017). Efficiency of The EU regulation on greenhouse gas emissions in Italy: The hierarchical cluster analysis approach. *Ecological Indicators, 81,* 115–123.

Audirac, I. (2002). Information technology and urban form. *Journal of Planning Literature, 17(2),* 212–226.

Aziz, K., Haque, M.M., Rahman, A., Shamseldin, A.Y., & Shoaib, M. (2017). Flood estimation in ungauged catchments: Application of artificial intelligence-based methods for Eastern Australia. *Stochastic Environmental Research and Risk Assessment, 31(6),* 1499–1514.

Bach, J. (2020). When artificial intelligence becomes general enough to understand itself. Commentary on Pei Wang's paper "on defining artificial intelligence". *Journal of Artificial General Intelligence, 11(2),* 15–18.

Batty, M. (2018). Artificial intelligence and smart cities. *Environment and Planning B,* https://doi.org/10.1177/2399808317751169.

BQ. (2020). Who uses Twitter? *Business Queensland,* Accessed on 10 November 2020 from https://www.business.qld.gov.au/running-business/marketing-sales/marketing-promotion/online-marketing/twitter/who.

Caprotti, F., & Liu, D. (2020). Emerging platform urbanism in China: Reconfigurations of data, citizenship and materialities. *Technological Forecasting and Social Change, 151,* 119690.

Cearley, D., Burke, B., Searle, S., & Walker, M.J. (2018). Top 10 strategic technology trends for 2018. Accessed on 16 November 2020 from http://brilliantdude.com/solves/content/GartnerTrends2018.pdf.

Chang, D.L., Sabatini-Marques, J., Da Costa, E.M., Selig, P.M., & Yigitcanlar, T. (2018). Knowledge-based, smart and sustainable cities: A provocation for A conceptual framework. *Journal of Open Innovation: Technology, Market, and Complexity, 4(1),* 5.

Chanthadavong, A. (2020). Australian and Korean researchers warn of loopholes in AI security systems. Accessed on 15 November 2020 from https://www.zdnet.com/article/australian-and-korean-researchers-warn-of-loopholes-in-ai-security-systems.

Chaudhry, S., & Dhawan, S. (2020). AI-based recommendation system for social networking. In: *Soft Computing: Theories and Applications,* Springer, Singapore, 617–629.

CSIRO. (2020). Australia's AI roadmap. Accessed on 10 November 2020 from https://research.csiro.au/robotics/australias-ai-roadmap-launched-solving-problems-growing-the-economy-and-improving-our-quality-of-life.

Cugurullo, F. (2020). Urban artificial intelligence: From automation to autonomy in the smart City. *Frontiers in Sustainable Cities, 2*, 38.

Datta, A., Bhatia, V., Noll, J., & Dixit, S. (2018). Bridging the digital divide: Challenges in opening the digital world to the elderly, poor, and digitally illiterate. *IEEE Consumer Electronics Magazine, 8(1)*, 78–81.

Davenport, T.H. (2018). *The AI Advantage: How to Put the Artificial Intelligence Revolution to Work*. MIT Press, Boston, MA, USA.

Donald, M. (2019). *Leading and Managing Change in the Age of Disruption and Artificial Intelligence*. Emerald Group Publishing, London.

Dyer, M., Dyer, R., Weng, M.H., Wu, S., Grey, T., Gleeson, R., & Ferrari, T.G. (2019). Framework for soft and hard city infrastructures. *Proceedings of the Institution of Civil Engineers-Urban Design and Planning, 172(6)*, 219–227.

Fan, W., & Gordon, M.D. (2014). The power of social media analytics. *Communications of the ACM, 57(6)*, 74–81.

Fast, E., & Horvitz, E. (2020). Long-term trends in the public perception of artificial intelligence. Accessed on 20 November 2020 from https://arxiv.org/pdf/1609.04904.pdf.

Gao, S., He, L., Chen, Y., Li, D., & Lai, K. (2020). Public perception of artificial intelligence in medical care: Content analysis of social media. *Journal of Medical Internet Research, 22(7)*, e16649.

Girasa, R. (2020). *AI as a Disruptive Technology*. Springer, Cham, Switzerland.

Gu, Y., Qian, Z., & Chen, F. (2016). From twitter to detector: Real-time traffic incident detection using social media data. *Transportation Research Part C, 67*, 321–342.

Hengstler, M., Enkel, E., & Duelli, S. (2016). Applied artificial intelligence and trust: The case of autonomous vehicles and medical assistance devices. *Technological Forecasting and Social Change, 105*, 105–120.

Hu, S.H. (2020). Analysis of the effect of the digital divide on the digital daily life of the elderly. *Journal of Digital Convergence, 18(9)*, 9–15.

IDC. (2020) The next generation of intelligence. Accessed on 15 November 2020 from https://www.idc.com/itexecutive/research/topics/ai.

Jackson, P.C. (2019). *Introduction to Artificial Intelligence*. Courier Dover Publications, New York.

Janbi, N., Katib, I., Albeshri, A., & Mehmood, R. (2020). Distributed artificial intelligence-as-a-service (DAIaaS) for smarter IoE and 6G environments. *Sensors, 20(20)*, 5796.

Kankanamge, N., Yigitcanlar, T., Goonetilleke, A., & Kamruzzaman, M. (2019). Can volunteer crowdsourcing reduce disaster risk? A systematic review of the literature. *International Journal of Disaster Risk Reduction, 35*, 101097.

Kankanamge, N., Yigitcanlar, T., & Goonetilleke, A. (2020a). How engaging are disaster management related social media channels? The case of Australian state emergency organizations. *International Journal of Disaster Risk Reduction*, 101571.

Kankanamge, N., Yigitcanlar, T., Goonetilleke, A., & Kamruzzaman, M. (2020b). Determining disaster severity through social media analysis: Testing the methodology with South East Queensland flood tweets. *International Journal of Disaster Risk Reduction, 42*, 101360.

Kankanamge, N., Yigitcanlar, T., Goonetilleke, A., & Kamruzzaman, M. (2020c). How can gamification be incorporated into disaster emergency planning? A systematic review of the literature. *International Journal of Disaster Resilience in the Built Environment, 11*(4), 481–506.

Kassens-Noor, E., & Hintze, A. (2020). Cities of the future? The potential impact of artificial intelligence. *AI, 1*(2), 192–197.

Kirwan, C.G., & Zhiyong, F. (2020). *Smart Cities and Artificial Intelligence.* Elsevier, London.

Liu, H. (2020). *Smart Cities: Big Data Prediction Methods and Applications*, Springer, Singapore, 1–314

Lutz, C.V. (2019). Digital inequalities in the age of artificial intelligence and big data. *Human Behavior and Emerging Technologies, 1*(2), 141–148.

Mah, D.N., van der Vleuten, J.M., Hills, P., & Tao, J. (2012). Consumer perceptions of smart grid development: Results of a Hong Kong survey and policy implications. *Energy Policy, 49*, 204–216.

Musikanski, L., Rakova, B., Bradbury, J., Phillips, R., & Manson, M. (2020). Artificial intelligence and community well-being: A proposal for an emerging area of research. *International Journal of Community Well-Being, 3*(1), 39–55.

Nagenborg, M. (2018). Urban robotics and responsible urban innovation. *Ethics and Information Technology, 22*, 345–355.

Neri, H., & Cozman, F. (2019). The role of experts in the public perception of risk of artificial intelligence. *AI & Society, 35*, 663–673.

Ortega-Fernández, A., Martín-Rojas, R., & García-Morales, V.J. (2020). Artificial intelligence in the urban environment: Smart cities as models for developing innovation and sustainability. *Sustainability, 12*(19), 7860.

Pan, Y., Tian, Y., Liu, X., Gu, D., & Hua, G. (2016). Urban big data and the development of city intelligence. *Engineering, 2*(2), 171–178.

Panda, G., Upadhyay, A.K., & Khandelwal, K. (2019). Artificial intelligence: A strategic disruption in public relations. *Journal of Creative Communications, 14*(3), 196–213.

Paulin, A. (2018). *Smart city Governance.* Elsevier, London.

Press, G. (2020). Top 10 hot artificial intelligence (AI) technologies. Accessed on 10 November 2020 from https://www.forbes.com/sites/gilpress/2017/01/23/top-10-hot-artificial-intelligence-ai-technologies.

Pueyo, S. (2018). Growth, degrowth, and the challenge of artificial superintelligence. *Journal of Cleaner Production, 197*, 1731–1736.

Quan, S.J., Park, J., Economou, A., & Lee, S. (2019). Artificial intelligence-aided design: Smart design for sustainable city development. *Environment and Planning B, 46*(8), 1581–1599.

Rahmati, O., Falah, F., Dayal, K.S., Deo, R.C., Mohammadi, F., Biggs, T., & Bui, D.T. (2020). Machine learning approaches for spatial modeling of agricultural droughts in the south-east region of Queensland Australia. *Science of the Total Environment, 699*, 134230.

Rathore, M.M., Ahmad, A., Paul, A., & Rho, S. (2016). Urban planning and building smart cities based on the internet of things using big data analytics. *Computer Networks, 101*, 63–80.

Schalkoff, R.J. (1990). Artificial Intelligence: An Engineering Approach, New York: McGraw-Hill, 529–533.

Taddeo, M., McCutcheon, T., & Floridi, L. (2019). Trusting artificial intelligence in cybersecurity is a double-edged sword. *Nature Machine Intelligence, 1*, 557–560.

Theodorou, A., & Dignum, V. (2020). Towards ethical and socio-legal governance in AI. *Nature Machine Intelligence, 2(1),* 10–12.

Thirgood, J., & Johal, S. (2017). Digital disruption. *Economic Development Journal, 16(2),* 25–32.

Ullah, Z., Al-Turjman, F., Mostarda, L., & Gagliardi, R. (2020). Applications of artificial intelligence and machine learning in smart cities. *Computer Communications, 154,* 313–323.

Vilajosana, I., Llosa, J., Martinez, B., Domingo-Prieto, M., Angles, A., & Vilajosana, X. (2013). Bootstrapping smart cities through a self-sustainable model based on big data flows. *IEEE Communications Magazine, 51(6),* 128–134.

Wah, B.W., Huang, T.S., Joshi, A.K., Moldovan, D., Aloimonos, J., Bajcsy, R.K., & Fahlman, S.E. (1993). Report on workshop on high performance computing and communications for grand challenge applications: Computer vision, speech and natural language processing, and artificial intelligence. *IEEE Transactions on Knowledge and Data Engineering, 5(1),* 138–154.

Webb, T., & Dayal, S. (2020). Building the wall: Addressing cybersecurity risks in medical devices in the USA and Australia. *Computer Law & Security Review, 33(4),* 559–563.

Williams, M.A. (2019). The artificial intelligence race: Will Australia lead or lose? *Journal and Proceedings of the Royal Society of New South Wales, 152(471/472),* 105–114.

Wirtz, B.W., Weyerer, J.C., & Geyer, C. (2019). Artificial intelligence and the public sector: Applications and challenges. *International Journal of Public Administration, 42(7),* 596–615.

Wu, N., & Silva, E.A. (2010). Artificial intelligence solutions for urban land dynamics: A review. *Journal of Planning Literature, 24(3),* 246–265.

Yellow. (2018). Yellow social media report 2018: Part one–consumers. Accessed on 10 November 2020 from https://www.yellow.com.au/wp-content/uploads/2018/06/Yellow-Social-Media-Report-2018-Consumer.pdf.

Yigitcanlar, T. (2010). *Rethinking Sustainable Development: Urban Management, Engineering, and Design.* IGI Global, Hersey, PA, USA.

Yigitcanlar, T., Butler, L., Windle, E., Desouza, K.C., Mehmood, R., & Corchado, J.M. (2020). Can building "artificially intelligent cities" safeguard humanity from natural disasters, pandemics, and other catastrophes? An urban scholar's perspective. *Sensors, 20(10),* 2988.

Yigitcanlar, T., & Cugurullo, F. (2020). The sustainability of artificial intelligence: An urbanistic viewpoint from the lens of smart and sustainable cities. *Sustainability, 12(20),* 8548.

Yigitcanlar, T., Desouza, K.C., Butler, L., & Roozkhosh, F. (2020). Contributions and risks of artificial intelligence (AI) in building smarter cities: Insights from a systematic review of the literature. *Energies, 13(6),* 1473.

Yigitcanlar, T., & Kamruzzaman, M. (2015). Planning, development and management of sustainable cities: A commentary from the guest editors. *Sustainability, 7(11),* 14677–14688.

Yigitcanlar, T., Kankanamge, N., Preston, A., Gill, P.S., Rezayee, M., Ostadnia, M., & Ioppolo, G. (2020). How can social media analytics assist authorities in pandemic-related policy decisions? Insights from Australian states and territories. *Health Information Science and Systems, 8(1),* 37.

Yigitcanlar, T., Kankanamge, N., & Vella, K. (2020). How are smart city concepts and technologies perceived and utilized? A systematic geo-Twitter analysis of smart cities in Australia. *Journal of Urban Technology, 28*(1–2), 135–154.

Yun, J.J., Lee, D., Ahn, H., Park, K., & Yigitcanlar, T. (2016). Not deep learning but autonomous learning of open innovation for sustainable artificial intelligence. *Sustainability, 8*(8), 797.

Zhang, F., Zhou, B., Liu, L., Liu, Y., Fung, H.H., Lin, H., & Ratti, C. (2018). Measuring human perceptions of a large-scale urban region using machine learning. *Landscape and Urban Planning, 180*, 148–160.

Zhou, J., Liu, T., & Zou, L. (2020). Design of machine learning model for urban planning and management improvement. *International Journal of Performability Engineering, 16*(6), 958–1005.

Part III

Platforms

This part of the book concentrates on providing examples and insights into platforms for urban analytics. These platform examples include social media analytics platform, cyber-physical data analytics platform, crowd detection platform, City-as-a-Platform, and city as a sensor for platform urbanism.

DOI: 10.1201/9781003278986-10

8

Social Media Analytics Platforms

8.1 Introduction

8.1.1 Smart Cities, Transportation and Social Sensing

Smart cities and societies aim to revolutionise our daily lives and improve social, economic, and environmental sustainability through increased technology penetration, participatory governance, and wise use of natural and other resources (Alomari et al., 2020). Smart urban and rural developments require timely sensing and analysis of diverse data produced by various edge sensors, smart devices, GPS, cameras, and the Internet of Things (IoT) (Hashem et al., 2016). Social media such as Twitter have become an important class of sensors for smart urban and rural developments (Zheng et al., 2015), and in many sectors of smart cities and societies, it is increasingly being seen as a conveniently available and relatively inexpensive source of information compared to physical sensors (Alomari et al., 2019). Road transportation which is considered the backbone of modern economies is one such sector. It costs globally 1.25 million deaths and 50 million human injuries annually and therefore it is a research and development area of high significance.

Increased urbanisation is giving rise to the evolution of cities into megacities where traffic congestion is a leading problem causing devastating economic, social, and ecological losses. The annual cost of congestion in the US is $305 billion, not to mention the damages to health and the number of deaths. Congestion is caused due to the steadily growing traffic in the cities over the years, road damages, roadworks, traffic accidents, bad weather, and other contingencies. There is a need to detect these causes or events to enable timely planning and operations.

Many times, congestion is caused due to events that are beyond the direct scope of physical road sensors, and therefore physical sensors cannot detect these events until the effects of these events are visible on the roads and can be sensed by the on-road sensors. For example, a football match in a city is likely to disrupt the traffic and increase pressure on the road network in certain segments of the city. Such an event can be detected through social media in advance of the event and timely intervention may reduce the aggravation of congestion in the city. Events such as a major football event may have already

DOI: 10.1201/9781003278986-11

been known to the authorities. However, social media can also detect events that are being arranged on ad hoc bases—such as social gatherings, small sports gatherings—and, though these are small, there can be many of these in a city and can create an aggregately large pressure on the city roads. Similarly, unpredictable events such as a fire in a city segment may also disrupt the city traffic and such events can also be detected automatically on social media before their effects on the roads are visible. Moreover, historical analysis of social media data can reveal hidden information related to the traffic that may have not known otherwise and can be used for urban planning (Kurniawan et al., 2016; Mohammad & Qawasmeh, 2016; Xu et al., 2017; Usman et al., 2019b).

Twitter is one of the most popular microblogging media used for communication and sharing personal status, events, news, and so on (Huang et al., 2019). Twitter allows users to post short text messages called tweets. A massive amount of real-time data is posted by millions of users on various topics including transportation and real-time road traffic (Alomari et al., 2019; 2020b; Alotaibi et al., 2020; Yigitcanlar et al., 2020). In the recent decade, the use of Twitter and other social media by researchers and practitioners to study different issues in many application domains and sectors has steadily increased). Transportation is no exception where social media has been used to study various aspects such as for analysing travel behaviours (Agarwal & Toshniwal, 2019), recognising mobility patterns (Assem et al., 2017), congestion detection (Cárdenas-Benítez et al., 2016), and event detection (Alomari et al., 2019; 2020a; 2020b; Agarwal et al., 2018). Due to the microblogging and real-time nature of Twitter, people are likely to communicate information about small and large-scale social gatherings, sports events, or events such as a fire, weather, allowing such information to be extracted in real-time (Yigitcanlar et al., 2021). Such information can allow the detection of transportation-related events and their causes for timely planning and operations. However, while manifesting great potential, several major challenges need to be overcome before its wide adoption in transportation and other areas.

8.1.2 Aim and Approach

This work aims to develop big data technologies for detecting road traffic-related events (i.e., events that may affect road traffic) from Twitter data in the Arabic language with a focus on Saudi Arabia. Over the past few years, we have continued to build a detailed literature review on social media analytics in transportation. We have learnt from the literature review that the cutting-edge on big data-enabled social media analytics for transportation-related studies is limited. Many more studies are needed to improve the breadth and depth of the research on the subject in several aspects to establish maturity in this area. The research gaps related to the focus of the studies, the size and diversity of the data, the applicability and performance of the machine learning methods, the diversity in terms of the social media languages, the scalability of the computing platforms, and others (Alomari et al., 2020a;

Yigitcanlar et al., 2021; Usman et al., 2019a) The maturity of research in this area will allow the development, commercialisation, and wide adoption of the tools for transportation planning and operations (for the literature review and research gap, see Section 8.2).

This chapter brings a range of technologies together to detect road traffic-related events using big data and distributed machine learning. This chapter contributes to most of the above-mentioned research gaps. The most specific contribution of this research is an automatic labelling method for machine learning-based traffic-related event detection from Twitter data. In principle, the method itself is generic and can be applied for natural language process-ing (NLP) in any language. However, in this chapter, the method is applied to Twitter data in the Arabic language. One of the approaches to detecting events from social media requires text classification using supervised clas-sification algorithms (Xu et al., 2017.) Supervised classification requires the labelling of data for the training phase. For big data, the manual labelling process is time-consuming and labour-intensive (Kankanamge et al., 2020). Using the automatic labelling techniques developed in this chapter we are able to deal with over an order of magnitude larger dataset compared to our earlier work in (Alomari et al., 2020c). We are able to detect several real events in Saudi Arabia without any prior knowledge including a fire in Jeddah, rains in Makkah, and an accident in Riyadh.

The proposed automatic labelling method uses predefined dictionaries to reduce the effort, time, and cost of manual labelling of tweets. The diction-aries have been generated automatically for each event type using the top vocabularies extracted from the manually labelled dataset. Then, the diction-aries are adjusted manually to add synonyms and make sure that we do not miss any important vocabulary. After that, we divide them into levels based on the importance and the degree of relevance to the event type. Then, we calculate the weight for each labelled tweet (see Section 8.3 for details of the tool design including the automatic labelling method).

The proposed method has been implemented in a software tool called Iktishaf+ (an Arabic word meaning discovery) that is able to detect traffic events automatically from tweets in the Arabic language using distributed machine learning over Apache Spark. The tool is built using nine compo-nents that are used for nine specific functions namely data collection and storage, data pre-processing, tweets labelling, feature extraction, tweets fil-tering, event detection, spatio-temporal information extraction, reporting and visualisation, and internal and external validation. The architectural blocks of the Iktishaf+ system are depicted in Figure 8.1 (we will describe in detail the system architecture including its nine components in Section 8.3). Iktishaf+ is built using a range of technologies including Apache Spark, Spark ML, Spark SQL, NLTK, PowerBI, Parquet, and MongoDB.

The Iktishaf+ tool uses Iktishaf Stemmer that we had introduced in (Alomari et al., 2020a). It is a light stemmer for the Arabic language developed by us. It is designed to strip affixes based on the length of the tokens. It allows

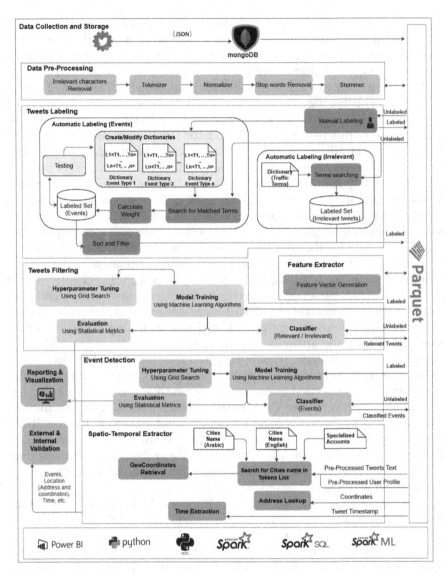

FIGURE 8.1

Iktishaf+: proposed system architecture.

reducing the feature space and minimising the number of removed letters from the token to prevent changes in meaning or losing important words. We also use in this work a location extractor developed by us that helps to find the location of the detected events. It uses multiple methods to extract the event location. The location is extracted from the tweet text where the place name is explicitly mentioned in the message or is included as hashtags. Additionally, the event locations are identified from the account names using a predefined list of account names that are specialised in posting about traffic conditions in different cities in Saudi Arabia. If no information is found, the other attributes associated with the tweets JSON object such as coordinates, and user profiles are checked for the location information. These methods have allowed us to extract and visualise spatio-temporal information about the detected events (Suma et al., 2020).

The specific data used in this work comprises 33.5 million tweets collected from Saudi Arabia using the Twitter API for over a year. We have not used this data in any of the earlier works. The findings show the effectiveness of the Twitter media in detecting important events, and other information in time, space, and information structure with no earlier knowledge about them. The detected events are validated using internal and external sources (Alsulami & Mehmood, 2018).

Iktishaf+ is an enhanced version of our tool Iktishaf that was introduced in (Alomari et al., 2020a). The tool Iktishaf+ extends the functionality, capacity, and testing of our earlier work on traffic event detection. The earlier work on event detection has reported analyses of 2.5 million tweets. The number of tweets was limited by our ability to manually label the tweets. We have also applied the Iktishaf tool to detect government measures and public concerns related to CVOID-19 using unsupervised learning [13]. Our earlier work on big data social media analytics has also focused on application areas including public sentiments analysis of government services (Alomari et al., 2021), logistics (Suma et al., 2017; Mehmood et al., 2017), and healthcare (Alotaibi et al., 2020) in both Arabic and English languages.

The Iktishaf+ tool uses open-source big data distributed computing technologies that enable the scalability and integration of transportation software systems with each other and with other smart city systems such as smart healthcare and urban governance systems. An elaboration of the novelty, contributions, and utilisation of this work is given in Section 8.2.4.

The organisation of this chapter is as follows. Section 8.2 highlights the related work, in which we review different techniques for traffic events detection from social media in addition to the existing approaches for labelling large-scale datasets. Section 8.3 describes the proposed methodology and details the tool design and architecture. Section 8.4 explains the analysis results, which is followed by conclusions and future work reported in Section 8.5.

8.2 Literature Review

Digital societies could perhaps be characterised by their increasing desire to express themselves and interact with others, and this is done through various digital platforms (Mehmood et al., 2017). The core ingredients of these digital societies, or digital platforms that enable these societies include a range of emerging technologies and their convergence. The technologies include big data (Arfat et al., 2020a; Usman et al., 2020), high-performance computing (HPC) (Muhammed et al., 2019; Alyahya et al., 2020; Usman et al., 2020), artificial intelligence (Mehmood et al., 2017; Alam et al., 2019; Alshareef et al., 2020; Yigitcanlar et al., 2021), cloud, fog, and edge computing (Schlingensiepen et al., 2014; Muhammed et al., 2018; Janbi et al., 2020), social sensing (Lau, 2017; Pandhare & Shah, 2017; Salas et al., 2017; Garg et al., 2019), and Internet of Things (IoT) (Mehmood et al., 2017; Alam et al., 2017; Muhammed et al., 2018; Lin et al., 2018; Muhammed et al., 2020). The applications include transportation (Kumar et al., 2013; Aqib et al., 2019a; Miglani & Kumar, 2019; Alomari et al., 2019; Alsolami et al., 2020), healthcare (Mehmood & Graham, 2015; Alotaibi & Mehmood, 2017; Alamoudi et al., 2020; Alotaibi et al., 2020), and others (Al-Dhubhani et al., 2017; Khanum et al., 2017; Garg et al., 2019; Alkhamisi & Mehmood, 2020). The pulse for sensing and engaging with the environments are provided by social media and IoT. Sentiment analysis, or opinion mining, is a vital tool in natural language processing (NLP) (Liu, 2012), and many of the notable works on sentiment analysis rely on artificial intelligence, Twitter, and other social media.

Over here we review the literature related to the topics of this chapter, which is the detection of events related to road traffic using Twitter in the Arabic language. We begin with the literature about traffic event detection and then we discuss the solutions for automatic labelling. We discuss in Section 8.2.1 the works that have been developed for event detection in any language whether they use big data or not. Section 8.2.2 discusses works in the Arabic language and since works for Arabic are very limited, we introduce the studies related to detecting any type of events and not only traffic events. In Section 8.2.3, we present the solutions for labelling large datasets. Finally, Section 8.2.4 reveals the research gap.

8.2.1 Traffic Events Detection Using Social Data (Any Language)

Sakaki et al. (2010) proposed an earthquake reporting system using Japanese tweets. They classified real-time tweets into positive (event-related) and negative (not related to events) classes using an SVM classifier. To prepare the training set, they used three groups of features for each tweet, which are keywords in a tweet, the number of words, and the words before and after the target-event words. Furthermore, they extended their work to extract events from tweets referring to driving information (Sakaki, 2012). They collected tweets using a list of keywords about traffic-related events such as heavy traffic, traffic restriction, police checkpoints, parking, and rain mist. As in their previous work, they prepared the features using different methods and then they selected the best features to train a classifier using the SVM algorithm. Moreover, Klaithin and Haruechaiyasak (2016) analysed tweets in the Thai language to extract traffic events. They trained a classifier using Naïve Bayes to classify the tweets into 6 categories, which are accident, announcement, question, request, sentiment, and traffic condition. They applied a machine learning classifier based on the Naive Bayes Model.

Kumar et al. (2014) trained a sentiment classification model to detect negative sentiment about a road Hazard from Twitter. The data is collected using search filtering with specific terms that relate to traffic. Then, Naïve Bayes, K-nearest-neighbour, and the Dynamic Language Model (DLM) are used to build models to classify the tweets into a hazard and not hazard. Semwal et al. (2015) applied real-time spatio-temporal analysis on Facebook data to detect traffic insights. They designed a module to detect the occurrence of events based on the spike in the number of posts at a specific time period and location. When the number is more than a threshold, the posts associated with that time and location are analysed to evaluate their sentiments. Further, a random forest classifier was used to predict the most dominant issue for the next day. To address the problem of having an imbalanced dataset, they used SMOTE. Tejaswin et al. (2015) and also used a random forest classifier to predict traffic incidents. The traffic incidents are clustered and predicted using spatio-temporal data from Twitter. The location information is extracted using NLP and background knowledge by using Freebase API, which is a community-curated structured database containing a large number of entities and each one defied by multiple properties and attributes that helps in entity disambiguation.

Moreover, D'Andrea et al. (2015) collected real-time Italian tweets and classified them after applying text mining techniques. The tweets are classified into three classes namely, traffic due to an external event, traffic congestion or crash, and non-traffic. They built a set of traffic events detected from official news websites or local newspapers and then they compared the time of detecting an event from these official sites with the time of detection from Twitter's stream fetched by their system.

None of the above-discussed approaches have used big data technology. Salas et al. (2017) used apache spark to process tweets and train the model using an SVM classification algorithm to classify them into traffic and non-traffic related tweets. To extract location information, they used a combination of Name Entity Recognition (NER) such as Stanford NER and a knowledge base such as Wikipedia.

Suma et al. (2017) built a classification model using logistic regression with stochastic gradient descent to detect events related to road traffic from English tweets using Apache Spark. Lau (2017) used the Latent Dirichlet Allocation (LDA) topic modelling module to filter traffic messages. In addition, they used the Spark MLib library and trained classifiers using SVM, KNN and NB to detect traffic events. A detailed survey of event detection techniques using Twitter data can be found in Atefeh & Khreich, 2015).

8.2.2 Traffic Events Detection Using Social Data (Arabic Language)

A very limited number of research has been proposed to analyse Arabic social information for traffic event detection. So, we review first the studies about detecting any event not necessarily related to traffic. Then, we review the works that focus on transport and traffic events. Finally, we discuss the works that use big data. Alkouz and Al Aghbari (2020) analysed English and Arabic data including standard Arabic and UAE dialectical posts from Twitter and Instagram to detect and predict traffic jams. They filtered the collected data to keep only traffic-related data. They used about 2.4 million tweets and 319,125 traffic-related image captions from Instagram. Further, the text is cleaned, tokenised and then stemmed using the NLTK root stemmer. Then, they used a predefined list of keywords to classify the posts into reporting posts or non-reporting posts where reporting posts contain at least one vocabulary from the list. They developed a tool to identify locations from the text of posts and/or GPS locations. Further, they employed a linear regression model to predict future traffic jams. Moreover, Alkhatib et al. (2019) analysed tweets written in Modern Standard Arabic and Dialect Arabic analysis for the purpose of incident and emergency reporting. To detect incidents and disasters occurring in the UAE, they collected tweets in real-time using specific keywords, which are a car accident, earthquake, drought, hailstorm, heatwave, building collapse, riot and civil disorder. They labelled 8,000 tweets manually to generate a training set and collected 82,150 tweets as a testing set. They built classification models using five machine learning algorithms, which are Polynomial Networks (PN), NB, KNN, Rachio (RA) and SVM. Moreover, they applied root stemmer and the results showed that it improves the classification accuracy. Further, they built the NER corpus using Wikipedia to identify certain types of NEs such as building name, event risk and impact level, and number of casualties. To extract location information, they built a dictionary of terms related to location names in Dubai city.

Other researchers have proposed a solution to detect events but their main focus was not on traffic. Al-Qawasmeh et al. (2016) extracted events about technology, sports, and politics using the unsupervised rule-based technique. Alsaedi and Pete (2015) developed a solution using Naïve Bayes and online clustering algorithms to detect disruptive events. Alabbas et al. (2017) detected a high-risk flood using an SVM classifier.

However, none of the above-discussed approaches for event detection from Arabic have used big data technologies. Alomari and Mehmood (2017) developed a dictionary-based approach using SAP HANA, which is an in-memory processing platform to analyse Arabic tweets related to traffic congestion in Jeddah city. Additionally, they extracted traffic congestion causes. Furthermore, they extended their work and applied sentiment analysis on traffic-related tweets (Alomari et al., 2020c). Moreover, they developed a supervised classification model using the Apache Spark platform to detect eight types of traffic events, which are accident, roadwork, road closure, road damage, road condition, fire, weather, and social events. The results show that SVM achieves better results compared to logistic regression and the Naive Bayes algorithm. Subsequently, they extended their work and validate the ability of the proposed Iktishaf tool (Alomari et al., 2020a) in detecting various events, their locations and times, with no earlier knowledge about the events from about 2.5 million tweets. Further, they designed a new light stemmer, Iktishaf Stemmer, for Arabic text and study the effect of using it on the performance. The results show that the performance of the trained model with and without using the proposed stemmer is almost similar. On the other hand, compared to other light stemmers such as Tashaphyne, and ISRI, Iktishaf Stemmer helps to minimise the number of letters removed and eliminate changes in the meaning, especially for the words that related to transportation.

8.2.3 Solution for Labelling Large-Scale Dataset (Any Language)

Manual labelling is a very challenging and expensive process, especially with having a very large dataset and thus supervised learning is hard to apply on big social data. One of the solutions is crowdsourcing by cooperating with freelancers but one of the issues is the quality of the work (Kankanamge et al., 2019). Besides, crowdsourcing is not a fully automatic approach. In this section, we discuss the existing works that are similar to us and enables labelling text automatically to eliminate the need for human experts to label all the training set.

Pandey and Natarajan (2016) proposed a system to extract Situation Awareness (SA) information and location from Twitter during disaster events. They suggested using semi-supervised classification instead of the traditional supervised machine learning approach, which would be tedious and time-consuming in terms of labelling. For creating a semi-supervised model, they manually labelled a small set of tweets and then fed them to the SVM to classify them into situation awareness and non-situation awareness. Then, they used the result from this initial classification to self-train the model. However, their model achieved very low precision and recall value for the situation awareness class.

Shafiabady et al. (2016) suggested using an unsupervised clustering approach such as Self-Organising Maps (SOM) and Correlation Coefficient (CorrCoef) to group the unlabelled documents and use them as labelled data to train the SVM for text classification. However, their approach was applied on documents not on short text such as tweets. Ghahreman and Dastjerdi (2011) applied semi-automatic labelling by combining co-training algorithms with the similarity evaluation measure. They labelled a small set of data manually, then they used the SVM algorithm to classify the unlabelled document. After that, based on the threshold, part of the output is selected. Then, they calculated the similarity between the selected documents and manually labelled documents

Xu et al. (2017) suggested labelling a few documents automatically using external semantic resources e.g., HowNet. Then, they combined the labelled data and most of the unlabelled training data to train the classifier by semi-supervised learning. To label the documents automatically, they obtained the knowledge of the category name using lexical databases as external semantic resources and then they generated a set of features for the corresponding category. Further, they extracted features from the documents as a corresponding feature vector. After that, the similarity between each category name and each text document are calculated to rank the documents and classify them into the corresponding category. Triguero et al. (2015) provided a taxonomy for the self-labelled techniques. One of the techniques is the addition mechanism. It consists of a variety of schemes, including incremental, batch and amending.

8.2.4 Research Gap, Novelty, Contributions and Utilisation

It can be seen from the literature review provided in this section that the works that use big data technology for traffic-related event detection are limited. To the best of our knowledge, none of the existing works for Arabic have used big data technology and platforms. Furthermore, none of them have used automatic labelling to address the problem of manual labelling of large datasets. The cutting-edge on big data-enabled social media analytics for transportation-related studies is limited. Many more studies are needed to improve the breadth and depth of the research on the subject in several aspects to establish maturity in this area. The research gaps relate to the focus of the studies, the size and diversity of the data, the applicability and performance of the machine learning methods, the diversity in terms of the social media languages, the scalability of the computing platforms, and others (Alomari, 2021; Yigitcanlar et al., 2021). The maturity of research in this area will allow the development, commercialisation, and wide adoption of the tools for transportation planning and operations.

The range of technologies that we have incorporated in the Iktishaf+ tool advances the state-of-the-art on big data social media analytics in the Arabic language, in a number of ways (some of these contributions related to big data analysis apply also to English and other languages). Firstly, the extended tool Iktishaf+ has contributed multiple big data pipelines and architectures for event detection (in transportation and other sectors) from social media using cutting-edge technologies including data-driven distributed machine learning and high-performance computing. Secondly, it incorporates a novel pre-processing pipeline for Saudi dialectical Arabic that includes irrelevant characters removal, tokeniser, normaliser, stop words removal, and an Arabic light stemmer to improve event detection and overall performance. This will help many other works in the Arabic language to benefit from our work. Thirdly, the tool incorporates a range of lexicon-based, supervised, and unsupervised machine learning methods for event detection from social media in the Arabic language to enable smarter transportation and smarter societies.

Using these methods, we have detected various physical and conceptual events such as congestion, fire, weather, government measures, and public concerns. Fourthly, the extended tool incorporates an automatic labelling method to reduce the effort, time, and cost of manual labelling of large datasets. We are not aware of any automatic labelling work in the Arabic language. Fifthly, we have developed and incorporated methods in the tool for spatial and temporal information from Twitter data to allow spatio-temporal clustering and visualisation of detected events. Sixthly, we have developed methods for validating the detected events using internal and external sources. None of the existing works in English and other languages, particularly Arabic, have reported a similar analysis of Twitter data for event detection in terms of the richness of the methods, depth of analysis, and significance of findings. To the best of our knowledge, no work in the Arabic language exists that has used automatic labelling or big data tools or has reported analysis of a large number of tweets such as we have in this chapter.

The scalability of the software systems for big data analytics is critical and is being hampered due to the challenges related to the management, integration, and analysis of big data (the 4V challenges). The use of big data distributed computing technologies is important because it will allow the scalability and integration of transportation software systems with each other and with other smart city systems. The ability of the Iktishaf+ tool to execute in parallel could save a month of computing time for the specific dataset size and the problem addressed in our work and speed up the development process (Alomari et al., 2021). For larger datasets, executing sequential codes may not even be possible, or distributed computing could save years of development time.

The utilisation possibilities of our tool are many. For example, governments could learn about the various events, public concerns, and reactions related to certain government policies, measures, and actions (in pandemic and normal times) and develop policies and measures to address these concerns. The public could raise their concerns and give feedback on government policies. The public could learn about various public and industry activities (such as fires, social events, and other events, and economic activities detected by our tool in the earlier work (Alomari et al., 2021) and get involved in these to address financial, social, and other difficulties. The standardisation and adoption of such tools could lead to real-time surveillance and the detection of transportation-related or other events, or disease outbreaks (and other potentially dangerous phenomena) across the globe and allow governments to take timely actions to prevent various risks, the spread of diseases, and other disasters. The international standardisation of such tools could allow governments to learn about the impact of policies of various countries and develop best practices for a national and international response.

8.3 Methodology and Design

Figure 8.1 illustrates Iktishaf+ architecture. It consists of nine components, which are: (1) Data Collection and Storage Component, (2) Data Pre-Processing Component, (3) Tweets Labelling Component, (4) Feature Extractor Component, (5) Tweet Filtering Component, (6) Event Detection Component, (7) Spatio-Temporal Extractor Component, (8) Reporting and Visualisation

Component, and (9) External & Internal Validation Component. The next sub-section explains the tools and libraries used to develop Iktishaf+. Subsections 8.3.2 to 8.3.10 elaborate each component in detail.

8.3.1 Tools and Libraries

Iktishaf+ is built over the Apache Spark platform, which enables in-memory processing on distributed data. The main libraries that have been used are Spark ML and Spark SQL. Spark.ML is a new package introduced in Spark 1.2. Unlike the Spark.MLlib package that was built on top of RDDs, Spark. ML contains a higher-level API built on top of DataFrames creating and tuning practical machine learning pipelines. Moreover, the script was written using Python and runs on Aziz supercomputer, a Fujitsu 230 TFLOPS machine comprising around 500 nodes, each with 24 cores. Besides, Fujitsu Exabyte File System (FEFS) has been used to provide high-performance storage space as well as Scalable I/O performance. FEFS is a scalable parallel file system based on Lustre. Aziz supercomputer supports running Spark with YARN, which allocates resources across applications.

Figure 8.2 shows the architecture of Apache Spark with YARN. Spark applications can run as independent sets of processes on a cluster. It acquires Executors on cluster nodes. The SparkContext is responsible for coordinating the application and enabling connecting YARN. Then, it sends tasks to the executors to run computations for the application.

8.3.2 Data Collection and Storage Component

We collected the data using the Twitter REST API, which enables collecting historical data. The returned data by the Twitter API are encoded using

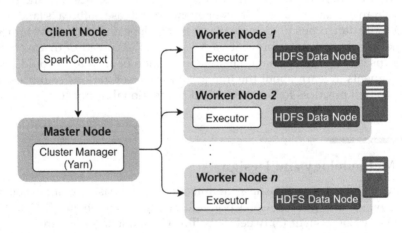

FIGURE 8.2
Spark application run on Yarn.

JavaScript Object Notation (JSON). Each tweet object includes a unique ID, the text content itself, a timestamp that represents when it was posted, and many child objects such as 'user' and 'place'. Based on their documentation (Twitter, 2019), a tweet can have over 150 attributes associated with it. Each child object encapsulates attributes to describe it. For instance, the 'user' object contains 'name', 'screen_ name', 'id', 'followers_count', and others. Some of the attributes that belong to the 'user' object can be filled in manually by the user such as 'description' and 'location'. Additionally, each tweet includes the 'entities' object, which encapsulates several attributes such as 'hashtags', 'user_mentions', 'media', and 'links'. The example below shows the core attributes of a tweet object.

```
"tweet" : {
      "created_at" : "Fri Oct 05 20:36:52 +0000 2018",
      "id" : NumberLong(10483110771954688010),
      "id_str" : "10483110771954688010",
      "full_text" : "@JeddahAmanah طفشنا من زحمة التحلية و فلسطين ..
      ماقي خطوط سريعة كفاية من الشرق للغرب ... الاهم من المناظر الجمالية",
      "entities" : {
            "hashtags" : [],
            "symbols" :   [],
            "user_mentions" : [
                        "screen_name" : "JeddahAmanah",
                        "name" : "أمانة محافظة جدة",
                        "id" : 58427580,
                        "id_str" : "58427580",                       ],
            "urls" : []
      },
      "user" : {
            "id" : 720346162200,
            "id_str" : "720346162200",
            "name" : "ahmadd",
            "screen_name" : "ahd1109",
            "location" : "جدة",
            "description" : "",
            "url" : null,
            "entities" : {
                  "description" : {
                        "urls" : []
                  }
            },
      "coordinates" : null,
      "place" : null,

      }
}
```

We fetch Arabic tweets posted by the users in Saudi Arabia by using geo-filtering. Besides, we searched for tweets using hashtags that included the city's name. Both methods ensure collecting tweets about Saudi Arabia or posted from any place inside it, but not necessarily related to road traffic. Moreover, we created a list of specialised accounts that post about transportation and traffic condition in Saudi Arabia and then use them to obtain traffic-related tweets. We collected data in the period between September 2018 and October 2019. The total number of the collected tweets is 33.5 million. After that, we clean the data by removing duplicates and the retweets.

For storing the collected tweets, we need a storage method that provides flexible schemas to store/retrieve the data. So, we found that the NoSQL databases are more appropriate compared to the traditional table structures in relational databases. One of the common types of NoSQL databases is a document-oriented database. In this type, each key is paired with the document of various document data types, such as XML and JSON. One of the most widely used document-oriented databases is MongoDB. Thus, we used MongoDB to store the fetched tweets using Twitter API.

Moreover, we use parquet file storage. The Parquet is a column-oriented format. It is supported by many data processing systems including Apache Spark. Furthermore, it enables very efficient compression. We select it to store the output after each stage because it is efficient and provides good performance for both storage and processing. Besides, Spark SQL supports both reading and writing Parquet files that automatically preserves the schema of the original data. After reading data from the Parquet file, it is stored in Spark DataFrames, which is equivalent to a table in a relational database or a data frame in R/Python. However, it provides richer optimisations.

8.3.3 Data Pre-processing Component

We use pre-processing component proposed in our earlier work, Iktishaf [6]. Figure 8.3 shows the algorithm. It received the collected tweets, the Arabic diacritics [D], punctuations [P], and Arabic stop words [SW] as an input while the output is clean, normalised, and stemmed tokens. The collected tweets are exported from MongoDB and stored in Apache Spark DataFrame. The next subsections explain the main pre-processing steps.

8.3.3.1 Irrelevant Characters Removal

We removed Arabic diacritics, punctuation marks. English letters and numbers. for Arabic diacritics, we created a list of all the three forms of diacritics suggested by Diab et al. (2007). The first form is Vowel Diacritics. It refers to the three main short vowels, named in Arabic as Fatha (ﹷ), Damma (ﹹ) and Kasra (ﹻ) as well as the Sukun diacritic (ﹿ), which indicates the absence of any vowel. The second form is Nunation Diacritics, which are named in Arabic as Fathatan (ﹰ), Dammatan (ﹲ) and Kasratan (ﹴ). They represent the

Algorithm: Pre-Processing

Input : tweets; [D]; [P]; [SW]
Output: Clean, normalized and stemmed tokens
1   *spark* ← createSparkSession()
2   *tweets_DF* ← spark.read(tweets)
3   **foreach** *tweet* ∈ *tweets_DF['text']* **do**
    // Remove Irrelevant Characters
4   *clean_tweets* ← ""
5   **for** *char in tweet* **do**
6   **if** *char not in [D] AND char not in [P] AND not char.isdigit()*
       AND not char.isEnglishChar() **then**
7   *clean_tweets.append*(char)
8   **end**
    // Tokenize
9   *tokens* ← [ ]
10   *tokens* ← clean_tweets.split()
    // Normalize
11   *normalized_tokens* ← [ ]
12   **for** *token in tokens* **do**
13   **for** *alif in ['إ' , 'أ' , 'آ']* **do**
14   **if** *alif in token* **then**
15   *token* ← token.replace(alif, 'ا')
16   **end**
17   **if** *token.endswith('ي ') or token.endswith('ى ')* **then**
18   *token* ← token.replaceLastCharWith('ي ')
19   **if** *token.endswith('ة ')* **then**
20   *token* ← token.replaceLastCharWith('ه ')
     // Remove Stop Words
21   **if** *token not in [SW]* **then**
22   *normalized_tokens.append*(token)
23   **end**
    // Stemmer
24   *stemm_tokens* ← stemmer(normalized_tokens)
25 **end**

FIGURE 8.3
Iktishaf+: pre-processing algorithm.

doubled version of the short vowels. The third form is called Shadda (germination) and refers to the consonant-doubling diacritical (ّ). It also can be merged with diacritics from the two previous types and result in a new diacritic such as (ً), (ٍ). Therefore, the total number of Arabic diacritics is thirteen diacritical marks. All of them will be removed from the text.

Furthermore, we created a list of all the punctuation marks such as commas, period, colons, both Arabic and English semi-colons, and question marks, in addition to the different types of brackets, slashes and mathematical symbols as well as the other signs such as $, %, &, and @. For the hashtags, we strip only the hash (#) and underscore (_) symbols and keep the keywords because they may contain useful information such as the place or event name.

8.3.3.2 Tokeniser and Normaliser

To divide the text into a list of words (tokens), we used a split() method in python, which returns a list of substrings after breaking the giving string by a specified separator, in our case the separator is any white space in the text. After that, the tokens are passed to the normaliser to replace letters that have different forms into the basic shape. The letter (١) pronounced Alif had three forms (آ, إ, أ). It will be normalised to bare Alif (١). Besides, the letter (ي) pronounced Yaa will be normalised to dotless Yaa (ى). In addition, the letter (ة) pronounced Taa marbutah will be normalised to (ه).

8.3.3.3 Stop-Words Removal

The Natural Language Toolkit (NLTK) (Loper & Bird, 2002) provided a stop-word list for the Arabic Language. However, it was designed for the formal Modern Standard Arabic. Therefore, we modified the list and added new stop-words that usually used in dialectical Arabic such as "ليش", "اللي" and others. Subsequently, we considered common grammar mistakes. For instance, the preposition "متى" might be written "متا" and "لكن" might be written "لاكن". Besides, we added the common words that are used in Du'aa (prayer) such as "يارب", "اللهم", "الله" because they are frequently used and keeping them is not necessary, in our particular case. before using the final generated stop-words list, we normalised them because they will be stripped from normalised tweets.

8.3.3.4 Stemmer

The existing Arabic stemmer tools can be categorised into two types, which are root-based stemmer and light stemmer. The first type extracts the root of the words while the light stemmers strip affixes (prefixes and suffixes). However, root-based stemmers are heavy stemmers and known to have some weaknesses such as increasing word ambiguity. Thus, in this work, we decided to use a light stemmer. However, most of the existing Arabic light stemmers can lead to removing important parts of the word which results in a few letters with no meaning. Therefore, we used the developed Arabic Light Stemmer, Iktishaf Stemmer (Alomari et al., 2020a). It is designed to strip affixes based on the length of the word to reduce the chance of stripping important letters which could lead to change the meaning or losing important words, particularly the words that are related to transportation. Figure 8.4 shows the algorithm of the proposed stemmer. It gets the normalised tokens, the lists of prefixes [P], and suffixes [S] as input. For prefixes,

---

Algorithm: Stemmer

    Input : normalized_tokens; [P1]; [P2]; [P3]; [S1]; [S2]; [S3]
    Output: Stemmed tokens

1 *stemm_tokens* ← [ ]
2 **foreach** *nToken* ∈ *normalized_tokens* **do**
       // Remove Prefix
3   **if** *nToken.length()* > *4* **then**
4   **if** *nToken.length()* > *5* and *nToken.startWithany([P1])* **then**
5 | *nToken* ← *nToken.removeStartWith*([P1])
6   **if** *nToken.length()* > *5* and *nToken.startWithany([P2])* **then**
7 | *nToken* ← *nToken.removeStartWith*([P2])
8   **if** *nToken.startWithany([P3])* **then**
9 | *nToken* ← *nToken.removeStartWith*([P3])
       // Remove Suffix
10   **if** *nToken.length()* > *5* **then**
11   **if** *nToken.endWithany([S1])* **then**
12   *nToken* ← *nToken.removeEndsWith*([S1])
13   **if** *nToken.endWith('ا')* **then**
14 | nToken=nToken.removeEndWith('ا')
15   **if** *nToken.endWith('ت')* **then**
16 | nToken=nToken.replaceWith('ه')
17   **if** *nToken.endWithany([S2])* **then**
18   *nToken* ← *nToken.removeEndWith*([S2])
19   **if** *nToken.endWith('ا')* **then**
20 | nToken=nToken.removeEndWith('ا')
21   **if** *nToken.endWith('ت')* **then**
22 | nToken=nToken.replaceWith('ه')
23   **if** *nToken.endWithany([S3]* **then**
24 | *nToken* ← *nToken.removeEndWith*([S3])
25   **if** *nToken.endWithany('ت ا')* **then**
26   nToken=nToken.replaceWith('ه')
27   **if** *nToken.endWith('ت')* **then**
28 | nToken=nToken.replaceWith('ه')
29   **if** *nToken.length()* > *1* **then**
30 | *stemm_tokens.append*(nToken)
31 **end**

FIGURE 8.4
Iktishaf+: stemmer algorithm.

we divide them into three lists, each list contains specific prefixes that do not usually come together in one word. P1 includes prefixes such as "ك", "و", "ف", "ب" whereas P2 contains "ما", "ي" and P3 includes prefixes such as "ال", "لل", "وال", "فال", "كال", "هال". Both P1 and P2 will be removed only if the token length is greater than 5 to decrease the chance of making mistakes and stripping important letters that are part of the token. For instance, "بريده" city starts with "ب" but the length is greater than 5 so it will not be affected by stemmer. On the other side, any prefixes in P3 will be stripped if the length of the word is greater than 4. Moreover, we take into consideration that the word may contain more than one prefix, so the first list of prefixes contains the prefixes that come at the beginning of the word. For instance, the word "ﻤﺎﻳﻨﺎﺳﺐ'" contains two prefixes: 'ﺏ', which is in P1 and 'ﻣﺎ', which is in P2 so 'ﻣﺎ' will be stripped after 'ﺏ'.

Similarly, for suffixes, we have three lists. S1 contains suffixes such as, "ﻫﺎ", "ﻛﻢ", "ﻛﻦ", "ﻫﻢ", "ﻫﻦ", "ﻧﺎ", "ﻧﻲ", "ﻣﺎ", "ﺗﻦ" while S2 contains "ﻳﻦ", "ﻭﻥ", "ﺍﻥ", "ﻭﺍ". To clarify, we give an example of the verb "ﻳﻌﺮﻑ". It can be ended with any of the following suffixes: ﻫﻢ, ﻕ, ﻫﺎ, ﻧﺎ, ﻫﻦ, ﻭﻥ, ﻛﻢ. It may also contain two suffixes like in "ﻳﻌﺮﻓﻮﻧﻬﻢ", which contains "ﻭﻥ" and "ﻫﻢ". So, "ﻫﻢ" will be removed first because it is in S1 and then "ﻭﻥ" will be removed in the next step.

After removing any suffix from the previous lists, we check the last letter in the word to see if it becomes end with 'ﺕ' to replace it with 'ﻩ'. For example, the word "ﺳﻴﺎﺭﺗﻬﻢ" (their car) will become "ﺳﻴﺎﺭﺕ" after removing "ﻫﻢ" but the correct spelling is "ﺳﻴﺎﺭﻩ" so we need to replace 'ﺕ' with 'ﻩ'.

Subsequently, the stemmer removes suffix in S3, which are 'ﻩ', 'ﻱ' only if the length of the word is greater than 5 and thus, we reduce the chance of stripping them if they are part of the word like the 'ﻩ' in the previous example "ﺳﻴﺎﺭﻩ". It will not be removed because the word consists of 5 letters. After that, we check if the new stemmed token ends with 'ﺕ' to replace it with 'ﻩ'. For example, the words "ﺳﻴﺎﺭﻱ" (my car) or "ﺳﻴﺎﺭﺗﻪ" (his car) will become after stemming "ﺳﻴﺎﺭﺕ", so we need to replace the last letter to make it "ﺳﻴﺎﺭﻩ". The final suffix is 'ﺍﺕ' and it will be replaced with 'ﻩ'. For instance, "ﺳﻴﺎﺭﺍﺕ" (cars) will become "ﺳﻴﺎﺭﻩ". Finally, we check the length of the word after striping suffixes and prefixes and keep only words that have at least 2 characters.

8.3.4 Tweets Labelling Component

To generate a training set for the classifiers, we need labelled tweets. Since we have a very large dataset of around 33.5 million tweets, manual labelling will be a very expensive and time-consuming process. We manually labelled approximately twenty thousand tweets of the total 33.5 million tweets and then we combined them with automatically labelled tweets using the automatic labelling approach. The manually labelled tweets also help us to generate dictionaries for automatic labelling since it is a lexical based approach. The following subsections explain the proposed approach for labelling tweets about event classifiers and tweets filtering classifiers. Even though we detect events after filtering tweets, we will start with labelling events because the output will be used later on to label the tweets into relevant and irrelevant.

8.3.4.1 Automatic Labelling for Events Tweets

8.3.4.1.1 Creating Dictionaries

For each event type, we automatically generated a dictionary that contains the top frequent terms using the manual labelled tweets. We manually updated each dictionary to include the missing terms related to each event type in addition to add synonyms. Both manually and automatically added terms in the dictionaries are passed to the stemmer since the search for matching terms will be applied to the tweet after pre-processing. We used Iktishaf light stammer (see Section 8.3.3.4).

The dictionaries contain a group of terms but we cannot use them directly to search for matching tweets because the degree of relevance to the event type is not equal for all the terms. Therefore, for each event type, we created an N number of terms list. Each list is considered as a level. So, we have N number of levels (L_1, L_2, ..., L_n). Each term T in the event dictionary is assigned to a level based on the degree of the importance of this term to the event. Thus, the terms that are highly related to the event and almost exist in each report about this event are assigned to the first level (L_1) while the last level contains terms that are least related to the event.

Furthermore, we gave each list a weight W based on the level it belongs to, which means we have N weights (W_1, W_2, ..., W_n). W_n is the highest weight so it is assigned to L1 which contains the most important terms. In this work, we used 4 levels of terms. To clarify, for Accident event, Level 1 includes terms such as Accident (حادث) and crash (صدم), Level 2 contains terms such as car (سياره), driver (سائق) and, road (طريق), Level 3 include Ambulance (اسعاف) and death(وفاه) while the last level (Level 4) contains the less important/relevant terms such as cause (يسبب).

Figure 8.5 illustrates the automatic labelling algorithm. It receives the pre-processed tweets (tweets_P), term dictionaries (terms_D), and event types (event_T) as input and provides the labelled tweets as an output. Apache Spark is used, and the pre-processed tweets are stored in Spark Dataframe (tweets_DF). For each token in the tweet, it searched for the matched term in the terms dictionary. Section 8.3.4.1.2 explains the process of searching for the matching terms. After that, weight is calculated for each labelled tweet. Section 8.3.4.1.3 clarifies the process of weight calculation. The last step is sorting and filtering the labelled tweets based on the calculated weight, see Section 8.3.4.1.4 for further details.

8.3.4.1.2 Find Matching Terms

For each tweet, we applied the pre-processing steps explained in Section 8.3.3 to remove irrelevant characters, divide the text into tokens, normalise the tokens, remove the stop words, and apply stemmer. The output is N number of clean normalised and stemmed tokens (K1, K2, ..., Kn). Moreover, we iterated over each tweet and for each token K, we searched for the match terms in the term levels (L_1, L_2, ..., L_n). The output is a list of existing terms in each level as shown below where Tx is the matching term.

$$Lx_1 = [Tx_1, Tx_2, ..., Tx_n], ..., Lx_n = [Tx_1, Tx_2, ..., Tx_n] \tag{8.1}$$

Algorithm: Automatic Labeling

Input : tweets_P; terms_D ; event_T
Output: Labeled tweets
1 *spark* ← createSparkSession()
2 *tweets_DF* ← spark.read(tweets_P)
3 *n* ← get_levels_num(terms_D)
4 **foreach** *tweet* ∈ *tweets_DF* **do**
5   *tokens* ← get_tokens(tweet)
6   **foreach** *event* ∈ *event_T* **do**
7   *term_levels* ← terms_D[event]
8   **foreach** *token* ∈ *tokens* **do**
9           $l \leftarrow 1$
10   *stopSearch* ← False
11   **while** $l < n$ **do**
12   **if** *!stopSearch* **then**
13   **foreach** *term* ∈ *term_levels*[l] **do**
14   **if** *term.isEqual(token)* **then**
15   *matchedTerms* ← add(term,l)
16   *stopSearch* ← True
17   break
18   **end**
19             $l \leftarrow +1$
20   **end**
21   **end**
22   *tweet_weight*[*event*] ← calculate_weight(matchedTerms)
23   **end**
24   *tweets_DF*['*weight*'] ← tweet_weight
25 **end**
26 *tweets_label_DF* ← sort_and_filter(tweets_DF['weight'])

FIGURE 8.5
Automatic labelling algorithm for events.

8.3.4.1.3 *Weight Calculation*

We filtered the tweets to keep only the tweets containing at least one term from the high-level (L1), except for roadwork/damage event type, we keep tweets that contain at least one term from level (L1) and at least one term from level (L2). For roadwork/damage event, L1 includes terms such as maintenance (صيانة), development (تطوير) while L2 include terms such as road (طريق), street(شارع). So at least on terms from each level should be found to assign a label to a tweet. After that, the weight is calculated using the following equation:

$$W_E = \left\{ \left(size(Lx_1) \times W_n \right) + \left(size(Lx_2) \times W_{n-1} \right) + \cdots + \left(size(Lx_n) \times W_1 \right) \right\} \quad (8.2)$$

where W_E is the total weight for the event E, Lx is the list of matching terms and W is the weight assigned for this level. Since we have 4 levels, the highest weight is 4, so, each of the term Tx that was found in Level Lx_1 has a weight equal to 4.

8.3.4.1.4 *Sort and Filter Automatic Labelled Tweets*

We used the weight to sort the labelled tweets and then we filtered them. Furthermore, we specified a threshold to discard labelled tweet that has low weight and kept tweets that have high weight because they are most likely related to the event. The same process is repeated for each event type. We take into consideration during this process that the tweet can have multiple labels.

8.3.4.1.5 *Testing and Evaluation*

The testing and evaluation of the proposed automatic labelling tool are performed in two stages. The first stage is in the beginning in order to update and modify the list of terms in each level in the dictionary such as moving terms from one level to another level or adding new terms. After each initial labelling iteration, we extracted the top vocabularies to search for the new important terms that are not yet included in the dictionary of that event. For instance, for the first iteration, most of the weather event is about rains so the automatic generated dictionary contains terms related to rains. So, this stage is important to insert missing terms and then we manually update the dictionary to add their synonyms if they exist. The second stage is applied to randomly selected tweets to make sure that the tweets are labelled correctly. The main goal is reducing the number of false-positive (labelled as an event but it is not) more than the number of false negatives (event but labelled as not related) to reduce the chance of making mistakes and including none event tweets in the training set of events classifiers. Besides, missing a few events tweets will not have a major effect on the size of the training set.

8.3.4.2 Automatic Labelling for Irrelevant Tweets

Before detecting the event, we need to train a classifier to classify the tweets into relevant and irrelevant to traffic. The training set contains positive tweets (related to traffic) and negative tweets (not related). Even though we train the filtering classifiers before the events classifiers, we generate the training set for the event before filtering classifiers. The output from the automatic event labelling process is used for a positive class for tweet filtering. For the negative class, we applied another automatic filtering approach by searching for the tweets that do not contain any terms related to traffic and transportation. We searched in the tweets collected by geo-filtering, and we excluded tweets posted by any account related to traffic.

8.3.5 Feature Extractor Component

We used CountVectorizer and IDFModel algorithms provided in the Spark ML package to generate the feature vectors and rescale them. IDFModel applied TF-IDF (Term Frequency-Inverse Document Frequency), which reflects the importance of a token to a document (tweet) in a corpus. The TF-IDF is the product of TF and IDF where TF (t, d) is the frequency of the appearance of token t in document d while the IDF is calculated using Equation (8.3). A detailed explanation was given in our earlier study [6].

$$IDF(t, D) = log \frac{|D| + 1}{DF(t, D) + 1} \qquad (8.3)$$

8.3.6 Tweets Filtering Component

8.3.6.1 Model Training

To filter tweets into related to road traffic and not related, we built a classifier using ML supervised classification algorithms. After labelling the tweets using both automatic and manual labelling approaches, we used the Spark ML library to build and train the models. We built three models using SVM, Naive Bayes and Logistic Regression algorithms. We have an imbalanced dataset because, in our work, the number of samples for the negative class (not related to traffic) is much higher than the positive class (traffic-related). This will lead to misleading evaluation results, especially for accuracy. To address this issue, we applied a random under-sampling approach to randomly remove some tweets from the negative class.

8.3.6.2 Hyperparameter Tuning

After data processing and feature extraction, we need to tune the parameters to obtain the best performance model. Grid search is one of the well-known ways to search for the best tuning parameter values. To do that, we need to specify a set of candidate tuning-parameter values and then evaluate them. Cross-validation can help to generate samples from the training set to evaluate each distinct parameter value combination and see how they perform. After that, we can get the best tuning parameter combination and use them with the entire training set to train the final model.

Spark ML supports model selection using tools such as CrossValidator to select a relatively reasonable parameter setting from a grid of parameters. We used 5-folds cross-validation. So CrossValidator will generate 5 (training, testing) dataset pairs. Then, the average evaluation metric for the five models will be computed and the best parameter will be founded. In the future, we plan to improve our method and use 10-fold validation.

8.3.6.3 Classification Model Evaluation

We compare the performance using the common evaluation metrics, which are accuracy, recall, precision and f-score. The model that achieves higher results is selected for the final classification of tweets. Since we are using binary classification to classify into relevant (class 1) and irrelevant (class 0), tuning the prediction threshold is very important. The default threshold is 0.5 and it can be any value in the range [0, 1]. If the estimated probability of class label 1 is greater than the specified threshold, the prediction result will be 1, otherwise, it will be class 0. Thus, specifying a high threshold value will encourage the model to predict 0 more often and vice versa. In our case, we need to minimise the chance of making mistakes and predicting 0 (irrelevant) as 1 (relevant) so we set the threshold to 0.8.

8.3.7 Events Detection Component

We focus in this work on detecting the following event types: Fire, Weather, Social, Traffic Condition, Roadwork/Road Damage, and Accident. The tweets are labelling using the labelling method explained in Section 8.3.4. The classes are not mutually exclusive where the tweet can be about multi-events at the same time. For instance, the tweet might explain the accident that occurs due to bad weather. Hence, two labels will be assigned to this tweet, which are accident and weather. To address the issue, we used a binary classification. We trained a model for each event type. For each model, we need positive and negative samples. Assume we have event type T, the tweets that are labelled as T are considered as positive samples while all the remaining tweets that belong to the other events types are considered negative samples. Moreover, tweet that has more than one label such as accident and weather will be included in the positive class in the training set of accident as well as weather during training both classifiers. However, as the number of tweets in the negative class is very large compared to the positive because it includes all the tweets about the other events types, we have an imbalance dataset problem. To address this problem, we followed the same approach explained in 3.6.1 by applying a random under-sampling approach.

8.3.8 Spatio-Temporal Extractor Component

The location is the foremost matter of interest in transportation analysis and event detection domain. Thus, we applied different techniques for location extraction from the Tweet object.

8.3.8.1 Text, Hashtag and Username

The main approach is extracting location details which are mentioned within the post. It might be explicitly mentioned in the tweet's message or it might exist as part of the hashtags or accounts name especially if the tweets are posted by a specialised account that posts about the events and traffic conditions in the cities. We created a list of cities names in Saudi Arabia to search for cities name in the tweet message. We pass the Arabic name list to the stemmer before using them to extract the place name from text because we extract them from the pre-processed text. In addition, we searched for the cities name in English to extract them from accounts or hashtags using a pre-defined list of cities' names in English. We also created a list of specialised accounts that post about traffic in Saudi Arabia cities and does not include a city name. After that, we use this list to find the city name based on the username.

8.3.8.2 Tweets Geo Attributes

One of the approaches is obtaining coordinates in geotagged tweets by getting latitude and longitude from 'coordinate' or 'place' objects. The 'place' child object consists of several attributes including 'place_type', 'pl ce_name', 'country_code'. The place type is either city or point of interest (poi). However, a small fraction of tweets are geotagged because most of the users used to disable location services in their smartphones for privacy reasons.

8.3.8.3 User Profile

The location information is also extracted from user profiles where they usually manually write the country and city name. We have to consider that this information might be written in Arabic or English and they use different spelling. For instance, Makkah can be written as Makkah or Mecca. The text is tokenised and then passed to the stemmer before searching for the city name using the created dictionaries.

We cannot rely on the geo attributes alone because geo coordinates information might not have been provided especially for users who disable location services in their smartphones where the value will be 'null' in this case, as shown in the JSON example in Section 8.3.2. Similarly, we cannot rely on profile information alone because users do not always fill in these fields with accurate information. In addition, they might travel to another city/country so the profile information, does not reflect the current location. Besides, both approaches do not necessarily represent the place of the event because users might post about events that occur in other cities.

In this work, we considered the text as the main source of location information because it is more accurate than the other attributes besides, we need to find the location where the events occur not where they were posted. If the information does not exist, we extract them from coordinates or place attributes. The last option is to find location from the profile because it is less accurate than the other since users specify their information in the profile manually and they do not usually update them whenever they travel to another city. For visualisation, the geospatial coordinates of the detected locations are extracted to enable plotting them on the map.

Algorithm: Peak Events Detection

Input : event_Tweets; event_Types; threshold; duration
Output: Peak events list
1 **for** *event in event_Types* **do**
2   **for** *d in duration* **do**
        // Duration can be Hours, Days or Months
3   *peakEvent* ← []
4   **for** *tweet in event_Tweets[event]* **do**
5   **if** *tweet.intensity() >threshold* **then**
6   *peakEvent.append*(tweet)
7   **end**
8   **end**
9 **end**

FIGURE 8.6
Peak events reporting algorithm.

8.3.9 Reporting and Visualisation Component

This component supports plotting the output of the spatio-temporal information extraction component and event detection components to show the detected events and their location and time of occurrence. Also, it supports finding peak events based on configurable parameters as well as visualises the results. Figure 8.6 shows the peak events reporting algorithm. It enables searching for hourly, daily and monthly peak events when the tweet's intensity exceeds a specific threshold value.

Moreover, this component supports visualising the results of the model evaluation (See Section 8.3.6.3) for both tweet filtering and event detection components to illustrate which algorithm achieved better results.

8.3.10 External and Internal Validation Component

To validate the Iktishaf+ tool and its ability to detect events and their spatial and temporal nature. We searched against various sources on the web including news media. Then, we compared the information extracted by our tool with the information in the web sources. However, news media do not report all the existing events and even if they report them, they might not mention the time of occurrence. In this case, we searched in the tweets we have, related to the event, to find the validation information we need. We consider this process as an internal validation because it is based on the collected tweets. To find time information, we go back to the earliest tweet we have about the event and if the time is not mentioned explicitly in the tweet text, we refer to the time of posting the tweet as the starting time of the event. The process of searching in the external sources was done manually, but we plan to automate it in the future.

8.4 Analysis and Results

8.4.1 Detected Events

8.4.1.1 Validation of Detected Events

To validate the ability of Iktishaf+ and verify if a detected event really happened on the same detected date and location, we searched against external validation sources (news media) or an internal source (Twitter) (see Section 8.3.10). Table 8.1 shows a comparison between information extracted by Iktishaf+ and information from external/internal sources. We cannot discuss all the detected events, due to the limited number of pages allowed and the large period we are covering in this work (September 2018–October 2019). So, we selected samples of different event types that occurred at different times and locations. Column 1 shows the event types. Column 2 lists the location (city name) where the event occurs as we found from searching in various external sources as well as the location extracted by our tool. Column 3 gives the date when the events occur. Column 4 gives the time of occurrence to assess the ability of our tool to detect the time. We compared the starting time mentioned in the web sources with the peak time shown by Iktishaf+. As explained in Section 8.3.10 the time information may not be mentioned in the news reports. So, in this case, we searched in the collected tweet and get the earliest tweet about this event. Then, we extracted the time from the timestamp attached to the tweet.

Moreover, we drew charts to display the time extracted by Iktishaf+ for each event in the table. Further, the locations of each event are overlayed on top of the Saudi Arabia map.

Row 1 shows the "Fire" event on 1st October 2018. Figure 8.7 illustrates the locations. Note the largest circle in Riyadh city, this matches the information

TABLE 8.1

Example of Validation

Event Type	Location		Date		Time	
	Validation Sources	Iktishaf+	Validation Sources	Iktishaf+	Validation Sources	Iktishaf+
Fire	Riyadh		1/10/2018		Started at 3 pm	Found peak around 4 pm
	Jeddah		29/9/2019		Started at 12:35 pm	Found peak around 12 pm
Weather	Makkah and Jeddah		23/11/2018		Started at dawn (before 5:42 am)	Found peak around 4 am
Accident	Riyadh		8/10/2018		Started around 4:48 am	Found peak around 5 am

FIGURE 8.7
Fire event on 1 October 2018.

found in the newspaper, where they reported about a huge fire breaking out at a power plant in Riyadh (Was, 2018). They also mentioned that the Saudi Civil Defence received notification about the fire at 3 pm. Figure 8.8 shows the time extracted by our tool. It can be seen that the intensity started raising at 3 pm and the highest peak was at 4 pm.

Row 2 validates another "Fire" event. As we found in the web source (NDTV, 2019), it was a massive fire ripped through the main station of Haramain High-speed Railways in Jeddah city on 29 September 2019. It was started at 12:35 pm according to the Haramain High-speed Railways' Twitter account. Further, it remains for hours before it was brought under control.

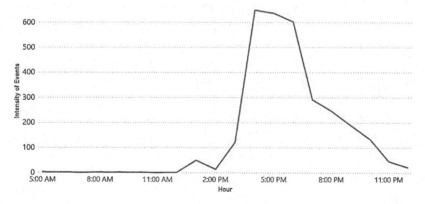

FIGURE 8.8
Intensity of detected fire event in Riyadh (1 October 2018).

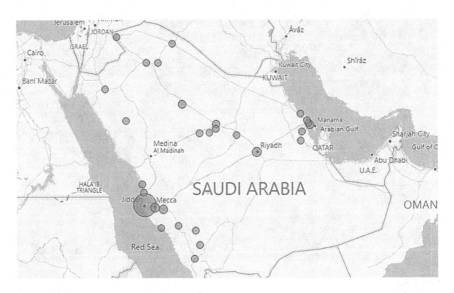

FIGURE 8.9
Fire event on 29 September 2019.

Figure 8.9 and Figure 8.10 show the location and time information extracted by Iktishaf+. Note the largest circle in Jeddah city, as well as the peak time as shown in Figure 8.10, are around noon.

Furthermore, Row 3 validates the "Weather" event on 23 November 2018. This was due to the rains in Makkah and Jeddah cities as reported in the newspaper. Figure 8.11 plots the locations of weather events on that date. Note the largest circles are in Jeddah and Makkah cities. The news article we found was posted around 5:42 am and they mentioned that the rains were

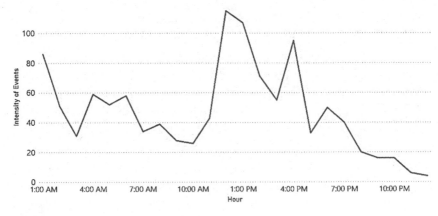

FIGURE 8.10
Intensity of detected fire event in Jeddah (29 September 2019).

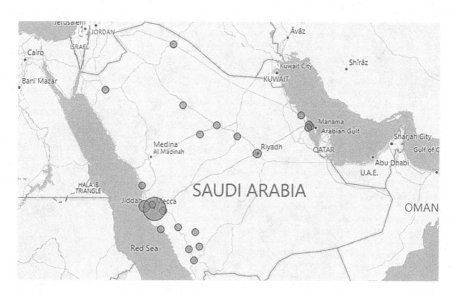

FIGURE 8.11
Weather event on 23 November 2018.

started at dawn. This validates the time extracted by our tool. Figure 8.12 shows a peak at 4 am. As we know, Twitter users almost post about events like rain immediately once it happened and most likely earlier than the newspapers.

Finally, Row 4 illustrates the "Accident" event on 8 October 2018. Note the largest circle in Riyadh shown in Figure 8.13. The time of occurrence is not available on the newspaper website so in this case, we went back to the tweets and searched for the earliest tweet that mentioned information

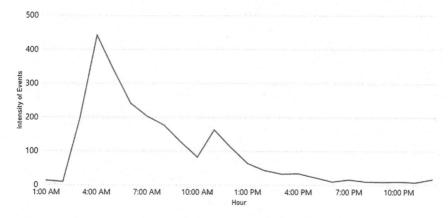

FIGURE 8.12
Intensity of detected weather event in Makkah (23 November 2018).

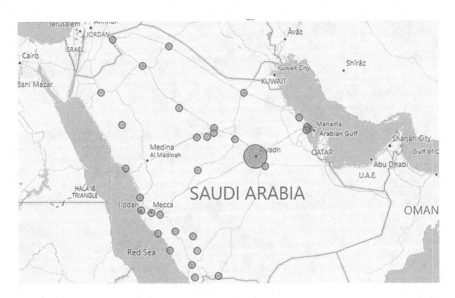

FIGURE 8.13
Accident event on 8 October 2018.

about the same accident we want to validate. Then, we extracted the time from the timestamp (created_at attribute) included with the tweet object and assumed that it was the time of occurrence (see Section 8.3.10). This is the English translation for the earliest tweet we found about this event "Congestion in every street and accident in the Alwashm bridge, stations crowded, crowded everywhere in Riyadh #Riyadh_now". The time attached to this tweet is "Mon Oct 08 04:48:17 +0000 2018" and the first peak time detected by Iktishaf+ as shown in Figure 8.14 is at 5 am. Therefore, it can be

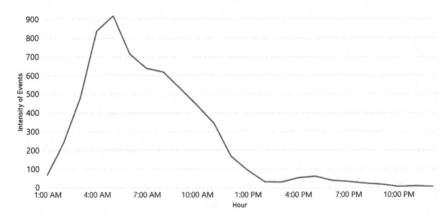

FIGURE 8.14
Intensity of detected accident event in Riyadh (8 October 2018).

seen from the discussed results above that the information from external or internal validation sources matches the information detected by Iktishaf+, which proves the ability of our tool to automatically detect events and their location and time without prior knowledge.

8.4.1.2 Spatial Analysis

Figure 8.15 depicts the percentage of the extracted location information using different approaches explained in Section 8.3.8. As shown in the pie chart, 44% of the information is extracted from tweet text while 16% are extracted using the information in the user's profile. However, 27% of tweets about events did not include any information about the location where it occurs. Besides, only 5% are extracted from geo attributes. This could be because few tweets are geo-tagged because, users usually turn off the location service in their smartphones. Also, we only look into the geo attributes if the location does not mention in the text because we mainly focus on where the event occurs not where it has been posted.

After inferring cities' names from the tweets, we group them by province. Figure 8.16 gives the number of tweets for each event type in the large provinces in Saudi Arabia. It shows the aggregated number of tweets for the whole period (from September 2018 to October 2019). It can be seen that the number of events detected in Riyadh is higher than the events in other provinces. This could be because Riyadh is the capital and one of the largest cities. Besides, based on the latest report published by INREX (INRIX, 2020), Riyadh is the most congested city in Saudi Arabia, which may explain the results we got.

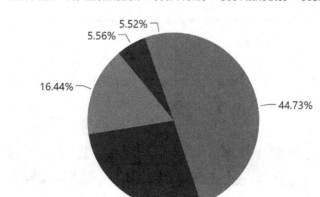

FIGURE 8.15
Number of tweets using different location extraction approaches.

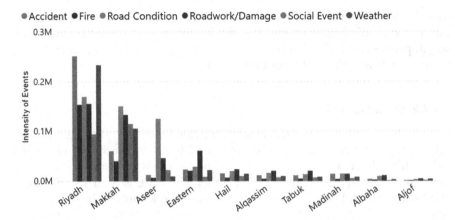

FIGURE 8.16
Number of detected events in different provinces.

8.4.1.3 Spatio-Temporal Analysis

Figure 8.17 shows the hourly distribution for the aggregated number of tweets for the whole period. We plot only the provinces that show high number of events to eliminate having too much data in the chart since we have 13 provinces in Saudi Arabia. As shown in this figure, the number of tweets starts raising in the morning and becomes very high by the time of coming back from school and work, which is usually between 12 pm and 5 pm. Further, the number goes down after 8 pm, which is expected because usually the traffic flow and activities during daytime are higher than the nighttime because of work and schools.

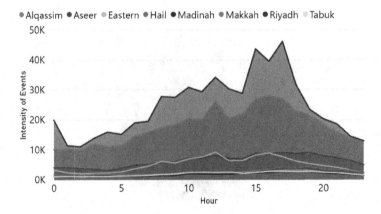

FIGURE 8.17
Hourly distribution of tweets divided by provinces (aggregated).

8.4.2 Evaluation: Tweet Filtering Classifiers

To evaluate the trained model for the Tweets Filtering Component (TFC), we used the common statistical metrics, accuracy, precision, recall, f-score (see Section 8.3.6.3). Most of the tweets we have are irrelevant to traffic, so we have an imbalanced dataset. So, to eliminate the effect on the evaluation results, we have two options either oversampling the majority class that represents the irrelevant tweets or under-sampling the minority class that represents the traffic tweets. In our particular case, it is better to have a large number of samples for both classes. Therefore, we decided to apply oversampling on positive (traffic-related) class. We simply duplicate the number of the tweet in the positive class (see Section 8.3.6.3). Figure 8.18 shows that SVM achieved higher results compared to the other algorithms. It achieved 91% for both accuracy and f1-score, 90% for precision and 89% for recall. The difference between the results achieved by SVM and LR is approximately 1%. However, we selected SVM where it performed better.

8.4.3 Evaluation: Event Classifiers

We numerically evaluated the built binary classifiers in the Event Detection Component (EDC). For each event type, we trained three models using NB,

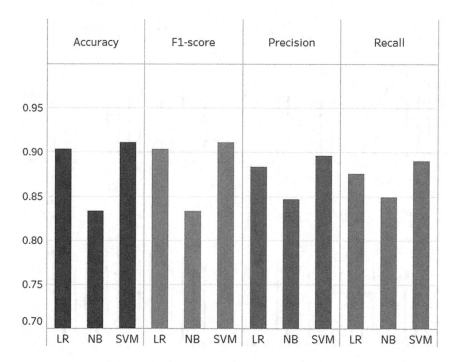

FIGURE 8.18
Numerical evaluation (tweets filtering).

SVM, and LR algorithms and then we selected the algorithm that achieved higher results in most evaluation metrics (accuracy, precision, recall and f1-score). We have used the four-performance metrics as discussed before in the previous section (also see Section 8.3.6.3).

Figure 8.19 illustrates the evaluation results for the four-performance metrics (left to right: Accuracy, Precision, Recall, and F-score) in four separate figures. The results show that SVM performs better than other algorithms for Weather, Roadwork and Traffic condition events while NB performed the best for Fire event. Besides, for accident events, SVM achieved higher results for accuracy, precision and f1-score while NB performed slightly better for the recall where SVM achieves 86% whereas NB achieves 88%. However, since the SVM performed better for most metrics, we selected SVM for accident event. For Social events, NB achieved higher recall and precision while SVM performed better for accuracy and f1-score. However, we selected NB for Social events since the accuracy and f1-score achieved by SVM are approximately 1% higher than NB. To summarise, SVM has been used for all the event types except Fire and Social where we used NB. Moreover, the highest results we got in all metrics were achieved by SVM for the Weather event where it achieved 98% for both accuracy and f1-score and 97% for recall and

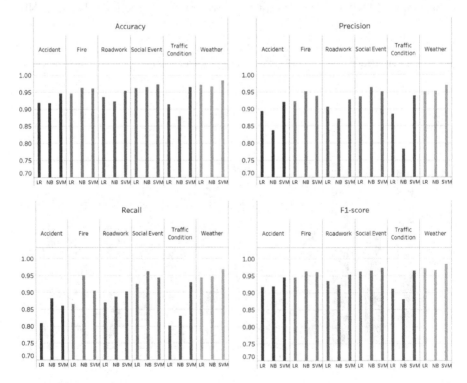

FIGURE 8.19
Numerical evaluation (events classification).

precision. We assume that the reason is we have a larger number of tweets for the training set of weather event since it occurs more often, and a lot of users post about it compared with other event types such as accidents and roadwork/damage.

8.5 Conclusion[1]

Digital societies could be characterised by their increasing desire to express themselves and interact with others. This is being realised through digital platforms such as social media that have increasingly become convenient and inexpensive sensors compared to physical sensors in many sectors of smart societies. One such major sector is road transportation, which is the backbone of modern economies and costs globally 1.25 million deaths and 50 million human injuries annually. The cutting-edge on big data-enabled social media analytics for transportation-related studies is limited.

In this chapter, we introduced the Iktishaf+ tool that uses big data and distributed machine learning to automatically detect road traffic events from Arabic tweets. Manual labelling is a time-consuming process that makes supervised classification hard to apply to big data. In order to address this problem; we proposed an automatic labelling approach to reduce the effort and time of generating a training set for training supervised classification models. The traditional manual labelling for text is usually achieved by looking for specific terms to decide whether the text is relevant to the topic or not. Hence, our tool was designed to follow the same procedure. We built a dictionary for each event type that contains lists of terms that are usually used when posting about the events. The dictionaries were generated automatically using the top vocabularies extracted from the manual labelled tweets. Then, we updated them manually to add synonyms and missing vocabulary. After that, we divided them into levels based on the degree of importance and relevance to the event type. Subsequently, the tool looked up the matched terms and labels the tweets based on that. Finally, the tool calculated weight for each labelled tweet, and only tweets that are highly related to the event are included in the training set.

Furthermore, we developed a location extractor to find the location of the events allowing spatio-temporal information extraction and visualisation of the events. Moreover, using a stemmer is necessary for our work not only to minimise feature space for model training but it is also very helpful especially

---

[1] This chapter, with permission from the copyright holder, is a reproduced version of the following journal article: Alomari, E., Katib, I., Albeshri, A., Yigitcanlar, T., & Mehmood, R. (2021). Iktishaf+: a big data tool with automatic labeling for road traffic social sensing and event detection using distributed machine learning. *Sensors*, 21(9), 2993.

for terms searching during automatic labelling and location extraction. The existing Arabic stemmers are not efficient in our case where they might lead to removing an important letter from the word and then cause losing or changing the meaning of important words. Therefore, we designed a light stemmer that enables affix stripping with fewer changes in the word meaning.

We built and trained models to filter out irrelevant tweets to traffic events. We focused on six events that might affect road traffic which are accident, fire, weather, roadwork/damage, road condition, and social events. Furthermore, we built classifiers to automatically classify tweets into different events. We used three machine learning algorithms, which are SVM, NB, and logistic regression. Then, we selected the algorithm that achieves better results in terms of accuracy, recall, precision, and f-score. Moreover, we applied external validation using online sources such as newspapers. We selected the highest peaks from the detected events and find whether they occurred or not. The results show that our tool can automatically detect events and their spatial and temporal nature without prior knowledge.

The ability of the Iktishaf+ tool to use big data distributed computing technologies could save days, months, or years of computing time proportional to the size of the data. Moreover, it enables the scalability and interworking of big data analytics software systems. The utilisation possibilities of our tool are many such as detection of transportation-related events for planning and operations, detection of causes of road congestion, understanding public concerns and their reactions to government policies and actions, and many more. An elaboration of these aspects of our work (the novelty, contributions, and utilisation) was given in Section 8.2.4.

We have shown good evidence of the use of automatic labelling, machine learning, and other methods. However, more work is needed to improve the breadth and depth of the work with regards to what can be detected, the diversity of data and machine and deep learning methods, the accuracy of detection in space and time, and the real-time analysis of the tweets.

The real-time operation of the proposed system could depend on a number of factors. Firstly, the definition of the term "real-time" per se depends on the application and the requirements at hand. Some applications may require reactions within sub-second periods while others may tolerate a few minutes or more. Moreover, taking preventive actions also depends on the event and the action being taken. In this particular context, and considering the example of a car accident, the Iktishaf system once trained can detect an accident from tweets instantaneously provided the tweets are available in real-time for the software to process. This can be achieved, for instance, by running the software at the edge or fog layers. The reactive actions, in this case, can mean to inform the police and ambulance services, which can be done in real-time by the software automatically through an automatic emergency call to 911, by sending tweets or other messages to the concerned bodies, or by other emergency strategies available in the area. The messages related to the particular actions in this context can also be propagated using vehicular ad hoc networks (VANETs), DSRC (Dedicated Short-Range Communications), etc. A more interesting and lucrative work would be to detect certain events (such as car chases or certain patterns in the traffic that may lead to accidents or certain social events that may cause congestion) before these happen and take actions to prevent the events before they happen. These will require further research and adding additional functionalities to the Iktishaf tool. Our future work will look into these areas.

Digitally and data-driven methods while bringing many benefits to the research and practice have their risks and disadvantages as is the case for anything else. These include issues related to security, privacy, data ownership, lack of standards describing ethical requirements from digital methods and compliance to these standards, the safety of the stakeholders involved in data-driven and digital methods, vulnerabilities of digital platforms, and the digital divide. For a detailed discussion of these issues, see Section 11, (Alam et al., 2021), and the references therein. As regards the specific privacy issues of Twitter data, the data we use is openly available. The information about the location of these tweets is also public. However, we have not disclosed any personal information through our analysis. The information we detected and published is of a general nature and therefore does not infringe on individual privacy. However, generally speaking, it is possible to detect information from Twitter data that affects individuals' privacy. Our earlier works (Ayres & Mehmood, 2010; Al-Dhubhani et al., 2017; Al-Dhubhani et al., 2019) have looked into privacy and we plan to extend this to investigate Twitter data privacy in the future.

Our focus in this work is on Saudi Arabia. The tool hence currently works with tweets only in the Arabic language. The tool can be used in other Arabic language-speaking countries, such as Egypt, Kuwait, Bahrain, and UAE. The system methodology and design of the tool developed in this chapter are generic, and therefore the tool can be extended to other countries globally. This will require the adaptation of the tool with additional languages, such as English, Spanish, or Chinese, by additional modules in the pre-processing and clustering modules.

This line of our work deals with the use of Twitter data as a virtual sensor to detect transportation-related events. It is necessary to look also into other sources and methods of sensing in transportation systems, such as inductive loops, floating car data, automatic vehicle locators, virtual loop detectors, cooperative driving, and so on. The real vision and potential of smart transportation systems will be realised when different sensing systems will be integrated within the transportation systems as well as with other urban systems. Our other strands of research have looked into different traffic sensing methods such as GPS (Alsolami et al., 2020), inductive loops (Aqib et al., 2019a), cooperative decision-making for autonomous vehicles (Alam et al., 2019), and urban travel data from travel cards and other sources (Aqib et al., 2019b). Our future work will look into integrating these sensing methods along with other urban sensing systems, such as healthcare (Alotaibi et al., 2020).

References

Agarwal, A., & Toshniwal, D. (2019). Face off: Travel habits, road conditions and traffic city characteristics bared using twitter. *IEEE Access, 7,* 66536–66552.

Agarwal, S., Mittal, N., & Sureka, A. (2018). Potholes and bad road conditions: mining Twitter to extract information on killer roads. In *Proceedings of the ACM India Joint International Conference on Data Science and Management of Data,* 67–77.

Al-Dhubhani, R.S., Cazalas, J., Mehmood, R., Katib, I., & Saeed, F. (2019). A framework for preserving location privacy for continuous queries. In *International Conference of Reliable Information and Communication Technology,* Springer.

Al-Dhubhani, R., Mehmood, R., Katib, I., & Algarni, A. (2017). Location privacy in smart cities era. In *International Conference on Smart Cities, Infrastructure, Technologies and Applications,* Springer.

Alabbas, W., al-Khateeb, H.M., Mansour, A., Epiphaniou, G., & Frommholz, I. (2017). Classification of colloquial Arabic tweets in real-time to detect high-risk floods. In *2017 International Conference On Social Media, Wearable And Web Analytics,* IEEE.

Alam, F., Almaghthawi, A., Katib, I., Albeshri, A., & Mehmood, R. (2021). IResponse: An AI and IoT-enabled framework for autonomous COVID-19 pandemic management. *Sustainability, 13*(7), 3797.

Alam, F., Mehmood, R., Katib, I., Albogami, N.N., & Albeshri, A. (2017). Data fusion and IoT for smart ubiquitous environments: A survey. *IEEE Access, 5,* 9533–9554.

Alam, F., Mehmood, R., Katib, I., Altowaijri, S.M., & Albeshri, A. (2019). TAAWUN: A decision fusion and feature specific road detection approach for connected autonomous vehicles. *Mobile Networks and Applications,* 1–17.

Alamoudi, E., Mehmood, R., Albeshri, A., & Gojobori, T. (2020). A survey of methods and tools for large-scale DNA mixture profiling. In *Smart Infrastructure and Applications.* Springer.

Alkhamisi, A.O., & Mehmood, R. (2020). An ensemble machine and deep learning model for risk prediction in aviation systems. In *2020 6th Conference on Data Science and Machine Learning Applications,* IEEE.

Alkhatib, M., El Barachi, M., & Shaalan, K. (2019). An Arabic social media-based framework for incidents and events monitoring in smart cities. *Journal of Cleaner Production, 220,* 771–785.

Alkouz, B., & Al Aghbari, Z. (2020). SNSJam: Road traffic analysis and prediction by fusing data from multiple social networks. *Information Processing & Management, 57*(1), 102139.

Alomari, E., & Mehmood, R. (2017). Analysis of tweets in arabic language for detection of road traffic conditions. In *International Conference on Smart Cities, Infrastructure, Technologies and Applications,* 98–110, Springer, Cham.

Alomari, E., Katib, I., & Mehmood, R. (2020a). Iktishaf: A big data road-traffic event detection tool using Twitter and spark machine learning. *Mobile Networks and Applications,* 1–16.

Alomari, E., Katib, I., Albeshri, A., & Mehmood, R. (2021). COVID-19: Detecting government pandemic measures and public concerns from Twitter Arabic data using distributed machine learning. *International Journal of Environmental Research and Public Health, 18*(1), 282.

Alomari, E., Mehmood, R., & Katib, I. (2019). Road traffic event detection using twitter data, machine learning, and apache spark. In *2019 IEEE Smart World, Ubiquitous Intelligence & Computing, Advanced & Trusted Computing, Scalable Computing & Communications, Cloud & Big Data Computing, Internet of People and Smart City Innovation*. Italy.

Alomari, E., Mehmood, R., & Katib, I. (2020b) *Smart Infrastructure and Applications: Foundations for Smarter Cities and Societies.* EAI/Springer Innovations in Communication and Computing, Springer International Publishing, Springer Nature Switzerland.

Alomari, E., Mehmood, R., & Katib, I. (2020c). Sentiment analysis of Arabic tweets for road traffic congestion and event detection. In *Smart Infrastructure and Applications*, 37–54, Springer, Cham.

Alotaibi, S., & Mehmood, R. (2017). Big data-enabled healthcare supply chain management: opportunities and challenges. In *International Conference on Smart Cities, Infrastructure, Technologies and Applications*, Springer.

Alotaibi, S., Mehmood, R., Katib, I., Rana, O., & Albeshri, A. (2020). Sehaa: A big data analytics tool for healthcare symptoms and diseases detection using twitter, apache spark, and machine learning. *Applied Sciences*, 10(4), 1398.

Al-Qawasmeh, O., Al-Smadi, M., & Fraihat, N. (2016). Arabic named entity disambiguation using linked open data. In 2016 7th International Conference on Information and Communication Systems (ICICS), pp. 333–338, IEEE.

Alsaedi, N., & Burnap, P. (2015). Arabic event detection in social media. In *International Conference on Intelligent Text Processing and Computational Linguistics*, Springer,

Alshareef, A., Albeshri, A., Katib, I., & Mehmood, R. (2020). Road traffic vehicle detection and tracking using deep learning with custom-collected and public datasets. *International Journal of Computer Science and Network Security*, 20(11), 9–21.

Alsolami, B., Mehmood, R., & Albeshri, A. (2020). Hybrid statistical and machine learning methods for road traffic prediction: A review and tutorial. *Smart Infrastructure and Applications*, 115–133.

Alsolami, B., Mehmood, R., & Albeshri, A. (2020). Hybrid statistical and machine learning methods for road traffic prediction: A review and tutorial. *Smart Infrastructure and Applications*, 115, 1.

Alsulami, M., & Mehmood, R. (2018). Sentiment analysis model for arabic tweets to detect Users' opinions about government services in Saudi Arabia: Ministry of education as a case study. In *Al Yamamah Information and Communication Technology Forum*, 1–8.

Alyahya, H., Mehmood, R., & Katib, I. (2020). Parallel iterative solution of large sparse linear equation systems on the Intel MIC architecture. In *Smart Infrastructure and Applications*. Springer.

Aqib, M., Mehmood, R., Alzahrani, A., Katib, I., Albeshri, A., & Altowaijri, S.M. (2019a). Smarter traffic prediction using big data, in-memory computing, deep learning and GPUs. *Sensors*, 19(9), 2206.

Aqib, M., Mehmood, R., Alzahrani, A., Katib, I., Albeshri, A., & Altowaijri, S.M. (2019b). Rapid transit systems: Smarter urban planning using big data, in-memory computing, deep learning, and GPUs. *Sustainability*, 11(10), 2736.

Arfat, Y., Suma, S., Mehmood, R., & Albeshri, A. (2020c). Parallel shortest path big data graph computations of US road network using apache spark: Survey, architecture, and evaluation. In *Smart Infrastructure and Applications*. Springer.

Arfat, Y., Usman, S., Mehmood, R., & Katib, I. (2020a). Big data tools, technologies, and applications: A survey. In *Smart Infrastructure and Applications*. Springer.

Arfat, Y., Usman, S., Mehmood, R., & Katib, I. (2020b). Big data for smart infrastructure design: Opportunities and challenges. *Smart Infrastructure and Applications*, 491–518.

Assem, H., Buda, T.S., & O'sullivan, D. (2017). RCMC: Recognizing crowd-mobility patterns in cities based on location based social networks data. *ACM Transactions on Intelligent Systems and Technology (TIST)*, 8(5), 1–30.

Atefeh, F., & Khreich, W. (2015). A survey of techniques for event detection in twitter. *Computational Intelligence*, 31(1), 132–164.

Ayres, G., & Mehmood, R. (2010). LocPriS: A security and privacy preserving location-based services development framework. In *International Conference on Knowledge-Based and Intelligent Information and Engineering Systems*, Berlin, Heidelberg.

Cárdenas-Benítez, N., Aquino-Santos, R., Magaña-Espinoza, P., Aguilar-Velazco, J., Edwards-Block, A., & Medina Cass, A. (2016). Traffic congestion detection system through connected vehicles and big data. *Sensors*, 16(5), 599–1005.

D'Andrea, E., Ducange, P., Lazzerini, B., & Marcelloni, F. (2015). Real-time detection of traffic from twitter stream analysis. *IEEE Transactions on Intelligent Transportation Systems*, 16(4), 2269–2283.

Diab, M., Ghoneim, M., & Habash, N. (2007). Arabic diacritization in the context of statistical machine translation. In *Proceedings of MT-Summit*, Japan.

Garg, S., Kaur, K., Kumar, N., & Rodrigues, J.J. (2019). Hybrid deep-learning-based anomaly detection scheme for suspicious flow detection in SDN: A social multimedia perspective. *IEEE Transactions on Multimedia*, 21(3), 566–578.

Garg, S., Kaur, K., Kumar, N., Kaddoum, G., Zomaya, A.Y., & Ranjan, R. (2019). A hybrid deep learning-based model for anomaly detection in cloud datacenter networks. *IEEE Transactions on Network and Service Management*, 16(3), 924–935.

Ghahreman, N., & Dastjerdi, A.B. (2011). Semi-automatic labeling of training data sets in text classification. *Computer and Information Science*, 4(6), 48.

Hashem, I.A.T., Chang, V., Anuar, N.B., Adewole, K., Yaqoob, I., Gani, A., Ahmed, E., & Chiroma, H. (2016). The role of big data in smart city. *International Journal of Information Management*, 36(5), 748–758.

Huang, W., Xu, S., Yan, Y., & Zipf, A. (2019). An exploration of the interaction between urban human activities and daily traffic conditions: A case study of Toronto, Canada. *Cities*, 84, 8–22.

INRIX, (2020). *INRIX Global Traffic Scorecard*, INRIX, Accessed on 16 October 2021 from http://inrix.com/scorecard/ (accessed Mar. 19, 2021).

Janbi, N., Katib, I., Albeshri, A., & Mehmood, R. (2020). Distributed artificial intelligence-as-a-service (DAIaaS) for smarter IoE and 6G environments. *Sensors*, 20(20), 5796.

Kankanamge, N., Yigitcanlar, T., & Goonetilleke, A. (2020). How engaging are disaster management related social media channels? The case of Australian state emergency organizations. *International Journal of Disaster Risk Reduction*, 48, 101571.

Kankanamge, N., Yigitcanlar, T., Goonetilleke, A., & Kamruzzaman, M. (2020). Determining disaster severity through social media analysis: Testing the methodology with South East Queensland flood tweets. *International Journal of Disaster Risk Reduction*, 42, 101360.

Kankanamge, N., Yigitcanlar, T., Goonetilleke, A., & Kamruzzaman, M. (2019). Can volunteer crowdsourcing reduce disaster risk? A systematic review of the literature. *International Journal of Disaster Risk Reduction, 35,* 101097.

Khanum, A., Alvi, A., & Mehmood, R. (2017). Towards a semantically enriched computational intelligence (SECI) framework for smart farming. In *International Conference on Smart Cities, Infrastructure, Technologies and Applications,* Springer.

Klaithin, S., & Haruechaiyasak, C. (2016). Traffic information extraction and classification from Thai Twitter. In *2016 13th International Joint Conference on Computer Science and Software Engineering (JCSSE),* IEEE, 1–6.

Kumar, A., Jiang, M., & Fang, Y. (2014). Where not to go? Detecting road hazards using Twitter. In *Proceedings of the 37th international ACM SIGIR conference on Research & development in information retrieval.*

Kumar, N., Chilamkurti, N., & Park, J.H. (2013). ALCA: Agent learning–based clustering algorithm in vehicular ad hoc networks. *Personal and Ubiquitous Computing, 17*(8), 1683–1692.

Kurniawan, D.A., Wibirama, S., & Setiawan, N.A. (2016, October). Real-time traffic classification with Twitter data mining. In *2016 8th International Conference on Information Technology and Electrical Engineering (ICITEE).*

Lau, R.Y. (2017). Toward a social sensor based framework for intelligent transportation. In *2017 IEEE 18th International Symposium on A World of Wireless, Mobile and Multimedia Networks,* IEEE.

Lin, C., He, D., Kumar, N., Choo, K.K.R., Vinel, A., & Huang, X. (2018). Security and privacy for the internet of drones: Challenges and solutions. *IEEE Communications Magazine, 56*(1), 64–69.

Liu, B. (2012). Sentiment analysis and opinion mining. *Synthesis Lectures on Human Language Technologies, 5*(1), 1–167.

Loper, E., & Bird, S. (2002). Nltk: The natural language toolkit. Accessed on 16 October 2021 from https://www.nltk.org/

Mehmood, R., & Graham, G. (2015). Big data logistics: A health-care transport capacity sharing model. *Procedia Computer Science, 64,* 1107–1114.

Mehmood, R., Alam, F., Albogami, N.N., Katib, I., Albeshri, A., & Altowaijri, S.M. (2017). UTiLearn: A personalised ubiquitous teaching and learning system for smart societies. *IEEE Access, 5,* 2615–2635.

Mehmood, R., Bhaduri, B., Katib, I., & Chlamtac, I. (2017). Smart Societies, Infrastructure, Technologies and Applications, In *First International Conference, SCITA 2017,* Jeddah, Saudi Arabia.

Miglani, A., & Kumar, N. (2019). Deep learning models for traffic flow prediction in autonomous vehicles: A review, solutions, and challenges. *Vehicular Communications, 20,* 100184.

Mohammad, A.S., & Qawasmeh, O. (2016). Knowledge-based approach for event extraction from Arabic tweets. *International Journal of Advanced Computer Science & Applications, 1*(7), 483–490.

Muhammed, T., Mehmood, R., Albeshri, A., & Alzahrani, A. (2020). HCDSR: A hierarchical clustered fault tolerant routing technique for IoT-based smart societies. In *Smart Infrastructure and Applications.* Springer.

Muhammed, T., Mehmood, R., Albeshri, A., & Katib, I. (2018). UbeHealth: A personalized ubiquitous cloud and edge-enabled networked healthcare system for smart cities. *IEEE Access, 6,* 32258–32285.

Muhammed, T., Mehmood, R., Albeshri, A., & Katib, I. (2019). SURAA: A novel method and tool for loadbalanced and coalesced SpMV computations on GPUs. *Applied Sciences, 9*(5), 947.

NDTV (2019). *5 Injured As Fire Breaks Out At High-Speed Train Station In Saudi Arabia*, Accessed on 16 October 2021 from https://www.ndtv.com/world-news/fire-breaks-out-at-haramain-high-speed-train-station-in-saudi-arabia-2109171

Pandey, N., & Natarajan, S. (2016). How social media can contribute during disaster events? Case study of Chennai floods 2015. In *2016 International Conference on Advances in Computing, Communications and Informatics*, IEEE.

Pandhare, K.R., & Shah, M.A. (2017). Real time road traffic event detection using Twitter and spark. In *2017 International conference on inventive communication and computational technologies*, IEEE.

Sakaki, T., Matsuo, Y., Yanagihara, T., Chandrasiri, N.P., & Nawa, K. (2012). Real-time event extraction for driving information from social sensors. In *2012 IEEE International Conference on Cyber Technology in Automation, Control, and Intelligent Systems*, IEEE.

Sakaki, T., Okazaki, M., & Matsuo, Y. (2010). Earthquake shakes twitter users: real-time event detection by social sensors. In *Proceedings of the 19th international conference on World wide web*, North Carolina, USA

Salas, A., Georgakis, P., Nwagboso, C., Ammari, A., & Petalas, I. (2017). Traffic event detection framework using social media. In *2017 IEEE International Conference on Smart Grid and Smart Cities*, IEEE.

Schlingensiepen, J., Mehmood, R., Nemtanu, F.C., & Niculescu, M. (2014). Increasing sustainability of road transport in European cities and metropolitan areas by facilitating autonomic road transport systems (ARTS). In *Sustainable Automotive Technologies 2013*. Springer.

Semwal, D., Patil, S., Galhotra, S., Arora, A., & Unny, N. (2015). STAR: real-time spatio-temporal analysis and prediction of traffic insights using social media. In *Proceedings of the 2nd IKDD Conference on Data Sciences*, Bangalore.

Shafiabady, N., Lee, L.H., Rajkumar, R., Kallimani, V.P., Akram, N.A., & Isa, D. (2016). Using unsupervised clustering approach to train the support vector machine for text classification. *Neurocomputing, 211*, 4–10.

Suma, S., Mehmood, R., & Albeshri, A. (2017). Automatic event detection in smart cities using big data analytics. In *International Conference on Smart Cities, Infrastructure, Technologies and Applications*, Springer.

Suma, S., Mehmood, R., & Albeshri, A. (2020). Automatic detection and validation of smart city events using HPC and apache spark platforms. *Smart Infrastructure and Applications*, 55–78.

Suma, S., Mehmood, R., Albugami, N., Katib, I., & Albeshri, A. (2017). Enabling next generation logistics and planning for smarter societies. *Procedia Computer Science, 109*, 1122–1127.

Tejaswin, P., Kumar, R., & Gupta, S. (2015). Tweeting Traffic: Analyzing Twitter for generating real-time city traffic insights and predictions. In *Proceedings of the 2nd IKDD Conference on Data Sciences*, Bangalore.

Triguero, I., García, S., & Herrera, F. (2015). Self-labeled techniques for semi-supervised learning: Taxonomy, software and empirical study. *Knowledge and Information Systems, 42*(2), 245–284.

Twitter, (2019). *Tweet objects*, Accessed on 16 October 2021 from https://developer.twitter.com/en/docs/tweets/data-dictionary/overview/intro-to-tweet-json.

Usman, S., Mehmood, R., & Katib, I. (2020). Big data and HPC convergence for smart infrastructures: A review and proposed architecture. *Smart Infrastructure and Applications*, 561–586.

Usman, S., Mehmood, R., Katib, I., & Albeshri, A. (2019a). ZAKI+: A machine learning based process mapping tool for SpMV computations on distributed memory architectures. *IEEE Access*, 7, 81279–81296.

Usman, S., Mehmood, R., Katib, I., Albeshri, A., & Altowaijri, S.M. (2019b). ZAKI: A smart method and tool for automatic performance optimization of parallel SpMV computations on distributed memory machines. *Mobile Networks and Applications*, https://doi.org/10.1007/s11036-019-01318-3.

Was, S. (2018). *Civil Defense in Riyadh Conducts Cooling Operations for Burnt Transformers in Al-Nafal Neighborhood*. Accessed on 16 October 2021 from https://saudiga-zette.com.sa/article/599725

Xu, Z., Li, J., Liu, B., Bi, J., Li, R., & Mao, R. (2017). Semi-supervised learning in large scale text categorization. *Journal of Shanghai Jiaotong University (Science)*, 22(3), 291–302.

Yigitcanlar, T., Corchado, J.M., Mehmood, R., Li, R.Y.M., Mossberger, K., & Desouza, K. (2021). Responsible urban innovation with local government artificial intelligence (AI): A conceptual framework and research agenda. *Journal of Open Innovation: Technology, Market, and Complexity*, 7(1), 71.

Yigitcanlar, T., Kankanamge, N., & Vella, K. (2021). How are smart city concepts and technologies perceived and utilized? A systematic geo-twitter analysis of smart cities in Australia. *Journal of Urban Technology*, 28(1–2), 135–154.

Yigitcanlar, T., Kankanamge, N., Preston, A., Gill, P.S., Rezayee, M., Ostadnia, M., Xia, B., & Ioppolo, G. (2020). How can social media analytics assist authorities in pandemic-related policy decisions? Insights from Australian states and territories. *Health Information Science and Systems*, 8(1), 1–21.

Yigitcanlar, T., Kankanamge, N., Regona, M., Ruiz Maldonado, A., Rowan, B., Ryu, A., Desouza, K.C., Corchado, J.M., Mehmood, R., & Li, R.Y.M. (2020). Artificial intelligence technologies and related urban planning and development concepts: How are they perceived and utilized in Australia? *Journal of Open Innovation: Technology, Market, and Complexity*, 6(4), 187.

Zheng, X., Chen, W., Wang, P., Shen, D., Chen, S., Wang, X., Zhang, Q., & Yang, L. (2015). Big data for social transportation. *IEEE Transactions on Intelligent Transportation Systems*, 17(3), 620–630.

Xu, Z., Li, J., Liu, B., Bi, J., Li, R., & Mao, R. (2017). Semi-supervised learning in large scale text categorization. *Journal of Shanghai Jiaotong University (Science)*, 22(3), 291–302.

9

Cyberphysical Data Analytics Platforms

9.1 Introduction

A smart city is an environment that uses innovative technologies to make networks and services more flexible, effective, and sustainable with the use of information, digital and telecommunication technologies, improving the city operations for the benefit of its citizens. However, where does the concept of smart cities and smart territories stand currently? The United Nations Educational, Scientific and Cultural Organization (UNESCO) gives us a fairly accurate view on this situation: "All the cities and territories who claim the smart city status are merely patchworks of opportunistic modernization, which is not always coherent and is sometimes juxtaposed without any real unity of function or meaning" (UNESCO, 2019). This proposal has been fully developed on the basis of this statement and the PIs have accordingly guided the choice of the concepts to be developed in this project.

It is estimated that in 2030, the population density will increase by 30% in most cities, 60% of the world population will live in cities, and there will be 43 megacities; these metropolitan zones will have more than 10 million residents (UN, 2018). Most experts agree on the fact that such population densities promote sustainable economic growth, which explains the increased mobility of the population from rural to urban areas. The downside of these advantages is the rise of uncontrollable sociological phenomena, such as urban violence and unhealthy crowding. Most cities face these issues, regardless of their political or economic regime. To counteract negative consequences, the emerging SCs have to adapt measures that will guarantee their economic attractiveness, and most importantly, they must meet the population's high expectations regarding the quality of life.

Contrary to the initial smart city concept, which favoured the modernisation of leading cities in developed countries, the new trend consists in deploying smart micro territories (or villages) within megacities and in their neighbouring regions, serving as smart satellites. The ideas presented in this proposal follow this smart city deployment policy. The majority of smart city projects aim to achieve sustainability and control economic growth by avoiding the loss of the already invested resources, by maintaining an ecology-friendly

DOI: 10.1201/9781003278986-12

environment and by striving towards social equity. However, in reality, this turns out to be very utopian, and several worldwide experiences show that this theoretical balance has never been successful at the practical level. As a result, smart city development tends to be geared towards only one of all the objectives, failing to adapt a comprehensive approach.

We conceive the smart city concept as a smart, realistic and technically balanced combination of the objectives and values described above. A smart city should be thought out and deployed following the principles of modular design, where each module is implemented, tested and deployed independently so that it can be easily modified, replaced or exchanged. Thus, modules are defined as dynamic and evolutionary. Each module is dedicated to a particular task within the smart city, such as Transportation Control, Logistics Planning, Traffic Control, Crowd Management, E-Health, etc. All modules interact and exchange the information collected within the smart city through a centralised Management Platform. Deepint.net is the platform presented in this chapter that is able to work independently and/or in collaboration with other (existing) smart city platforms/IoT systems. Furthermore, the platform is equipped with the vast majority of the required connectors, facilitating its integration.

Such is the added value of the data that not only cities/territories but also users and companies in all sectors have been interested in AI-based data analysis and visualisation methodologies. This is because they are fully aware of the benefits of those processes. As a result, the Artificial Intelligence sector has enjoyed high demand in recent years.

In this research, a platform has been developed that is capable of applying the most well-known techniques within the data analysis sector in a way that is simple and user-friendly. The platform's design makes it fully prepared for the management of SCs and territories, regardless of the size of the territories and the origin of the data. Deepint.net not only processes data, but also automates its intake, visualisation and integration with any other platform and dashboard.

This platform is easy to use and does not require specialists in artificial intelligence, edge computing or machine learning. Deepint.net has been designed to provide managers with tools for data analysis and to help them generate models efficiently with no need for specialised data analysts or developers.

The platform aids the data analysis process at different levels: (a) It gives computer support so that cities do not have to invest in infrastructure; (b) It offers mechanisms for the ingestion of data from different sources (relational and non-relational databases, files, repositories based on CKAN, streaming data, multi-functional IoT sensors, social networks, etc.) and in different formats; (c) It offers data processing mechanisms to all users who do not have knowledge of programming (information fusion, data filtering, etc.); (d) It offers information representation techniques based on interactive graphics to help understand data, the results of analysis and rapid decision-making; and (e) It helps select the methodologies that can be applied to the

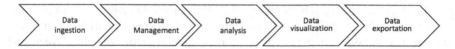

FIGURE 9.1
Data management flow in Deepint.net.

data provided by the user and automatically searches for the configuration that provides the best results (through cross-validation) so that the user does not have to configure anything at all. The data management flow can be found in Figure 9.1.

The platform, therefore, includes signal processing methods capable of transforming and using data (even real-time data) from any given source: IoT sensors, advanced multi-functional sensors, smart edge nodes, next-generation networks, etc. or even the data from relational and non-relational databases. The platform helps the users select and use the most adequate combination of mathematical models; dynamic data assimilation and neuro-symbolic artificial intelligence systems are capable of working with knowledge and data; they adapt to new time constraints and can explain why a certain decision has been taken. Research into the creation of explainable adaptive mixtures of expert systems is the key innovation of this project together with its application in the smart logistics field.

The platform has been used to develop several smart territory projects in the cities of Santa Marta and Carbajosa (Spain), in Caldas (Colombia), in Panama City, in Istanbul (Turkey), etc. The state of the art is reviewed in Section 2. Section 3 presents Deepint.net as a platform for managing smart territory projects. The results obtained from the use of the platform in Paris (France) are outlined in Section 4. Finally, the conclusions and future lines of research are described in Section 5.

9.2 Smart Territory Platforms and the Edge Computing Approach

It is expected that the world population will reach 9.7 billion in 2050. By then, two-thirds of the population will live in urban environments (UNESCO, 2019). The United Nations estimates that by 2030 there will be 43 megacities (defined as metropolitan areas with a population greater than 10 million), most of them in developing countries. Critical social and ecological challenges that cities will face may include urban violence, inequality, discrimination, unemployment, poverty, unsustainable energy and water use, epidemics, pollution, environmental degradation, and increased risk of natural disasters.

The concept of SCs, which emerged in the early 2000s, attempts to provide solutions to these challenges by implementing information and communication technologies, improving the socio-ecological network of urban areas and the quality of life of its citizens. The initial concept of smart cities focused on the modernisation of megacities. However, most of the so-called smart cities are just cities with several smart projects (UNESCO, 2019). The main reason for this is that existing cities are difficult to modernise, mostly because buildings are too old to renovate, or they are heritage-listed buildings (due to their historical value), so they cannot be rebuilt or demolished. To overcome these limitations, different approaches have been proposed. The most promising trend is the creation of smart micro-territories, defined as hi-tech small towns, districts or satellite towns near megacities (UNESCO, 2019). Real-life examples include Songdo City; a satellite village near Seoul, or the Cyberabad District in Hyderabad (India). This chapter presents Deepint.net as a platform for the efficient and dynamic management of smart territories.

Given the availability of large amounts of data, the challenge is to identify intelligent and adaptive ways of combining the information to create valuable knowledge (Silva et al., 2018). However, the implementation of SCs still poses several challenges, such as design and operational costs, sustainability, or information security. Thus, over the last few years, platforms have been designed and developed to provide innovative solutions to these problems. These platforms combine the data collected by electronic devices (sensors and actuators) with the data that has been generated by citizens and is stored on different types of databases.

In general, smart city management platforms focus on one or several of the following dimensions: Crowd Management, Traffic Control and Smart Logistics, or resource prioritisation in emergency scenarios, etc. These modules interact and exchange information among them. Figure 9.2 illustrates an architecture that is typical of these platforms, which normally work independently and/or in collaboration with other existing platforms and IoT systems.

Smart mobility is probably considered one of the main dimensions of smart cities. With the rapid population growth and its high concentration in urban environments, urban traffic congestion (which significantly lengthens waiting times) has a significant impact on the citizens' daily life. To monitor and manage the state of road traffic, sensors are employed on road intersections and public transport vehicles, measuring location, speed, and density. Aimed at supporting local authorities in traffic control, recent studies propose different systems and platforms which improve the safety and security of the commuter (Latif et al., 2018; Rehena & Janssen, 2018; Ning et al., 2019; Pan et al., 2019; Yao et al., 2019; Kapser & Abdelrahman, 2020). Another important aspect of Smart Mobility is last-mile delivery. With the exponential growth of e-commerce, the logistics sector is experiencing efficiency difficulties. Technologies such as the Internet of Things or Autonomous Delivery Vehicles are expected to have a positive impact on this industry (Luo et al., 2020).

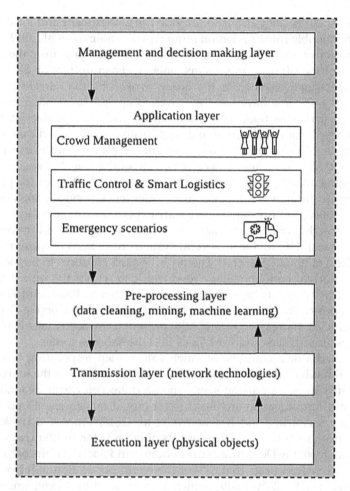

FIGURE 9.2
Smart city management architecture.

In a smart transportation system, crowd management is a key variable, not only during commutes and regular travel, but also when an event takes place. Major events with large crowd gatherings (sports events, concerts, protests, etc.) are celebrated in urban areas every year. Overcrowding and the poor management of crowds can lead to threatening and unsafe situations, such as injuries, stampedes and crushing. Therefore, effective crowd management is a crucial task. Crowd management systems have been developed to support services and infrastructures devoted to managing and controlling crowds at any time, so that in case of emergency situations, crowds are well managed, while the dangers and risks are minimised. Current studies focus on crowd counting and monitoring models (Luo et al., 2020) and algorithms (Kumar et al., 2018), and crowd flow prediction architectures

(Zhao et al., 2019), their aim is to provide the government and local authorities with valuable information on large crowds (Solmaz et al., 2019).

The objective of many smart city projects is to prioritise the efficient use of resources: Irrigation systems, energy consumption, or dealing with emergency scenarios, such as the one provoked by the current pandemic. Thousands of people have lost their lives in epidemics, pandemics, natural disasters (hurricanes, floods, fires) and human-induced disasters (stampedes, terrorist attacks or communicable diseases), and it is believed that a reasonable number of these fatalities are associated with the poor management of crowds and slow response to accidents. One of the key challenges involved in managing an emergency is minimising the time it takes for the personnel and supplies to arrive at the scenario. Emergency services, such as health services, police, and fire departments, are expected to make critical decisions and to correctly prioritise the use of resources, using limited time and information. To facilitate this task, several systems have been proposed in recent years. Rego et al. (2018) introduced an IoT-based platform that modifies the routes of normal and emergency road traffic to reduce the time it takes for resources to arrive at the scenario of an emergency. Rajak and Kushwaha (2019) propose a framework capable of creating a "Green Corridor" for emergency vehicles. Ranga and Sumi (2018) present a traffic management system that helps ambulances and fire trucks find the shortest routes.

Social media data could be of much value when responding to an emergency. Alkhatib et al. (2019) propose a novel framework for the management of incidents in SCs by using social media data; Perez and Zeadally (2019) present a communication architecture for crowd management in disruptive emergency scenarios, and Kousiouris et al. (2018) propose a tracking and monitoring system that identifies events of interest for Twitter users.

Statistics from the Department of Economic and Social Affairs of the United Nations, DESAP, indicate that 68% of the world population will live in cities or urban areas by 2050 (2019), which means rapid and even uncontrolled growth with consequent challenges for governments, for example: Pollution, limited mobility due to traffic and congestion; high cost of housing, food and basic services; as well as security problems (Liu et al., 2019).

To address this growth, the smart city concept emerged as the integration of the urban environment with information and communication technologies (ICTs), attracting the interest of all major sectors (governments, universities, research centres, etc.) in presenting solutions or developments that would make up a smart city (Ullah et al., 2020). The objective of this paradigm is the effective management of the challenges associated with the growth of urban areas through the adoption of ICTs in developments, solutions, applications, services, or even in the design of state policies (Chamoso et al., 2020).

Currently, the term smart city is widely used, for example, in the systematic reviews of the literature, there are more than 36 definitions that address different dimensions of the urban environment such as: Mobility, technology, public services, economy, environment, quality of life or governance (Laufs et al., 2020). One of the most widely used definitions is the one proposed by Elmaghraby and Losavio (2014): "an intelligent city is one that incorporates information and communication technologies to increase operational efficiency, shares information independently within the system and improves the overall effectiveness of services and the well-being of citizens". However, the growth of the Internet of Things and the devices permanently connected to the Internet has led to a growing interest in data management (Chamoso et al., 2015) and security (Kitchin & Dodge, 2019) new urban management challenges emerge.

Ensuring the security of information, devices, infrastructure and users in an environment where large volumes of data are managed in real-time is the objective of state-of-the-art research, because it is a critical element of any solution aimed at smart cities/territories (O'Dwyer et al., 2019). This challenge has generated a research trend: Edge Computing and its integration with IoT, which is reflected in statistics and the interest of large corporations in research, development and implementation opportunities in smart territory scenarios, so that they can increase their profits and market shares (Jia et al., 2017; Schneider et al., 2017; Taleb et al., 2017; Premsankar et al., 2018; Hussain et al., 2019; Khan et al., 2020; Gheisari et al., 2020). Table 9.1 lists the researches that have employed Edge Computing in different smart city scenarios. These proposals evidence the interest in this technology.

In this context, most cities are not prepared and do not have the policies required to understand and ensure the confidentiality of a huge amount

TABLE 9.1

Edge Computing Applied in Smart City/Territory Environments

Field	Solution	Author
Mobility	• The study considered an SC/Territory scenario where vehicles ran applications that take data from the environment and send them to edge computing servers through roadside units. • The authors conduct a case study on the fog and edge computing requirements of the intelligent traffic light management system.	Premsankar et al. (2018) Hussain et al. (2019)
Tourism	Mobile edge computing potential in making cities/territories smarter.	Taleb et al. (2017)
Industry and Augmented Reality	Proposes the use of Edge Computing to enable intelligent management of industrial tasks.	Schneider et al. (2017)
Smart District (manhole cover)	Edge computing servers interact with corresponding management personnel through mobile devices based on the collected information. A demo application of the proposed IMCS in the Xiasha District of Hangzhou, China, showed its high efficiency	Jia et al., (2017)

of data, as well as their correct processing and storage. Another important factor is the application of artificial intelligence techniques for the extraction of information which facilitates the management of key infrastructures, systems and devices in a district, making them functional and efficient. However, rapid response time is fundamental for the functioning of a Smart Territory. In addition, the large volume of data that is sent from a Smart Territory directly to the cloud has high associated and variable costs, forcing cities to seek solutions that reduce the cost of using cloud services, energy and bandwidth.

In a Smart Territory scenario, the proposed architecture should be capable of managing the heterogeneity of the IoT devices in order to ensure the management system's safety and efficiency. Although there are many proposals in the state of the art, Figure 9.3 represents a general model of most architectures, where Blockchain technology may be implemented to preserve the safety and reliability of the sensitive data generated by IoT devices at the edge of the network. Edge nodes are also included in architectures of this type, using artificial intelligence and deep learning algorithms for filtering, real-time data processing and low latency (Sittón-Candanedo et al., 2019a).

Figure 9.3 shows a basic schema of an edge-computing architecture with edge nodes that allow user application processes to be executed closer to the data sources (Sittón-Candanedo et al., 2019b). The edge nodes perform computing tasks such as filtering, processing, caching, load balancing, requesting services and information, and reducing the amount of data that are sent or received from the cloud.

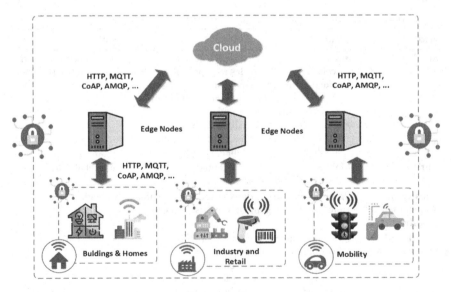

FIGURE 9.3
Edge computing for smart cities. (Derived from Sittón-Candanedo et al., 2019a.)

9.2.1 Smart City Vertical Markets and Tools

The development of a Smart City involves a series of phases, from planning to the selection of the most suitable tools. Both the citizens and the private sector have to be involved in the development of a Smart City, resulting in a connected, innovative, digital and successful city.

The projects that constitute a Smart City can be classified as follows: Smart Governance, Smart Economy, Smart Mobility, Smart Environment, Smart People and Smart Living. On the basis of these indicators, a number of rankings classify the most advanced Smart Cities, which are the fruit of governance oriented towards innovation and digital inclusion. The highest scores have been obtained by London, Singapore, Seoul, New York and Helsinki. It should be noted that these cities also stand out for having one of the best open data portals, another Smart City pillar that favours innovation. In particular, the high quality of data available in several US cities has led to a number of Data Science competitions on the Kaggle platform to predict future demand for city bikes.

In addition, Europe's profits from the use of AI-based software are expected to reach a value of more than $1.5 billion by 2025, five times the amount obtained in 2020. Several companies have presented proposals related to smart city platforms and architectures, highlighting the Huawei Horizon@ City, Toyota and NTT smart city platform and IBM City Operations Platform reference architecture proposals. The Deepint.net tool has been created as the starting point for the solution to these problems, facilitating the rapid and efficient development of the infrastructure that any Smart City requires. Smart City vertical markets and their domains can be found in Table 9.2.

9.3 Deepint.net: A Platform for Smart Territories

Today, cities/territories are the largest data producers, and all major sectors can extract knowledge and benefit considerably from data analyses. Thanks to advances in computing such as distributed processing techniques, improved processing capabilities and cheaper technology, current artificial intelligence techniques can be applied to large volumes of data at a very fast pace; this would have been unthinkable less than a decade ago.

As a result, large investments are being made in the information and computing sector, either through the acquisition of technology that allows for the recovery and processing of information, or by investing in hiring highly qualified scientists to carry out precise studies. Such staff is not always easy to find due to the scientific complexity involved and the peculiarities of the problem domain.

Deepint.net is a platform that seeks to cover the current "gap" between the need to create smart territories and the big expenses that this normally

TABLE 9.2

The Vertical Markets and Domains of Smart Cities

Vertical Markets	Domain
Smart Governance	• Participation • Social Services • Transparency
Smart Economy	• Innovation • Productivity • Entrepreneurship • Flexible labour market
Smart Mobility	• Connected public transport • Multimodality • Logistics • Accessibility
Smart Environment	• Environmental protection • Resources management • Energy efficiency
Smart People	• Digital education • Creativity • Inclusive society
Smart Living	• Tourism • Security • Healthcare • Culture

entails in terms of tools and data scientists. This platform has been created for the managers of intelligent cities/territories, facilitating all aspects of data management, processing and visualisation.

Deepint.net is a platform deployed in a self-adapting cloud environment, which enables users to apply artificial intelligence methodologies to their data using the most widespread techniques (random forest, neural networks, etc.), even if they lack knowledge of their operation/configuration, or even programming skills. Deepint.net facilitates the construction of models for data processing, guiding the user through the process. It indicates how to ingest data, work with the data, visualise the information, apply a model and, finally, obtain, evaluate, interpret and use the results. The platform incorporates a wizard that automates the process, it is even able to select the configuration for the artificial intelligence methodology that will provide the best solution to the problem the user is trying to solve.

Furthermore, additional features enable users to exploit all the results through dynamic, reusable dashboards that can be shared and used by other smart city tools. Moreover, the results can be exported in different formats for simple integration, for example, in a report. Figure 9.4 shows elements and tools that can be used along the process of data management, from data intake, to the creation of scorecards or data exploitation.

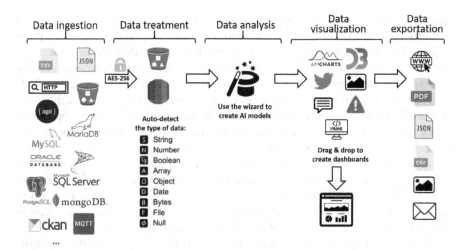

FIGURE 9.4
Data analysis flow and elements.

Deepint.net is a platform created for managing and interpreting data in an efficient and simple way. It has been structured in five different functional layers as shown in Figure 9.4. Figure 9.5 presents the elements of the data ingestion layer of Deepint.net.

On Deepint.net, both static and dynamic data may be incorporated into the tool. Dynamic data are constantly updated. The data are stored as 'data sources' as presented in Figure 9.5. The data sources on Deepint.net are elementary because they are the starting point of the rest of the functions that can be applied. To create a data source from data that are available elsewhere, the wizard asks the user to specify the type of media in which the original

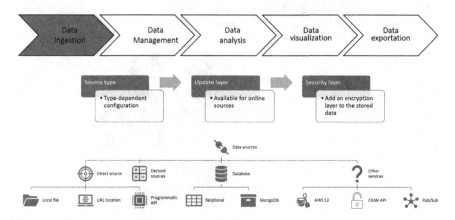

FIGURE 9.5
Data ingestion layer description.

data is found, and the configuration associated with that type of media. For example, if it is a database, the user must indicate the host, username, password, database name and the SQL query to be executed. After indicating the configuration of the data source, the wizard requests information on the data update frequency in the case of dynamic data. Finally, it is possible to encrypt the data in a data source on Deepint.net. This option slightly slows down all operations, as the user is asked to perform a decryption operation every time they want to make use of the data. Nevertheless, it provides an extra layer of security that other tools on the market do not offer.

Regarding the type of support in which the original data are found, the following are allowed: (i) direct sources: CSV or JSON files containing the data to be imported from local files, URLs or calls to existing endpoints; (ii) derived sources: New data sources obtained from existing data sources (very useful for the next step of the flow, data management); (iii) databases: Both relational and NoSQL databases; (iv) Other services: For data coming from well-known services such as AWS S3, CKAN or data streaming (such as MQTT).

Deepint.net offers multiple functionalities to users for the management of the information contained in data sources (Figure 9.6). To begin with, the system automatically detects the type of data and the format (for decimal data or dates), thus, the user does not have to spend time specifying it. However, in the case of certain graphs or models, it may be important to specify the type of data and Deepint.net allows users to specify it manually or change the type that has been detected automatically. It also allows the user to generate features from existing fields using user-defined expressions. At this point in the flow, the creation of derived data sources from existing data sources is possible, as discussed in the previous section. More

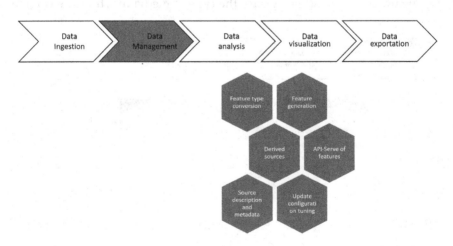

FIGURE 9.6
Data management layer.

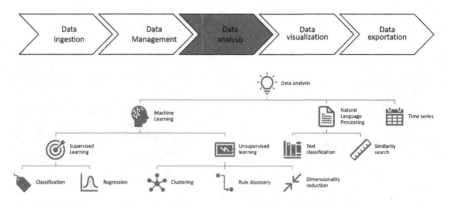

FIGURE 9.7
Data analysis layer.

specifically, different types of operations may be performed on the different data sources, such as filters on records or parameters in a data source, merging two data sources with the same parameters, and much more. The tool also offers the possibility of working with data sources from an API to edit them programmatically.

The platform provides tools for knowledge extraction within the context of various learning methodologies, as shown in Figure 9.7. We can find in it multiple supervised learning methodologies, both for classification and regression problems, using algorithms such as Decision Tree, Random Forest, Gradient Boosting, Extreme Gradient Boosting, Naive Bayes, Support Vector Machines, and linear and logistic regressions. In all of the cases, the configuration of the algorithms can be adjusted to achieve better performance. Additionally, there are unsupervised learning techniques available, including clustering methods (k-means, DBSCAN, and others), as well as association rule learning or dimensionality reduction techniques, for example, principal component analysis (PCA).

Another field of application of the platform is Natural Language Processing, which involves processes such as text classification, text clustering, and similarity-based retrieval.

The tool offers a wizard that facilitates the process of creating dynamic and interactive graphs. It only takes a few simple steps, as presented in Figure 9.8. In the first step, the user is asked to specify the data source they want to use to create the visualisation. They can create as many visualisations of a data source as they wish. In the same step, the source can be filtered to represent a subset that meets the conditions specified by the user (conditions can be nested with AND and OR operations). Similarly, the user can select a subset of the sample, which is ordered randomly or by the user in situations where large volumes of data are represented with pivot charts which may slow down the user's computer (since these are

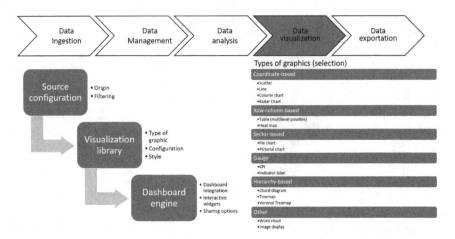

FIGURE 9.8
Data visualisation layer.

pivot charts developed in JavaScript, the processing power is provided by the client). The next step that the user has to do is to select the type of chart they want and configure it. The configuration depends specifically on each of the types of graphs and there are more than 30 different graphs. Likewise, the information to be represented can be configured, the style (title, legend, series, colours, etc.) can be easily set using the wizard.

Once the visualisations are created, they can be added to interactive dashboards and placed in the positions that the user wants by means of drag and drop. Different forms can be added with which the user can interact to filter the information that is represented (a second level of filtering in addition to the filtering performed when creating the visualisation). This offers multiple benefits when it comes to controlling cities and monitoring only the information that is relevant at any given time. The user can also add other elements to the dashboards, such as the results of the machine learning models, iframes, images or content through WYSIWYG editors, among many other possibilities.

A very important aspect of data analysis is being able to export the obtained results, as well as the data used as input. This feature facilitates, for example, the use of other types of tools and enables the scientific community to reproduce the system. Deepint.net allows exporting all data sources to CSV or JSON files, as well as the results of the developed artificial intelligence models or visualisations (such as static PNG images) to, for example, be able to incorporate them in documents or reports (Figure 9.9).

However, one of the most powerful features of the tool is the possibility of sharing the dashboards that have been created, both with the users of the tool, and with those that receive a unique link from the user. Through this link, all the functionality incorporated in the dashboards can be accessed in

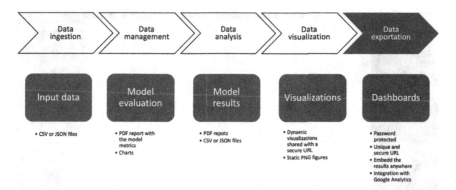

FIGURE 9.9
Data exportation layer.

real-time and it is even possible to integrate the dashboards in third-party tools through the use of iframes or WebViews, for example.

Figure 9.10 shows some screenshots of data ingestion. In short, the platform covers all the usual flow of data analysis from the intake of information to the exploitation of the results. However, unlike other existing tools, its user does not need to have any knowledge of programming or data analysis. Figure 9.11 shows a screenshot of the process of creating a supervised model for data analysis.

Deepint.net offers mechanisms for the management of all the information provided by the user, enabling the creation of different projects. Figure 9.12 shows a screenshot of the process of creating a model for data visualisation, which as you can see, is extremely simple, since it consists of selecting the type of model to display the data, the data set and the selected parameters. Figure 9.13 gives a screenshot of the dashboards created for the visualisation of city information, Panama (top) and Istanbul (bottom). Similarly, the creation of users and permissions is allowed so that all the group members/employees can exploit the results of the analysis, displaying them on dynamic and interactive dashboards. Deepint.net is a versatile, multipurpose platform, whose utility for smart territory or city management is of special interest.

These are some of the functionalities of Deepint.net:

- User management functionality which offers plans that are customised to the needs of the cities.
- Integration of multi-source data, prioritising the most common sources: Formatted local and internet (CSV/JSON) files, databases (NoSQL and SQL), streaming data (MQTT, among others), CKAN-based repositories, etc.
- Automatic detection of the data type to facilitate analysis and representation.

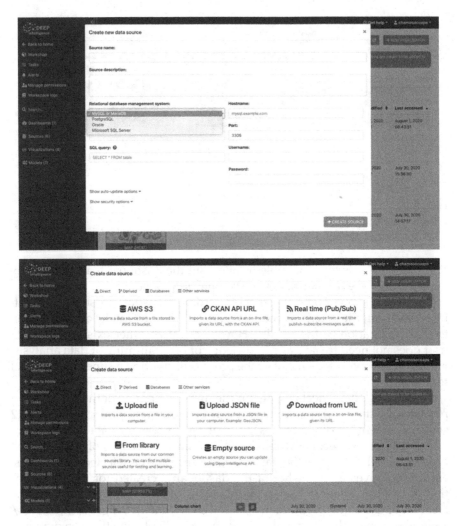

FIGURE 9.10
Data ingestion.

- Mechanisms for data processing (filtering records according to a criterion, eliminating fields, merging sources, creating compound fields, etc.).
- Guided mechanisms that facilitate the representation of the information provided by the user.
- Mechanisms for the guided creation of data analysis models, suggesting the best configuration to the users while allowing advanced users to carry out this process themselves if they wish.
- Simple evaluation of the results of the model according to different metrics.

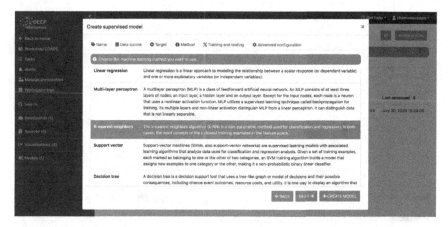

FIGURE 9.11
Intelligent model selection.

- Dashboard definition by inserting created visualisations, model results, etc. through 'drag and drop' so that users can customise how they want to work with the tool.

- Structuring the user's projects so that with one account the tool can be used in different areas or for different clients.

- Creation of city users with different roles so that all employees can use the platform as specified by the administrator.

- Exportation of results for easy integration in reports, etc.

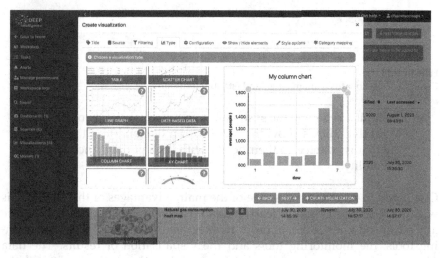

FIGURE 9.12
Screenshot of the process of creating visualisation models.

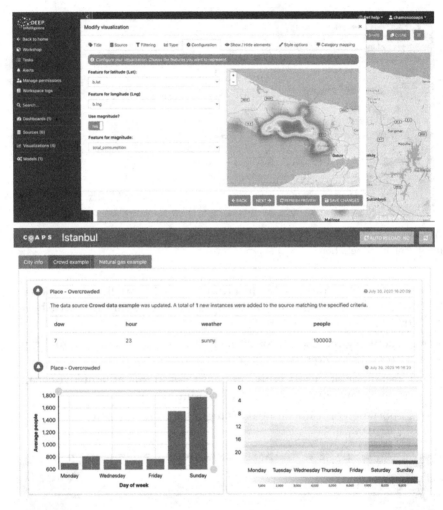

FIGURE 9.13
Creation of dashboards. Panama (top) and Istanbul (bottom).

- Possibility to deploy the system in a commercial cloud environment (AWS) that allows providing services on demand to all users, in a way that is adapted to their needs, with high performance and high availability.

Compared to its competitors, one of the main advantages of this platform is wizards. Users just need to learn how to use them, which does not require any advanced knowledge, in order to integrate the results of machine learning tools, the monitoring tools and the visualisation of results. The data accuracy of all data science tasks depends directly on the input and the selected algorithms. The accuracy of both generic and specific algorithms is considered constant independently of the platform. The volume of data that the platform can manage depends on its architecture, which is introduced in the following section.

9.3.1 Platform Architecture

The platform architecture can be deployed in an on-premise environment or in a commercial cloud environment.

The on-premise solution has been designed for situations in which it is not possible to process information in the infrastructures of third-party companies due to, for example, restrictive data protection policies.

Nevertheless, the solutions advertised on the platform web page are all hosted in commercial cloud environments (other solutions require a custom study and deployment).

Figure 9.14 provides a high-level representation of the architecture to be deployed in AWS (Amazon Web Services). Clients can connect to the application through the internet, available on app.deepint.net. The load balancer redirects the traffic to the corresponding EC2 instance. The users of the free version share resources, while the users of the paid version have private EC2 instances and do not share resources, which guarantees a good processing capacity at all times.

In each EC2 there is a web server and task workers, which are managed by a Redis server for event management on the platform (for the cache and the pub/subsystem).

These resources access the serverless systems when they stop dealing with information. For the processing of information on Deepint, a relational database is used, in this case, an Aurora DB as it is the serverless relational system of AWS. In addition, the system uses the storage system S3 to deploy all the data sources that the users upload on the system. The deployment can be encrypted with AES-256 if the user specifies it.

As the cloud environment of AWS is used, there is no limit on the volume of data and the response times depend directly on the type of EC2 chosen by the client. In case the client needs to improve the response times, they can increase their expenditure on resources or migrate to an on-premise solution.

The main technical challenges considered during the platform design are: Parallelisation aspects, availability of on-demand resources and a serverless solution which allows the user to work with no size restrictions.

9.4 Case Study

This platform can be adapted for the development of vertical markets, as part of smart city management. In general, vertical markets are associated with mobility, security, pollution, etc.

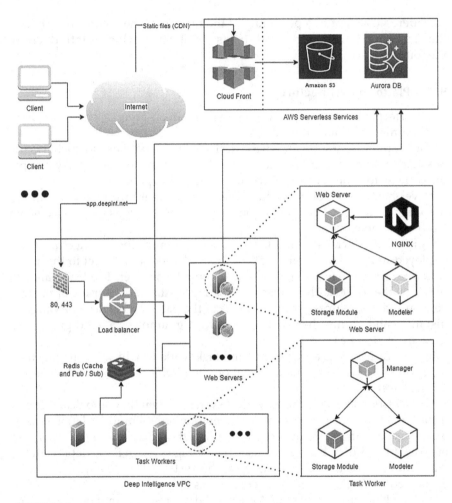

FIGURE 9.14
High-level representation of the platform architecture.

The following is a case study on the use of the platform to develop a system for bicycle rental management in Paris. It allows the user to identify the areas of Paris in which they are more likely to find bicycles using historical data in order to predict areas with the highest bicycle density in real-time. The process is carried out using the Pareto optimal location algorithm.

9.4.1 Pareto Optimal Location Algorithm

In this section, we present an algorithm for optimal geographically distributed resource selection.

Let $\{C_i\}$I be a set of locations offering the resources a user is seeking. For example, the resources might be public bike-sharing stands. The user is

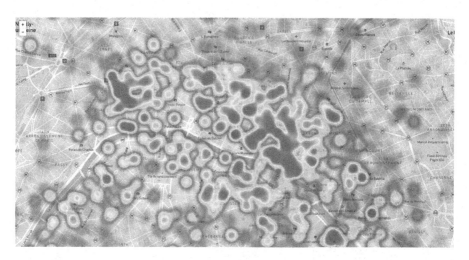

FIGURE 9.15
The heat map of a probability model for the availability of bikes in the City of Paris. A smoothed plot has been generated by overlapping Gaussian kernels weighted with the estimated availability probability.

interested in borrowing a bike, but they risk arriving at a location where there are no bikes available. The probability of one of those resources can be modelled as a set of functions $\{pi(t)\}i$, where t is the time.

Such functions can be approximated using an existing dataset, where further dependence on other variables is allowed. For example, a set of models $\{pi(weekday, hour, weather)\}I$ can be built using machine learning prediction algorithms. An example made with the Vélib dataset, available from the open data Paris portal, is shown in Figure 9.15.

While these models can be used to suggest the resource locations to the user, to maximise the probability of satisfying their need, it is necessary to address the interplay between distance to the resource and the likelihood of finding an available bike. A notion of Pareto optimality (Morris, 2012) can be introduced to reduce the choice to a smaller set of points. A resource location j dominates another one I if the following conditions apply:

$$\left\{ (d(x, Ci) \geq d(x, Cj) pi(t + d(x, Ci)) \leq pj(t + d(x, Cj)) \right\} \Leftrightarrow Ci \leq Cj \quad (9.1)$$

Where d is the estimated time to arrive at a given location, x is the user's location, and, on the right-hand side, a notation for this domination condition has been introduced. A location Ci in a set $\{Ci\}(i \in I)$, Pareto is optimal if there is no other point dominating it, i.e.,

$$\exists / j \in I : j \neq i, Ci \leq Cj \quad (9.2)$$

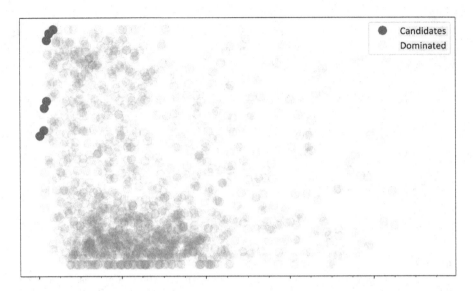

FIGURE 9.16
Pareto optimal points on the time-probability plane.

A natural approximation for simplifying the model assumes the variations of probability are negligible on the time scale of displacement, i.e.,

$$pi(t + d(x, Ci)) \approx pi(t) \qquad (9.3)$$

This allows to reduce the notion to a regular Pareto condition on the plane $(d(x,Ci),pi)$. An example is shown in Figure 9.16, where optimal points are found in the upper left corner.

A representation of the points in terms of real-world coordinates is shown in Figure 9.17.

Finally, an ordered list of recommendations can be provided to the user by introducing a risk-aversion parameter $\omega \in R$, so

$$vi = pi - d(x, Ci)\omega \qquad (9.4)$$

defines a metric that serves to order the Pareto optimal points. Users with higher risk-aversion (larger ω) tend to choose options with greater probabilities, while users with higher risk-tolerance (smaller ω) tend to choose the closest resources. The choice of reasonable values for ω is scale-dependent and can be tuned by presenting sets of Pareto optimal points to the user and asking for their preference.

9.4.2 Implementation with Deepint.net

The algorithm described in the previous section was implemented using the Deepint.net platform, as well as specific deployments. An outline of the process is described in this section.

Firstly, a prediction algorithm was built using tabulated historical data. A simple example of such data is shown in Figure 9.18. These data could be used to predict the probability of availability (ratio) as a function of the station, the weather conditions, and the date (here only distinguishing weekdays and weekends for simplicity).

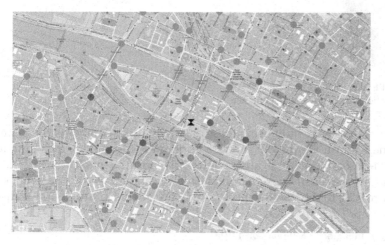

FIGURE 9.17
Real-world coordinates of the Pareto optimal points. The location of the user is shown as the black cross. Pareto-optimal choices are shown as dark dots, while sub-optimal locations are shown in light dots

FIGURE 9.18
Data uploaded on Deepint.net to build a prediction model.

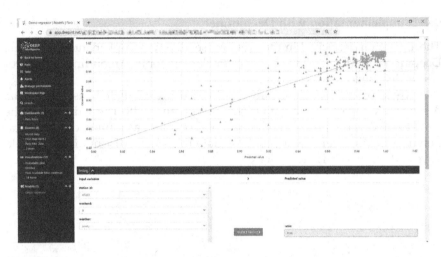

FIGURE 9.19
Prediction model built on Deepint.net.

Regressors were built using these data with the assistance of the platform's online wizard. Figure 9.19 shows a Random Forest model, including a predicted-observed diagram and an interactive form to invoke the model.

Finally, a specially designed mobile application used the Deepint.net API (Figure 9.20) to retrieve the model predictions. This information was used to

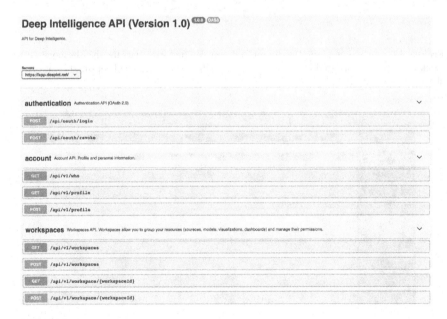

FIGURE 9.20
Online documentation of the Deepint.net API.

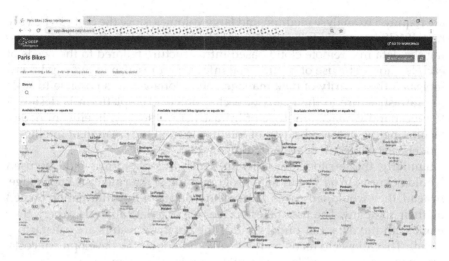

FIGURE 9.21
System dashboard built using the Deepint.net platform.

perform the Pareto optimisation as described in the previous section, providing the user with an interactive map where they could choose their preferred option.

The integration of the platform was completed with the construction of a set of dashboards which allowed to monitor the information, as shown in Figure 9.21.

9.5 Conclusion[1]

Deepint.net is a platform that facilitates knowledge management and the creation of intelligent systems for managing territories efficiently. The platform facilitates the use of centralised intelligence and edge architectures, with intelligent nodes, allowing for both decentralised and centralised analyses.

The implementation of smart territory management systems involves a reduction in costs associated with maintenance and resource management. Depending on its application, the platform can facilitate traffic optimisation, create systems for analysing the opinions of citizens on social networks, or help assess and prevent pollution, and so on.

In general, the use of a platform of this type, which allows for the use of any cloud, reduces initial investment needs. Normally, costly infrastructures

---

[1] This chapter, with permission from the copyright holder, is a reproduced version of the following journal article: Corchado, J.M., Chamoso, P., Hernández, G., Gutierrez, A.S.R., Camacho, A.R., González-Briones, A., ... & Omatu, S. (2021). Deepint. net: A rapid deployment platform for smart territories. *Sensors, 21*(1), 236.

are required to analyse medium and large volumes, since the cost can be very high if 1GB is exceeded. This cost would be significantly reduced by processing the data in a remote cloud-based infrastructure tailored to the needs of each territory. The use of commercial infrastructures also reduces risks and increases the security of data management. Moreover, it is possible to scale the infrastructure to the needs of each moment. The platform is designed to ingest and manage any type of infrastructure, such as intelligent nodes, facilitating the decentralisation of intelligence and the creation of intelligent models distributed in edge computing mode.

Similarly, the territories or cities in which this platform would be used would not need to have staff with programming or data analysis knowledge, instead, they would only need to have knowledge of the information owned by their company. The user takes on the role of a data analysis expert; they work with the data and understand if the obtained results are satisfactory or not. This allows to focus on the result and not on the development costs, which would be negligible thanks to the proposed system.

The system may be operated in real-time by any user in the city. Users with no computer knowledge would only display the information on a real-time dashboard while managers would be in charge of monitoring the general performance of the company. All city stakeholders can benefit.

The wizards offered by Deepint.net for the integration of data sources, creation of visualisations, dashboards and modelling, cover the entire ecosystem within the data analysis life cycle. This proposal has an advantage over other commercial data analysis solutions which are much more limited in functionality and usability.

The development process of this platform has been made efficient thanks to the use of Deepint.net. The platform also facilitated the carrying out of the case study in the city of Paris. Moreover, Deepint.net is highly versatile and it is currently undergoing further development in order to incorporate new functionalities which can adapt to a wider range of smart territories, eventually aiming to become a comprehensive agent capable of speeding up the development of any smart city. Furthermore, an in-depth research is being carried out on the many technologies which form Deepint.net and the findings will be shared with the scientific community in future studies.

References

Alkhatib, M., El Barachi, M., & Shaalan, K. (2019). An Arabic social media-based framework for incidents and events monitoring in smart cities. *Journal of Cleaner Production, 220,* 771–785.

Chamoso, P., González-Briones, A., De La Prieta, F., Venyagamoorthy, G.K., & Corchado, J.M. (2020). Smart city as a distributed platform: Toward a system for citizen-oriented management. *Computer Communications, 152,* 323–332.

Chamoso, P., Prieta, F.D.L., Paz, F.D., & Corchado, J.M. (2015). Swarm agent-based architecture suitable for internet of things and smartcities. In *Distributed Computing and Artificial Intelligence, 12th International Conference* (pp. 21–29). Springer, Cham.

Elmaghraby, A.S., & Losavio, M.M. (2014). Cyber security challenges in smart cities: Safety, security and privacy. *Journal of Advanced Research, 5*(4), 491–497.

Gheisari, M., Wang, G., & Chen, S. (2020). An edge computing-enhanced internet of things framework for privacy-preserving in smart city. *Computers & Electrical Engineering, 81*, 106504.

Hussain, M.M., Alam, M.S., & Beg, M.S. (2019). Fog computing model for evolving smart transportation applications. *Fog and Edge Computing: Principles and Paradigms, 22*(4), 347–372.

Jia, G., Han, G., Rao, H., & Shu, L. (2017). Edge computing-based intelligent manhole cover management system for smart cities. *IEEE Internet of Things Journal, 5*(3), 1648–1656.

Kapser, S., & Abdelrahman, M. (2020). Acceptance of autonomous delivery vehicles for last-mile delivery in Germany–Extending UTAUT2 with risk perceptions. *Transportation Research Part C: Emerging Technologies, 111*, 210–225.

Khan, L.U., Yaqoob, I., Tran, N.H., Kazmi, S.A., Dang, T.N., & Hong, C.S. (2020). Edge-computing-enabled smart cities: A comprehensive survey. *IEEE Internet of Things Journal, 7*(10), 10200–10232.

Kitchin, R., & Dodge, M. (2019). The (in) security of smart cities: Vulnerabilities, risks, mitigation, and prevention. *Journal of Urban Technology, 26*(2), 47–65.

Kousiouris, G., Akbar, A., Sancho, J., Ta-Shma, P., Psychas, A., Kyriazis, D., & Varvarigou, T. (2018). An integrated information lifecycle management framework for exploiting social network data to identify dynamic large crowd concentration events in smart cities applications. *Future Generation Computer Systems, 78*, 516–530.

Kumar, S., Datta, D., Singh, S.K., & Sangaiah, A.K. (2018). An intelligent decision computing paradigm for crowd monitoring in the smart city. *Journal of Parallel and Distributed Computing, 118*, 344–358.

Latif, S., Afzaal, H., & Zafar, N.-A. (2018). Intelligent traffic monitoring and guidance system for smart city. In *Proceedings of the International Conference on Computing, Mathematics and Engineering Technologies (iCoMET)*, Sukkur, Pakistan.

Laufs, J., Borrion, H., & Bradford, B. (2020). Security and the smart city: Systematic review. *Sustainable Cities and Society, 55*, 102023.

Liu, Y., Yang, C., Jiang, L., Xie, S., & Zhang, Y. (2019). Intelligent edge computing for IoT-based energy management in smart cities. *IEEE Network, 33*(2), 111–117.

Luo, A., Yang, F., Li, X., Nie, D., Jiao, Z., Zhou, S., & Cheng, H. (2020). Hybrid graph neural networks for crowd counting. In *Proceedings of the AAAI Conference on Artificial Intelligence*, California USA.

Morris, P. (2012). *Introduction to Game Theory*. Springer Science & Business Media.

Ning, Z., Huang, J., & Wang, X. (2019). Vehicular fog computing: Enabling real-time traffic management for smart cities. *IEEE Wireless Communications, 26*(1), 87–93.

O'Dwyer, E., Pan, I., Acha, S., & Shah, N. (2019). Smart energy systems for sustainable smart cities: Current developments, trends and future directions. *Applied Energy, 237*, 581–597.

Pan, X., Zhou, W., Lu, Y., & Sun, N. (2019). Prediction of network traffic of smart cities based on DE-BP neural network. *IEEE Access, 7*, 55807–55816.

Perez, A.J., & Zeadally, S. (2019). A communication architecture for crowd management in emergency and disruptive scenarios. *IEEE Communications Magazine*, 57(4), 54–60.

Premsankar, G., Ghaddar, B., Di Francesco, M., & Verago, R. (2018). Efficient placement of edge computing devices for vehicular applications in smart cities. In *NOMS 2018–2018 IEEE/IFIP Network Operations and Management Symposium*. IEEE.

Rajak, B., & Kushwaha, D.S. (2019). Traffic control and management over IoT for clearance of emergency vehicle in smart cities. In *Information and Communication Technology for Competitive Strategies*, Springer, Singapore.

Rego, A., Garcia, L., Sendra, S., & Lloret, J. (2018). Software-defined network-based control system for an efficient traffic management for emergency situations in smart cities. *Future Generation Computer Systems, 88*, 243–253.

Rehena, Z., & Janssen, M. (2018). Towards a Framework for Context-Aware Intelligent Traffic Management System in Smart Cities. In *Proceedings of the Companion Web Conference*, Lyon, France.

Schneider, M., Rambach, J., & Stricker, D. (2017). Augmented reality-based on edge computing using the example of remote live support. In *Proceedings of 2017 IEEE International Conference on Industrial Technology (ICIT)*. IEEE.

Silva, B.N., Khan, M., & Han, K. (2018). Towards sustainable smart cities: A review of trends, architectures, components, and open challenges in smart cities. *Sustainable Cities and Society, 38*, 697–713.

Sittón-Candanedo, I., Alonso, R.S., García, Ó, Muñoz, L., & Rodríguez-González, S. (2019a). Edge computing, iot and social computing in smart energy scenarios. *Sensors, 19*(15), 3353.

Sittón-Candanedo, I., Alonso, R.S., Corchado, J.M., Rodríguez-González, S., & Casado-Vara, R. (2019b). A review of edge computing reference architectures and a new global edge proposal. *Future Generation Computer Systems, 99*, 278–294.

Solmaz, G., Wu, F.J., Cirillo, F., Kovacs, E., Santana, J.R., Sánchez, L., Sotres, P., & Munoz, L. (2019). Toward understanding crowd mobility in smart cities through the internet of things. *IEEE Communications Magazine*, 57(4), 40–46.

Sumi, L., & Ranga, V. (2018). Intelligent traffic management system for prioritizing emergency vehicles in a smart city. *International Journal of Engineering, 31*(2), 278–283.

Taleb, T., Dutta, S., Ksentini, A., Iqbal, M., & Flinck, H. (2017). Mobile Edge computing potential in making cities smarter. *IEEE Communications Magazine*, 55(3), 38–43.

Ullah, Z., Al-Turjman, F., Mostarda, L., & Gagliardi, R. (2020). Applications of artificial intelligence and machine learning in smart cities. *Computer Communications, 154*, 313–323.

UN. (2018). *The World's Cities in 2018: Data Booklet*; United Nations, New York, USA, Accessed on 31 December 2020 from https://www.un.org/en/events/citiesday/assets/pdf/the_worlds_cities_in_2018_data_booklet.pdf.

UNESCO (2019). *Smart Cities: Shaping the Society of 2030*. United Nations Educational, Scientific and Cultural Organization. Netexplo, París, France.

Yao, H., Gao, P., Wang, J., Zhang, P., Jiang, C., & Han, Z. (2019). Capsule network-assisted IoT traffic classification mechanism for smart cities. *IEEE Internet of Things Journal, 6*(5), 7515–7525.

Zhao, L., Wang, J., Liu, J., & Kato, N. (2019). Routing for crowd management in smart cities: A deep reinforcement learning perspective. *IEEE Communications Magazine*, 57(4), 88–93.

10

Crowd Detection Platforms

10.1 Introduction

Statistics from the Department of Economic and Social Affairs of the United Nations, DESAP, indicate that 68% of the world's population will live in cities or urban areas by 2050 (O'Dwyer et al., 2019), which means rapid and even uncontrolled growth with consequent challenges for governments, for example: Pollution, problems of travel due to traffic and congestion; high costs of housing, food and basic services; as well as security problems (Liu & Liu., 2019). In particular, noise pollution is becoming a growing concern as it is the second most important pollutant after air—it has been discovered to have great effects on both the health of adults (Basner et al., 2014) and children (Lercher et al., 2003).

To address the abovementioned problems, the smart city concept emerged over the last years, which refers to the integration of the urban environment with information and communication technologies (ICTs). This concept has attracted the interest of all sectors (governments, universities, research centres, etc.) to present solutions or developments to achieve a smart city (Ullah et al., 2020). The objective of the smart city paradigm is the effective management of challenges related to the growth of urban areas through the adoption of ICTs in developments, solutions, applications, services, or even in the design of state policies (Chamoso et al., 2020).

Modern models of municipal governance promote the creation of public value through articulated initiatives involving citizens. In this context, the generation of useful information for citizens is essential and citizens are increasingly demanding that it be accessible via the Internet. Making data open and mobilising collective knowledge is increasingly important to enable the creation of sustainable solutions for cities. It is in this context that the concept of City-as-Platform emerges, which is associated with the movement for open government and the application of digital technologies to expand the possibilities for the co-production of public services (Repette et al., 2021). The city-as-platform is the technological and governmental infrastructure that enables society to play a direct and broader role in the life of cities. Digital technologies are applied to promote an open space for collaboration and

DOI: 10.1201/9781003278986-13

democratisation of information and knowledge, which requires governance that is consensual, transparent, responsive, efficient, effective, equitable and inclusive. In order to promote this type of initiative, it is essential to have tools such as the one presented in this chapter, in order to have dynamic, efficient and fast mechanisms to facilitate the analysis of information and to provide it to citizens. This platform makes it easy to capture data from IoT platforms, open data, etc. and process them using artificial intelligence techniques, augmented reality, etc (Chamoso et al., 2018a, b).

Currently, a smart city is a broadly used term, for example, in systematic reviews of the literature, more than 36 definitions are identified that address different dimensions of the urban environment such as: Mobility, technology, public services, economy, environment, quality of life or governance (Ramaprasad et al., 2017; Trindade et al., 2017; Laufs et al., 2020). One of the most widely used definitions is the one proposed by Elmaghraby and Losavio (2014): "An intelligent city is one that incorporates information and communication technologies to increase operational efficiency, shares information independently within the system and improves the overall effectiveness of services and the well-being of citizens". However, the growth of the Internet of Things from 2017 onwards has led to a large number of devices being permanently connected to the Internet. This has led to increased interest in overcoming the challenges posed to effective data management and security and opened up a debate regarding their importance in urban management and the wellbeing of the population (Ramaprasad et al., 2017; Reddy et al., 2018; Kitchin et al., 2019).

Security is a very important element in cities, it is vital to guarantee a safe environment for both the citizen and the data that is generated. Any city must implement security measures to ensure full protection of the citizens' data, and the data generated by the urban infrastructure and sensors, etc. Given the seriousness of the current pandemic, it is also important to facilitate compliance with security measures that protect citizens and that, for example, they have an adequate social distance. For this reason, imaginative systems that allow us to identify those areas where there is less density of pedestrians can be of great interest, for example, to facilitate the leisure of families who want to go out and enjoy the city. Smart cities need a secure and flexible platform for managing data coming from city sensors, service providers, citizens etc., (O'Dwyer et al., 2019). Data coming from real-time sensors, smart nodes, relational or non-relational databases. Especially small to medium cities or territories that need scalable platforms, that are easy to deploy and manage and that do not require specialised data analysts, which they do not normally have (Khan et al., 2019). The construction of a smart city is a dynamic process, and the management platforms have to be ready not just for real-time data ingestion but also for the inclusion of data from different sources, to manage such data, to analyse it, to create different visualisation models and to integrate different datasets. It is also of great relevance to exploit the data, to be able to develop classification, optimisation, prediction, etc. models and to develop secure dashboards that can be integrated into the control system of a city or county council or any other entity responsible for the management of the smart city. All these challenges must be tackled while developing a smart city, therefore slowing down the process and arising several problems for the developers. How to accelerate the development of Smart Cities, reducing costs, time and troubles?

This chapter presents the deepin.net platform (Corchado et al., 2021) and how it has been used to implement a model that facilitates the maintenance of social distance when walking around a city. Many cities have cameras to guarantee security and/or facilitate decision-making with respect to, for example, traffic, frequency of cleaning, etc. In this case, we show how a model with a facial recognition algorithm has been implemented on images captured in real-time and another regressive one. This collects images from security cameras and identifies the number of pedestrians on a street, calculates the density and on the basis of historical data predicts what the density of pedestrians will be in the future. The HOG algorithm (Histogram of Oriented Gradients Algorithm) is used to detect pedestrians and calculate their density on a street. The XGBoost algorithm (Chen, 2016) is used to predict the future. The facility that deepint.net has to incorporate sensor data, in this case from camera images, and to implement these algorithms makes it very simple to build mechanisms for automated decision-making processes. With this information, citizens will be able to plan their walks, know the density of pedestrians on a street at a given time and what is likely to happen in the future.

One of the main advantages of deepint.net against similar platforms is its serverless design, based on the cloud environment of AWS. This results in no volume restrictions for the data and response times corresponding to the AWS machine chosen by the client. Moreover, its ease of use makes it possible for anyone with basic knowledge to take part in the development of a smart city, greatly speeding up the developing and deployment phases.

This chapter is organised as follows: Section 10.2 describes the concept of the smart city, presents some tools for managing them; these are the verticals on which they can be structured and for which a greater number of use cases are carried out. Section 10.3 describes deepint.net and Section 10.4 presents the hybrid model used to identify pedestrian areas with an accumulation of citizens. Once the results have been analysed, the conclusions are presented.

10.2 Smart Cities

Cities are constantly evolving and regardless of their size, they are seeking solutions to improve the quality of life of their citizens, to be more efficient and to optimise their resources. Information and Communication Technology (ICT) is a basic element in the development of intelligent cities and numerous projects have been launched to create information management systems especially adapted to the needs of cities (Repette et al., 2021).

In all these developments it is essential to take into account aspects that are closely related to the citizens such as human capital/education, social and relational capital, the environment, etc. For smart city models to be useful and progress together with their citizens it is necessary for them to be efficient, flexible, easy and rapid to implement and to integrate with other smart city tools or technologies (Cardullo & Kitchin, 2019; Chamoso et al., 2020). Many countries are making a considerable effort to develop a 'smart' urban growth strategy in its metropolitan areas (Cardullo & Kitchin, 2019). The Intelligent Community Forum conducts research on the local effects of ICTs that are now available worldwide.

The role of innovation in the ICT sector is fundamental in the development of the infrastructure that provides a city with intelligence and of tools for the sustainable, citizen-oriented, realistic and coherent management that is required (Peris-Ortiz et al., 2017). The scope of research is extraordinarily broad in this field and there are numerous options for the implementation of intelligent cities. It is therefore important to know all of them and make the right choices. Interesting options have been presented for smart cities in the fields of wireless sensor networks (Toutouh & Alba, 2017; Hashim et al., 2018), agriculture (González-Briones et al., 2018a, 2018b), energy optimisation (Chamoso et al., 2018a; González-Briones et al., 2018c, 2018d, 2018e), optimal resource allocation (Enayet et al., 2018)], risks and challenges of EV adoption (Potdar et al., 2018), vehicle networks (Rivas et al., 2018; Toutouh & Alba, 2018) and route optimisation (Chamoso et al., 2018b; González-Briones et al., 2018d, 2018f).

The Internet of Things is a basic element in the development of intelligent cities (Arasteh et al., 2016; Chamoso et al., 2020). City data, especially if accessible in real-time, can be used to effectively transform and manage the city and promote urban planning and development (García et al., 2015). Appropriate real-time solutions and systems capable of making decisions to solve run-time problems are elements that can improve the efficiency of smart cities (Chatterjee et al., 2018). The present chapter is an example of how the data extracted from real-time images can be used to identify areas where pedestrians can walk, maintaining adequate social distance.

Any platform for smart city management must have a robust system to acquire and process data from multiple data sources (databases, trackers-thirdpartyy applications, sensors, intelligent nodes). Architectures require flexible and scalable computing power to process large volumes of data. Today, thanks to technological advances and lower storage and sensor prices, the amount of generated and stored data is huge and growing exponentially. Multicore processing (in the form of symmetric multiprocessing (SMP) and asymmetric multiprocessing (AMP)) is becoming common, with embedded multicore CPUs expected to grow by a factor of $x6$ in the next years (Venture Development Corporation). In addition, Field Programmable Gate Arrays (FPGAs) have grown in capacity and decreased in cost, providing the high-speed functionality that could only be achieved with Application-Specific Integrated Circuits (ASICs) (Trimberger, 2018). In addition, virtualisation is driving the development of large scalable systems and blurring the connection between hardware and software by allowing multiple operating systems to run on a single processor.

There are numerous platforms for the management of smart cities, which facilitate both massive and secure data intake and processing. These platforms have mechanisms for information analysis, data transmission, information fusion, pre-processing, etc. In addition, these platforms must be prepared for integration with other platforms, with information management systems, etc. Some of the platforms used for the management of smart cities are presented in Table 10.1.

TABLE 10.1

Main Platforms Used for the Management of Smart Cities

Platform Name	Description	Key Features
Deepint.net	Platform for data acquisition, integration, preprocessing and modelling. Incorporates a complete suite of artificial intelligence techniques for data analysis: Clustering, forecasting, optimisation, etc. It is scalable and easy to implement.	Scalable, easy-to-use, versatile, smart city development focus.
ICOS	It is an open repository of solutions for smart cities, offering a set of existing applications and projects that can be reused for application creation.	Open-source, active forum, re-usable solutions.
Webinos	Web application platform that allows developers to access native resources through APIs. Webinos makes it easy to connect to any IoT device.	Open-source, independent software components.
Sofia2	Middleware that enables interoperability between multiple systems and devices, offering a semantic platform that makes real-world information available to smart, mainly IoT-oriented applications	IoT focus, Interoperability among systems.
Kaa	An initiative that defines an open and efficient cloud platform to provide IoT solutions. Among the most common solutions is the connection of all types of sensors that can be found or deployed in a smart city.	Focus on road infrastructure, public service facilities, and smart buildings.
Altair SmartWorks	PaaS-type platform designated for IoT and M2M. It can be used to connect the information-providing infrastructure to a smart city. However, the platform remains at this level, without offering user-oriented services, a layer that would have to be created independently of the platform.	PaaS platform, good IoT protocols support.
FIWARE	A platform that provides a series of APIs for the development and deployment of Internet applications, targeting a number of verticals. Many of these sectors are responsible for providing a variety of smart city services.	Open-source, powerful APIs, strong ecosystem.

Although much research is being done on smart cities, a compact system is still needed that is efficient and scalable, easy to implement and integrate with other platforms. The platforms presented in the previous tables offer many options and some of them are quite flexible for data management. They all have been analysed and some of them are more efficient in modelling data, others are better at acquiring data from sensors but the most interesting one, that the biggest potential is deepint.net (Corchado et al., 2021)

Deepint.net offers all the necessary elements to build a system for collecting and managing data using all the power of Artificial Intelligence. Deepint. net simplifies the development of the management systems of a smart city and also offers the possibility of integrating data from any source.

Deepint.net offers user-centred services and facilitates the creation of intelligent dashboards without the need for knowledge of intelligent systems, as it has an intelligent tutor that guides experts in city management to develop their own models. The platform is ready to integrate new management models and facilitates the composition of intelligent hybrid or expert mixing systems, so that different algorithms work together to obtain results from integrated or heterogeneous data sources.

Moreover, one of the main characteristics of smart cities is the heterogeneity of all their components (Paskaleva, 2011), both in the final applications and in the technology used in the deployed infrastructure. For example, within the IoT sector, there are many manufacturers, protocols and communication technologies (Sandulli et al., 2017; Ferraris, 2019; González García et al., 2019). As detailed below, one of the main advantages of the platform presented in this document is that it is compatible with any technology or manufacturer.

Deepint.net incorporates the elements required for the management of any smart city without the need for ICT professionals or expert data analysts, and it has been developed under the concept of 'Smart City-as-a-Platform'. The platform includes artificial intelligence techniques for the extraction of information that is useful in the management of infrastructures, systems and devices, making the city functional and efficient. Moreover, maintaining a rapid response time is fundamental for the functioning of a smart city. Without deepint.net, the large volume of data collected from a smart city is normally sent directly to the cloud; this has high associated and variable costs, forcing cities to seek solutions that reduce the costs of payments to cloud service providers, as well as energy and bandwidth consumption. Deepint.net is a scalable, easy to use and dynamic platform that has a fast response time, is capable of satisfying the immediate needs of any city or territory.

10.2.1 Smart Cities as a Platform: Verticals and Domains of Smart Cities

The development of a smart city must be based on certain foundations, which range from a well-defined planification phase to the selection of the most suitable tools (Yigitcanlar et al., 2020). In many cases, key aspects such as an

TABLE 10.2

Verticals and Domains of Smart Cities

Verticals	Domains
Smart governance	Social services, participation, transparency…
Smart economy	Innovation, productivity, entrepreneurship, flexible labour market…
Smart mobility	Connected public transport, multimodality, logistics, accessibility…
Smart environment	Environmental protection, resources management, energy efficiency…
Smart people	Digital education, creativity, inclusive society…
Smart living	Tourism, security, healthcare, culture…

in-depth review of the human factors of the city or the validation of market-ready technologies, have been left out. This can result in a slow adoption of new systems and unsuccessful smart city projects. Vertical markets and tools for smart cities are often classified following the principles of Table 10.2, which provides a solid structure upon which a smart city must be built.

10.3 A Platform for Smart Cities

Today, all sectors can extract knowledge and benefit considerably from data analysis, with cities or territories being the largest producers of data that exist today. Thanks to advances in computing such as distributed processing techniques, improved processing capabilities and cheaper technology, artificial intelligence techniques can now be applied to large volumes of data, offering rapid results, this was unthinkable less than a decade ago.

Deepint.net offers functionalities that cover the entire data analysis flow: A wizard for data ingestion from multiple sources and in multiple formats, a wizard for data management (pre-processing, filtering, etc.), a wizard for applying proprietary data analysis methodologies with the advantage that no algorithm needs to be programmed or configured, a wizard for creating fully customised dynamic visualisations and dashboards using drag and drop techniques, and finally, mechanisms for exporting data and visualisation results, allowing, for example, for the interactive sharing of analyses with any Internet user. The architecture of the platform includes the 5 different layers described in Figure 10.1.

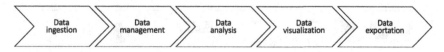

FIGURE 10.1
Deepint.net architecture layers.

Deepint.net is a platform that can be used to create data collection and management systems for members efficiently and without the need for data scientists, which is difficult to find nowadays, as it includes many data analysis algorithms created with artificial intelligence techniques. It is a platform created for the managers of smart cities, it facilitates all the aspects related to data management, processing and visualisation.

Deepint.net is a platform deployed in a self-adapting cloud environment, which allows users to apply artificial intelligence methodologies to their data, using the most widespread techniques (random forest, neural networks, etc.). The user does not have to know how these techniques work, nor how to configure them, it is not even necessary to have programming skills. Deepint.net facilitates the construction of models for data processing in a guided and clear way, indicating how to ingest data, work with the data, visualise the information to understand the data, apply a model and, finally, obtain, evaluate, interpret and use the results. The platform incorporates a wizard that automates the process, selecting the configuration for the artificial intelligence methodology that provides the best solution to the problem the user is addressing.

Figure 10.2 shows which elements and tools can be used throughout the data and information management process, from data entry, to the creation of dashboards or data exploitation at the end. Deepint.net allows users to exploit all results through dynamic, reusable dashboards that can be shared and used within other tools available to the city, such as exporting results in different formats for easy reporting, for example.

It is a platform that covers all the usual flow of data analysis from the intake of information to the exploitation of the results, but unlike other existing tools, the user has no knowledge of programming or data analysis but is only an expert in smart cities (Corchado et al., 2021).

Some of the most outstanding features of this platform are related to its plans tailored to the needs of cities, its ability to integrate datasets from

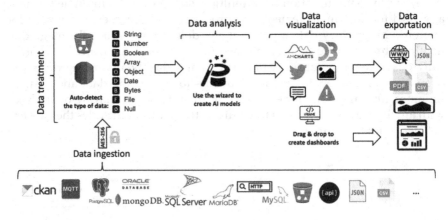

FIGURE 10.2
Flow and elements of data analysis.

different sources, prioritising the most common: Formatted files (CSV/JSON) both local and available on the Internet, databases (NoSQL and SQL), streaming data (MQTT, among others), repositories based on CKAN, etc., the inclusion of models for the automatic detection of the type of data, the use of automatic mechanisms for data processing (filtering records according to a criterion, eliminating fields, merging sources, creating compound fields, etc.), guided mechanisms that facilitate the representation of the information provided by the user, mechanisms for the creation of data analysis models in a guided manner, suggesting the best configuration to users. Meanwhile, the platform has advanced features which can be used by the users who have knowledge of data analysis; the use of metrics that allow the model results to be evaluated in a simple manner, the definition of dashboards by inserting created visualisations, model results, etc. by means of 'drag & drop' so that users can personalise how they want to work with the tool, etc.

In addition, Deepint.net allows users to create different roles, structure user projects in such a way that with one account the tool can be used in different environments or for different clients, exploit results for the creation of reports, etc, and deploy the system in a commercial cloud environment (i.e., AWS) that allows all users to be served in a way that is adapted to their needs, on-demand, with high performance and high availability.

10.4 A Case Study: Melbourne

In this section, a model is presented for real-time crowd detection and future crowd prediction using video surveillance footage. The use case is set in the city of Melbourne and focuses on the ability to detect the most crowded streets of the city and the streets which have the lowest number of pedestrians. This information is of critical importance to both, government institutions and citizens, especially during the current COVID-19 pandemic. Crowds may contribute to the spread of the Coronavirus if the social distance among people is not adequate, and maintaining such distance is rather difficult. The information generated by the presented model may help citizens and city authorities take decisions.

The method allows the user to identify the areas of Melbourne in which crowds will appear using historical and real-time data from the video surveillance cameras of the city. The process is carried out using a hybrid algorithm with two modules: A face recognition unit and a regression unit.

10.4.1 Input Data

The method is designed in such a way that constant image flow is the only required input. Camera footage is analysed every 2 minutes by the face

TABLE 10.3

The Face Recognition Algorithm Applied to a Frame of a Crowd at a Country Fair. The Average Number of Faces Detected Per Frame Is Used to Estimate the People Density in the Area

Year	Month	Date	Day	Time	Sensor_ID	Hourly_Counts	Latitude	Longitude
2019	September	20	Friday	2	57	16	−37.8164124	144.9558028
2017	March	9	Thursday	2	40	6	−37.8150015	144.95226225
2014	October	8	Wednesday	14	9	507	−37.818124	144.953581
2011	February	9	Wednesday	12	3	2.297	−37.81000274999995	144.96259436892453
2013	June	16	Sunday	8	12	64	−37.8145826	144.9422374
2018	January	4	Thursday	11	33	182	−37.8217763	144.9519159

recognition unit and the number of detected faces is fed to the regressor unit, which is re-trained once a month. This creates a well-labelled dataset and provides real-time insight to the users. So as to test both units separately, the use case presented in this chapter uses independent data for each unit.

The Regressor Unit has been trained using a dataset that contains hourly pedestrian counts from 5 January 2009 to 31 October 2020 from pedestrian sensor devices located across the city of Melbourne (link is provided in the Data Availability Statement). It is formed by 3,391,523 data instances and contains information about each sensor's location, the time of the measurement and the number of pedestrian hourly counts. The data is considered reliable, up-to-date and publicly available.

As for the Face Recognition Unit, data protection laws do not permit the publishing of open datasets of street surveillance footage without blurring the face of the people involved (Huang et al., 2007, 2008). This obstacle has been overcome by using a well-tested algorithm which provided a good performance in a vast variety of datasets (Dalal et al., 2005; Huang et al., 2012; Dadi et al., 2016)

An example of the data used is shown below (Table 10.3)

10.4.2 Crowd Detection Method

The goal of this solution is to accurately describe and predict the location of crowds in any developed smart city. To achieve this, security camera footage is processed using a face recognition algorithm which calculates the number of individuals in each frame. This process is carried out every two minutes and the obtained number is extrapolated to estimate the people density surrounding the considered sensor. The obtained information is useful for monitoring crowd behaviours and creating a training dataset. An output describing the areas of the city by "low, medium or high density of pedestrians" is generated.

Afterwards, a machine learning algorithm is trained with the labelled dataset and used for predicting the behaviour of crowds in the near future.

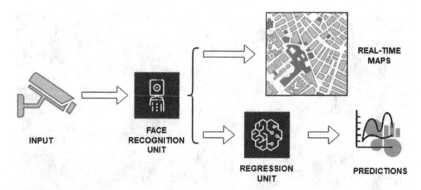

FIGURE 10.3
Flow and elements of the crowd detection method.

An output describing the density of pedestrians in the different areas of the city is generated after one hour and after two hours.

The overall process is described in Figure 10.3.

10.4.3 Face Recognition Unit

The main aim of this module is to transform the input, which consists of camera images, into a consistent dataset of people density. To achieve this, the number of faces in each frame is obtained and the average number of people over a period of time is calculated. This results in a dataset of people density in the location of each camera, which is used for training a regression unit.

This unit makes usage of the HOG algorithm (Histogram of Oriented Gradients Algorithm) due to its good performance for human face image detection. This algorithm obtains a near-perfect separation on the original MIT pedestrian database and an 89% accuracy in other more complex datasets (Dalal et al., 2005).

The face recognition process is as follows (also see Figure 10.4):

- Convert the image to grayscale and calculate the gradient of each pixel. This creates a common ground for all images. Changes in brightness do not affect the algorithm anymore.
- The gradients are stored in an array, divided into 16x16 pixel squares and the direction of the greatest gradients of each square is selected.
- A trained linear Support Vector Machine (SVM) is used to find face patterns.

The algorithm produces a series of locations within the image which contain people's faces. A visual example of the output of the algorithm is shown in Figure 10.5. The accuracy of the algorithm reaches 99.38% on the Labelled Faces in the Wild benchmark (Huang et al., 2012).

FIGURE 10.4
The face recognition algorithm applied to a frame of a crowd at a country fair. The average number of faces detected per frame is used to estimate the people density in the area. This public image has been chosen to illustrate the concept to be represented. In order to comply with data protection legislation, actual security camera footage has not been used.

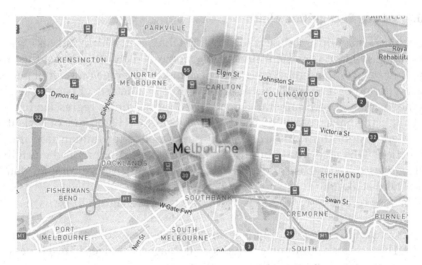

FIGURE 10.5
The heat map of a probability model of crowds in the City of Melbourne. A smoothed plot was generated by overlapping Gaussian kernels weighted with the estimated crowd probability.

10.4.4 Regression Unit

The regression unit in this case makes use of the XGBoost algorithm. This method stands out as it has shown a very powerful performance, accuracy, and it has good interpretability. The goal is to model the previously obtained dataset and use it to predict future crowds as well as to monitor the current ones (Figure 10.6).

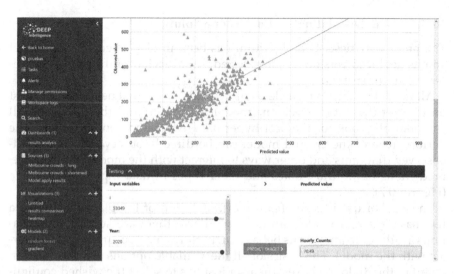

FIGURE 10.6
Predicted-observed diagram of the trained model and wizard for interactive predictions.

XGBoost is an optimisation method which makes use of regularisation and a loss function as described in (Chen et al., 2016). It addresses the problem of traditional Euclidean space optimisation methods and achieves a gradient tree boosting method. The (simplified) objective function is defined as:

$$\Lambda^{(t)} = \sum_{i=1}^{n} l\left(y_i, \overline{y}_i^{(t-1)} + f_t(x_i)\right) + \Omega(f_t) \tag{10.1}$$

where l is the loss function, y_i is the real observed value, $\overline{y}_i^{(t-1)}$ is the previously predicted value, $f_t(x_i)$ is the function to optimise in step i, and $\Omega(f_t)$ is the regurgitation factor of the function.

This is defined as a computational-enhanced version of the Tailor Theorem which, in addition, can apply Euclidean space optimisation techniques.

Similarly, if we consider the second-order Taylor approximation, we obtain the truly used goal function:

$$\Lambda^{(t)} = \sum_{i=1}^{n} \frac{1}{2} h_i \left(f_i(x_i) - \frac{g_i}{h_i} \right)^2 + \Omega(f_t) + C \tag{10.2}$$

where $g_i = \dfrac{\partial l\left(y_i, \overline{y}_i^{(t-1)}\right)}{\partial \overline{y}_i^{(t-1)}}$ and $h_i = \dfrac{\partial^2 l\left(y_i, \overline{y}_i^{(t-1)}\right)}{\partial \left(\overline{y}_i^{(t-1)}\right)^2}$ are the first and second order gradient statistics of the loss function and C is a constant.

The usage of this function results in a lower computational complexity as compared to the random forest and traditional tree ensemble models.

10.4.5 Using Deepint.net to Construct a Solution

The previously described algorithm has been implemented on deepint.net and its deployed version has been tested. An overview of the process is presented in this section.

All the data analysis is made using wizards on deepint.net. The user must only select the data source, the model to be used and the platform will automatically look for the best hyper-parameters and configurations. The performance of the created model can be directly observed in predicted-observed diagrams and other ways to interact with the model. For example, predictions of arbitrary dates and other types of data input can be made (Figure 10.7).

The ease of use is a key feature of the design of the platform. In just a few basic steps, a model can be created and there are several visualisations available to analyse its behaviour, performance, accuracy and to interact with the model. The basics of all the available options are described in detail in the dialogue boxes, the user just has to select the wished configuration. Furthermore, advanced data scientists can fine-tune the parameters manually if they wish, while using the functionalities of deepint.net via an API REST.

After the models have been created and connected within the smart territory, the design of the platform allows the user to create a set of dashboards for real-time monitoring of the sensors (Figure 10.7). Furthermore, heatmaps as shown in Figure 10.6 can be added to new dashboards.

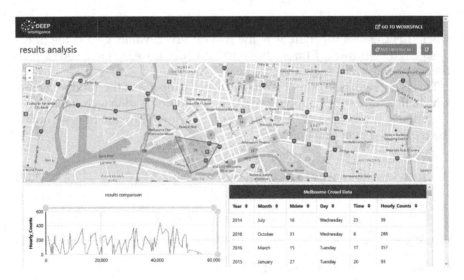

FIGURE 10.7
System dashboard for real-time monitoring of crowds, created using Deepint.net.

10.5 Results

Deepint.net is a platform which eases the development and monitoring of intelligent systems in smart territories while providing robust results. The developed applications can be operated in real-time by any user in the city: both a pedestrian who wants to plan a quiet walking route and a manager who has to decide where to reinforce the street cleaning routines. Moreover, during the current COVID19 pandemic it would allow pedestrians to keep a safety distance among themselves, as well as help the authorities keep a lower infection rate within their territory. All city stakeholders can benefit.

The wizards offered by Deepint.net for the integration of data sources, creation of visualisations, dashboards and modelling, cover the entire ecosystem within the data analysis life cycle. This proposal has this key advantage over other commercial data analysis solutions which are more limited in functionality and usability.

The algorithm used for prediction was XGBoost as it is an optimised distributed gradient boosting library designed to be highly efficient, flexible and portable. It implements machine learning algorithms under the Gradient Boosting framework, which provide fast and accurate results for most data science problems. It is widely used nowadays as it has achieved better accuracy than other tree ensemble algorithms and even outperformed newer algorithms such as LightGBM (Liang et al., 2020). The discussed use case, designed as a mock-up version to test the platform's possibilities, has used a reduced version of the dataset (first 57,000 instances out of the 2,281,353 total instances) and obtained a mean relative error of 0.314. As it can be seen in Figure 10.7, most values can be found near the predicted-observed line, with only a small amount of them far away. This performance corresponds with the basic results obtained when the platform automatically configures all the parameters, equivalent to a beginner user without any experience using it. For more advanced users, the wizards make it possible to boost this performance by manually fine-tuning the parameters and testing multiple configurations.

The face recognition algorithm applied in the use case has been selected due to its high performance, accuracy and popularity; resulting in a trustworthy algorithm. A comparison with other algorithms is shown in Table 10.4. HOG algorithm stands out as the one with the higher detection rate, and it has been shown to work well with subsequent algorithms withing a complex task (Dalal et al., 2005; Huang et al., 2012; Dadi et al., 2016).

10.5.1 Limitations

The proposed system assumes that the cameras used for crowd detection are located in relevant locations with an angle to capture pedestrians—a camera facing a wall could confuse the classifier and distort the heatmaps. Furthermore, the model trained in this use case is designed to emulate the

TABLE 10.4

Comparison of Different Face Recognition Algorithms
(Adouani et al., 2019)

		Methods		
		HAAR	**HOG**	**LBP**
Metrics	Detected frames	653,484	772,954	503,516
	Detected faces	652,451	772,954	503,350
	TPR (%)	78.23	92.68	60.37
	FNR (%)	21.76	7.31	39.64

process performed by the most basic user. If a model wants to be used in a real-world scenario, it will need to be fine-tuned by a data scientist.

10.6 Conclusion[1]

The proposed model makes use of advanced machine learning algorithms for face recognition and an ensemble learning method that successfully predicts the present and future location of crowds within cities, as evidenced by the results. The developed platform is the cornerstone of Smart Territory development, enabling any user to achieve equivalent results seamlessly and to implement them in real-life scenarios, facilitating the entire development process. Deepint.net made the creation of an advanced crowd detection dashboard possible and greatly reduced the development time—a few working days as opposed to the typical months of R&D for creating a system from the ground up. Most methods are based on well-established Python libraries, providing a high degree of reliability to any developed system.

The platform has a much greater potential than specialised tools with regards to providing strong, resilient models to a wider public; without dropping in performance. As the number of smart cities around the world continues to increase, such advancements are more needed than ever. Deepint.net is capable of reducing the costs associated with maintenance and resource management in smart territories while accelerating their development.

Current technological advantages are changing our cities from many different perspectives, and an efficient data management model is required. Such changes constitute a key challenge to any smart city, and they constantly make platforms become obsolete and full of limitations. As a result,

---

[1] This chapter, with permission from the copyright holder, is a reproduced version of the following journal article: Garcia-Retuerta, D., Chamoso, P., Hernández, G., Guzmán, A.S.R., Yigitcanlar, T., & Corchado, J.M. (2021). An efficient management platform for developing smart cities: Solution for real-time and future crowd detection. *Electronics*, 10(7), 765.

deepint.net and any other such platform must include constant upgrades and incorporate new, promising ideas and algorithms.

The concept of 'City-as-a-platform' has been successfully introduced and is driving the development of smart cities, efficient in the use of data and boosting the development of smart applications. In this sense, it is not sufficient to have mechanisms for data processing and solution development; it is necessary to have platforms that allow for the construction of these systems in an efficient, fast and secure way. The availability of 'open-data' platforms, sensors capable of providing secure and continuous data and the demand for solutions for each of the verticals identified by the many smart cities under development. It seems clear that what impedes municipal governments from undergoing a definitive and disruptive transformation is the use of inappropriate platforms. This hindrance has been addressed in this chapter, by demonstrating that deepint.net is a platform with great potential for information capture, visualisation, management, modelling and representation. Municipal governance implies a systematic and definitive boost in the use of technologies such as those presented in this chapter. The presented user-friendly platform employs AI to manage data originating from IoT architectures.

References

Adouani, A., Henia, W.M.B., & Lachiri, Z. (2019, March). Comparison of Haar-like, HOG and LBP approaches for face detection in video sequences. In *Proceedings of 2019 16th International Multi-Conference on Systems, Signals & Devices*, IEEE.

Arasteh, H., Hosseinnezhad, V., Loia, V., Tommasetti, A., Troisi, O., Shafie-khah, M., & Siano, P. (2016). Iot-based smart cities: A survey. In *Proceedings of 2016 IEEE 16th International Conference on Environment and Electrical Engineering (EEEIC)*. IEEE.

Basner, M., Babisch, W., Davis, A., Brink, M., Clark, C., Janssen, S., & Stansfeld, S. (2014). Auditory and non-auditory effects of noise on health. *The Lancet, 383*(9925), 1325–1332.

Briones, A.G., Chamoso, P., Rivas, A., Rodríguez, S., De La Prieta, F., Prieto, J., & Corchado, J.M. (2018). Use of gamification techniques to encourage garbage recycling. a smart city approach. In *Proceedings of International Conference on Knowledge Management in Organizations*, Springer, Cham.

Cardullo, P., & Kitchin, R. (2019). Smart urbanism and smart citizenship: The neoliberal logic of 'citizen-focused'smart cities in Europe. *Environment and Planning C: Politics and Space, 37*(5), 813–830.

Chamoso, P., González-Briones, A., De La Prieta, F., Venyagamoorthy, G.K., & Corchado, J.M. (2020). Smart city as a distributed platform: Toward a system for citizen-oriented management. *Computer Communications, 152*, 323–332.

Chamoso, P., González-Briones, A., Rivas, A., Bueno De Mata, F., & Corchado, J.M. (2018a). The use of drones in Spain: Towards a platform for controlling UAVs in urban environments. *Sensors, 18*(5), 1416.

Chamoso, P., González-Briones, A., Rodríguez, S., & Corchado, J.M. (2018b). Tendencies of technologies and platforms in smart cities: A state-of-the-art review. *Wireless Communications and Mobile Computing*, 1–17.

Chatterjee, S., Kar, A.K., & Gupta, M.P. (2018). Success of IoT in smart cities of India: An empirical analysis. *Government Information Quarterly, 35*(3), 349–361.

Chen, T., & Guestrin, C. (2016). Xgboost: A scalable tree boosting system. In *Proceedings of the 22nd acm sigkdd international conference on knowledge discovery and data mining*.

Corchado, J.M., Chamoso, P., Hernández, G., Gutierrez, A.S.R., Camacho, A.R., González-Briones, A., & Omatu, S. (2021). Deepint. net: A rapid deployment platform for smart territories. *Sensors, 21*(1), 236; https://doi.org/10.3390/s21010236

Dadi, H.S., & Pillutla, G.M. (2016). Improved face recognition rate using HOG features and SVM classifier. *IOSR Journal of Electronics and Communication Engineering, 11*(04), 34–44.

Dalal, N., & Triggs, B. (2005). Histograms of oriented gradients for human detection. In *Proceedings of EEE computer society conference on computer vision and pattern recognition (CVPR'05)*. IEEE.

Elmaghraby, A.S., & Losavio, M.M. (2014). Cyber security challenges in Smart Cities: Safety, security and privacy. *Journal of Advanced Research, 5*(4), 491–497.

Enayet, A., Razzaque, M.A., Hassan, M.M., Alamri, A., & Fortino, G. (2018). A mobility-aware optimal resource allocation architecture for big data task execution on mobile cloud in smart cities. *IEEE Communications Magazine, 56*(2), 110–117.

Ferraris, A., Erhardt, N., & Bresciani, S. (2019). Ambidextrous work in smart city project alliances: Unpacking the role of human resource management systems. *The International Journal of Human Resource Management, 30*(4), 680–701.

García, M., Eizaguirre, S., & Pradel, M. (2015). Social innovation and creativity in cities: A socially inclusive governance approach in two peripheral spaces of Barcelona. *City, Culture and Society, 6*(4), 93–100.

González García, C., Núñez Valdéz, E.R., García Díaz, V., Pelayo García-Bustelo, B.C., & Cueva Lovelle, J.M. (2019). A review of artificial intelligence in the internet of things. *International Journal of Interactive Multimedia and Artificial Intelligence, 5*.

González-Briones, A., Castellanos-Garzón, J.A., Mezquita Martín, Y., Prieto, J., & Corchado, J.M. (2018a). A framework for knowledge discovery from wireless sensor networks in rural environments: A crop irrigation systems case study. *Wireless Communications and Mobile Computing*, 1–14.

González-Briones, A., Chamoso, P., De La Prieta, F., Demazeau, Y., & Corchado, J.M. (2018b). Agreement technologies for energy optimization at home. *Sensors, 18*(5), 1633.

González-Briones, A., De La Prieta, F., Mohamad, M.S., Omatu, S., & Corchado, J.M. (2018c). Multi-agent systems applications in energy optimization problems: A state-of-the-art review. *Energies, 11*(8), 1928.

González-Briones, A., Prieto, J., Corchado, J.M., & Demazeau, Y. (2018d). EnerVMAS: virtual agent organizations to optimize energy consumption using intelligent temperature calibration. In *International Conference on Hybrid Artificial Intelligence Systems*, Springer.

González-Briones, A., Prieto, J., De La Prieta, F., Herrera-Viedma, E., & Corchado, J.M. (2018e). Energy optimization using a case-based reasoning strategy. *Sensors, 18*(3), 865.

González-Briones, P., Chamoso, H.Y., & Corchado, J.M. (2018f). Greenvmas: Virtual organization based platform for heating greenhouses using waste energy from power plants. *Sensors, 18*(3), 861–897.

Hashim Raza Bukhari, S., Siraj, S., & Husain Rehmani, M. (2018). Wireless sensor networks in smart cities: Applications of channel bonding to meet data communication requirements. *Transportation and Power Grid in Smart Cities: Communication Networks and Services,* 247–268, https://doi.org/10.1002/9781119360124.ch9.

Huang, G.B., Mattar, M., Berg, T., & Learned-Miller, E. (2008, October). Labeled faces in the wild: A database for studying face recognition in unconstrained environments. In *Workshop on faces in 'Real-LifeReal-LifeImages: detection, alignment, and recognition.*

Huang, G., Ramesh, M., Berg, T., & Learned-Miller, E. (2007). Faces in the wild: A database for studying face recognition in unconstrained environments. *Technical Report,* 07–49.

Huang, D., Wang, P., & Niyato, D. (2012). A dynamic offloading algorithm for mobile computing. *IEEE Transactions on Wireless Communications, 11*(6), 1991–1995.

Khan, J.S., Jibb, L.A., Busse, J.W., Gilron, I., Choi, S., Paul, J.E., McGillion, M., Mackey, S., Buckley, D.N., Lee, S.F., & Devereaux, P.J. (2019). Electronic versus traditional data collection: A multicenter randomized controlled perioperative pain trial. *Canadian Journal of Pain, 3*(2), 16–25.

Laufs, J., Borrion, H., & Bradford, B. (2020). Security and the smart city: A systematic review. *Sustainable Cities and Society, 55,* 102023.

Lercher, P., Evans, G.W., & Meis, M. (2003). Ambient noise and cognitive processes among primary schoolchildren. *Environment and Behavior, 35*(6), 725–735.

Liang, W., Luo, S., Zhao, G., & Wu, H. (2020). Predicting hard rock pillar stability using GBDT, XGBoost, and LightGBM algorithms. *Mathematics, 8*(5), 765.

Liu, J., & Liu, Z. (2019). A survey on security verification of blockchain smart contracts. *IEEE Access, 7,* 77894–77904.

O'Dwyer, E., Pan, I., Acha, S., & Shah, N. (2019). Smart energy systems for sustainable smart cities: Current developments, trends and future directions. *Applied Energy, 237,* 581–597.

Paskaleva, K.A. (2011). The smart city: A nexus for open innovation? *Intelligent Buildings International, 3*(3), 153–171.

Peris-Ortiz, M., Bennett, D.R., & Yábar, D.P.B. (2017). Sustainable smart cities. In *Innovation, Technology, and Knowledge Management,* Springer International Publishing Switzerland, Cham.

Potdar, V., Batool, S., & Krishna, A. (2018). Risks and challenges of adopting electric vehicles in smart cities. In *Smart Cities,* Springer, Cham.

Ramaprasad, A., Sánchez-Ortiz, A., & Syn, T. (2017). A unified definition of a smart city. In *International Conference on Electronic Government* (pp. 13–24). Springer, Cham.

Reddy, K.J., Menon, K.R., & Thattil, A. (2018). Academic stress and its sources among university students. *Biomedical and Pharmacology Journal, 11*(1), 531–537.

Repette, P., Sabatini-Marques, J., Yigitcanlar, T., Sell, D., & Costa, E. (2021). The evolution of City-as-a-platform: Smart urban development governance with collective knowledge-based platform urbanism. *Land, 10*(1), 33. https://doi.org/10.3390/land10010033

Rivas, A., Chamoso, P., González-Briones, A., & Corchado, J.M. (2018). Detection of cattle using drones and convolutional neural networks. *Sensors, 18*(7), 2048.

Sandulli, F.D., Ferraris, A., & Bresciani, S. (2017). How to select the right public partner in smart city projects. *R&D Management, 47*(4), 607–619.

Toutouh, J., & Alba, E. (2017). Parallel multi-objective metaheuristics for smart communications in vehicular networks. *Soft Computing, 21*(8), 1949–1961.

Toutouh, J., & Alba, E. (2018). A swarm algorithm for collaborative traffic in vehicular networks. *Vehicular Communications, 12*, 127–137.

Trimberger, S.M.S. (2018). Three ages of FPGAs: A retrospective on The first thirty years of FPGA technology: This paper reflects on how Moore's law has driven The design of FPGAs through three epochs: The age of invention, The age of expansion, and The age of accumulation. *IEEE Solid-State Circuits Magazine, 10*(2), 16–29.

Trindade, E.P., Hinnig, M.P.F., Moreira da Costa, E., Marques, J.S., Bastos, R.C., & Yigitcanlar, T. (2017). Sustainable development of smart cities: A systematic review of the literature. *Journal of Open Innovation: Technology, Market, and Complexity, 3*(3), 11.

Yigitcanlar, T., Kankanamge, N., Regona, M., Maldonado, A., Rowan, B., Ryu, A., & Li, R.Y.M. (2020). Artificial intelligence technologies and related urban planning and development concepts: How are they perceived and utilized in Australia? *Journal of Open Innovation: Technology, Market, and Complexity, 6*(4), 187.

11

City-as-a-Platform

11.1 Introduction

Since the 1990s, with the beginning of the popularisation of internet use, the rapid expansion of technology has changed the social, political, economic, environmental, and legal scenarios of the world in which we live, with repercussions and changes that directly impact cities urban development (Chang et al., 2018). This has led many governments focusing on online planning and incorporating online platforms for citizen participation in the local or urban decision-making process (Yigitcanlar et al., 2006). The greater connectivity between people, organisations and governments through the internet—where it is combined with the exponential generation of data, due to Internet-of-Things (IoT), big data, ubiquitous technologies, location-based services, augmented reality (AR), and artificial intelligence (AI) (Yigitcanlar et al., 2020)—increases the complexity of cities but also provides new development perspectives, with real possibilities of transforming them into more human, intelligent, and sustainable places (Anttiroiko, 2016; Yigitcanlar et al., 2015).

In a recent systematic review of the literature on the contributions and risks of AI for building smart cities, it was emphasised how new technologies can support governments in governance and city planning with the participation of society in urban decision-making processes and public policies definition (Yigitcanlar et al., 2020). The current model of thinking about cities simply as physical places governed by a conventional, closed, and bureaucratic administrative structure is under great pressure to evolve (Bollier, 2016), as it does not present itself as a compatible option with the necessary response speed for cities' economic development, the society's desire for participation, and the required transparency and accountability for governments (Gabriel, 2017).

Contemporary models of public governance advocate the creation of public value through articulated initiatives involving governments and society. In these, one of the main roles of the government is to provide information and services online, to allow and encourage popular participation in decision-making and the definition of public policies. The opening up of data and the mobilisation of collective knowledge is becoming more important to enable the co-creation of sustainable solutions for cities [9]. It is in this context that

DOI: 10.1201/9781003278986-14

the concept of City-as-a-Platform (CaaP) emerges, which is associated with the government's opening movement and with the application of digital technologies to expand the possibilities of co-production of public services (Walravens, 2011; Bollier, 2016). CaaP is portrayed in the literature as the technological and political infrastructure that allows society to play a direct and broader role in the life of cities. Digital technologies are applied to promote an open space for the collaboration and democratisation of information and knowledge, requiring consensual, transparent, responsive, efficient, effective, equitable, and inclusive governance (Meijer & Bolívar, 2016). Moreover, the development and popularity of CaaP has led to a new urbanism approach: So-called 'platform urbanism' (Van der Graaf & Ballon, 2019).

In this work, platformisation—platform urbanism in general and CaaP in particular—is conceptualised as a model of sociotechnical governance supported by digital architecture technologies with open and modular standards that provide the connection between government and society for the co-creation of services and policies of high public value.

With the advancement of digital technologies, new models of value production emerge, culminating recently in the perspective of business models based on platforms. This model advocates the feasibility of new flows of value production, bringing actors together in multilateral arrangements, promoting the addition of value through the interaction between these parties (O'Reilly, 2011). The discussion of platform-based models received even more attention with the essays on the economic perspective of platforms, and Jean Tirole was awarded the Nobel Memorial Prize in Economic Sciences in 2014 for his work on platformisation (Rochet & Tirole, 2003). In the context of cities, digital platforms are treated as tools for enabling open and participatory urban governance models (Zhuang et al., 2019). The opening of public administration to citizens marks the transition from party politics to representative governance, from centralised management to public and democratic engagement, aiming at promoting the community to participate in the construction of their own cities (Anttiroiko, 2016; Bollier, 2016; Gil-Garcia et al., 2016; Pereira et al., 2018). As a result, digital platforms support new ways of interacting in communities and through mediated co-creation (De Reuver et al., 2018; Harmaala, 2015).

According to (Barns, 2018), cities are living organisms, and their prosperity is based on their resilience and in their ability to adapt to changes, and emerging technologies can be used as allies in urban planning. In this sense, the more fluid and synergistic interaction between the four assets that make up cities—(a) people, (b) data, (c) infrastructure, and (d) technology—is considered essential and desirable (Bollier, 2016). The openness of the government and the engagement of the population in the discussion of local needs and the co-production of public policies is described in the literature as a promising way to make cities more humane, intelligent, and sustainable and for more inclusive economic and social development (Anttiroiko, 2016; Bollier, 2016; O'Reilly, 2011; Yigitcanlar, 2010).

Smart governance is the main challenge for smart city initiatives, which is an emerging field of research and practice (Chourabi et al., 2012; Yigitcanlar et al., 2020). In this sense, this chapter aims to address the following question: "How can platform urbanism support local governance efforts in the development of smarter cities?" Through an integrative review of articles published in the last ten years, the evolution of the concept of City-as-a-Platform was analysed, as well as its relationship with knowledge-based development, making it possible to identify elements that can categorise different levels of cities as platforms (Anttiroiko et al., 2014; Caprotti & Liu, 2019; Graham, 2020). In addition, the main opportunities and challenges identified in the literature for the realisation of the transformative and disruptive impact on the government and society of the platform model are presented.

11.2 Methodology

Integrative reviews provide a comprehensive view on a given research topic, including several theoretical and experimental data sources and types of publications, which contribute to a systemic understanding of the topic of interest (Whittemore & Knafl, 2005). Nowadays, the vast availability of publications in the computerised databases makes the selection of journal articles that have high scientific quality and that are relevant to the research complex and challenging. The application of integrative review methodologies ensures greater rigor in the bibliographic selection and analysis process, enabling the researcher to better understand and clarify the state of the art in relation to the researched topic. In this work, a combination of the methods was used (Whittemore & Knafl, 2005; Botelho, 2011), which prescribe a set of pre-defined steps for carrying out an integrative literature review.

The research question that guided the definition of terms to compose the Boolean search equation (Table 11.1) in the databases was: "How can the use

TABLE 11.1

Boolean Search Equations

Search no	Boolean Search Equations
1st search	TITLE-ABS-KEY ("smart cit*" OR "future cit*" OR "intelligent cit*" OR "digital cit*" AND governance OR "e-governance" OR "digital governance" OR "smart governance" AND platform OR "e-platform" OR "online platform*" OR "platformization" OR "mobile platform*") AND (LIMIT-TO (DOCTYPE, "ar") OR LIMIT-TO (DOCTYPE, "re")) AND (LIMIT-TO (LANGUAGE, "English"))
2nd search	TITLE-ABS-KEY ("smart cit*" OR "future cit*" OR "intelligent cit*" OR "digital cit*" AND "collective intelligence" OR "innovation" OR "co-creation" AND "systematic review" OR "review") AND DOCTYPE (re) AND PUBYEAR > 2009 AND PUBYEAR < 2021

TABLE 11.2

Eligibility Criteria

Inclusion Criteria	Exclusion Criteria
• Publication date: Published between 2010 and 2020 • Publication type: Journal research and review articles • Publication focus: Topics that align well with the identified research aim	• Language: Other than English language journal articles • Access: Articles not available online and full-text

of online platforms by local governments support urban governance for the development of smarter cities?" The first literature review was carried out in May 2020, and due to the need to complement the research of the journal articles found in the first survey, a second search was carried out in June 2020, including new terms. Table 11.1 shows the Boolean equations that guided the searches. Table 11.2 illustrates the eligibility criteria (inclusion and exclusion) applied in both databases searches. Figure 11.1 illustrates the increase in publications on the topic in the Scopus database in the first search performed, corroborating the adequacy of the defined investigation period.

The bases consulted were Scopus, Web of Science, and Science Direct, and to evaluate the most cited articles and authors, we used the computational tool Publish or Perish, which retrieves and analyses academic citations from various data sources and presents them by the total number of articles and the number of citations, in addition to other metrics. The research and review articles found by applying the aforementioned Boolean equations were previously selected based on their titles, according to Table 11.3. We included publications that brought a direct link to the researched topic or that were relevant to the research. The most suitable articles for the research were

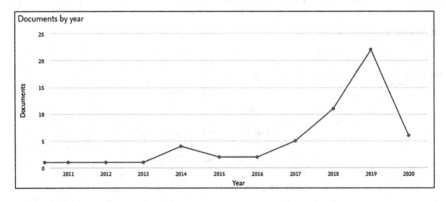

FIGURE 11.1

Number of publications in relation to the Boolean research equation over time.

TABLE 11.3

Source and Number of Articles Selected for Review

Criteria for Selection	Researched Database Results					
	Scopus		Science Direct		Web of Science	
	1st Search	2nd Search	1st Search	2nd Search	1st Search	2nd Search
Articles published between 2010 and 2020	118	127	8	8	85	90
Research and review articles only	41	55	7	7	53	58
Pre-selected articles by title, except duplicates	34	36	7	7	37	37
Final selection of articles for review	30					

selected based on the evaluation of the keywords and the abstracts reading. Recent publications were prioritised, with exceptions for the reference literature on the topic.

In total, 30 articles were selected for this integrative review, as shown in Table 11.4, which included theoretical and experimental studies. Some citations found in the articles read, due to their relevance to the topic, as well as seminal articles, were included in the research. Grey literature produced by research institutions and government, in electronic format not controlled by scientific or commercial editors, due to their connection with the theme or originality, were also incorporated into the study (Table 11.5).

The data extraction happened from the careful reading of the selected publications. In order to help the understanding of the articles, a matrix was elaborated with the important aspects raised in each theoretical framework, trying to create topics or categories that could compose the research structure. Matrices displays were used to order, summarise, and categorise the information, which allows a more complete interpretation, comparison, as well as evidence synthesis (Whittemore & Knafl, 2005). In Section 11.3.1, the evolution of the concept of City-as-a-Platform is analysed, as well as its relationship with knowledge-based development, making it possible to identify elements that can categorise different levels of cities as platforms. To exemplify the proposed categorisation, we brought some commercial online engagement platforms that bring communities and local governments together, and also, governments that have developed their own city platforms. In both cases, the objectives are nearly the same: To bring together the public and city leaders to improve and innovate together, making use of available government open data.

The main opportunities and challenges identified in the literature for the realisation of the transformative and disruptive impact on the government and society of the platform model are presented in the following section.

TABLE 11.4

Selected Journal Articles for Review

#	Author	Year	Title	Journal
1	Borghys, Van Der Graaf, Walravens, and Van Compernolle	2020	Multi-stakeholder innovation in smart city discourse: Quadruple helix thinking in the age of "platforms"	*Frontiers in Sustainable Cities*
2	Chamoso, González-Briones, De La Prieta, Venyagamoorthy, and Corchado	2020	Smart city as a distributed platform: Toward a system for citizen-oriented management	*Computer Communications*
3	Panori, Kakderi, Komninos, Fellnhofer, Reid, and Mora	2020	Smart systems of innovation for smart places: Challenges in deploying digital platforms for co-creation and data-intelligence	*Lan Use Policy*
4	Richardson	2020	Coordinating the city: platforms as flexible spatial arrangements	*Urban Geography*
5	Sabatini-Marques, Yigitcanlar, Schreiner, Wittmann, Sotto, and Inkinen	2020	Strategizing smart, sustainable, and knowledge-based development of cities: Insights from Florianópolis, Brazil	*Sustainability*
6	Stehlin, Hodson and McMeekin	2020	Platform mobilities and the production of urban space: Toward a typology of platformization trajectories	*Environment and Planning A: Economy and Space*
7	Törnberg and Uitermark	2020	Complex control and the governmentality of digital platforms	*Frontiers in Sustainable Cities*
8	Van Dijck	2020	Governing digital societies: Private platforms, public values	*Computer Law & Security Review*
9	Yigitcanlar and Cugurullo	2020	The sustainability of artificial intelligence: An urbanistic viewpoint from the lens of smart and sustainable cities	*Sustainability*
10	Yigitcanlar, Kankanamge, and Vella	2021	How are smart city concepts and technologies perceived and utilized? A systematic geo-twitter analysis of smart cities in Australia	*Journal of Urban Technology*
11	Bouzguenda, Alalouch, and Fava	2019	Towards smart sustainable cities: A review of the role digital citizen participation could play in advancing social sustainability	*Sustainable Cities and Society*

(Continued)

TABLE 11.4 *(Continued)*

Selected Journal Articles for Review

#	Author	Year	Title	Journal
12	Gil, Cortés-Cediel and Cantador	2019	Citizen participation and the rise of digital media platforms in smart governance and smart cities	Int. Journal of E-Planning Research (IJEPR)
13	Ismagilova, Hughes, Dwivedi and Raman	2019	Advances in research: An information systems perspective	Int. Journal of Information Management
14	Meijer, Lips and Chen	2019	A new paradigm for understanding urban governance in an information age	Frontiers in Sustainable Cities
15	Park	2019	Strategy for Building Smart City-as-a-Platform of the 4th Industrial Revolution	Journal of Digital Convergence
16	Rotta, Sell, dos Santos Pacheco and Yigitcanlar	2019	Digital commons and citizen coproduction in smart cities: Assessment of Brazilian municipal e-government platforms	Energies
17	Barns	2018	Smart cities and urban data platforms: Designing interfaces for smart governance	City, Culture and Society
18	Chang, Sabatini-Marques, Da Costa, Selig and Yigitcanlar	2018	Knowledge-based, smart and sustainable cities: A provocation for a conceptual framework	Journal of Open Innovation: Technology, Market, and Complexity
19	Gil-Garcia, Zhang and Puron-Cid	2016	Conceptualizing smartness in government: An integrative and multi-dimensional view	Government Information Quarterly
20	Mergel, Kleibrink and Sörvik	2018	Open data outcomes: U.S. cities between product and process innovation	Government Information Quarterly
21	Pereira, Parycek, Falco and Kleinhans	2018	Smart governance in the context of smart cities: A literature review	Information Polity

(Continued)

TABLE 11.4 (Continued)

Selected Journal Articles for Review

#	Author	Year	Title	Journal
22	Srivastava and Mostafavi	2018	Challenges and opportunities of crowdsourcing and participatory planning in developing infrastructure systems of smart cities	Infrastructures
23	Brown, Fishenden, Thompson and Venters	2017	Appraising the impact and role of platform models and government as a platform (GaaP) in UK Government public service reform: Towards a platform assessment framework	Government Information Quarterly
24	De Reuver, Sørensen and Basole	2018	The digital platform: a research agenda	Journal of Information Technology
25	Anttiroiko	2016	City-as-a-platform: towards citizen-centred platform governance	Sustainability
26	Meijer and Bolívar	2016	Governing the smart city: A review of the literature on smart urban governance	International Review of Administrative Sciences
27	Harmaala	2015	The sharing city as a platform for a more sustainable city environment?	International Journal of Environment and Health
28	Yigitcanlar and Dur	2013	Making space and place for knowledge communities: Lessons for Australian practice	Australasian Journal of Regional Studies
29	Paskaleva	2011	The smart city: a nexus for open innovation?	Intelligent Buildings Int.
30	O'Reilly	2010	Government as a platform	Innovations

TABLE 11.5

Selected Documents on Grey Literature

#	Author	Year	Title	Source
1	Bollier	2016	The city as platform: How digital networks are changing urban life and governance	The Aspen Institute
2	Ulrich, Marshment-Howell and Van Geest	2016	Open governance in the smart city	ICLEI (Global Network of Local Governments for Sustainability)
3	Chourabi, Nam, Walker, Gil-Garcia, Mellouli, Nahon, Pardo and Scholl	2012	Understanding smart cities: An integrative framework	45th Hawaii International Conference on System Sciences
4	Komninos, Schaffers and Pallot	2011	Developing a policy roadmap for smart cities and the future internet	eChallenges e-2011 Conference
5	Nam and Pardo	2011	Conceptualizing smart city with dimensions of the technology, people, and institutions	12th International Digital Government Research Conference
6	Walravens	2011	The City-as-a-Platform	15th International Conference on Intelligence in Next Generation Networks

11.3 Results

11.3.1 Knowledge-based Urban Development and Smart Cities

The relationship between urban development and knowledge emerged for the first time in 1995 (Knight, 1995), when researchers argued about the need for a new approach to the development of cities with a focus on development based on knowledge resources, which would provide the basis and foundation for sustainable development. The four pillars of knowledge-based urban development (KBUD) encompass the domains of economic, sociocultural, environmental, urban, and institutional development. It is a "new development paradigm of the knowledge era that aims to bring prosperity, to produce cities purposefully designed to encourage the production and circulation of knowledge, in an environmentally conserved, economically safe, socially just and well governed human environment" (Yigitcanlar & Dur, 2013).

In KBUD's conceptual framework, shown in Figure 11.2, economic development is associated with the transformation of individuals' technical knowledge, skills, and creativity into product and service innovations, which generate economic benefits for cities. In the aspect of socio-cultural development, there is an appreciation of social and human capital in the sense of

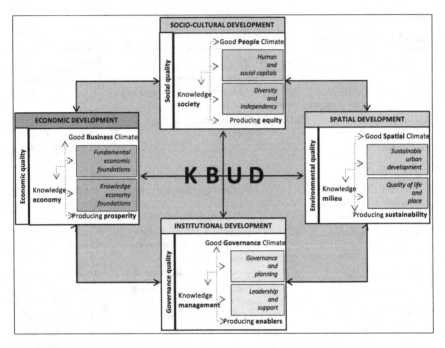

FIGURE 11.2
Knowledge-based urban development (KBUD) conceptual framework. (Adapted from Sabatini-Marques et al., 2020.)

creating a society where knowledge can be generated, distributed, and used for the common good. KBUD's perspective for environmental and urban development is related to making urban development compatible with environmental preservation, in order to promote and guarantee a better quality of life in cities, now and for the next generations. Finally, institutional development represents the governance to be exercised by governments to lead, unite, and orchestrate the main actors and information that, together, will contribute to the strategic planning and formation of cities (Yigitcanlar & Dur, 2013).

Eight interrelated aspects can positively influence the development of cities and make them smarter, namely, governance, people or communities, natural environment, infrastructure, economy, technology, management, and politics, with emphasis on the fundamental role of technology for the success of all other aspects (Chourabi et al., 2012). Considering a combination of knowledge and technology, smart cities are a space with knowledge-intensive activities and based on innovation, where there are integrated social cooperation routines that allow knowledge to be acquired and adapted, supported by an information and communication infrastructure capable of managing knowledge in public digital spaces to solve city problems (Komninos et al., 2011; Sabatini-Marques et al., 2020).

A city is smart when it "invests in its human and social capital in conjunction with the communication and information infrastructure, to fuel sustainable economic growth and improve the population's quality of life, for example through the proper management of natural resources and participatory governance" (Caragliu et al., 2009). Although there is no single meaning for smart cities that is specific and widely recognised in academia, the literature on smart cities has gradually been configured in a balance between social intelligence and digital technologies. Smart cities are not just a network of sensors and data and communication connections (D'Amico et al., 2020), but mainly those where citizens are interested in engaging and collaborating to define guidelines for the planning and functioning of cities, in order to add public value to a common good, becoming an essential part of the process (Yigitcanlar et al., 2020).

Technology, despite being increasingly evolved, disseminated, and accessible to the population, does not replace human responsibility in the planning and governance process of cities (Yigitcanlar, 2016). However, it can assist in solving complex problems, by providing greater interactivity, quality, and efficiency in urban services, reducing costs and improving connections between governments and society (Gil et al., 2019). Therefore, smart cities are supported by a combination of technological infrastructure, human skills, knowledge management, and innovation (Komninos, 2009).

The main characteristics of smart cities are: (a) Infrastructure network, which allows good connectivity; (b) Strategic vision, to develop the city's competitiveness through new technologies and the involvement of multiple actors; and (c) Adoption of a sustainable and inclusive urban development approach that emphasises social capital in urban development (Paskaleva, 2019). Open innovation is a new paradigm for building smart cities, where governments and software developers take advantage of the experience, skills, and knowledge of citizens to develop digital services that are relevant to users of the urban environment (Komninos, 2009; Paskaleva, 2019). The technology supports open innovation and eliminates boundaries between companies, society, and government, enabling the transfer of innovation into and out of the urban environment, driving research and the development of partnerships.

Three factors enable the formation of smart cities—technology (hardware and software infrastructures), people (creativity, diversity, and education), and institution (governance and politics) (Park, 2019). Technologies are applied in smart cities to boost social interaction and bring society closer in collaborative networks. In the scope of governance, digital platforms enable the creation of ecosystems of urban innovation that make cities increasingly intelligent, human, and sustainable (Paskaleva, 2011; Park, 2019). According to Nam and Pardo (2011), investments in human and social capital, added to the adequate technological infrastructure and intelligent governance, can boost the sustainable growth of cities. Good governance to manage and mediate the network of public and private actors, with the definition of responsibilities of the parties involved and the establishment of regulatory policies is the main challenge of smart cities initiatives (Chourabi et al., 2012), as will be presented in the next section.

11.3.2 Smart Urban Governance

The intelligence of a city is related to its ability to attract and mobilise human capital in collaborations through information and communication technology (ICT) tools (Yigitcanlar et al., 2020). Governance is not a purely technological issue but rather a complex process of institutional change of a sociotechnical nature (Meijer & Bolivar, 2006). Based on a systematic review of the literature (Meijer & Bolivar, 2006), the authors admit that city governance is a strong collaboration network between government and stakeholders. In this sense, they understand governance from two perspectives: as a result, and also as a process.

As a result, governance focuses on the content of government actions, which should support the research and development of technology and public services that can improve citizens' quality of life. The smart cities governance seen as a process implies stakeholder participation and engagement in the production of the common good, with the exploration of collective intelligence, experiences, and knowledge (Meijer & Bolivar, 2006; Yigitcanlar et al., 2019). The governance process involves the creation of rules and the coordination of political decision-making that encompasses different actors, social groups, and institutions in a specific context, to achieve objectives discussed and defined collectively in fragmented and complex environments (Tasan-Kok & Vranken, 2011). Urban governance is a means to achieve integrated urban development, and it can be achieved through an integrated approach that combines: (a) The existence of a multidimensional plan that considers ecological, social, cultural, and organisational aspects = objective; (b) Forms of communication between different levels of structured and continuous governance = communication; (c) Bottom–up participation that produces relevant information = popular engagement and (d) Political agenda that supports integrated urban development at different levels (local, regional, and national) = integration (Tasan-Kok & Vranken, 2011).

Assuming the idea of governance as a sociotechnical process, under the social aspect, smart city governance allows citizens to articulate their interests, measure their differences, and exercise their rights and duties in decision-making, in a responsibility shared with the government, with the aim of improving life in cities (Gil et al., 2019). From a technical point of view, governance aims to establish an environment with technological and legal infrastructure that allows the connection between government and society. In this sense, the digital transformation is changing governance models in a disruptive way (Gil et al., 2019). At the same time that new technologies have increased the complexity of cities, they have provided new ways for actors involved in urban development to organise, demand, and offer solutions (Ulrich et al., 2016).

The consolidation of the web gave rise to e-governance and enabled new means of government interaction with citizens and companies and making government internal operations more agile (O'Reilly 2011; Gil et al., 2019). A wide range of electronic services have been offered by the government in an increasing way in recent years for citizens (G2C—'government to citizens'), companies (G2B—'government to business'), and governments (G2G—'government to government'). Conversely, it is also allowing access for citizens and companies to the government and among themselves, in technological options for C2G, B2G, and B2C interaction (Gil et al., 2019).

The introduction of technological tools that enable open and massive collaboration in the urban ecosystem at a low cost with the objective of solving complex problems in cities with the contribution of collective knowledge is known as smart cities open governance (Meijer et al., 2019). The authors emphasise that traditional governance paradigms, with government as the protagonist, are no longer applicable to collective initiatives enabled by technology, in which complex problems can be more effectively solved by the digitally connected actors in the urban ecosystem, in more horizontal and collaborative partnerships with the government. In this context, the network connections provided by technology can change the government's roles as solely responsible for decisions about the future of cities, transforming citizens into co-creators and co-responsible for urban development, as a third driving force, public and private (Bollier, 2016).

Open governance in smart cities should be based on three pillars: (a) Open data—where information is considered a collective asset, which is worth collecting, using, preserving, and sharing; (b) Data quality—which must be reliable; and (c) Open participation—which has in collective knowledge a valuable asset, responsible for improving the effectiveness of public policies and the results of decision-making processes in favour of increasing the quality of life in cities (Meijer et al., 2019). The city's open government structure is an essential requirement of smart cities, being composed of open data, open governance, open programs and services, and open involvement, which can be enabled through digital platforms that bring together corporate governance (Anttiroiko, 2016).

The idea of CaaP presents itself as the technological and political infrastructure that allows society (citizens, companies, organised groups) to play a direct and larger role in the life of cities, hence realising platform urbanism. The platforms created by governments are an open space for the collaboration and democratisation of information and knowledge that, while providing channels for cooperation and participation, demand governance that is consensus-oriented, transparent, responsive, efficient, effective, equitable, and inclusive (Tasan-Kok & Vranken, 2011)

Urban governance through platforms is characterised by being open, collaborative, intelligent, and electronic (Hwang, 2020). This governance can be evolutionary depending on the desire and the need for transformation and government opening. Different levels of governance are directly related to the levels of government opening, which can range from e-government as a simple information channel and online service provision, through enabling social participation via crowdsourcing, reaching a radical public data opening for the development of innovative applications that improve the quality of life in cities [11,40]. This theme will be further discussed in this chapter and, below, a brief description of the concept of digital e-government platforms is presented.

11.3.3 Digital E-government Platforms

The term 'Government-as-a-Platform' (GaaP) was coined for the first time in 2010 by Tim O'Reilly, based on the understanding that government should position itself as a facilitator and manager of its interactions with society, acting as the provider of a platform, where citizens would co-produce innovative solutions for the government derived from their experience, knowledge, and collective intelligence (O'Reilly, 2011).

O'Reilly (2011) proposed a change in the government's view as the sole provider of services to society, with centralised control of proposals and actions, for a government that would allow, through electronic platforms, the involvement of society in proposing services and public policies in an environment of digital commons. The government as a platform is based on seven premises (O'Reilly, 2011):

- Open platforms: the adoption of open-source software platforms and open data structures, allowing the combination of products and services that are oriented to meet the current demands of society;
- Autonomy: Offer participants ways to create, generate, implement, or produce new content, without additional help or information from the platform's original creators
- Participatory design, with clear rules and interoperable systems architecture, with an emphasis on standardisation, modularity, and component reuse, which facilitates the assembly line of new applications;
- Open mind: The best ideas will not necessarily come from the creators of the platform, but from those who break the rules (hackers), combining data in an unexpected and creative way to make useful mashups for users;
- Exploring user behaviour: Data mining can be applied to get to know users' interests and extract from their participation new ways to boost the creation of services that meet their demands;
- Agile development: Reduction of barriers to experimentation, embracing failure, experimentation, and iteration in real-time, continuously improving applications, without worrying about having perpetual beta versions. Platform thinking is an antidote to complete

specifications, as the cost of experimentation is reduced, and it is possible to discard products and services that do not suit users;

- Leadership by example: Building platforms with remarkable resources and making available a set of applications that allow developers to add value to the platform's ecosystem.

Digital platforms are a new business model driven by ICT. The internet is responsible for connecting people, companies, and governments, and for providing a rich database on servers and in the clouds, and it has been also providing the development of multilateral networked arrangements that maximise the approximation between producers and consumers and the generation of value through interaction between these parts (Rochet & Tirole, 2003; Stehlin et al., 2020). O'Reilly's idea aligns, to a certain extent, with the performance of large organisations in this fourth era of innovation that, in the face of the inability to innovate quickly due to their rigid and complex organisational structures, seek partnerships with startups, which inject new knowledge, knowledge, and ideas and, through agile methodologies, propose innovations in the market (O'Reilly, 2011).

In city administration, government and society partnership is sought through the configuration of an ecosystem that combines technological infrastructure, made available by the platform owner (government), with a wide range of external participants (individuals and companies), who will have the opportunity to participate or even complement the platform with innovative services and applications, using data provided by the government (Brown et al., 2017).

Unlike the private sector, the motivating reasons for the adoption of platforms by the government go beyond economic issues, focusing on how to serve citizens well and how to develop public policies for the common good at a time characterised by rapid technological, social, and economical changes. It is not a matter of delegating its competence as a government to third parties but to develop ways of articulating new competences in society that are capable of guaranteeing a dynamic, agile, innovative, and efficient performance in the provision of services and definition of public policies, which meets citizen's expectations. Table 11.6 summarises the relationships between stakeholders— government, citizens, and companies—derived from the research of 13 digital media platforms for e-governance and smart city initiatives (Gil et al., 2009).

Themes such as e-government and innovation are being connected to urban governance to develop approaches that can make cities smarter (Nam & Pardo, 2011; Rotta et al., 2019). Two Finnish cities adopted open platforms to encourage citizens and stakeholder participation in the construction of urban economic renewal, showing that it is possible to reach economic development through open innovation (Anttiroiko, 2016). The platforms facilitated self-expression and interactive processes among participants, allowing for a more natural connection that evidenced the tendency to democratise innovation and participatory change in public governance (Anttiroiko, 2016).

TABLE 11.6

Electronic Governance by Platform Categories

Government to Citizens (G2C)	Citizens to Government (C2G)
• Provides information and online services to citizens efficiently and economically. • Strengthens the relationship between government and citizens through ICT. • G2C services allow citizens to access government documents (laws and regulations), carry out transactions (payment of municipal taxes and fees), and perform bureaucratic tasks (updating registration, changing address, requesting facilities and subsidies).	• Share distributed information or collaborate in the formulation of public policies through platforms. • Send messages directly to public administrators, conduct remote electronic voting, propose, discuss, and vote on public initiatives.
Government to Business (G2B)	**Government to Government (G2G)**
• Facilitates interaction between government and corporate bodies and private sector organisations. • Provides business, information, and advice on best e-commerce practices. • G2B services allow entrepreneurs to access information online about laws and regulations needed to comply with government regulatory requirements for their business (corporate tax reporting and government procurement).	• Facilitates non-commercial online interaction between government organisations, departments, and authorities with the aim of reducing costs, bureaucracy, excessive communication, and human resources.

Source: Adapted from Gil et al. (2019).

The term platform can be understood as a sociotechnical set that encompasses social elements (participation of stakeholders in the development of services and public policies that generate value to society) and technical elements (existence of an infrastructure information and communication technology with open, evolving, and adaptable standards of architecture) (De Reuver et al., 2018). According to the author, platforms that only broker different groups of users but do not offer an open-source base should not be considered digital platforms. An open data platform in smart cities contains semantically enriched databases, application development kits, and reusable application components aimed at web application developers (De Reuver et al., 2018). Therefore, in this work, CaaP is conceptualised as a model of sociotechnical governance supported by digital architecture technologies with open and modular standards that, through government regulation and moderation, provide the connection between government and society for the co-creation of services and policies of high public value.

The mentality of CaaP has profound repercussions for public administration, as it impacts all aspects of governance, power distribution, and democratic citizenship, enhancing the possibility of obtaining better results in all aspects of urban planning in cities—transport, energy, security, health, economic development, education, and culture, among others (Bollier, 2016).

11.4 City-as-a-Platform

11.4.1 The Evolution of City-as-a-Platform

The evolution of CaaP presupposes a new form of urban governance that is more open and participatory, with the use of technology in the organisation and intermediation of the collaboration of different actors in society. This smart governance refers to the introduction of technological tools that enable open and massive collaboration in the urban ecosystem, with the aim of solving complex problems in cities based on data sharing and contributions from collective knowledge (Meijer et al., 2019). In CaaP, the government's role in the provision of services and in the definition of public policies is no longer unique or protagonist but becomes the mediator or orchestrator, both in terms of data availability and the participation of actors that enable the cities ecosystem. Table 11.7 illustrates the evolution of institutional governance paradigms that still coexist and interact, showing open governance as an emerging form of massive and mediated collaboration between individuals and the government (Meijer et al., 2019).

Open data are the most valuable opportunities that governments can offer to cities. Internally to the government, data based on open and interoperable standards increases the inter- and trans-departmental cooperation of public administrations by sharing systems and information and, externally, with society, they signal transparency, responsibility, and trust in the government, in addition to allowing civic participation in the use of data, with the opportunity to innovate and improve the efficiency of the services provided

TABLE 11.7

Open Governance as a New Paradigm

Paradigm	Nature of the State	Focus	Emphasis	Resource Allocation Mechanism	Nature of the Service System	Value Base
Old Public Administration (OPA)	Unitary	Political system	Policy development and implementation	Hierarchy	Closed	Public sector ethos
New Public Administration (NPA)	Regulatory	Service organisation	Management of organisational resources and performance	Market	Calculated openness	Performance
New Public Governance (NPG)	Plural	Governance network	Negotiation of values, meaning, and relationships	Network	Negotiated openness	Constructed in networks
Open Governance (OG)	Open	Network of individuals	Massive collaborative production of information	Platform	Radical openness	Collaborative around a shared value

Source: Adapted from Meijer et al. (2019).

(Rochet & Tirole, 2003; Rotta et al., 2019). From the literature review, considering a triad composed of government, technology, and people for the formation of smart cities, two aspects are important to classify the evolution of CaaP—the forms of participation and engagement of individuals and the availability of data opened by governments. In our perception, the interaction between government and society in a CaaP can occur in different ways: (a) Simple provision of information and services; (b) Possibility of holding popular consultations; (c) Incorporation of citizens in a more effective participation processes; and (d) Provision of open data for developers and start-ups to create new technologies that will impact and transform the way people live in cities.

Based on these levels of interaction, on O'Reilly's premises of government as a platform (O'Reilly, 2011), on the spectrum of popular participation developed by the International Association for Popular Participation (IAP2, 2020) and on a large survey developed to analyse municipal Brazilian portals (Rotta et al., 2019), we propose a categorisation of CaaP in four levels, as shown in Table 11.8 (Anttiroiko, 2016; Ulrich et al., 2016; Gil et al., 2019). Some examples of commercial engagement platforms for cities and city platforms developed by governments are presented.

- *Level 1 platform (low G2C–low C2G):* It is characterised by a low level of popular engagement and low government opening. The government's role is restricted to providing information to society and making services available online. The path is unidirectional, from the government to society. Technological tools are not available to enable the direct involvement of social actors with the government to propose ideas related to services or public policies. The government does not provide open data via Application Programming Interface (API). The platforms inform and provide digital services to the population, such as information about the existence of problems on public roads, and allow online monitoring by the citizen of the registration of their request/information. At this level, the platform's objective is to deliver greater convenience to citizens by reducing the time, effort, and costs of accessing the government, offering information and services in a simplified and organised manner. An example of this type of platform is Cityopen (*www.cityopen.com.br*) in Brazil.

- *Level 2 platform (average G2C–average C2G):* The purpose of platforms at level 2 is to provide cities and governments with a digital participation platform to consult and include citizens in decision-making, assisting governments in their decisions. To this end, they allow consultation with citizens and minimal crowdsourcing actions, representing an average level of citizen participation and average government openness. There is a higher level of interaction on these platforms in the G2C (e.g., consultations for the approval of projects and referrals) and C2G (e.g., project proposals, ideas, and

TABLE 11.8

The Evolution of City-as-a-Platform

	Public Engagement Level (C2G)			
Government openness level (G2C)	Low	Medium	High	High
	Low	Medium	Medium	High
	Information and Services	Public Consultation	Government and Society Involvement	Collaboration and Application Development
Platform rating	❶	❷	❸	❹
Government objectives	Provide information and services online.	Obtain feedback, analysis, opinions, or decisions on proposals or actions.	Work directly with the public to ensure that their concerns and aspirations are understood and considered.	Provide open data in machine language, for the development of applications that facilitate and improve the quality of life in cities.
				Provide open data that enable innovation in the formulation of solutions that can be made available to society.
Government deliveries to society	Keep society informed and offer services online.	Keep society informed, listen and acknowledge their concerns and aspirations, provide feedback on how their views influence the government's decision.	Ensure that society's concerns and aspirations are reflected in the alternatives developed and provide feedback on how their contributions influence the government's decision.	
Does it involve open data?	No	No	No	Yes

(Continued)

TABLE 11.8 *(Continued)*

The Evolution of City-as-a-Platform

	Public Engagement Level (C2G)			
	Low	Medium →	High →	High →
Does it involve direct popular participation?	No	Yes	Yes	Yes
G2C/C2G benefits	Convenience Reduction of time, effort, and costs, simplification, organisation, information.	Access Exposition of opinions and ideas, manifestation of will.	Access and reach Exposure of opinions and ideas with the government's counterpart through virtual or face-to-face meetings with specialists.	Public value Provision of open data for the development of web and/or mobile applications by developers.
Examples of commercial online cities' platforms	Cityopen (Brazil)	Citizenlab (France) Mind Mixer (USA and Canada)	Bang the Table (Australia, Canada, USA, UK, New Zealand) Your Priorities (Europe, Canada, and USA)	Consul (International) Decidim (Barcelona) Opengov (USA) Mysidewalk (USA) vTaiwan (Taiwan) Deepint.net (International)
Facilities provided by platforms	Information and availability of digital services.	Crowdsourcing.	Crowdsourcing and virtual or face-to-face living labs.	Crowdsourcing, virtual or face-to-face living labs, hackathons, and the possibility of creating mashups through open data combination.
Brazilian cities eGov platforms (Rotta et al., 2019)	Almost half of the Brazilian cities.	44.08% of the Brazilian cities.	21.96% of the Brazilian cities.	Only 2% of Brazilian cities.

public policies). These platforms provide society with access to the government through direct, convenient, and interactive participation, in addition to offering the government the possibility to select specific target audiences in certain surveys when necessary. Analytics resources are present with real-time monitoring of data collected in society through panels. These platforms do not offer functionality related to open government data. They contribute to the strengthening of democracy, to the increase of transparency, and the confidence of citizens in governments. Some examples of type 2 platforms are MindMixer (*www.mindmixer.com*), which is used by cities in the United States and Canada, and Citizenlab (*www.citizenlab.co*), which is based in Belgium and adopted by several European cities.

- *Level 3 platform (medium G2C–high C2G):* These platforms have all the functionality of level 2 platforms, but additionally, they allow the organisation of virtual events with expert panels or government servers, such as virtual workshops, which give participants the opportunity to discuss a topic in small groups before sharing with a larger group of people. They also offer tools for the ideation of new projects, making it possible to gather ideas from as many people as possible, as if they were virtual living labs, that is, iterative ecosystems of open innovation centered on the user. On these platforms, the level of interaction between government and society is high, but there is no possibility, through the platform, to access open government data to propose new solutions for services and applications. The values of these platforms are centred on the access and reach of opinions and ideas, in addition to manifesting citizens' wishes, with more direct and close involvement of the government through virtual or face-to-face meetings. Examples of this type of platform are Bang the Table (*www.bangthetable.com*), adopted by cities in the United States, Canada, Australia, the United Kingdom, and New Zealand; YourPriorities (*www.yrpri.org*), developed in Iceland as an open-source platform, being used by cities in the United States, Canada, United Kingdom, Portugal, Spain, Amsterdam, and several other European countries.

- *Level 4 platform (high G2C - high C2G):* The platforms at this level present the same functionalities as level 3 platforms in terms of public engagement, with the difference of allowing the production of software and applications from a link to the open data made available by governments, via programmable interface applications (API—Application Programming Interface). In addition, some platforms at this level have free code allowing the proposals to be made available to be audited and inspected by anyone with technical knowledge. The amounts delivered by governments that use these platforms go far beyond crowdsourcing or living labs and include hackathons and the possibility of creating software and applications for web or mobile through the combination of data from government and non-government sources, which can lead to services for citizens with high public value. Examples of this type of platform are Consul (*www.consulproject.org*), an open-source and free use platform developed in Spain and currently used by more than 35 countries in Latin America, South America, Africa, and Europe; Decidim (*www.decidim. barcelona*), created and used in the city of Barcelona, Spain; Opengov (*www.opengov.com*) and Mysidewalk (*www.mysidewalk.com*), both developed and used in the United States; vTaiwan (*www.vtaiwan.tw*), created and applied in Taiwan. Additionally, noteworthy to mention that two city platforms are created through government initiatives: London/ UK (*www.london.gov.uk*) and Singapore (*www.gov.sg*).

Urban governance through platforms is a stimulus to the development of cities based on collective knowledge, being operationalised through the following: (a) Crowdsourcing: Raising the knowledge of people who contribute to decision-making in relation to public policies; (b) Participatory democracy: Collective decisions through direct citizen voting; (c) Co-creation: Not just listening to citizens' demands and desires, but making them part of the solution, increasing their effectiveness and acceptance; and (d) Data and information: Sharing and inviting the use of open data, aiming at creating applications that contribute to the more human, intelligent, and sustainable development of cities [39].

In Brazil, (Rotta et al., 2019) evaluated 903 municipal eGov platforms, and the results revealed that the majority of them have a low level of digital maturity, with low citizenship co-production and fewer opportunities for city smartness. In the proposed categorisation above, almost half of the Brazilian cities analysed are still in level 1, offering simple information or services in a unidirectional fashion. A significant number of cities analysed (44.08%) fit in the second level of maturity, and 21.96% of the portals analysed have some type of functionality that allows the co-production of public services as recommended by level 3. Only 2% of the portals of Brazilian cities analysed have characteristics of the fourth platform level.

The adoption of some of the platform models presented above represents an economic advantage for local governments, as they have the technological infrastructure ready and available for use, sometimes in open source. In addition, they provide data management and analytical resources, with presentation of information on dashboards to support the management of local administrators. The platforms do not replace human importance in the governance of cities and do not exclude the possibility of maintaining face-to-face civic meetings for discussion, ideation, and voting on proposals related to policies for urban development. However, they are important allies for a more open, participatory, and intelligent public governance.

Although the model of CaaP provides real opportunities and benefits for better urban governance, rejuvenating civic life and stimulating better government performance, its inclusion in the sphere of city administration poses new challenges in terms of government, political, and civic arrangements. Citizen participation represents changes in the structures of power, wealth, and voice, and the availability of open data creates uncertainties regarding the security, privacy, and reliability of information (Bollier, 2016).

In the next section, opportunities and challenges for urban development based on collective knowledge in CaaP are discussed.

11.4.2 Opportunities and Challenges for the Development Based on Collective Knowledge in City-as-a-Platform

Based on the literature review, the CaaP vision presents promising opportunities, but with several challenges, of a political, economic, technical, and cultural nature in the spheres of government, society, and technology, as summarised in Table 11.9. From the perspective of the government as an institution, the obstacles will be related to its strongly hierarchical and departmentalised organisational structure, which will hinder the synergy of actions, the resistance to change of teams, the lack of behavioural skills of civil servants for a more direct relationship with the citizen, and low technology training.

CaaP presupposes new governance models focused on communication, interaction, collaboration, and participation in decision-making, facilitating openness and transparency and promoting direct democracy (Pereira et al., 2018). The governance model will need to be based on rules for participation and content exposure, with the definition of sanctions, in a document available to participants. The government should exercise mediation power on the platform, ensuring that in all projects, real public value is achieved (Van Dijck et al., 2020). Regulations and laws that involve urban planning and the definition of public policies should be revisited, considering a new society that is digital and participatory.

Openness to co-production is an essential requirement in CaaP for the provision of the common good in arrangements involving citizens, government, and organisations. Common goods are conceptualised by (Ostrom, 1990) as goods for collective use shared by individuals and subject to social conflicts. The principles of common goods can guide the structuring of the governance model in CaaP initiatives, establishing guidelines for the participation of stakeholders in decision-making processes in a given context, delimiting rights, monitoring the behaviour of members, defining sanctions, and promoting conflict resolution, with governmental autonomy in multiple layers of participation and responsibility (Ostrom, 1990).

In this sense, (Rotta et al., 2019) established a model to analyse the level of adherence to the principles of the common good and to identify the potential of digital platforms to promote the common good. The model was applied in digital platforms in Brazilian cities and identified the limitation of the platforms analysed in the incorporation of the principles of the common good. Only 7% of the analysed platforms were able to identify elements that refer to

TABLE 11.9

Opportunities and Challenges of City-as-a-Platform

	Opportunities	Challenges
Government	• Improvement of services delivered to society. • Harnessing collective intelligence and knowledge. • Improvement in decision-making process quality, with diversified views. • Increased citizens' co-responsibility. • Monitoring of city indicators—transport, health, education, and economic development, among others. • Cost reduction and speed in service provision. • Greater satisfaction of service users—companies and citizens.	• Hierarchical and departmentalised institutional culture. • Development of server behavioural skills. • Training public servants and adapting to change. • Open and participatory governance (leadership and mediation). • Changes in regulations and laws. • Open data as standard (with security, privacy, reliability, and quality guarantee) and systems interoperability. • Financial resources for investments in platform technology. • Ethics in data analysis and use. • Provision of broad and equitable access to technological infrastructure. • Ensuring diversity and representativeness in participation and decisions, preferably involving all stakeholders—citizens, the private sector, and academia.
Society	• Possibility of participation and engagement in the proposition and choice of public policies. • Exercise of rights and duties as a citizen. • Feeling of belonging in the contribution to the city's development process. • Monitoring and control of government actions.	• Absence of a culture of participation and engagement. • Lack of knowledge and access to digital technologies (computer, broadband internet). • Lack of motivation or incentive to participate. • Lack of confidence and legitimacy in technological tools. • Lack of confidence or security in online deliberations. • Respect for online participation (digital etiquette). • Lack of face-to-face interaction that can impair bonding and empathy.
Technology	• Simpler and easier online interactions. • Use of artificial intelligence to support data and information processing. • Reach a larger number of participants at a relatively low cost.	• Ensuring cybersecurity, privacy, and data quality reliability. • Ambiguities and confusion in data analysis, requiring human supervision. • Exponential increase in data collected daily. • Information transparency. • Participant diversity and non-discrimination.

civic engagement, inclusion, shared responsibility, accountability, data opening, and co-production of the society for the common good. Most platforms
offer information and electronic transactions characteristic of the first 2 levels of our platform categorisation.

Based on the work analysed in the literature review, it is possible to understand that CaaP's motivations involve (a) promoting the improvement of
public services, making them more adherent to the needs of society; (b) the
definition of public policies supported by collective knowledge; (c) the creation of innovative digital applications in partnership with developers and
start-ups, facilitating and improving the quality of life of people in cities.
In fact, many of the municipal platforms analysed in (Rotta et al., 2019) do
not provide the information required by law, or provide it in an incomplete,
unstructured, or difficult to understand manner, compromising the transparency and publicity of actions taken in the public sector. According to
(Rotta et al., 2019), the absence of services and information, or the difficulty
in locating and understanding them, distances citizens from public administration and prevents manifestations, requests, criticisms, suggestions, or
praise. The lack of inclusion of interested parties and the low understanding
of the functioning of public services hamper citizen participation and the
co-production of the public good. To achieve the objectives of a networked
city, delivering results that effectively meet the wishes of the majority of
society, it will be up to the government to carefully analyse the data generated by the platform, especially due to the ambiguities and confusions
that they may eventually present. Human interaction in conjunction with
artificial intelligence is essential to evaluate the data in order to recognise
its real meaning, since misinterpreted data may lead to incorrect decisions
(Bollier, 2016). Still, with regard to data, the government's concern should
also be focused on protecting citizens' privacy and connected infrastructure against cyber-attacks. Technologies such as blockchain and cryptogra-
phy can alleviate concerns about data security and contribute to increasing
transparency and trust in relation to online systems (Yigitcanlar et al., 2020).

In countries with greater social inequalities, another challenge for governments is related to the provision of technological infrastructure for broad
and equitable access to popular participation in order to achieve greater
diversity and social representativeness in the issues under discussion on the
platform. In the case of Brazil, (Lima et al., 2020) describes the importance
of digital inclusion policies to enable community participation in the public consultations required by national legislation. The authors describe that
internet access remains a challenge for the expansion of popular participation in Brazilian cities (Lima et al., 2020).

From the perspective of society, the engagement of citizens in the processes
of defining or choosing public policies and in the design and creation of
public services brings the possibility of exercising a direct democracy, without intermediaries, with greater opportunities for monitoring and controlling government actions, increasing the level of confidence in government.

The real contribution to the urban development of the place where they live provides people with a sense of belonging, ensuring greater commitment to the solutions chosen and legitimising the defined public policies.

The platforms, as a link of communication and collaboration between government and citizens, allow people to exercise their role as part of the quadruple innovation helix (society + government + academia + private sector) and have their voices heard, contributing to the construction of proposals that arise from the consensus of the analysis of different perspectives that are capable of building a fairer, more inclusive, and sustainable urban environment (Bouzguenda et al., 2019; Borghys et al., 2020).

Nonetheless, there are obstacles to be overcome in the popular participation aspect. For example, platforms that use crowdsourcing encounter problems related to the human aspect, such as the lack of motivation or incentive for participation, the lack of digital equality between different social strata (in terms of age, gender, income, and skills), as well as the level of knowledge on the themes of the proposals (Srivastava & Mostafavi, 2018). Allied to this, there are other issues that can prevent people's participation, such as the lack of confidence in the virtual deliberative processes, the feeling of uncertainty regarding the security and privacy of technological tools, and the discomfort related to participating in the platforms due to the lack of knowledge of technology.

From a technology point of view, although platforms create an environment that supports the involvement of multiple actors, there are challenges related to the opacity, complexity, unpredictability, and partially autonomous behaviour of digital systems. Such challenges can make it difficult to guarantee the fundamental rights of citizens, such as privacy, security, and non-discrimination systems (Ismagilova et al., 2019; Yigitcanlar et al., 2020).

Aspects related to transparency, participants' privacy, reliability, and data quality were also identified in relation to crowdsourcing (Srivastava & Mostafavi, 2018). Technology can have negative impacts on the democratic process if there are no forms of control and punishment. In this sense, although digital platforms seem to provide freedom, in reality, there is a mediation layer in their architecture that guides interaction, allowing certain forms of action and preventing others systems (Lim & Yigitcanlar, 2022). It is as if technological control through behaviour modelling, incorporated into the interaction rules of the platform, extends to parts of social life, with the power in the subtle adjustment of some technical code. Hence, the importance of adopting platforms that have open and auditable sources.

On the other hand, with the use of new information and communication technologies, it is possible to reach the participation of a large number of people, regardless of their geographical location, in the urban development processes of cities, in a more friendly and interactive way, counting, still, with the ease of compiling the results through strategies based on AI systems (Yigitcanlar et al., 2020b). In addition, digital tools allow participants to monitor the status of the proposed recommendations and the impact they have had on final decision-making.

In cities organised as platforms, it is possible to take advantage of the creativity, intelligence, and knowledge of a large and indefinite group of people, increasing the likelihood of generating original ideas for urban development (Panori et al., 2020). For the authors, the main contribution of digital technologies is the rise and interconnection of various types of intelligence—(a) artificial, (b) human, and (c) collective— supported by good public governance, to build smarter, more human, and more sustainable cities.

The idea here is that no single governance rule or specific platform model is applicable to every city. There is no one size fits all. The choice between the platform models presented in this chapter will depend on the technological maturity of the governments, their organisational structure, the available resources and, mainly, the culture of participation of the population.

There is no roadmap or project on how to organise CaaP or a ready recipe for implementing open, participatory and intelligent governance processes (Ulrich et al., 2016). Nevertheless, the authors provide some guidelines, which are listed below:

- Clearly define the objectives to be achieved and seek to solve real problems, with technology being only a tool; if the problems to be solved are not relevant to the city's population, the use of new technologies alone will not motivate them to get involved;

- Configure a new platform and link it to existing systems, which users know; combine online and offline formats for stakeholder access;

- Plan and reserve sufficient resources, as it is not enough to just create the platform, since discussions will need to be moderated, the platform maintained, proposals transferred to decision-makers, requests answered, information prepared, and much more;

- Prepare for change, as the structure of CaaP not only requires different resources and team capacity but also generates changes in internal workflows, organisational culture, and self-conception by local governments;

- Keep governance processes open, accessible, and inclusive;

- Be transparent and follow the defined objectives and goals; initiating a process, creating expectations, and subsequently, disregarding the contribution of citizens and stakeholders must be avoided in all circumstances, as this undermines the trust and credibility of open governance processes;

- Build future innovation through open-source codes, which allow greater cooperation with other codes and flexibility for adaptations, helping to avoid technological blockages.

Additionally, analysing the results of (Rotta et al., 2019) and the good practices of the platforms positioned at levels 3 and 4 identified in Table 11.8, Table 11.10 describes complementary principles for CaaP platforms:

TABLE 11.10

Principles for the Design of City-as-a-Platform

Principle	Description	Example
Intuitive interface	Use design standards that favor access to services of interest to the user, including service guidelines and recommendations according to user profiles	Organisation of services and information adopted by London/UK and Singapore platforms
Responsibilities	Make clear the policies for the use of services, informing interested parties of their rights, responsibilities, and penalties	Decidim's social contract; government terms in Singapore platform
Social eGov	Promote the integration of content and services with social media to facilitate the dissemination or incorporation of content on the platform	London/UK Media Centre and social media resources of Singapore platform
Accountability	Provision of services for government transparency	In my area at London/UK platform; Dashboard automation in mySidewalk
Open data	Apply open government practices, making open data available, with the possibility of downloading and reading by machine	Openness and transparency section of London/UK platform and data dissemination strategy of mySidewalk
Interoperability	Enable the integration of platform services or external resources through APIs and interoperability programs	List of API of London/UK and Consul platforms
Communication	Provide channels of interaction with stakeholders	Communication features available in London/UK and Singapore platforms
Knowledge management	Include resources for knowledge management and sharing	KM resources available in London/UK Get involved section
Conflict resolution	Offer quick access channels for complaints of inappropriate use of resources and mediation of conflicts between different actors on the platform	Terms of service and consultation in getting involved sections of London/UK platform
Co-production	Availability of resources that enable the participation of society in the discussion of priorities and the co-production of public policies	Talk London in London/UK; Debates in Consul platform; participatory budgeting/participative processes in Decidim; open consultation process of vTaiwan

11.5 Conclusion[1]

In recent years, one of the significant developments was the coining of the concept of City-as-a-Platform (CaaP) as part of the platform urbanism movement (Gil et al., 2019; Richardson, 2020; Leszczynski, 2020; Fields et al., 2020). The concept is rapidly gaining popularity, as more and more platform thinking applications become available to the city context—where open data and the participatory innovation opportunity of these platforms contribute to identifying and solving critical urban issues (De Waal et al., 2017; Chamoso et al., 2020). Nonetheless, this topic is an understudied area of urban research. Hence, the study attempted to evaluate the use of digital media platforms by local governments (particularly along the notion of CaaP) as a tool to support urban governance for the development of smart cities by answering the aforementioned research question of this study. Through an integrative review of scholarly articles published during the last decade (2010–2020), combined with research on websites of some platforms in existing cities, it was shown how these platforms have been organised and used, classifying them according to the level of involvement citizens and government opening, also presenting the opportunities and challenges arising from its adoption.

Our review has found that CaaP is an emerging field of research and practice and, therefore, more prospective studies are needed to consolidate knowledge on the topic (Sadowski, 2020). The complexities of the digital age and the rapid expansion of disruptive technologies are creating the need to better understand the economic, social, environmental, philosophical, and legal implications of their development, adoption, and use for the most human, intelligent, and sustainable development of cities (Ekman, 2018; Salvati, 2020). This includes a deeper understanding of the opportunities and risks associated with adopting CaaP.

The use of technology is fundamental and irreversible, but innovation itself is a human undertaking (Van den Bergh et al., 2016; Shiode, 2000). In this sense, the organisation of cities in the platform model requires analysis of their transformative and disruptive impact on government and society, since they alter the power structure and the relationship between participants in this ecosystem.

Among the principles identified in the literature to guide the governance strategy in CaaP, we highlight those pointed out by (Meijer, 2016; Rotta et al., 2019) linked to the promotion of the common good, such as the following: (a) Training all stakeholders, taking into account their roles and responsibilities; (b) Defining mechanisms for resolving conflicts; (c) Understanding the

---

[1] This chapter, with permission from the copyright holder, is a reproduced version of the following journal article: Repette, P., Sabatini-Marques, J., Yigitcanlar, T., Sell, D., & Costa, E. (2021). The evolution of City-as-a-Platform: Smart urban development governance with collective knowledge-based platform urbanism. *Land*, 10(1), 33.

context for designing sustainable initiatives; (d) Taking co-production and citizen participation as key principles; (e) Considering that public goods are a collective responsibility; and (f) Establishing rules to govern diffuse and collective interests and monitor the interactions of the actors. Regarding the technological perspective, a number of important aspects will need to be addressed:

- Maximise society's equitable access to digital technologies and relevant urban platforms to form collective knowledge to tackle issues.
- Promote digital literacy and mitigate the digital divide to prevent the growth of socioeconomic inequalities.
- Design, develop, and deploy technologies that positively affect the behaviour of citizens in relation to common goods.
- Promote information security and privacy so that technologies are used with complete confidence.
- Understand the reality of online city governance and establish mechanisms to promote the automation of platform decisions in a secure manner.
- Make open data available and ensure the transparency, security, and privacy of that data.

Lastly, the challenges for the implementation of CaaP are immense for governments and societies (De Waal et al., 2017; Caprotti & Liu, 2019). Nevertheless, tackling these challenges is critical, and opportunities are already here for researchers, since countless studies and experiments are on the rise in the fields of digital media, urban planning and development, open and big data, public services, sustainable governance, and smart collaboration. Platform urbanism has the potential to contribute to the efforts in expanding the benefits for citizens and their quality of life in cities, where its contribution is also essential for shaping the smarter urban development governance and achieving the smart urbanism goals with collective knowledge (Bissell, 2020; Corchado et al., 2021).

References

Anttiroiko, A.V. (2016). City-As-a-platform: The rise of participatory innovation platforms in Finnish cities. *Sustainability, 8*(9), 922.

Anttiroiko, A.V., Valkama, P., & Bailey, S.J. (2014). Smart cities in the new service economy: Building platforms for smart services. *AI & Society, 29*(3), 323–334.

Anttiroiko, A.V., Valkama, P., & Bailey, S.J. (2014). Smart cities in the new service economy: Building platforms for smart services. *AI & Society, 29*(3), 323–334.

Barns, S. (2018). Smart cities and urban data platforms: Designing interfaces for smart governance. *City, Culture and Society, 12,* 5–12.

Bissell, D. (2020). Affective platform urbanism: Changing habits of digital on-demand consumption. *Geoforum, 115,* 102–110.

Bollier, D. (2016). *The city as Platform: How Digital Networks Are Changing Urban Life and Governance.* The Aspen Institute, Washington, DC.

Borghys, K., Van Der Graaf, S., Walravens, N., & Van Compernolle, M. (2020). Multi-stakeholder innovation in smart City discourse: Quadruple helix thinking in the age of "Platforms". *Frontiers in Sustainable Cities, 2,* 5.

Botelho, L.L.R., Cunha, C.D.A., & Macedo, M. (2011). The integrative review method in organizational studies. *Rev Eletr Gestão Soc, 5*(11), 121–36.

Bouzguenda, I., Alalouch, C., & Fava, N. (2019). Towards smart sustainable cities: A review of the role digital citizen participation could play in advancing social sustainability. *Sustainable Cities and Society, 50,* 101627.

Brown, A., Fishenden, J., Thompson, M., & Venters, W. (2017). Appraising the impact and role of platform models and government as a platform (GaaP) in UK government public service reform: Towards a platform assessment framework (PAF). *Government Information Quarterly, 34*(2), 167–182.

Caprotti, F., & Liu, D. (2019). Emerging platform urbanism in China: Reconfigurations of data, citizenship and materialities.

Caragliu, A., & Del Bo, C. (2009, October). Nijkamp.: P. Smart cities in Europe. In *Proceedings of the 3rd Central European Conference in Regional Science. Košice, Slovak Republic.*

Chamoso, P., González-Briones, A., De La Prieta, F., Venyagamoorthy, G.K., & Corchado, J.M. (2020). Smart city as a distributed platform: Toward a system for citizen-oriented management. *Computer Communications, 152,* 323–332.

Chang, D.L., Sabatini-Marques, J., Da Costa, E.M., Selig, P.M., & Yigitcanlar, T. (2018). Knowledge-based, smart and sustainable cities: A provocation for a conceptual framework. *Journal of Open Innovation: Technology, Market, and Complexity, 4*(1), 5–28.

Chourabi, H., Nam, T., Walker, S., Gil-Garcia, J.R., Mellouli, S., Nahon, K., Pardo, T.A., & Scholl, H.J. (2012). Understanding smart cities: An integrative framework. In *Proceedings of 2012 45th Hawaii international conference on system sciences,* IEEE.

Corchado, J.M., Chamoso, P., Hernández, G., Gutierrez, A.S.R., Camacho, A.R., González-Briones, A., Pinto-Santos, F., Goyenechea, E., Garcia-Retuerta, D., Alonso-Miguel, M., & Hernandez, B.B. (2021). Deepint. net: A rapid deployment platform for smart territories. *Sensors, 21*(1), 236.

D'Amico, G., L'Abbate, P., Liao, W., Yigitcanlar, T., & Ioppolo, G. (2020). Understanding sensor cities: Insights from technology giant company driven smart urbanism practices. *Sensors, 20*(16), 4391.

De Reuver, M., Sørensen, C., & Basole, R.C. (2018). The digital platform: A research agenda. *Journal of Information Technology, 33*(2), 124–135.

De Waal, M., De Lange, M., & Bouw, M. (2017). The hackable city: Citymaking in a platform society. *Architectural Design, 87*(1), 50–57.

Ekman, U. (2018). Smart city planning: Complexity. *International Journal of E-Planning Research, 7*(3), 1–21.

Fields, D., Bissell, D., & Macrorie, R. (2020). Platform methods: Studying platform urbanism outside the black box. *Urban Geography, 41*(3), 462–468.

Gabriel, A.G. (2017). Transparency and accountability in local government: Levels of commitment of municipal councillors in Bongabon in the Philippines. *Asia Pacific Journal of Public Administration, 39*(3), 217–223.

Gil, O., Cortés-Cediel, M.E., & Cantador, I. (2019). Citizen participation and the rise of digital media platforms in smart governance and smart cities. *International Journal of E-Planning Research (IJEPR), 8*(1), 19–34.

Gil, J., Tobari, E., Lemlij, M., Rose, A., & Penn, A.R. (2009). The differentiating behaviour of shoppers: clustering of individual movement traces in a supermarket. Royal Institute of Technology (KTH).

Gil-Garcia, J.R., Zhang, J., & Puron-Cid, G. (2016). Conceptualizing smartness in government: An integrative and multi-dimensional view. *Government Information Quarterly, 33*(3), 524–534.

Graham, M. (2020). Regulate, replicate, and resist–the conjunctural geographies of platform urbanism. *Urban Geography, 41*(3), 453–457.

Harmaala, M.M. (2015). The sharing city as a platform for a more sustainable city environment? *International Journal of Environment and Health, 7*(4), 309–328.

Hwang, J.S. (2020). The evolution of smart city in South Korea: The smart City winter and the City-as-a-platform. In *Smart Cities in Asia*. Edward Elgar Publishing.

IAP2 (2020). Spectrum of Public Participation. International Association of Public Participation. Accessed from https://www.iap2.org/page/pillars on 7 June 2020.

Ismagilova, E., Hughes, L., Dwivedi, Y.K., & Raman, K.R. (2019). Smart cities: Advances in research—An information systems perspective. *International Journal of Information Management, 47*, 88–100.

Knight, R.V. (1995). Knowledge-based development: Policy and planning implications for cities. *Urban Studies, 32*(2), 225–260.

Komninos, N. (2009). Intelligent cities: Towards interactive and global innovation environments. *International Journal of Innovation and Regional Development, 1*(4), 337–355.

Komninos, N., Schaffers, H., & Pallot, M. (2011, October). Developing a policy roadmap for smart cities and the future internet. In *eChallenges e-2011 Conference Proceedings, IIMC International Information Management Corporation*. IMC International Information Management Corporation.

Lim, S. B., & Yigitcanlar, T. (2022). Participatory Governance of Smart Cities: Insights from e-Participation of Putrajaya and Petaling Jaya, Malaysia. *Smart Cities, 5*(1), 71–89.

Lima, E.G., Chinelli, C.K., Guedes, A.L.A., Vazquez, E.G., Hammad, A.W., Haddad, A.N., & Soares, C.A.P. (2020). Smart and sustainable cities: The main guidelines of City statute for increasing the intelligence of Brazilian cities. *Sustainability, 12*(3), 1025.

Meijer, A.J., Lips, M., & Chen, K. (2019). Open governance: A new paradigm for understanding urban governance in an information age. *Frontiers in Sustainable Cities, 1*, 3.

Meijer, A., & Bolívar, M.P.R. (2016). Governing the smart city: A review of the literature on smart urban governance. *International Review of Administrative Sciences, 82*(2), 392–408.

Mergel, I., Kleibrink, A., & Sörvik, J. (2018). Open data outcomes: US cities between product and process innovation. *Government Information Quarterly, 35*(4), 622–632.

Nam, T., & Pardo, T.A. (2011, June). Conceptualizing smart city with dimensions of technology, people, and institutions. In *Proceedings of the 12th annual international digital government research conference: Digital government innovation in challenging times* (pp. 282–291).

O'Reilly, T. (2011). Government as a platform. *Innovations: Technology, Governance, Globalization, 6*(1), 13–40.

Ostrom, E. (1990). *Governing the Commons: The Evolution of Institutions for Collective Action.* Cambridge University Press.

Panori, A., Kakderi, C., Komninos, N., Fellnhofer, K., Reid, A., & Mora, L. (2020). Smart systems of innovation for smart places: Challenges in deploying digital platforms for co-creation and data-intelligence. *Land Use Policy, 111*, 104631.

Park, Y.J. (2019). Strategy for building smart City as a platform of the 4th industrial revolution. *Journal of Digital Convergence, 17*(1), 169–177.

Paskaleva, K.A. (2011). The smart city: A nexus for open innovation? *Intelligent Buildings International, 3*(3), 153–171.

Pereira, G.V., Parycek, P., Falco, E., & Kleinhans, R. (2018). Smart governance in the context of smart cities: A literature review. *Information Polity, 23*(2), 143–162.

Richardson, L. (2020). Coordinating the city: Platforms as flexible spatial arrangements. *Urban Geography, 41*(3), 458–461.

Rochet, J.C., & Tirole, J. (2003). Platform competition in two-sided markets. *Journal of the European Economic Association, 1*(4), 990–1029.

Rotta, M.J.R., Sell, D., dos Santos Pacheco, R.C., & Yigitcanlar, T. (2019). Digital commons and citizen coproduction in smart cities: Assessment of Brazilian municipal e-government platforms. *Energies, 12*(14), 2813.

Sabatini-Marques, J., Yigitcanlar, T., Schreiner, T., Wittmann, T., Sotto, D., & Inkinen, T. (2020). Strategizing smart, sustainable, and knowledge-based development of cities: Insights from florianópolis, Brazil. *Sustainability, 12*(21), 8859.

Sadowski, J. (2020). Cyberspace and cityscapes: On the emergence of platform urbanism. *Urban Geography, 41*(3), 448–452.

Salvati, L., & Carlucci, M. (2020). Shaping dimensions of urban complexity: The role of economic structure and socio-demographic local contexts. *Social Indicators Research, 147*(1), 263–285.

Shiode, N. (2000). Urban planning, information technology, and cyberspace. *Journal of Urban Technology, 7*(2), 105–126.

Srivastava, P., & Mostafavi, A. (2018). Challenges and opportunities of crowdsourcing and participatory planning in developing infrastructure systems of smart cities. *Infrastructures, 3*(4), 51.

Stehlin, J., Hodson, M., & McMeekin, A. (2020). Platform mobilities and the production of urban space: Toward a typology of platformization trajectories. *Environment and Planning A: Economy and Space, 52*(7), 1250–1268.

Tasan-Kok, T., & Vranken, J. (2011). *Handbook for Multilevel Governance in Europe.* European Urban Knowledge Network, Amsterdam, The Netherlands.

Törnberg, P., & Uitermark, J. (2020). Complex control and the governmentality of digital platforms. *Frontiers in Sustainable Cities, 2*, 6.

Ulrich, P., Marshment-Howell, J., & Van Geest, T. (2016). *Open Governance in the Smart City: A Scoping Report.* Smarticipate Project, London, UK.

Van den Bergh, J., & Viaene, S. (2016). Unveiling smart city implementation challenges: The case of Ghent. *Information Polity, 21*(1), 5–19.

van der Graaf, S., & Ballon, P. (2019). Navigating platform urbanism. *Technological Forecasting and Social Change, 142*, 364–372.

van Dijck, J. (2020). Governing digital societies: Private platforms, public values. *Computer Law & Security Review, 36*, 105377.

Walravens, N. (2011). The city as a platform. In: Proceedings of the 2011 15th IEEE International Conference on Intelligence in Next Generation Networks, 4–7 October, Berlin, Germany, 283–288.

Whittemore, R., & Knafl, K. (2005). The integrative review: Updated methodology. *Journal of Advanced Nursing, 52*(5), 546–553.

Yigitcanlar, T. (2006). Australian Local governments' practice and prospects with online planning. *URISA Journal, 18*(2), 7–17.

Yigitcanlar, T. (2016). *Technology and the City: Systems, Applications and Implications.* Routledge.

Yigitcanlar, T. (Ed.). (2010). *Rethinking Sustainable Development: Urban Management, Engineering, and Design.* IGI Global.

Yigitcanlar, T., & Cugurullo, F. (2020). The sustainability of artificial intelligence: An urbanistic viewpoint from the lens of smart and sustainable cities. *Sustainability, 12*(20), 8548.

Yigitcanlar, T., & Dur, F. (2013). Making space and place for knowledge communities: Lessons for Australian practice. *Australasian Journal of Regional Studies, 19*(1), 36–63.

Yigitcanlar, T., & Kamruzzaman, M. (2015). Planning, development and management of sustainable cities: A commentary from the guest editors, 14677–14688.

Yigitcanlar, T., Butler, L., Windle, E., Desouza, K.C., Mehmood, R., & Corchado, J.M. (2020). Can building "artificially intelligent cities" safeguard humanity from natural disasters, pandemics, and other catastrophes? An urban scholar's perspective. *Sensors, 20*(10), 2988.

Yigitcanlar, T., Desouza, K.C., Butler, L., & Roozkhosh, F. (2020b). Contributions and risks of artificial intelligence (AI) in building smarter cities: Insights from a systematic review of the literature. *Energies, 13*(6), 1473.

Yigitcanlar, T., Foth, M., & Kamruzzaman, M. (2019). Towards post-anthropocentric cities: Reconceptualizing smart cities to evade urban ecocide. *Journal of Urban Technology, 26*(2), 147–152.

Yigitcanlar, T., Kankanamge, N., & Vella, K. (2021). How are smart city concepts and technologies perceived and utilized? A systematic geo-twitter analysis of smart cities in Australia. *Journal of Urban Technology, 28*(1–2), 135–154.

Yigitcanlar, T., Kankanamge, N., Regona, M., Ruiz Maldonado, A., Rowan, B., Ryu, A., & Li, R.Y.M. (2020b). Artificial intelligence technologies and related urban planning and development concepts: How are they perceived and utilized in Australia? *Journal of Open Innovation: Technology, Market, and Complexity, 6*(4), 187.

Zhuang, T., Qian, Q.K., Visscher, H.J., Elsinga, M.G., & Wu, W. (2019). The role of stakeholders and their participation network in decision-making of urban renewal in China: The case of Chongqing. *Cities, 92,* 47–58.

12

City as a Sensor for Platform Urbanism

12.1 Introduction

Today, cities are at the forefront of increasing urbanisation and digitalisation pressures (Yigitcanlar, 2006; Arbolino et al., 2018; Ingrao et al., 2018), where they play a crucial role in supporting the transition towards a sustainable and smart urbanism practice (Zheng et al., 2013; Bettencourt, 2014; Bibri & Krogstie, 2017a). The current urban context is associated with numerous economic, social, and environmental issues, such as waste management (Huang & Hsu, 2003; Costi et al., 2004; Zamam & Lehmann, 2013; Aazam et al., 2016), energy efficiency (Glazebrook & Newman, 2018; Chui et al., 2018; Ghiani et al., 2018), renewable energy sources (Lund, 2014; Strielkowski et al., 2019), water management (Ler & Gourbesville, 2018), social, cultural, and health aspects (Nitschke et al., 2007; Lin, 2015; Jowell et al., 2017; Sodhro et al., 2018; Macke et al., 2019; Muzammal et al., 2020), material flows (Kennedy et al., 2007), biodiversity (Morimoto, 2010), transport (Arndt et al., 2013; Sadiku et al., 2017), land use optimisation (Kim et al., 2018), air and noise pollution prevention (Kamal-Chaoui et al., 2011; OECD, 2014; Peng et al., 2017), infrastructure mishaps [29], economic growth [30]. Policymakers, thus, need a paradigm shift, developing innovative, sustainable, and intelligent solutions to optimise urban processes and improve citizens' quality of life and sustainability of the city (Batty, 2013; Bibri, 2018a; Bibri & Krogstie, 2020; Young et al., 2021).

In recent years, the notion of 'sensor city' has emerged as a response to the future challenges of growing urbanisation and datafication (Batty, 2012; Postránecký & Svítek, 2017). This new version of the city—i.e., City 4.0—(thanks to the urban dashboards and platforms integrates Internet-of-Things (IoT) infrastructure (Wirtz et al., 2019), sensors (Arkian et al., 2017), real-time monitoring stations (Jardim-Gonçalves et al., 2020; Tekouabou et al., 2020), digital cameras (Liu & Xu, 2020), actuators (Bonomi et al., 2012), real-time tracking systems (Uhlemann et al., 2017; Rathore et al., 2018), big data analytical techniques (Al Nuaimi et al., 2015; Hashem et al., 2016; Bibri, 2019), information and communication technologies (ICTs) (Kramers et al., 2014; Palvia et al., 2018), cloud computing (Baucas & Spachos, 2020), smart grid (Witkowski, 2017; Daissaoui et al., 2020), artificial intelligence (AI) (Ullah et al., 2020;

Regona et al., 2022a, 2022b), autonomous shuttles (Faisal et al., 2020), and other digital appliances with physical objects that characterise urban context) improves the efficiency of resources usage.

Specifically, city dashboards accommodate visual/graphical and dynamic analysis suite capable of holistically combining urban infrastructures to view, integrate, and communicate real-time information on performance, trends, and future urban scenarios (Eicker et al., 2020; Caprotti & Liu, 2020). These dashboards are characterised by a high degree of interactivity with users, capable of combining, filtering, querying, and overlapping large amounts of urban data (Pettit & Leao, 2017; Bissell, 2020). Indeed, urban dashboards are implemented to facilitate an understanding of major urban issues and provide stakeholders with a sense of accountability and engagement in smart urban governance activities (Batty, 2015; Young et al., 2017; Young & Kitchin, 2020).

According to the forecasts of the "World Smart Cities Spending Guide" provided by the International Data Corporation (IDC, 2020), the total expenditure for smart urban solutions this year alone amounted to almost $124 billion. This is an increase of 18.9% compared to 2019 (IDC, 2020). Specifically, global cities such as Singapore, Tokyo, New York City, and London occupy the top of the ranks in terms of investments in smart urban initiatives (IDC, 2020). Furthermore, cities such as Toronto, Adelaide, Hamburg, Kansas City, Dallas, and Stockholm (see this chapter's Appendix) have implemented participatory and intelligent platforms that use ICTs to connect companies, local authorities, universities, start-ups, citizens, associations, and so on in order to support the decision-making process, allowing the collection, processing, monitoring, and analysis of large amounts of urban data (Lane et al., 2008; Perng et al., 2018; Kankanamge et al., 2020). In this sense, Bibri and Krogstie (2020) described cities as complex networks of holistic relationships that integrate smart and sustainable solutions in order to provide a suitable context for long-term urban strategic development (de Wijs et al., 2016).

Indeed, the rapid and pervasive development of ICTs taking place all over the world is transforming cities into centres of economic, social, environmental, and technological development with the aim of providing increasingly efficient, sustainable, and smart urban services (Batty, 2012; Kramers et al., 2014; Piro et al., 2014; Sharifi, 2020). In this regard, the United Nations (UN) Agenda 2030 defines ICTs as necessary tools to facilitate the transition towards sustainable development (United Nations General Assembly, 2015; Höjer & Wangel, 2015). Hence, policymakers use data and information sharing systems through IoT technologies for planning, monitoring, and evaluating the performance of urban policies, and for improving transparency, active participation of citizens, and awareness of urban issues (Yigitcanlar, 2010; Gabrys, 2014; Marsal-Llacuna & Segal, 2016). For example, cities such as Singapore, Zurich, Oslo, Geneva, Copenhagen, Auckland, Melbourne, Taipei, Helsinki, Bilbao, and Düsseldorf represent forward-looking cases regarding the use of ICTs in the urban area, occupying the first places in the ranking developed by the IMD World

Competitiveness Centre Smart City Observatory (International Institute for Management Development (IMD), 2019).

The current urban theoretical and managerial debates increasingly focus on the role of ICTs and their integration with various aspects related to sustainable urban development (Hilty et al., 2014; Kamble et al., 2018). Indeed, the literature provides several synonymous for sensor city such as a digital city (Ishida & Isbister, 2000; Stollmann, 2019; Colding et al., 2020), smart city (Talari et al., 2017; Yigitcanlar et al., 2018; Saborido & Alba, 2020), ubiquitous city (Lee et al., 2008; Shin, 2009; Wang et al., 2017), knowledge city (Lopez-Ruiz et al., 2014; Pancholi et al., 2015; Penco et al., 2020), intelligent city (Komninos, 2009; Liugailaité-Radzvickiené & Jucevičius, 2014), techno-centric city (Willis & Aurigi, 2017), creative city (Landry, 2008; Baum et al., 2009), sustainable city (Li et al., 2019; Sodiq et al., 2019), informational city (Mainka et al., 2011; Rutherford, 2020), smart sustainable city (Bibri, 2018b; Chang et al., 2018; Akande et al., 2019; Huovila et al., 2019), and artificially intelligent city (Yigitcanlar et al., 2020b), which express the importance of ICTs in the management of the cities of future.

Nevertheless, technology alone cannot be a panacea for all urban issues related to growing urbanisation (Ahvenniemi et al., 2017; Allam & Dhunny, 2019; Yigitcanlar et al., 2019). In particular, cities excessively connected to IoT and big data analytical solutions have often been criticised for being too techno-centric and for underestimating social and environmental aspects (Höjer & Wangel, 2015; Yigitcanlar et al., 2018; 2019). At the same time, sustainable cities struggle to integrate the technological approach with the social, environmental, and economic dimensions of sustainable development (Bibri & Krogstie, 2017b; Huovila et al., 2019). Specifically, the use of advanced techniques (e.g., real-time monitoring stations for energy consumption, location systems to guide urban traffic, cloud computing systems for sharing sensitive data between government departments, urban infrastructures such as smart bins, smart street lamps, and surveillance cameras) highlights a multitude of challenges related to the quality of the data used, level of protection of traditional and cybernetic urban security, necessary data integration between the various urban infrastructures, and ability to transform feedback from citizens and other stakeholders into innovative urban policies. Consequently, sensors and related ICT infrastructures are rapidly gaining strategic importance for sustainable and disruptive urban development (Hancke et al., 2012). They are not only enhancing in terms of technological aspects, but also social, environmental, and economic ones (Thomson & Newman, 2018).

This chapter aims to explore the main challenges related to sensor cities, emphasising the opportunities and critical issues of this growing datafication of urban contexts. In this sense, an integrated and holistic framework is proposed which includes a theoretical and managerial review of the main disruptive technological applications. The study, thus, identifies and compares IoT solutions based on sensors, big data analysis and other technologies related to ICTs adopted by different cities, to manage urban development in an innovative and computerised manner (Schintler & McNeely, 2019). This chapter generates insights from the current sensor city best practices by placing some renowned projects, implemented by Huawei, Cisco, Google, Ericsson, Microsoft, and Alibaba, under the microscope. With the objective to offer a detailed overview, this chapter adopts a mixed research approach, able to integrate a literature review and an in-depth analysis of several case studies. In this regard, the proposed framework provides users with greater knowledge and awareness of sensor cities' development.

This chapter is structured as follows. Section 12.2 introduces the mixed methodological approach used. Section 12.3 analytically describes the proposed framework, highlighting the technological factors such as IoT, big data analysis, AI, ICTs, real-time monitoring stations, sensors, cloud computing, digital platforms, and urban challenges that characterise sensor cities. Finally, Section 12.4 provides conclusions and some considerations on the contribution of sensor cities to future urban challenges.

12.2 Methodology

The development of this study is structured according to a mixed approach, characterise by a literature review and a detailed analysis on several case studies, in order to create a framework for policymakers that collect the forward-looking ICT urban initiatives, emphasising a data-focused method in the assessment of urban development. The implementation of this study is carried out in different phases and in this sense, the methodological approach followed is illustrated in Figure 12.1.

In Phase 1: *Identification*, the research question, keywords, and research databases are defined. Regarding the objective and the research question, the study aims to identify and analyse the main characteristics of sensor cities, highlighting the impacts of their technological applications on urban development.

The attention of the study has focused that have provided an interdisciplinary and/or transdisciplinary perspective to the development of sensor city. Specifically, these scientific disciplines include technology and innovation management, urban planning, policy, sustainable development, environmental management, data science, urban informatics, geography, urban development, strategic management, and urban statistics. Moreover, this chapter—through a qualitative approach—analyses in detail several sensor cities considered successful examples of disruptive urban actors, capable of integrating sensor strategies with the economic, social, and environmental aspects of urban development. As a result, the study includes peer-reviewed journal articles, book chapters, conference proceedings,

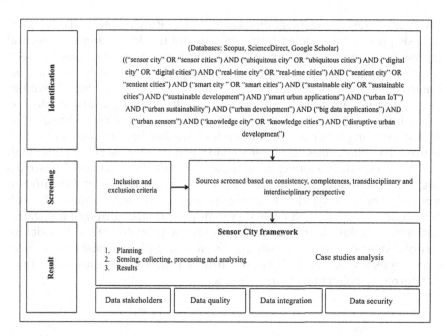

FIGURE 12.1
Methodological approach adopted.

grey literature such as government documents, and industry technical reports. In terms of databases, ScienceDirect, Google Scholar and cities' websites were utilised to achieve the analysis. Furthermore, the keywords searched include ("sensor city" OR "sensor cities") AND ("ubiquitous city" OR "ubiquitous cities") AND ("digital city" OR "digital cities") AND ("real-time city" OR "real-time cities") AND ("sentient city" OR "sentient cities") AND ("intelligent city" OR "intelligent cities") AND ("data-driven city" OR "data-driven cities") AND ("smart city" OR "smart cities") AND ("sustainable city" OR "sustainable cities") AND ("sustainable development") AND ("smart urban applications") AND ("urban IoT") AND ("urban sustainability") AND ("urban development") AND ("big data applications") AND ("urban sensors") AND ("knowledge city" OR "knowledge cities") AND ("disruptive urban development").

In Phase 2: *Screening*, the review aims to provide a clear and comprehensive definition of the concept of sensor city, introducing urban dimensions (e.g., governance, economy, environment, mobility, people, and living) and technological solutions (e.g., IoT, sensors, AI, ICTs, big data analytics) necessary for its implementation. In order to further refine the research, all the selected sources were screened following a set of inclusion and exclusion criteria, in line with the objective and the research question of the study. As exclusion criteria, sources with partial information and inconsistent with the topic of the study were not included in the search.

In Phase 3: *Result*, the integration between literature review and case study analysis provides a detailed framework useful for developing a theoretical approach to sensor cities, underlining the holistic relationships between urban sustainability and computerisation aspects. Nonetheless, it is important to consider that sensor cities, taken into consideration in the case studies analysis use non-uniform terminology and lack detailed quantitative data on sensor infrastructures. In this sense, a greater understanding and awareness of urban sensing is needed to develop forward-looking projects in line with future urban challenges. This research focused on 20 sensor cities, with high quality in social, economic, environmental, and technological infrastructures. Consequently, the sample analysed does not represent the different types of cities globally. Most cities around the world are not equipped to collect, monitor, analyse, and evaluate urban performance through innovative platforms and dashboards. In sum, this review provides: (a) A clear definition of sensor city; (b) A sensor city framework; (c) A detailed analysis of several sensor cities; and (d) Various different sensing policies and actions that currently policymakers have in place.

12.3 Results

Given the growing importance of sensor city solutions in the world panorama, technology giant companies (e.g., Huawei, Ericsson, Microsoft, Oracle, Alibaba, Deutsche Telekom, Samsung) are involved in numerous urban technological projects in order to provide platforms, products, and services in line with the necessary paradigm of shift (Yigitcanlar et al., 2021). Thus, sensor cities aim to involve citizens and companies in the process of planning, monitoring, and analysing urban processes and raising awareness and comprehension on environmental, social, and economic issues (Hasegawa et al., 2019; Yamagata et al., 2020). This chapter's Appendix presents some examples of cities equipped with real-time monitoring stations and sensors that analyse and collect urban performance.

Few (2006) in his book 'Information Dashboard Design: The Effective Visual Communication of Data' defines the dashboard as a visual, consolidated, and organised display on a single screen of the most important information needed to monitor, analyse, and achieve one or more urban objectives. Similarly, Kitchin (2014) explains urban dashboards as digital, physical, or mixed interfaces that allow users to actively or passively interact in urban data monitoring and management in order to improve understanding of urban systems. Kitchin and McArdle (2016) and Pettit (2018) describe urban dashboards as platforms that use dynamic and interactive graphic interfaces, maps, 3D models, augmented reality, bar charts, and so on, to support urban decision-making with the aim of monitoring, analysing, and interpreting performance and trends of cities. Thus, the sensor city is generally accepted as a digital platform where users are completely immersed.

Nevertheless, theoretically, the ideals that characterise sensor cities can be defined as universal and homogeneous, while contexts tend to be specific and heterogeneous (Karvonen et al., 2019). For example, cities have different social, economic, environmental, and technological infrastructures and are governed by different political and bureaucratic systems with interests that are difficult to combine in a single urban project. Furthermore, while urban data is increasingly easy to access, technical and digital skills are difficult to find in some urban contexts around the world, in order to manage, analyse and interpret urban data.

Urban contexts using IoT and/or ICT platforms require more initial efforts due to the assembly and maintenance of the infrastructure, in order to adapt it to increasingly complex urban scenarios (Sharma et al., 2020; Mocnej et al., 2018). In detail, it is a matter of integrating devices that are: (a) Heterogeneous, capable of generating different types of data; (b) Powered by different energy sources, such as a battery or renewable energy; (c) Dynamic and flexible, capable of analysing constantly changing urban scenarios; and (d) Unpredictable, in the sense that technological applications can provide conflicting results by analysing the same data, as they use different protocols and standards.

The significant costs of designing, installing, and maintaining monitor stations and sensor technologies represent a barrier to entry for smaller cities or those located in less developed regions (Yigitcanlar et al., 2008; Castell et al., 2017). The success of an urban sensor strategy depends essentially on the economic, social, and environmental characteristics of the urban context taken into consideration together with organisational, ethical and transdisciplinary factors of the actors involved (Karvonen et al., 2019).

The sensor city framework is illustrated in Figure 12.2. In detail, the operational phases, integrated into a holistic perspective of the urban context are divided into planning, sensing, collecting, processing, and analysis of urban data and results.

In Phase 1, or *planning*, the role of ICTs is highlighted, which allow citizens to participate in the decision-making process and to enhance systemic collaboration between stakeholders involved, contributing significantly to greater comprehension, transparency, and accountability (Ioppolo et al., 2016; de Wiis et al., 2016; Gil et al., 2019). Hence, planning activities through smart solutions permits a holistic and integrated approach of the various urban dimensions (e.g., governance, economy, environment, mobility, living, and people), reducing costs and time of the bureaucratic collaborations between departments and improving quality and efficiency of urban services (Ruhlandt, 2018). Nonetheless, most cities do not work like companies (e.g., IBM, Cisco, Google). They tend to be disorganised, e.g., departments do not collaborate on solutions (Dowling et al., 2019). On this point, Cugurullo (2018) elaborates

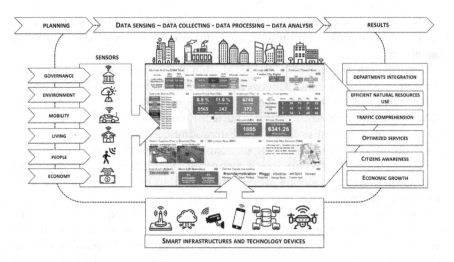

FIGURE 12.2
Sensor city framework.

that urban contexts promoted as examples of integrated and holistic urban planning are often fragmented and disconnected, characterised by several incompatible components.

The Digital Single Market strategy adopted by the European Commission (EC) represents one of the fundamental pillars of the policies for creating a digital single environment (European Commission (EC), 2020). Indeed, the strategy aims to ensure a better, secure, and uniform access for citizens to digital networks in order to improve technological knowledge and encourage greater social inclusion.

The *governance* dimension highlights the spread of social media (e.g., Facebook, Twitter, Instagram) and other data-sharing platforms that allow increasingly integrated and structured communications between stakeholders (Johnson et al., 2020). Thus, by adopting a bottom-up approach, these feedbacks generation, sharing and management tools transform citizens, companies, local authorities, and so on, into active participants in the governance of sensor cities (Yeh, 2017; Axelsson & Granath, 2018; Cardullo & Kitchin, 2019).

The *environmental* dimension involves various aspects of urban context such as:

- *Waste management,* capable of providing the real-time type and quantity of waste via cloud solutions, to optimise time and resources (Aazam et al., 2016; Ahad et al., 2020). With the development of new technology devices, electronic waste (e-waste) represents an environmental and health challenge due to its difficult disposal and potential impacts on the environment.

- *Energy efficiency,* which refers to all technologies able to reduce energy consumption. for example, street lighting networks equipped with sensors and public and private buildings equipped with real-time consumption monitoring systems represent the forward-looking urban infrastructures needed to manage urban activities efficiently (Chui et al., 2018; Ghiani et al., 2018; Shahidehpour et al., 2018).

- *Renewable energy sources,* such as solar, wind, thermal, and biogas, which represent a sustainable and efficient alternative to fossil fuels, capable of guaranteeing a stabilisation of energy prices and a sustainable source of energy supply for urban processes (e.g., public transport, heating of public and private buildings) (Lund et al., 2014; Strielkowski et al., 2019).

- *Water management,* which includes solutions capable of providing real-time data on the consumption and quality of water distribution systems, fundamental for the sustainability and efficiency of the urban system (Ler & Gourbesville, 2018).

- *Material flows,* that underline the exchange and transformation of resources (e.g., raw materials, by-products, waste) between various interested actors (Kennedy et al., 2007).

- *Biodiversity conservation,* which includes revitalisation actions for abandoned urban and industrial areas and the safeguarding of green and urban spaces (Morimoto, 2010).

- *Land use optimisation,* as support for urban agriculture and infrastructure (Kim et al., 2018).

- *Air and noise pollution prevention,* to reduce pollutant emissions through ICTs, sensors, and real-time monitoring stations, capable of providing high-definition videos and images to check environmental quality (Peng et al., 2017).

The *mobility* dimension includes, amongst others, smart and sustainable public transport system, availability of urban infrastructure suitable for autonomous vehicles, car-sharing stations for electric vehicles and ICTs relating to traffic and road monitoring (Sadiku et al., 2017; De et al., 2019; 180. Acheampong & Cugurullo, 2019; Cugurullo et al., 2021).

The aspects related to the *living* dimension include actions to improve the use of cultural and entertainment facilities (e.g., libraries, museums, schools, public parks, sport facilities) (Syed et al., 2019).

The *people* dimension includes policies aimed at promoting a 'sustainable' community, improving digital literacy, providing various assistance programs for citizens with special needs and quality healthcare system, ensuring gender equality in terms of pay and office positions and finally, safe and healthy work environments, and so on (Macke et al., 2019).

The *economic* dimension refers to the ability of the urban context to favour a path of growth through technological innovation, entrepreneurship and sustainability, attracting the most innovative companies, start-ups and talents, and capable of promoting a digitalised and collaborative development (Kumar & Dahiya, 2017).

In Phase 2, with the objective of *sensing, collecting, processing* and *analysing urban data*, the Chinese telecom company Huawei, for example, has developed 'Smart City Solution', a platform used in over 160 cities in 40 countries in Asia and Europe, capable of analysing large volume of real-time urban data and providing to policymakers a method of predictive analysis of future urban scenarios (Figure 12.3). Specifically, Lanzhou New Area represents the first new state-level development area in northwest China which, through the support of Huawei's network, was able to build the nation's first governmental IoT and wireless sensors network that integrates both broadband and narrowband communications, integrating 31 departments (e.g., public safety, finance, energy, transport, healthcare, education) with 45 eLTE stations. The program aims to improve the quality of life by optimising urban resources in a smart and sustainable manner (Huawei, 2020).

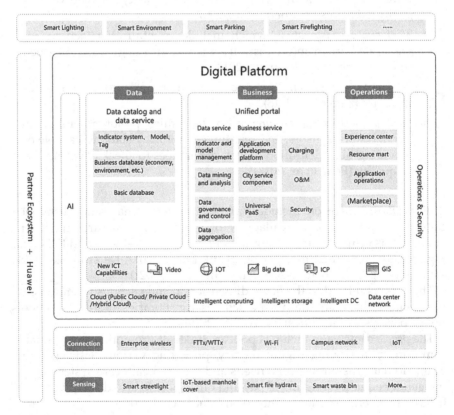

FIGURE 12.3
Huawei digital platform. (Derived from HDI, 2020.)

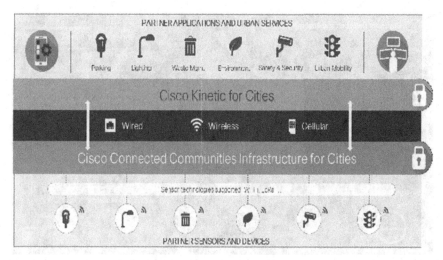

FIGURE 12.4
The Cisco smart + connected digital platform. (Derived from Cisco, 2020.)

Similarly, Cisco has developed the 'Cisco Kinetic for Cities' framework, an open and easy-to-use urban data-sharing platform that combines data provided by sensors, applications, and other third-party devices to create a dynamic sensor city infrastructure, encouraging the exchange of innovative urban initiatives between policymakers, companies, and citizens (Figure 12.4) (CISCO, 2020).

At the same time, Alibaba has developed the 'City Brain' program that has also become a useful tool for city managers, providing a holistic dashboard that can improve the perception of urban data and real-time processing capacity (Zhang et al., 2019). Figure 12.5 shows the real-time detection and analysis platform for city events. By integrating the data from the surveillance rooms, it is possible to coordinate traffic lights to give priority passage to response vehicles (e.g., police, fire-fighters, rescue, and other vehicles) in case of an emergency. Likewise, the program has been launched in several Chinese cities such as Hangzhou, Shanghai, Chongqing, Suzhou, Haikou, Beijing, Chengdu, Quzhou, and Jiaxing. Projects as CityBrain highlight the continuous interaction between local authorities and technology companies in managing urban governance. In fact, the Chinese platforms are largely owned by national technology companies (Caprotti & Liu, 2020).

Barcelona has changed its sensor city approach from top-down to bottom-up, involving its citizens in participating in innovative urban projects. For example, the Smart Citizen Kit is a dashboard that collects data on the environment such as air composition, temperature, light intensity, sound levels, and humidity through sensors and ICTs (SC, 2020). The data collected in real-time is sent via Wi-Fi to an open data platform and is used to create maps that display environmental conditions, equipping public and private

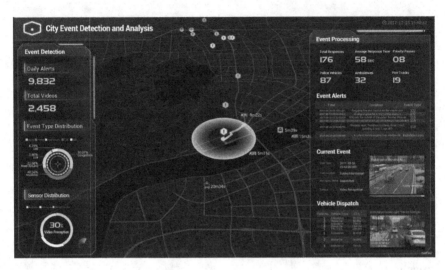

FIGURE 12.5
Alibaba city event detection and smart processing. (Derived from AC, 2020.)

stakeholders with urban data in order to develop and/or improve services for citizens (Camprodon et al., 2019). Telefonica—through the Valencia Smart City Project—aims to transform the city of Valencia into an intelligent ecosystem and fully connected via 350 sensors, allowing the management of public resources through a single ICT platform and improving several urban areas such as transport, energy, efficiency, and environmental services. The city of Santander has installed around 20,000 parking sensors in the streets, introducing intelligent waste containers capable of monitoring and measuring air pollution, rainfall, and traffic density. Through the integration and interpretation of the corresponding data, the Santander municipal administration optimises waste truck routes to save staff and fuel costs, or controls the irrigation of city parks to save water (Zaman & Lehmann, 2013; Gutiérrez-Bayo, 2016). Deutsche Telekom has implemented a similar dashboard, equipping urban physical objects (e.g., street lamps, bins, parking lots, traffic lights) with software, sensors, and connectivity systems integrated into a shared network. In this sense, the collection, monitoring, analysis, and interpretation of urban data allow the implementation of innovative service and business models (Figure 12.6).

In 2018, Deutsche Telekom and the city of Hamburg implemented around 11,000 parking spaces equipped with sensors that can provide the current availability status to users via the app (Telekom, 2020b). The local authorities of Gelsenkirchen (Germany) have decided to collaborate with Huawei and GELSEN-NET in order to implement a new open and shared urban governance system, developing an ICT infrastructure capable of integrating key data to improve the efficiency of the public services and the accuracy of the

FIGURE 12.6
Smart city dashboard developed by Deutsche Telekom for Hungary subsidiary. (Derived from Telekom, 2020a.)

decision-making process. In particular, the 'Safe City' program uses Huawei's extensive wired and wireless broadband network and the IoT that connects industrial parks, hospitals, schools, pedestrian areas, and urban centres, creating a sustainable ICT ecosystem. As part of the T-City project in Friedrichshafen (Germany), Deutsche Telekom has partnered with Alcatel-Lucent to provide hardware solutions and network devices for T-City. Specifically, Deutsche Telekom has developed over 40 pilot projects in several categories such as mobility, research, tourism, culture, health, and employment.

The LuxTurrim5G ecosystem in Espoo (Finland) aims to transform the Kera area into a sustainable and digitised urban neighbourhood, involving Nokia and several partners in order to create a multitude of urban digital services. The LuxTurrim5G platform is able to collect, store, manage, and share large amounts of urban data and solutions in a safe and efficient way between local authorities, companies and citizens. Specifically, the network developed by Nokia includes, among other things, over 50 Wi-Fi devices, 75 cameras, 49 different sensors that monitor air quality, climate, temperature, road surface conditions as well as CO2 levels, 9 radar devices, 7 information screens, a charging station for electric vehicles and a charging and landing station for drones.

Oracle through a partnership with the Indian state of Maharashtra has implemented a platform to design, develop, and analyse government-to-citizen and smart-business government services across the state. Maharashtra also aims to connect all its 113 million residents via fibre, including those in the more than 300 cities of Maharashtra and its 29,000 villages. Dallas has chosen to collaborate with Ericsson to implement an advanced traffic management system through a dashboard capable of monitoring, managing, analysing, and aggregating different data in real-time from traffic sensors and cameras to dynamically control the traffic lights. The goal of the city is to have an intuitive and shared analysis tool capable of integrating data from the various departments and agencies.

According to the report (LuxTurrim, 2020) 'The Future of Street Lighting', street lighting represents the main part (about 40%) of a city's overall electricity costs. In this sense, the replacement of conventional lamps with LED bulbs can reduce energy consumption by up to 80% when using a centralised management system. For example, the intelligent lighting platform of Cisco and Sensity in Kansas transforms each lamppost into a sensor connected to a broadband wireless network, creating a truly interconnected lighting network capable of collecting real-time data such as intelligent parking systems, electricity consumption, or air quality level. In this sense, the smart pole developed by Deutsche Telekom and Nokia represents a paradigm shift in the use of lighting poles as it goes beyond simple urban lighting and constitutes an essential component of the infrastructure of sensor cities (Figure 12.7).

The Hamburg Port Authority (HPA) through Cisco systems has developed sensors that monitor the use of resources (e.g., trucks, cranes, means of transport, ships) and infrastructures (e.g., roads, parking lots, storage warehouses) in one of the busiest and most important ports in Europe. In this sense, modernisation through IoT technological innovation allows the Port Road

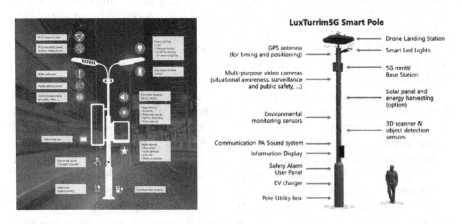

FIGURE 12.7
Smart street lighting models developed by Deutsche Telekom and Nokia. (Derived from Telekom, 2020b; LuxTurrim, 2020.)

Management Centre to plan future investments in the traffic infrastructure, optimising the flow of traffic and minimising the externalities of the port on the inhabitants of the city.

Ericsson aims to make Stockholm the smartest city in the world by 2040. With the water Monitoring Network project, Ericsson has the ability to design and implement a real-time water quality-monitoring network using an IoT sensor system located in the Stockholm water system. In addition, big data analytics are used that can analyse the data produced by the sensors and provide more information on changes in water quality such as pH and temperature.

In many cases, small towns do not need sophisticated public transportation solutions. In this sense, the challenge is to combine the departure time of buses, subways, railways, and so on, with data from traffic jams and road works on highways, showing the best alternative connections. As a partner of the Kooperation Östliches Ruhrgebiet, Deutsche Telekom helps to connect local public transport in the German state of North Rhine-Westphalia. In this regard, Deutsche Telekom's strategy allows not only meeting the needs of passengers in terms of both transparency in information (e.g., timetables, delays) and efficiency, sharing the same platform for multiple tasks. In Croatia, Deutsche Telekom's subsidiary, Hrvatski Telekom, has developed an electric vehicle charging network of 145 charging points in 101 charging stations in 70 cities. The project also integrates an ICT infrastructure that helps users to book and pay for vehicles top-ups and receive real-time availability information.

The final phase concerning the results explaining the decisive role of sensor solutions in terms of implementation of innovative urban processes (e.g., efficient use of natural resources, cross-departmental integration, real-time monitoring of traffic congestion and energy consumption, smart management of infrastructures), in order to strategically improve the contribution of sensor cities to disruptive urban development. Consequently, the optimisation of Quality of Experience (QoE) and Quality of Services (QoS) has become a crucial aspect in the implementation of urban services and processes (Alvarez et al., 2015). Particularly, QoE represents an evaluation of human experience when interacting with technology solutions and stakeholders in a given context. Therefore, a detailed analysis of the QoE should consider several actors interacting with each other at different levels (environmental, social, economic, technological) and with different goals. To do this, it is necessary to define the main interactions between citizens, companies, local authorities, social organisations, and so on. In sum, some QoE aspects related to sensor city are listed in Table 12.1.

In this regard, the challenge for policymakers will be the widespread use of several tools, such as devices, platforms, algorithms, and networks, to access, share, and integrate the largest number and type of urban data. The big data evolution process requires significant data gathering, highly specialised personnel, and infrastructures owned by different municipalities, agencies, corporations, and private companies (Bettencourt, 2014). This attention of ICT leads urbanist Mark Swilling to describe the sensor city as

TABLE 12.1

Impact of Quality of Experience on Sensor City

	Economic, Social and Privacy Implications	E-government	Health and Assisted Living	Intelligent Transportation Systems	Smart Grids, Energy Efficiency, and Environment
Quality of Experience	Usability Personalisation Transparency	Usability Personalisation Transparency	Usability Availability Personalisation Effectiveness Accessibility Efficiency	Usability Usefulness Effectiveness Accessibility Efficiency	Usefulness Accessibility Personalisation

Source: Derived from Alvarez et al. (2015).

a form of algorithmic urbanism (Allen et al., 2016). In this sense, concepts, such as big data analysis, ICT, sensors, real-time monitoring systems, smart infrastructures, IoT, represent necessary but not sufficient solutions (Kitchin, 2014; Hollands, 2015; Yigitcanlar et al., 2019). The reconfiguration of the urban system expresses the need to integrate the environmental, social, economic dimensions of smart technologies into an integrated, efficient, and computerised urban context (Shahrokni et al., 2015; Bifulco et al., 2016; Bibri & Krogstie, 2017b; Bibri, 2019).

12.4 Discussion

The perspective of implementing sensor cities based on IoT and on different urban technologies that permit the collection, monitoring, analysis, and integration of large amounts of urban data has developed new opportunities for policymakers regarding the ability to plan, combine, and evaluate social, environmental, and economic aspects in a holistic manner (Trilles et al., 2017; Jain et al., 2017; Bibri, 2018b).

The expansion of urban technologies has stimulated local authorities, technology companies, start-ups, citizens, municipal companies, and other actors involved, to develop increasingly innovative and sophisticated projects, devices, platforms, algorithms, systems, initiatives, and so on, especially in technologically and ecologically developed cities. Consequently, the use of advanced techniques such as real-time monitoring stations for energy consumption, location systems to guide urban traffic, cloud computing systems for sharing sensitive data between government departments, urban infrastructures such as smart bins, smart street lamps, and surveillance cameras, have great potential in transforming the way we understand and evaluate the urban context and, at the same time, highlight a multitude of challenges related to the quality of the data used, the level of protection

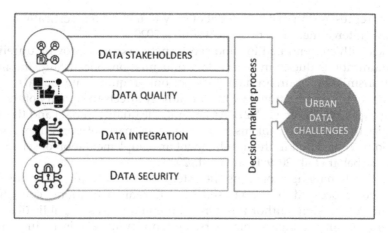

FIGURE 12.8
Future urban data challenges.

of traditional and cybernetic urban security, the necessary data integration between the various urban infrastructures and the ability to transform feedback from citizens and other stakeholders into innovative urban policies (Figure 12.8). In that perspective, sensor cities represent a sophisticated paradigm shift in the concept of the technical-urban context, necessary for a transition towards disruptive urban development (Li & Shahidehpour, 2017; Chatfield & Reddick, 2019; Habibzadeh, 2019).

The first challenge refers to the development of innovative urban policies in line with the needs of citizens, local authorities, companies, organisations, and so on. Hence, to use a significant amount of urban data according to the needs of the stakeholders involved, it is necessary to identify the relevant information and understand its consistency and validity. For example, citizens of the well-known German tourist destination, Heidelberg, in a survey identified traffic as the most urgent issue to be solved. In this sense, the efforts of local policymakers have focused on how to improve urban mobility. Thus, the identification, collection, and processing of information provided by the actors involved are crucial in the development of urban sensor projects (Certomà et al., 2020; De Guimarães et al., 2020; Wu, 2020).

The second challenge concerns the need to guarantee a certain level of data quality in order to develop efficient and innovative urban policies. For example, data collection sensors can produce incorrect, partial, or missing values as they use different standards or protocols, generating inconsistencies and differences between the data. For example, CityPulse described by (Puiu et al., 2016) is a real-time monitoring framework supported by the European Union (EU) that processes, integrates and adapts uncertain and incomplete data through quality of information techniques in order to develop reliable information capable of satisfying user requests. In this regard, the urban project represents a practical model of how to move from vertically to horizontally interconnected services (CityPulse, 2020).

Cities with concentrated IoT and sensor networks may provide unreliable communications due to incorrect data transmission. Specifically, the incorrect transmission of urban data does not only require time, but also incur retransmit the information flow that negatively affects the quality of the data (Jiang, 2020; Mocnej et al., 2021). As a result, the quality of data and the technologies to overcome problems of inconsistency, partiality, and unreliability should be considered in the development and implementation of sensor city projects (Babar et al., 2019; Engin et al., 2020).

The third challenge concerns the integration of different types of data, collected, processed, and analysed by different institutions, companies, and/or independent authorities. One of the main tasks of public decision-makers, urban managers, planners, and policymakers is to implement infrastructures, models, and networks capable of connecting data deriving from different urban sectors, promoting better communication between the various stakeholders involved (Yigitcanlar, 2010). For example, the dashboard implemented by Alibaba, illustrated in Figure 12.5, requires an information flow and systemic communication between government, security, and emergency service institutions. Hence, the holistic combination of data is necessary to plan and better understand the potential of sensor cities.

The fourth challenge involves the security of sensitive data. In this regard, ensuring maximum privacy protection is indispensable for developing urban policies based on sensors, video surveillance cameras, monitoring stations, cloud computing, and so on. Data security issues not only have isolated effects but also often affect all the urban dimensions (analysed in the previous section). Thus, data security is treated as a fundamental issue in the management of sensor cities (Sadgali et al., 2018; Borrion et al., 2020; Laufs et al., 2020). Through the collection and use of large amounts of data and technological solutions that analyse human behaviour, it is possible to influence not only the fight against crime through sensors that analyse movements or facial expressions, but also urban governance in terms of planning and attractiveness of the city (Cagliero et al., 2015; Rothkrantz, 2017; Sajjad et al., 2020). Nonetheless, the corresponding interventions are particularly controversial in terms of privacy, emphasising ethical requirements in the urban safety planning process (Parra & Lopez, 2017; Calzada, 2018). Therefore, integrating the problems related to traditional and cybernetic urban security into the planning and implementation projects of sensor cities is necessary to guarantee safe and digitalised urban development (Carter, 2020; Kumar et al., 2020).

The challenges explained in this section are related because the collection, processing, and analysis of data through IoT solutions, sensors, and big data analysis refer to interdependent urban dimensions (e.g., governance, environment, mobility, economy, life, and people). Nevertheless, this perspective requires a change in the structural paradigm of technical-scientific skills, greater organisational flexibility of government institutions, and a more aware and involved citizenship in urban administration.

12.5 Conclusion[1]

Sensor and IoT technologies are acquiring ever-increasing importance in the techno-spatial context by collecting, processing, analysing, and integrating a large amount of data to improve the healthy functioning of our cities. In this regard, the importance of the corresponding urban assessment tools is evidenced by the vast investment made by technology giants, such as Cisco, Google, Microsoft, Ericsson, Alibaba, Oracle, in prototype sensor cities. These initiatives are helping cities, such as Toronto, Valencia, Dallas, Singapore, Kansas City, Hamburg, Shenzhen, Adelaide, Dublin, integrate IoT and related applications for big data, and actively engaging in city sensor development. The sensing city model allows policymakers to benefit from bid data and urban analytics to improve urban policies, services, and operations.

The purpose of this chapter is to explore and integrate different sensor cities taken as case studies consistent with the research demand and to discuss technological solutions (e.g., sensors, devices, IoT, AI, platforms, digital infrastructures, computer models, ICTs), emphasising the economic, social, and environmental benefits of their practical application. Hence, the technological applications enabled by the IoT and ICTs, in general, have the potential to improve daily urban activities, providing a series of opportunities concerning urban dimensions such as governance, economy, environment, mobility, people, and life. In this perspective, the social, environmental, and economic challenges arising from the use of these tools have been explained. The study finds that disruptive urban technologies not only promote highly efficient and computerised urban processes and efficiency, but also improve the understanding of planning, monitoring, and analysis of the performance of sensor cities by increasing awareness of citizens, businesses, local authorities, and so on.

The framework of sensor cities (see Figure 12.2) illustrates and defines the process of detection, collection, processing, analysis of urban data up to their transformation into information necessary for urban policymakers. In this regard, the use of IoT platforms equipped with systems, devices, sensors, algorithms, platforms, models, and so on provides a complete and exhaustive

---

[1] This chapter, with permission from the copyright holder, is a reproduced version of the following journal article: D'Amico, G., L'Abbate, P., Liao, W., Yigitcanlar, T., & Ioppolo, G. (2020). Understanding sensor cities: Insights from technology giant company driven smart urbanism practices. *Sensors, 20*(16), 4391.

view of the future trends of urban performance measurement methodologies. Furthermore, these methodologies and approaches give rise to some important issues such as data quality and integrity, cyber security, digital data and information ethics and regulations. These are among the critical issues that prospective research to be tackled.

To recap the findings and conclude this chapter, we list the following highlights of the study (based on our analysis of the sensor city projects, see this chapter's Appendix Table 12.2): (a) The proposed framework improves the understanding of the cities' progress towards becoming sensing localities to address raising issues effectively and efficiently; (b) Achieving truly smart urbanism requires continuous monitoring trough urban platforms and dashboards; (c) The data-driven approach highlights a multitude of challenges related to urban governance; (d) Urban dashboards improve citizen accountability and awareness on urban issues; and (e) Data security, quality, integration, and stakeholders must be involved in the urban sensor strategy.

Appendix

TABLE 12.2

Sensor City Projects of High-Tech Companies Investigated

| Location | | High-tech | | | |
City	Nation	Company Partner	Sensor City Project	Focus	Source
Toronto	Canada	Google	Sidewalk Labs	Building, energy, waste, environment, water	(SL, 2020)
Hamburg Port	Germany	Cisco	smartROAD	Building, energy, water, mobility	(smartROADSR, 2020; Cisco Kinetic for Cities, 2020.
Gelsenkirchen	Germany	Huawei	Gelsenkirchen: A Small, Smart City with Big Plans	Mobility, environment, energy	(Huawei, 2020)
Adelaide	Australia	Cisco	Lighthouse City	Mobility, environment	(Lighthouse City, 2020)
Kansas City	U.S.A	Cisco	Smart+Connected Communities	Mobility, water, energy	(Smart+Connected Communities, 2020)
Singapore	Singapore	Google	Smarter Digital City 3.0	Mobility, living, people, finance, retail	(Ipsos, 2019)
Friedrichshafen	Germany	Deutsche Telekom	T-City Friedrichshafen	Energy, mobility, healthcare, building	(T-City Friedrichshafen, 2020)

(Continued)

TABLE 12.2 *(Continued)*

Sensor City Projects of High-Tech Companies Investigated

Location		High-tech Company Partner	Sensor City Project	Focus	Source
City	Nation				
Charlotte	U.S.A	Microsoft	Charlotte sustainability city	Energy, mobility, education, safety	(Americaninno, 2020)
Dublin	Ireland	IBM	SMART Dublin	Mobility, environment, building, water, energy	(IBM, 2015; Coletta et al., 2019)
Aspern Seestadt	Austria	Siemens	Aspern Smart City Research	Building, energy, environment, water	(ASCR, 2020)
Stockholm Port	Sweden	Ericsson	Stockholm Royal Seaport's Smart Energy City project	Water, environment, energy	(ERICSSON, 2020a)
Dallas	U.S.A	Ericsson	Factory of the Future	Mobility	(ERICSSON, 2020b)
Espoo	Finland	Nokia	Luxturrim5G Project	Environment, mobility, safety, energy	(EE, 2020)
Hangzhou	China	Alibaba	City Brain	Mobility, water, environment, healthcare	(Zhang et al., 2019)
Maharashtra	India	Oracle	Centre of Excellence	Mobility, water, education	(ORACLE, 2020)
Bari Matera	Italy	TIM	Bari Matera 5G	Tourism, culture, mobility, safety, environment, healthcare, agriculture	(BM, 2020)
Saemangeum	South Korea	Samsung	Green Energy Industrial Complex	Energy, education, agriculture, tourism, environment	(Green Energy Industrial Complex, 2020)
Shenzhen	China	Tencent	Tencent Campus	Energy, environment, mobility, education	(Hu, 2019)
Guiyang	China	Alibaba, Tencent, Apple	Guiyang Sunac City	Environment, mobility, recreation	(EKISTICS, 2020)
Valencia	Spain	Telefonica	Valencia Smart City Platform	Mobility, waste, environment, energy	(Valencia Smart City Platform, 2020)

References

Aazam, M., St-Hilaire, M., Lung, C.H., & Lambadaris, I. (2016, October). Cloud-based smart waste management for smart cities. In *Proceedings of 2016 IEEE 21st International Workshop on Computer Aided Modelling and Design of Communication Links and Networks*, IEEE.

AC (2020). *Alibaba City Event detection and Smart Processing*, Alibaba Cloud, Accessed from; www.alibabacloud.com (accessed on 06/06/2020)

Acheampong, R.A., & Cugurullo, F. (2019). Capturing the behavioural determinants behind the adoption of autonomous vehicles: Conceptual frameworks and measurement models to predict public transport, sharing and ownership trends of self-driving cars. *Transportation Research Part F: Traffic Psychology and Behaviour, 62*, 349–375.

Ahad, M.A., Paiva, S., Tripathi, G., & Feroz, N. (2020). Enabling technologies and sustainable smart cities. *Sustainable Cities and Society, 61*, 102301.

Ahvenniemi, H., Huovila, A., Pinto-Seppä, I., & Airaksinen, M. (2017). What are the differences between sustainable and smart cities? *Cities, 60*, 234–245.

Akande, A., Cabral, P., Gomes, P., & Casteleyn, S. (2019). The Lisbon ranking for smart sustainable cities in Europe. *Sustainable Cities and Society, 44*, 475–487.

Al Nuaimi, E., Al Neyadi, H., Mohamed, N., & Al-Jaroodi, J. (2015). Applications of big data to smart cities. *Journal of Internet Services and Applications, 6*(1), 1–15.

Allam, Z., & Dhunny, Z.A. (2019). On big data, artificial intelligence and smart cities. *Cities, 89*, 80–91.

Allen, A., Lampis, A., & Swilling, M. (2016). *Untamed Urbanisms*. Taylor & Francis.

Alvarez, O., Markendahl, J., & Martinez, L. (2015). Quality of Experience (QoE) – based service differentiation in the smart cities context: Business Analysis. In *Proceeding of ICCS 2015 – International Conference on City Sciences*. New architectures, infrastructures and services for future cities. Tongji University, Shanghai, China.

Americaninno (2020) Charlotte sustainability city, Americaninno. Accessed from www.americaninno.com (accessed on 12/06/2020).

Arbolino, R., De Simone, L., Carlucci, F., Yigitcanlar, T., & Ioppolo, G. (2018). Towards a sustainable industrial ecology: Implementation of a novel approach in the performance evaluation of Italian regions. *Journal of Cleaner Production, 178*(1), 220–236.

Arkian, H.R., Diyanat, A., & Pourkhalili, A. (2017). MIST: Fog-based data analytics scheme with cost-efficient resource provisioning for IoT crowdsensing applications. *Journal of Network and Computer Applications, 82*, 152–165.

Arndt, W.H., Schäfer, T., Emberger, G., Tomaschek, J., & Lah, O. (2013). Transport in megacities—development of sustainable transportation systems. In *Proceedings of the 13th World Conference on Transport Research*, Rio de Janeiro, Brazil.

ASCR (2020). Aspern Smart City Research, Aspern Smart City Research, Accessed from www.ascr.at on 12/06/2020.

Axelsson, K., & Granath, M. (2018). Stakeholders' stake and relation to smartness in smart city development: Insights from a Swedish city planning project. *Government Information Quarterly, 35*(4), 693–702.

Babar, M., Arif, F., Jan, M.A., Tan, Z., & Khan, F. (2019). Urban data management system: Towards big data analytics for internet of things based smart urban environment using customized Hadoop. *Future Generation Computer Systems, 96*, 398–409.

Batty, M. (2012). Smart cities, big data. *Environment and Planning B: Planning and Design, 39*(2), 191–193.

Batty, M. (2013). Urban informatics and big data. *A Report to the ESRC Cities Expert Group*, 1–36.

Batty, M. (2015). A perspective on city dashboards. *Regional Studies, Regional Science, 2*(1), 29–32.

Baucas, M.J., & Spachos, P. (2020). Using cloud and fog computing for large scale iot-based urban sound classification. *Simulation Modelling Practice and Theory, 101*, 102013.

Baum, S., O'Connor, K., & Yigitcanlar, T. (2009). The implications of creative industries for regional outcomes. *International Journal of Foresight and Innovation Policy, 5*(1–3), 44–64.

Bettencourt, L. (2014). The uses of big data in cities. *Big Data, 2*, 12–22.

Bibri, S.E. (2018a). A foundational framework for smart sustainable city development: Theoretical, disciplinary, and discursive dimensions and their synergies. *Sustainable Cities and Society, 38*, 758–794.

Bibri, S.E. (2018b). The IoT for smart sustainable cities of the future: An analytical framework for sensor-based big data applications for environmental sustainability. *Sustainable Cities and Society, 38*(1), 230–253.

Bibri, S.E., & Krogstie, J. (2017a). On the social shaping dimensions of smart sustainable cities: A study in science, technology, and society. *Sustainable Cities and Society, 29*, 219–246.

Bibri, S.E., & Krogstie, J. (2017b). Smart sustainable cities of the future: An extensive interdisciplinary literature review. *Sustainable Cities and Society, 31*, 183–212.

Bibri, S.E., & Krogstie, J. (2020). Smart eco-city strategies and solutions for sustainability: The cases of Royal Seaport, Stockholm, and Western Harbor, Malmö, Sweden. *Urban Science, 4*(1), 11–26.

Bibri, S.E. (2019). *Big Data Science and Analytics for Smart Sustainable Urbanism: Unprecedented Paradigmatic Shifts and Practical Advancements*, Springer, Germany.

Bifulco, F., Tregua, M., Amitrano, C.C., & D'Auria, A. (2016). ICT and sustainability in smart cities management. *International Journal of Public Sector Management, 29*, 132–147.

Bissell, D. (2020). Affective platform urbanism: Changing habits of digital on-demand consumption. *Geoforum, 115*, 102–110.

BM. (2020). Bari Matera 5G, Bari Matera, Accessed from; www.barimatera5g.it on 15/06/2020)

Bonomi, F., Milito, R., Zhu, J., & Addepalli, S. (2012). Fog computing and its role in the internet of things. In *Proceedings of the first edition of the MCC workshop on Mobile cloud computing*, New York, USA.

Borrion, H., Ekblom, P., Alrajeh, D., Borrion, A.L., Keane, A., Koch, D., & Toubaline, S. (2019). (2020). The problem with crime problem-solving: Towards a second generation POP? *The British Journal of Criminology, 60*(1), 219–240.

Cagliero, L., Cerquitelli, T., Chiusano, S., Garino, P., Nardone, M., Pralio, B., & Venturini, L. (2015). Monitoring the citizens' perception on urban security in smart City environments. In *Proceedings of IEEE International Conference on Data Engineering Workshops*, IEEE.

Calzada, I. (2018). (Smart) citizens from data providers to decision-makers? The case study of Barcelona. *Sustainability, 10*(9), 3252.

Camprodon, G., Gonzalez, O., Barberan, V., Pérez, M., Smari, V., de Heras, M.A., & Bizzotto, A. (2019). Smart citizen kit and station: An open environmental monitoring system for citizen participation and scientific experimentation. *HardwareX, 6,* e00070.

Caprotti, F., & Liu, D. (2020). Emerging platform urbanism in China: Reconfigurations of data, citizenship and materialities. *Technological Forecasting and Social Change, 151,* 2–15.

Cardullo, P., & Kitchin, R. (2019). Being a 'citizen'in the smart city: Up and down the scaffold of smart citizen participation in Dublin, Ireland. *GeoJournal, 84*(1), 1–13.

Carter, D.M. (2020). *Cyberspace and Cyberculture.* International Encyclopedia of Human Geography (Second Edition). 143–147.

Castell, N., Dauge, F.R., Schneider, P., Vogt, M., Lerner, U., Fishbain, B., Broday, D., & Bartonova, A. (2017). Can commercial low-cost sensor platforms contribute to air quality monitoring and exposure estimates? *Environment International, 99,* 293–302.

Certomà, C., Corsini, F., & Frey, M. (2020). Hyperconnected, receptive and do-it-yourself city. An investigation into the European "imaginary" of crowdsourcing for urban governance. *Technology in Society, 61,* 101229.

Chang, D.L., Marques, J., da Costa, E.M., Selig, P.M., & Yigitcanlar, T. (2018). Knowledge-based, smart and sustainable cities: A provocation for a conceptual framework. *Journal of Open Innovation: Technology, Market, and Complexity, 4*(1), 5.

Chatfield, A.T., & Reddick, C.G. (2019). *a framework for internet of things-enabled smart government: A case of IoT cybersecurity policies and use cases in U.S. Government Information Quarterly, 36*(2), 346–357.

Chui, K.T., Lytras, M.D., & Visvizi, A. (2018). Energy sustainability in smart cities: Artificial intelligence, smart monitoring, and optimization of energy consumption. *Energies, 11*(11), 2869.

CISCO (2020). *The Cisco Smart + Connected Digital Platform,* CISCO, Accessed from; www.cisco.com (accessed on 06/06/2020).

Cisco Kinetic for Cities; www.blogs.cisco.com (accessed on 06/06/2020)

CityPulse; www.ict-citypulse.eu/page/ (accessed on 08/06/2020)

Colding, J., Colding, M., & Barthel, S. (2020). Applying seven resilience principles on the vision of the digital City. *Cities, 103,* 102761.

Coletta, C., Heaphy, L., & Kitchin, R. (2019). From the accidental to articulated smart city: The creation and work of 'Smart Dublin'. *European Urban and Regional Studies, 26*(4), 349–364.

Costi, P., Minciardi, R., Robba, M., Rovatti, M., & Sacile, R. (2004). An environmentally sustainable decision model for urban solid waste management. *Waste Management, 24*(3), 277–295.

Cugurullo, F. (2018). Exposing smart cities and eco-cities: Frankenstein urbanism and the sustainability challenges of the experimental city. *Environment and Planning A: Economy and Space, 50*(1), 73–92.

Cugurullo, F., Acheampong, R.A., Gueriau, M., & Dusparic, I. (2021). The transition to autonomous cars, the redesign of cities and the future of urban sustainability. *Urban Geography, 42*(6), 833–859.

Daissaoui, A., Boulmakoul, A., Karim, L., & Lbath, A. (2020). IoT and big data analytics for smart buildings: A survey. *Procedia Computer Science, 170,* 161–168.

De Guimarães, J.C.F., Severo, E.A., Júnior, L.A.F., Da Costa, W.P.L.B., & Salmoria, F.T. (2020). Governance and quality of life in smart cities: Towards sustainable development goals. *Journal of Cleaner Production, 253,* 119926.

de Wijs, L., Witte, P., & Geertman, S. (2016). How smart is smart? Theoretical and empirical considerations on implementing smart city objectives–a case study of Dutch railway station areas. *Innovation: The European Journal of Social Science Research, 29*(4), 424–441.

De, M., Sikarwar, S., & Kumar, V. (2019). Strategies for inducing intelligent technologies to enhance last mile connectivity for smart mobility in Indian cities. In *Progress in Advanced Computing and Intelligent Engineering*, Springer, Singapore.

Dowling, R., McGuirk, P., & Gillon, C. (2019). Strategic or piecemeal? Smart City initiatives in Sydney and Melbourne. *Urban Policy and Research, 37*(4), 429–441.

EE (2020) Espoo Innovation Garden;, Enter Espoo, Accessed from www.espooinnovationgarden.fi/en/espoo on 24/07/2020).

Eicker, U., Weiler, V., Schumacher, J., & Braun, R. (2020). On the design of an urban data and modeling platform and its application to urban district analyses. *Energy and Buildings, 217,* 109954.

EKISTICS (2020). Guiyang Sunac City, Ekistics, Accessed from www.ekistics.com on 16/06/2020.

Engin, Z., van Dijk, J., Lan, T., Longley, P.A., Treleaven, P., Batty, M., & Penn, A. (2020). Data-driven urban management: Mapping the landscape. *Journal of Urban Management, 9*(2), 140–150.

ERICSSON (2020a). *Stockholm Royal Seaport's Smart Energy City project*, Ericsson, Accessed from www.ericsson.com on 12/06/2020).

ERICSSON (2020b). *Factory of the Future*, Ericsson, Accessed from www.ericsson.com on 12/06/2020).

European Commission (EC); www.ec.europa.eu (accessed on 06/06/2020)

Faisal, A., Yigitcanlar, T., Kamruzzaman, M., & Paz, A. (2020). Mapping two decades of autonomous vehicle research: A systematic scientometric analysis. *Journal of Urban Technology, 28*(3–4), 45–74.

Few, S. (2006). *Information Dashboard Design: The Effective Visual Communication of Data.* O'Reilly Media.

Gabrys, J. (2014). Programming environments: Environmentality and citizen sensing in the smart City. *Environment and Planning D: Society and Space, 32*(1), 30–48.

Ghiani, E., Serpi, A., Pilloni, V., Sias, G., Simone, M., Marcialis, G., Armano, G., & Pegoraro, P.A. (2018). A multidisciplinary approach for the development of smart distribution networks. *Energies, 11*(10), 2530.

Gil, O., Cortés-Cediel, M.E., & Cantador, I. (2019). Citizen participation and the rise of digital media platforms in smart governance and smart cities. *International Journal of E-Planning Research (IJEPR), 8*(1), 19–34.

Glazebrook, G., & Newman, P. (2018). The city of the future. *Urban Planning, 3*(2), 1–20.

Green Energy Industrial Complex; www.tecnologiaericerca.com (accessed on 15/06/2020)

Gutiérrez-Bayo, J. (2016). *International Case Studies of Smart Cities.* Inter-American Development Bank, Santander, Spain. Inter-American Development Bank.

Habibzadeh, H., Nussbaum, B.H., Anjomshoa, F., Kantarci, B., & Soyata, T. (2019). A survey on cybersecurity, data privacy, and policy issues in cyber-physical system deployments in smart cities. *Sustainable Cities and Society, 50,* 101660.

Hancke, G.P., Silva, B., & Hancke, G.P. Jr (2012). The role of advanced sensing in smart cities. *Sensors, 13*(1), 393–425.

Hasegawa, Y., Sekimoto, Y., Seto, T., Fukushima, Y., & Maeda, M. (2019). My City forecast: Urban planning communication tool for citizen with national open data. *Computer Environment and Urban Systems, 77,* 101255.

Hashem, I.A.T., Chang, V., Anuar, N.B., Adewole, K., Yaqoob, I., Gani, A., Ahmed, E., & Chiroma, H. (2016). The role of big data in smart city. *International Journal of Information Management, 36*(5), 748–758.

HDI (2020). *Digital platform drives innovative experiences*, Huawei Digital Platform. Accessed from; https://e.huawei.com/en/digital-platform/smart-city (accessed on 06/06/2020).

Hilty, L.M., Aebischer, B., & Rizzoli, A.E. (2014). Modeling and evaluating the sustainability of smart solutions. *Environmental Modelling and Software, 56,* 1–5.

Höjer, M., & Wangel, J. (2015). Smart sustainable cities: Definition and challenges. In *ICT Innovations for Sustainability* (pp. 333–349), Springer, Cham.

Hollands, R.G. (2015). Critical interventions into the corporate smart city. *Cambridge Journal of Regions, Economy and Society, 8*(1), 61–77.

Hu, R. (2019). The state of smart cities in China: The case of Shenzhen. *Energies, 12*(22), 4375.

Huang, S.-L., & Hsu, W.-L. (2003). Materials flow analysis and energy evaluation of Taipei's urban construction. *Landscape Urban Planning, 63,* 61–74.

Huawei (2020). Gelsenkirchen: A Small, Smart City with Big Plans, Huawei, Accessed from e.huawei.com/en/case-studies/global/2017/201709071445 on 11/06/2020.

Huawei; www.e.huawei.com (accessed on 06/06/2020)

Huovila, A., Bosch, P., & Airaksinen, M. (2019). Comparative analysis of standardized indicators for smart sustainable cities: What indicators and standards to use and when? *Cities, 89,* 141–153.

IBM (2015). Smarter Cities Challenge report, IBM. Dublin, Ireland.

Ingrao, C., Messineo, A., Beltramo, R., Yigitcanlar, T., & Ioppolo, G. (2018). How can life cycle thinking support sustainability of buildings? Investigating life cycle assessment applications for energy efficiency and environmental performance. *Journal of Cleaner Production, 201,* 556–569.

IDC. (2020). Worldwide Smart Cities Spending Guide, International Data Corporation.

International Institute for Management Development (IMD) (2019). *IMD Smart City Index 2019. World Competitiveness Center,* Lausanne.

Ioppolo, G., Cucurachi, S., Salomone, R., Saija, G., & Shi, L. (2016). Sustainable local development and environmental governance: A strategic planning experience. *Sustainability, 8*(2), 180.

Ipsos (2019). Smarter Digital City 3.0. Report commissioned by Google.

Ishida, T., & Isbister, K. (2000). *Digital Cities – Technologies, Experiences, and Future Perspectives.* Springer-Verlag, Berlin Heidelberg. 1765.

Jain, B., Brar, G., Malhotra, J., & Rani, S. (2017). A novel approach for smart cities in convergence to wireless sensor networks. *Sustainable Cities and Society, 35,* 440–448.

Jardim-Gonçalves, R., Sgurev, V., Jotsov, V., & Kacprzyk, J. (Eds.). (2020). *Intelligent Systems: Theory, Research and Innovation in Applications.* Springer Nature.

Jiang, D. (2020). The construction of smart city information system based on the internet of things and cloud computing. *Computer Communications, 150,* 158–166.

Johnson, P.A., Robinson, P.J., & Philpot, S. (2020). Type, tweet, tap, and pass: How smart city technology is creating a transactional citizen. *Government Information Quarterly, 37*(1), 101414.

Jowell, A., Zhou, B., & Barry, M. (2017). The impact of megacities on health: Preparing for a resilient future. *The Lancet Planetary Health, 1*(5), e176–e178.

Kamal-Chaoui, L., Grazi, F., Joo, J., & Plouin, M. (2011). The implementation of the Korean green growth strategy in urban areas, OECD Regional Development Working Papers 2011/02, OECD Publishing.

Kamble, S.S., Gunasekaran, A., & Gawankar, S.A. (2018). Sustainable industry 4.0 framework: A systematic literature review identifying the current trends and future perspectives. *Process Safety and Environmental Protection, 117,* 408–425.

Kankanamge, N., Yigitcanlar, T., Goonetilleke, A., & Kamruzzaman, M. (2020). Determining disaster severity through social media analysis: Testing the methodology with South East Queensland Flood Tweets. *International Journal of Disaster Risk Reduction, 42*(1), 101360.

Karvonen, A., Cugurullo, F., & Caprotti, F.(2019). Introduction: Situating smart cities, in Karvonen, A., Cugurullo, F., Caprotti, F. (eds) *Inside Smart Cities: Place, Politics and Urban Innovation*. London: Routledge. 1–12.

Kennedy, C., Cuddihy, J., Engel, & Yan, J. (2007). The changing metabolism of cities. *Journal of Industrial Ecology, 11*(2), 43–59.

Kennedy, C., Cuddihy, J., & Engel-Yan, J. (2007). The changing metabolism of cities. *Journal of Industrial Ecology, 11,* 43–59.

Kim, G., Miller, P.A., & Nowak, D.J. (2018). Urban vacant land typology: A tool for managing urban vacant land. *Sustainable Cities and Society, 36*(1), 144–156.

Kitchin, R. (2014). The real-time city? Big data and smart urbanism. *GeoJournal, 79,* 1–14.

Kitchin, R., & McArdle, G. (2016). Urban data and city dashboards: Six key issues. *Data and the City, 1,* 1–21.

Komninos, N. (2009). Intelligent cities: Towards interactive and global innovation environments. *International Journal of Innovation and Regional Development, 1*(4), 337–355.

Kramers, A., Höjer, M., Lövehagen, N., & Wangel, J. (2014). Smart sustainable cities–Exploring ICT solutions for reduced energy use in cities. *Environmental Modelling & Software, 56,* 52–62.

Kumar, H., Singh, M.K., Gupta, M.P., & Madaan, J. (2020). Moving towards smart cities: Solutions that lead to the smart City transformation framework. *Technological Forecasting and Social Change, 153,* 119281.

Kumar, T.V., & Dahiya, B. (2017). Smart economy in smart cities. In *Smart Economy in Smart Cities*, Springer, Singapore.

Landry, C. (2008). *The Creative City – A Toolkit for Urban Innovators*. London, Sterling, VA.

Lane, N.D., Eisenman, S.B., Musolesi, M., Miluzzo, E., & Campbell, A.T. (2008). Urban sensing: Opportunistic or participatory? In: *Proceedings of the 9th workshop on mobile computing systems and applications*. Napa Valley.

Laufs, J., Borrion, H., & Bradford, B. (2020). Security and the smart city: A systematic review. *Sustainable Cities and Society, 55,* 102023.

Lee, S.H., Yigitcanlar, T., Han, J.H., & Leem, Y.T. (2008). Ubiquitous urban infrastructure: Infrastructure planning and development in Korea. *Innovation, 10*(2–3), 282–292.

Ler, L.G., & Gourbesville, P. (2018). Framework implementation for smart water management. *EPiC Series in Engineering, 3,* 1139–1146.

Li, A., & Shahidehpour, M. (2017). Deployment of cybersecurity for managing traffic efficiency and safety in smart cities. *The Electricity Journal, 30*(4), 52–61.

Li, X., Fong, P.S., Dai, S., & Li, Y. (2019). Towards sustainable smart cities: An empirical comparative assessment and development pattern optimization in China. *Journal of Cleaner Production, 215,* 730–743.

Lighthouse City; www.iotjournal.com (accessed on 11/06/2020)

Lin, J. (2015). Urbanization and inequality in China's megacities: A perspective from Chinese industrial workers. In *Dialogues of Sustainable Urbanisation: Social Science Research and Transitions to Urban Contexts.* University of Western Sydney.

Liu, W., & Xu, Z. (2020). Some practical constraints and solutions for optical camera communication. *Philosophical Transactions of the Royal Society A, 378*(2169), 20190191.

Liugailaitė-Radzvickienė, L., & Jucevičius, R. (2014). Going to be an intelligent city. *Procedia-Social and Behavioral Sciences, 156,* 116–120.

Lopez-Ruiz, V.R., Alfaro-Navarro, J.L., & Nevado-Pena, D. (2014). Knowledge-city index construction: An intellectual capital perspective. *Expert Systems with Applications, 41*(12), 5560–5572.

Lund, H. (2014). *Renewable Energy Systems: A Smart Energy Systems Approach to the Choice and Modeling of 100% Renewable Solutions.* Academic Press.

Lund, H., Mathiesen, B., Connolly, D., & Østergaard, P. (2014). Renewable energy systems – A smart energy systems approach to the choice and modelling of 100% renewable solutions. *Chemical Engineering Transactions, 39,* 1–6.

LuxTurrim (2020). *LuxTurrim5G Smart Pole,* LuxTurrim5, Accessed from www.luxturrim5g.com on 08/06/2020.

Macke, J., Sarate, J.A.R., & de Atayde Moschen, S. (2019). Smart sustainable cities evaluation and sense of community. *Journal of Cleaner Production, 239,* 118103.

Mainka, A., Khveshchanka, S., & Stock, W.G. (2011). Dimensions of informational city research. *Digital CitiesCities7–Real WorldWorldExperiences.*

Mainka, A., Khveshchanka, S., & Stock, W.G. (2011). *Dimensions of Informational City Research.* Conference: Digital Cities 7 – Real-World Experiences. State Library of Queensland, Brisbane, Qld.

Marsal-Llacuna, M.L., & Segal, M.E. (2016). The intelligenter method (I) for making "smarter" City projects and plans. *Cities, 55,* 127–138.

Mocnej, J., Pekar, A., Seah, W.K., Papcun, P., Kajati, E., Cupkova, D., Koziorek, J., & Zolotova, I. (2021). Quality-enabled decentralized IoT architecture with efficient resources utilization. *Robotics and Computer-Integrated Manufacturing, 67,* 102001.

Mocnej, J., Seah, W.K., Pekar, A., & Zolotova, I. (2018). Decentralised IoT architecture for efficient resources utilisation. *IFAC-PapersOnLine, 51*(6), 168–173.

Morimoto, Y. (2010). Biodiversity and ecosystem services in urban areas for smart adaptation to climate change: "Do you Kyoto"? *Landscape and Ecological Engineering, 7*(1), 9–16.

Muzammal, M., Talat, R., Sodhro, A.H., & Pirbhulal, S. (2020). A multi-sensor data fusion enabled ensemble approach for medical data from body sensor networks. *Information Fusion, 53,* 155–164.

Nitschke, U., Ouan, N., & Peters, G. (2007). Megacities—A challenge for (German) development cooperation. *Asien, 103,* 79–87.

OECD. (2014). *Compact City Policies: Korea: Towards Sustainable and Inclusive Growth,* OECD Green Growth Studies, OECD Publishing.

ORACLE (2020) Centre of Excellence, Oracle, Accessed from www.blogs.oracle.com on 15/06/2020.

Palvia, P., Baqir, N., & Nemati, H. (2018). ICT for socio-economic development: A citizens' perspective. *Information & Management, 55*(2), 160–176.

Pancholi, S., Yigitcanlar, T., & Guaralda, M. (2015). Public space design of knowledge and innovation spaces: Learnings from Kelvin Grove Urban Village, Brisbane. *Journal of Open Innovation: Technology, Market, and Complexity, 1*(1), 13.

Parra, J., & Lopez, R. (2017). Application of predictive analytics for crime prevention: The case of the City of San Francisco. *Police: Global Perceptions, Performance and Ethical Challenges*, Nova Science Publishers, Inc.: New York, NY, USA, 85–109.

Penco, L., Ivaldi, E., Bruzzi, C., & Musso, E. (2020). Knowledge-based urban environments and entrepreneurship: Inside EU cities. *Cities, 96*, 102443.

Peng, H., Bohong, Z., & Qinpei, K. (2017). Smart City Environmental Pollution Prevention and Control Design based on Internet of Things. In *Proceedings of IOP Conference Series: Earth and Environmental Science, 94*, 012174.

Perng, S.Y., Kitchin, R., & Donncha, D.M. (2018). Hackathons, entrepreneurial life and the making of smart cities. *Geoforum, 97*, 189–197.

Pettit, T. (2018). *U.S. Patent No. 10,160,294*. U.S. Patent and Trademark Office, Washington, DC.

Pettit, C., & Leao, S.Z. (2017). Dashboard. Encyclopedia of Big Data.

Piro, G., Cianci, I., Grieco, L.A., Boggia, G., & Camarda, P. (2014). Information-centric services in smart cities. *Journal of Systems and Software, 88*, 169–188.

Postránecký, M., & Svítek, M. (2017). Smart city near to 4.0—an adoption of industry 4.0 conceptual model. In *2017 Smart City Symposium Prague*, IEEE.

Puiu, D., Barnaghi, P., Tonjes, R., Kumper, D., Ali, M.I., Mileo, A., Parreira, J.X., Fischer, M., Kolozali, S., & Farajidavar, N. (2016). Citypulse: Large scale data analytics framework for smart cities. *IEEE Access, 4*, 1086–1108.

Rathore, M.M., Paul, A., Hong, W.H., Seo, H., Awan, I., & Saeed, S. (2018). Exploiting IoT and big data analytics: Defining smart digital city using real-time urban data. *Sustainable Cities and Society, 40*, 600–610.

Regona, M., Yigitcanlar, T., Xia, B., & Li, R.Y.M. (2022a). Opportunities and adoption challenges of AI in the construction industry: A PRISMA review. *Journal of Open Innovation: Technology, Market, and Complexity, 8*(1), 45.

Regona, M., Yigitcanlar, T., Xia, B., & Li, R.Y.M. (2022b). Artificial intelligent technologies for the construction industry: How are they perceived and utilized in Australia? *Journal of Open Innovation: Technology, Market, and Complexity, 8*(1), 16.

Rothkrantz, L. (2017). Person identification by smart cameras. In *Proceedings of 2017 Smart City Symposium Prague (SCSP)*, IEEE.

Ruhlandt, R.W.S. (2018). The governance of smart cities: A systematic literature review. *Cities, 81*, 1–23.

Rutherford, J. (2020). Informational city, International Encyclopedia of Human Geography (Second Edition). 315–320.

Saborido, R., & Alba, E. (2020). Software systems from smart city vendors. *Cities, 101*, 102690.

Sadgali, I., Sael, N., & Benabbou, F. (2018). Detection of credit card fraud: State of art. *International Journal of Computer Science and Network Security, 18*(11), 76–83.

Sadiku, M., Shadare, A., & Musa, S. (2017). Smart transportation: A primer. *International Journal of Advanced Research in Computer Science and Software Engineering, 7*(1), 6–27.

Sajjad, M., Nasir, M., Muhammad, K., Khan, S., Jan, Z., Sangaiah, A.K., Elhoseny, M., & Baik, S.W. (2020). Raspberry pi assisted face recognition framework for enhanced law-enforcement services in smart cities. *Future Generation Computer Systems, 108*, 995–1007.

SC (2020). *Smart Citizen Kit*, Smart Citizen, Accessed from www.smartcitizen.me on 06/06/2020.

Schintler, L.A., & McNeely, C.L. (Eds.). (2019). *Encyclopedia of Big Data*, Springer International Publishing, Cham.

Shahidehpour, M., Li, Z., & Ganji, M. (2018). Smart cities for a sustainable urbanization: Illuminating the need for establishing smart urban infrastructures. *IEEE Electrification Magazine*, 6(2), 16–33.

Shahrokni, H., Lazarevic, D., & Brandt, N. (2015). Smart urban metabolism: Towards a real-time understanding of the energy and material flows of a city and its citizens. *Journal of Urban Technology*, 22(1), 65–86.

Sharifi, A. (2020). A typology of smart city assessment tools and indicator sets. *Sustainable Cities and Society*, 53, 101936.

Sharma, A., Singh, P.K., & Kumar, Y. (2020). An integrated fire detection system using IoT and image processing technique for smart cities. *Sustainable Cities and Society*, 61, 102332.

Shin, D.H. (2009). Ubiquitous city: Urban technologies, urban infrastructure and urban informatics. *Journal of Information Science*, 35(5), 515–526.

SL (2020). We build products and places to radically improve quality of life in cities for all, Sidewalk Labs, Accessed from www.sidewalklabs.com on 11/06/2020.

Smart City Dashboard developed by Deutsche Telekom for Hungary subsidiary; www.t-system.hu (accessed on 07/06/2020)

Smart+Connected Communities; www.newsroom.cisco.com (accessed on 11/06/2020)

smartROADSR (2020). Smart port – the intelligent port, Smart Road, Accessed from; www.hamburg-port-authority.de/en/hpa-360/smartport/ (accessed on 11/06/2020).

Sodhro, A.H., Sangaiah, A.K., Sodhro, G.H., Lohano, S., & Pirbhulal, S. (2018). An energy-efficient algorithm for wearable electrocardiogram signal processing in ubiquitous healthcare applications. *Sensors*, 18(3), 923.

Sodiq, A., Baloch, A.A., Khan, S.A., Sezer, N., Mahmoud, S., Jama, M., & Abdelaal, A. (2019). Towards modern sustainable cities: Review of sustainability principles and trends. *Journal of Cleaner Production*, 227, 972–1001.

Stollmann, J. (2019). Digital cities. *The Wiley Blackwell Encyclopedia of Urban and Regional Studies*, 1–4.

Strielkowski, W., Streimikiene, D., Fomina, A., & Semenova, E. (2019). Internet of energy (IoE) and high-renewables electricity system market design. *Energies*, 12(24), 4790.

Strielkowski, W., Streimikiene, D., Fomina, A., & Semenova, E. (2019). Internet of energy (IoE) and high-renewables electricity system market design. *Energies*.

Syed, L., Jabeen, S., Manimala, S., & Alsaeedi, A. (2019). Smart healthcare framework for ambient assisted living using IoMT and big data analytics techniques. *Future Generation Computer Systems*, 101, 136–151.

Talari, S., Shafie-Khah, M., Siano, P., Loia, V., Tommasetti, A., & Catalão, J.P. (2017). A review of smart cities based on the internet of things concept. *Energies*, 10(4), 421.

T-City Friedrichshafen; www.t-city.de/en (accessed on 11/06/2020)

Tekouabou, S.C.K., Cherif, W., & Silkan, H. (2020). Improving parking availability prediction in smart cities with IoT and ensemble-based model. *Journal of King Saud University-Computer and Information Sciences*, https://doi.org/10.1016/j.jksuci.2020.01.008

Telekom (2020a). *Deutsche Telekom city of Hamburg*, Telekom, Accessed from www.telekom.com on 07/06/2020).

Telekom (2020b). *Smart Street Lighting models developed by Deutsche,* Telekom, Accessed from www.deutschetelekom.com on 07/06/2020.

Thomson, G., & Newman, P. (2018). Urban fabrics and urban metabolism–from sustainable to regenerative cities. *Resources, Conservation and Recycling, 132,* 218–229.

Trilles, S., Calia, A., Belmonte, Ó, Torres-Sospedra, J., Montoliu, R., & Huerta, J. (2017). Deployment of an open sensorized platform in a smart city context. *Future Generation Computer Systems, 76,* 221–233.

Uhlemann, T.H.J., Lehmann, C., & Steinhilper, R. (2017). The digital twin: Realizing the cyber-physical production system for industry 4.0. *Procedia CIRP, 61,* 335–340.

Ullah, Z., Al-Turjman, F., & Mostarda, L. (2020). Cognition in UAV-aided 5G and beyond communications: A survey. *IEEE Transactions on Cognitive Communications and Networking, 6*(3), 872–891.

United Nations (UN) General Assembly (2015). Transforming our world: The 2030 Agenda for Sustainable Development.

Valencia Smart City Platform; www.smartcity.valencia.es (accessed on 16/06/2020)

Wang, J., Hui, L.C., Yiu, S.M., Wang, E.K., & Fang, J. (2017). A survey on cyber attacks against nonlinear state estimation in power systems of ubiquitous cities. *Pervasive and Mobile Computing, 39,* 52–64.

Willis, K.S., & Aurigi, A. (2017). *Digital and Smart Cities.* Routledge, New York.

Wirtz, B.W., Weyerer, J.C., & Schichtel, F.T. (2019). An integrative public IoT framework for smart government. *Government Information Quarterly, 36*(2), 333–345.

Witkowski, K. (2017). Internet of things, big data, industry 4.0–innovative solutions in logistics and supply chains management. *Procedia Engineering, 182,* 763–769.

Wu, W.N. (2020). Determinants of citizen-generated data in a smart city: Analysis of 311 system user behavior. *Sustainable Cities and Society, 59,* 102167.

Yamagata, Y., Yang, P.P., Chang, S., Tobey, M.B., Binder, R.B., Fourie, P.J., Jittrapirom, P., Kobashi, T., Yoshida, T., & Aleksejeva, J. (2020). Urban systems and the role of big data. In *Urban Systems Design.* Elsevier.

Yeh, H. (2017). The effects of successful ICT-based smart city services: From citizens' perspectives. *Government Information Quarterly, 34*(3), 556–565.

Yigitcanlar, T. (2006). Australian Local governments' practice and prospects with online planning. *URISA Journal, 18*(2), 7–17.

Yigitcanlar, T. (2010). *Rethinking Sustainable Development: Urban Management, Engineering, and Design.* IGI Global, Hersey, PA.

Yigitcanlar, T. (Ed.). (2010). *Sustainable Urban and Regional Infrastructure Development: Technologies, Applications and Management: Technologies, Applications and Management.* IGI Global.

Yigitcanlar, T., Butler, L., Windle, E., Desouza, K.C., Mehmood, R., & Corchado, J.M. (2020b). Can building "Artificially intelligent cities" safeguard humanity from natural disasters, pandemics, and other catastrophes? An urban Scholar's perspective. *Sensors, 20*(10), 2988.

Yigitcanlar, T., Desouza, K.C., Butler, L., & Roozkhosh, F. (2020b). Contributions and risks of artificial intelligence (AI) in building smarter cities: Insights from a systematic review of the literature. *Energies, 13*(6), 1473.

Yigitcanlar, T., Foth, M., & Kamruzzaman, M. (2019). Towards post-anthropocentric cities: Reconceptualizing smart cities to evade urban ecocide. *Journal of Urban Technology, 26*(2), 147–152.

Yigitcanlar, T., Han, H., Kamruzzaman, M., Ioppolo, G., & Sabatini-Marques, J. (2019). The making of smart cities: Are Songdo, Masdar, Amsterdam, San Francisco and Brisbane the best we could build? *Land Use Policy, 88,* 104187.

Yigitcanlar, T., Kamruzzaman, M., Buys, L., Ioppolo, G., Marques, J., Da Costa, M.E., & Yun, J.J. (2018). Understanding 'smart cities': Intertwining development drivers with desired outcomes in a multidimensional framework. *Cities, 81,* 145–160.

Yigitcanlar, T., Kamruzzaman, M., Foth, M., Marques, J., da Costa, E., & Ioppolo, G. (2018). Can cities become smart without being sustainable? A systematic review of the literature. *Sustainable Cities and Society, 45,* 348–365.

Yigitcanlar, T., Kankanamge, N., & Vella, K. (2021). How are smart city concepts and technologies perceived and utilized? A systematic geo-Twitter analysis of smart cities in Australia. *Journal of Urban Technology, 28*(1–2), 135–154.

Yigitcanlar, T., Velibeyoglu, K., & Baum, S. (Eds.). (2008). *Creative Urban Regions: Harnessing Urban Technologies to Support Knowledge City Initiatives: Harnessing Urban Technologies to Support Knowledge City Initiatives.* IGI Global.

Young, G.W., & Kitchin, R. (2020). Creating design guidelines for building city dashboards from a user's perspectives. *International Journal of Human-Computer Studies, 140,* 102429.

Young, G.W., Kitchin, R., & Naji, J. (2021). Building City dashboards for different types of users. *Journal of Urban Technology, 28*(1–2), 289–309.

Young, G.W., Naji, J., Charlton, M., Brunsdon, C., & Kitchin, R. (2017). *Future Cities and Multimodalities: How Multimodal Technologies can Improve Smart-Citizen Engagement with city Dashboards.* Institute of Sustainable urbanism Talks #05: Future Cities.

Zaman, A.U., & Lehmann, S. (2013). The zero-waste index: A performance measurement tool for waste management systems in a 'zero waste city'. *Journal of Cleaner Production, 50,* 123–132.

Zhang, J., Hua, X.S., Huang, J., Shen, X., Chen, X., Zhou, Q., Fu, Z., & Zhao, Y. (2019). City Brain: Practice of large-scale artificial intelligence in the real world. *IET Smart Cities, 1*(1), 28–37.

Zheng, Y., Liu, F., & Hsieh, H. (2013). U-Air: When urban air quality inference meets big data. In *Proceedings of the 19th ACM SIGKDD international conference on Knowledge discovery and data mining,* ACM.

Afterword

On 15 April 2013, two terrorists planted pressure-cooker bombs that detonated during the Boston Marathon. Three people lost their lives and over 250 other individuals were injured. In the immediate aftermath of the event, law enforcement personnel used social media to keep the public informed of events and seek information to apprehend the terrorists. This tragic event was one of the first to see the full-scale use of social media. Social media platforms have come a long way since 2013. Today, these platforms play a critical role in all aspects of our society. One only has to look at the recent past to understand the impact of social media platforms. From the current inquests into Facebook handled misinformation on its platform during the last US elections (TNYT, 2021) to the abusive and racist messages directed to black football players during recent tournaments (e.g., players representing England during the Euro 2020 final) (TG, 2021). On a more positive note, social media platforms have also been mobilised to drive social movements such as the over 3 million individuals who participated in the 2017 Women's March (TA, 2021) to #BlackLivesMatter.

There is a growing number of active observers and researchers of civic activity on social media. Some of their interests in social media platforms began with an examination of how digital platforms could be leveraged for crowdsourcing. Especially when the US federal government under President Obama's leadership launched Challenge.gov, some researchers studied this crowdsourcing platform (Desouza, 2012). Even during the early days of this platform, there was palatable interest in opening up how the public sector conducted innovation. Agencies posted challenges and competitions along with criteria to judge solutions and the public could contribute solutions. Some researchers also studied cities around the US that were designing digital participatory platforms for civic innovation (Desouza & Bhagwatwar, 2014) and the use of mobile apps to tackle urban challenges (Desouza & Bhagwatwar, 2012).

One of the earlier studies on the topic dates back to the early 2000s, such as the book entitled, *Managing Knowledge with Artificial Intelligence: An Introduction with Guidelines for Non-Specialist* (Desouza, 2002). More recent studies looked at activity on the Facebook pages of all candidates for the 2016 US elections (Brookings, 2021). This study focussed on tracking the tone of the discourse on the various candidates, to unpack the network dynamics behind posts and the individuals who contributed them, and to uncover how variances in topics discussed by candidates and other external factors (e.g., an offline event) shaped a candidate's image with the electorate. Other studies concentrated on the examination of analytics within the context of urban planning and the design and delivery of public services. For instance, one such project analysed reviews on childcare centres on Yelp.com across the 20 largest US cities. This project is concerned with uncovering how parents experienced childcare services and how these reviews shed light on the differences across those living in affluent and less affluent neighbourhoods (Herbst et al., 2020).

Cities are self-organising ecosystems. While a city's administration plays a critical role in shaping a city, there are a multitude of actors that influence a city's functioning. Information is critical to enable coordination among actors within the ecosystem. Information is generated from a host of objects, agents, and organisations within the ecosystem. Today, the amount of data and information generated continues to explode thanks to advances in technologies, e.g., artificial intelligence, drones, sensors, IoT, and digital twins, among others. Social media represents one of the most critical sources of data for cities.

Cities can use social media platforms to inform, source insights, and even drive innovation. Today, we need innovations that can leverage social media data to make our cities smarter, accessible, resilient, and sustainable. Social media data if leveraged adequately can promote citizen engagement, facilitate crowdsourcing of solutions, and increase the situational awareness of a city's functions, processes, and status. However, a city's ability to leverage social media is a function of its analytical capacity. Unfortunately, while most cities share and collect massive amounts of data on social media platforms, only a fraction of this is ever analysed. And even less is used to drive innovations in public services and the design or evaluation of public policies.

With social media data, and the underlying analytics, it is imperative that one accounts for privacy and ethical considerations. Just because one can analyse data that is available does not mean one should. Moreover, when analysing data, it is important to consider the various privacy and ethical conundrums that might arise, especially when social media data is overlayed or integrated with other data sources. Furthermore, it is vital to remember that not everyone is on social media. There are large sections of our communities that do not have a Facebook account or upload videos on TikTok or tweet. As such it is important to ensure that we do not use social media data as representative of all sections of our communities.

In an era where 'data is the new oil', this book, by Yigitcanlar and Kankanamge, brings a new breath to urban analytics with social media big data by 'cracking the codes' for understanding on the foundations, applications, platforms and implications of the subject matter. Authors have assembled a definite reader on urban analytics and social media. This book will be of interest to students, researchers, and practitioners who want to learn about analytical techniques, application domains, and platforms where social media analytics can create urban innovations.

Professor Kevin C. Desouza
School of Management and Centre for Future Enterprise
Queensland University of Technology, Brisbane, Australia

References

Brookings (2021). What is the tone of the 2016 presidential campaign on Facebook? Brookings, Accessed from https://www.brookings.edu/blog/techtank/2016/04/13/tracking-presidential-campaigns-on-facebook/ https://www.brookings.edu/blog/techtank/2016/05/19/which-topics-do-presidential-candidates-discuss-on-facebook/ https://www.brookings.edu/blog/techtank/2016/08/10/what-is-the-tone-of-the-2016-presidential-campaign-on-facebook/ on 10 November 2021.

Desouza, K.C. (2002). *Managing Knowledge with Artificial Intelligence: An Introduction with Guidelines for Nonspecialists.* Greenwood Publishing Group. https://www.amazon.com/Managing-Knowledge-Artificial-Intelligence-Nonspecialists/dp/1567204910.

Desouza, K.C., (2012). *Challenge.Gov: Using Competitions and Awards to Spur Innovation,* Arizona State University, Accessed from https://www.businessofgovernment.org/sites/default/files/Challenge.gov_.pdf on 10 November 2021.

Desouza, K.C., & Bhagwatwar, A. (2012). Citizen apps to solve complex urban problems. *Journal of Urban Technology, 19*(3), 107–136.

Desouza, K.C., & Bhagwatwar, A. (2014). Technology-enabled participatory platforms for civic engagement: The case of US cities. *Journal of Urban Technology, 21*(4), 25–50.

Herbst, C.M., Desouza, K.C., Al-Ashri, S., Kandala, S.S., Khullar, M., & Bajaj, V. (2020). What do parents value in a child care provider? Evidence from yelp consumer reviews. *Early Childhood Research Quarterly, 51,* 288–306.

TA (2021). *The significance of millions in the streets,* The Atlantic, Accessed from https://www.theatlantic.com/politics/archive/2017/01/the-significance-of-millions-in-the-streets/514091/on 10 November 2021.

TG (2021) *Revealed: Shocking scale of Twitter abuse targeting England at Euro 2020,* The Guardian, Accessed from https://www.theguardian.com/football/2021/jun/27/revealed-shocking-scale-twitter-abuse-targeting-england-euro-2020 on 10 November 2021.

TNYT (2021). *Internal alarm, public shrugs: Facebook's employees dissect its election role,* The New York Times. Accessed from https://www.nytimes.com/2021/10/22/technology/facebook-election-misinformation.html on 10 November 2021.

Index

Note: *Italicized* folios indicate figures and **bold** indicate tables in the text.

Printed in the United States
by Baker & Taylor Publisher Services

Printed in the United States
by Baker & Taylor Publisher Services